# TOEIC®テスト
# 大学生のための
# 頻出英単語

Z会編集部 編

TOEIC is a registered trademark of Educational Testing Service (ETS).
This publication is not endorsed or approved by ETS.

Z会

## はじめに

　日本人の英語学習経験の中で大きな割合を占めるのは「単語学習」ではないでしょうか。大学受験までの学習でも，1冊は単語集を持っていた人が大多数でしょう。また，「単語を覚えられなかったから，英語は苦手」という声も出るほど，「英語＝単語」というイメージが強いのではないでしょうか。

　では，学校でそれほどの時間を割き，努力を重ねて覚えてきた単語は，TOEIC テストには役立たないものなのでしょうか。

　そんなことはありません。むしろ，TOEIC テストで目にする単語の多くは，実はすでに学習し，知っているはずの単語ばかりなのです。学校で学んだ英語のうち，必要な単語だけを思い出し，TOEIC テスト特有の知識をプラスすれば，非常に効率的な単語学習ができます。

　本書は，TOEIC テストの公開データと模擬試験などのデータから，独自のコーパス（英文データベース）を作成し，それをもとに TOEIC テストに頻出の約 1700 語を厳選しました。すでに自分が持っている知識を TOEIC テストで使える知識に変換できるよう，それらの単語を大学受験用単語集『速読英単語　①必修編』（Z会出版）のリストにしたがって，以下のように分類しました。
① **学校で習った単語のうち，TOEIC テストでは別の意味や派生語で使われることが多い単語**
② **学校英語の知識がそのまま使える単語**
③ **TOEIC テスト特有の単語**
これらを効果的に配置し，今ある語彙力を最大限活かしてさらにステップアップできる構成にこだわりました。

　また，本書で扱う例文はすべて実際の TOEIC テストのレベル，関連ある内容に設定しました。「できる限り TOEIC テストの内容に近い例文を読む」ことを通して，単語力と TOEIC テストに対応できる読解力が身に付きます。「単語の意味を1つでも多く覚える」よりは，「例文を1つでも多く読む」ことを心がけてください。

　本書が読者の皆さまの語彙力向上に役立ち，TOEIC テストやその他さまざまな場面において効果を実感していただければ，これにまさる喜びはありません。

2013 年秋　Z会編集部

# CONTENTS

はじめに ································· 2

本書の構成と活用法 ······················· 4

## Chapter 1　学校英語を TOEIC にバージョンアップ　9
- **1-1** 意外な意味 ······················· 10
- **1-2** 関連語 ··························· 42

## Chapter 2　使える学校英語を総ざらい　67
- **2-1** 頻度 ★★★ ······················· 68
- **2-2** 頻度 ★★ ························ 128
- **2-3** 頻度 ★ ·························· 166

## Chapter 3　TOEIC 特有の頻出語を覚える　203
- **3-1** 頻度 ★★★ ······················ 204
- **3-2** 頻度 ★★ ························ 230

## Chapter 4　TOEIC 形式の長文で覚える　255
- **4-1** Part 4 形式 ······················ 256
- **4-2** Part 7 形式 ······················ 284

INDEX ··································· 338

# 本書の構成と活用法

## ■章構成

　これまでの英語学習ですでに学んだ知識を活かしながら，TOEIC レベルの語彙知識を効率よく習得しましょう。空所補充形式や長文での学習など，4段階でレベルアップし，最後まで単調にならずに学習できる構成になっています。

### Chapter 1　学校英語を TOEIC にバージョンアップ

TOEIC 頻出の単語には，すでに学校で習っている単語も多く含まれます。ただし，知識に少しアレンジを加える必要があります。ここでは，**知っている単語でも TOEIC ならではの意味を新たに覚える必要がある語，知っている単語の関連語として覚える語**など，すでにある語彙力を記憶のカギにできる単語をまとめて覚えましょう。

### Chapter 2　使える学校英語を総ざらい

学校で習った単語のうち，同じように TOEIC でも頻出の単語を確認しましょう。記憶に残っている単語も忘れてしまった単語もすべて，**TOEIC レベルの英文を使って，空所補充形式のテストに挑戦**しましょう。すぐに答えが浮かばなかった単語は隣のページで語義をチェック。必須語を総ざらいしましょう。

### Chapter 3　TOEIC 特有の頻出語を覚える

TOEIC に取り組むにあたり，新たに重要となる単語に取りかかりましょう。ビジネスや日常生活で使われる単語が中心になります。TOEIC レベルの例文を繰り返し読みながら覚えていきましょう。

### Chapter 4　TOEIC 形式の長文で覚える

TOEIC の Part 4 形式と Part 7 形式の長文の中で新出語を学習しましょう。各長文には Part 7 で実際に出題される語彙問題と同形式の問題がついていますので，確認に使用してください。**長文を通して単語学習をすることで，語彙力だけでなく読む力も強化できます**。また，音声をダウンロードして聞く力も一緒に鍛え，万全の状態で本番に臨みましょう。

## ■ページ構成

《Chapter 1-1》

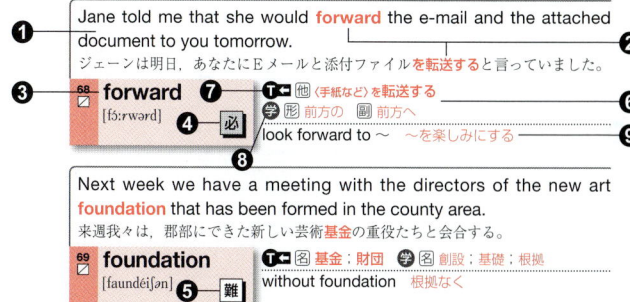

❶ **例文**…辞書や一般的な単語集のような短く抽象的な文ではなく，TOEIC レベルの例文を全見出し語に掲載しました。

❷ **赤太字**…赤シートで和訳中の赤字を隠して，見出し語の訳を覚えられるようになっています。

❸ **見出し語**…コーパスを参照し，頻度の高い語を1397語（派生語を含めると1712語）を選出しました。

❹ **必**…大学生が必ず覚えておきたい語です。

❺ **難**…大学生には難易度が高く，差のつく語です。

❻ **語義**…コーパスを参照し，TOEICに頻出の語義を厳選しました。例文を読んでから，確認用として利用してください。

❼ **T**…TOEICでよく使われる語義を掲載しました。違いを意識して学習しましょう。

❽ **学**…一般に大学受験までに学ぶ語義を掲載しました。忘れていた場合はあわせて思い出しましょう。

❾ **フレーズ**…TOEICに頻出のフレーズや，重要な語法を取り上げました。意味を赤シートで隠して，訳してみましょう。

《Chapter 1-2》

❿ ♂…学校で習う関連語を示しました。見出し語を覚える際の記憶のカギにしてください。

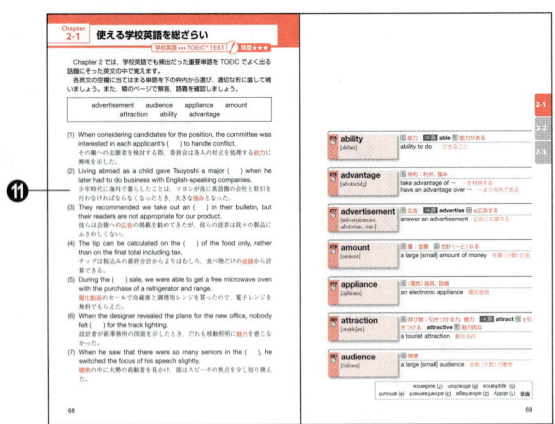

❶ **空所補充テスト**…枠内の単語から空所に入る語を選び，適切な形にして補いましょう。隣のページで解答，語義を確認しましょう。

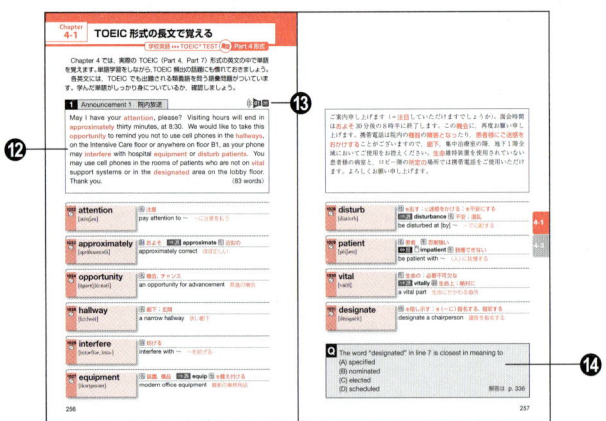

⓬ **長文**…TOEIC の Part 4，Part 7 形式の英文を掲載しました。「語彙力」と「読む力」を同時に強化しましょう。

⓭ **音声ファイル**…TOEIC のスピードで，長文部分を吹き込んでいます。

⓮ **クイズ**…各長文の見出し語のうち，いずれかについて TOEIC の Part 7 で出題される形式の単語クイズを掲載しています。文中での使われ方として適切なものを選び，解答を確認しましょう。

## ■効果的活用法

本書の特長である「大学受験までに習った語彙知識を使う」,「TOEIC レベルの例文,長文で覚える」という2点を最大限に有効活用し,効率的に学習しましょう。

### ① すでに持っている知識を TOEIC に対応させる

学校で習った語彙を覚えている人・英語が得意な人は,Chapter 1 でその知識に磨きをかけるところから始めましょう。知っている語でも,意外な意味があることに気づくでしょう。次に Chapter 2 では左側の空所補充形式のページを中心に,単語テストのつもりで進めてみましょう。それから例文だけを通して読むと,すでに知っている語もより一層定着します。

英語からしばらく遠ざかっていた人・英語が苦手な人は,Chapter 1 を例文を訳しながら順番に時間をかけて覚えていきましょう。Chapter 2 はテストとして解かなくても構いません。1回目は左右のページを同時に確認し,語彙知識の穴を埋めていきましょう。一通り学習を終えたあと,2回目の学習で単語テストに挑戦しましょう。

Chapter 3 では例文を中心に確認し,音読なども交えると効果的です。

最後に語彙力と読む力,聞く力を一緒に高めるため,Chapter 4 の長文を繰り返し読み,音声を何度も聞きましょう。

### ② 例文を使いこなす

どの Chapter の例文も,そのまま TOEIC 本番レベルの内容です。赤シートで和訳の赤字を隠しながら例文を読み,その意味をつかむことから始めてください。それから,見出し語の意味をチェックします。例文から語義を身につけ,さらにフレーズで知識を定着させましょう。

学習の始めは例文が難しく感じることもあるかもしれませんが,先に進むにつれ,この単語集の中で学習した語が繰り返し出てくることに気づくでしょう。例文を学習していてどこかで見たことがある語だと思ったら,索引で調べてその単語に戻って復習すると効果的です。TOEIC 本番の文脈・レベルに慣れ,確かな語彙力を手に入れましょう。

# ■本書で用いた記号

## 品詞
- 名 名詞
- 動 動詞
- 他 他動詞
- 自 自動詞
- 形 形容詞
- 副 副詞
- 前 前置詞

## その他
- ⇒派 派生語
- ≒類 類義語
- ⇔反 反意語
- → 関連語リンク
- 〔 〕 交換可能
- ～，… 名詞句，動詞，節の代用
- 〈 〉 結びつく主語や目的語の種類
- to do to 不定詞
- ...ing 動名詞または現在分詞
- **T←** 特に注意すべき TOEIC 特有の語義（Chapter 1-1 のみ）
- **学** 大学受験までにすでに学んだ語義（Chapter 1-1 のみ）
- **必** 必ずマスターしておきたい単語（Chapter 1-1 のみ）
- **難** 差がつく単語（Chapter 1-1 のみ）
- ♂ 記憶のカギになる関連語（Chapter 1-2 のみ）

## 【音声ファイルについて】
- Chapter 4 の音声ファイルを無料でダウンロードできます。
- 以下の URL にアクセスし，ファイルをダウンロードしてください。
  http://www.zkai.co.jp/books/uwords/
- 音声ファイル番号は，((　01 のマークで確認することができます。
- 本書では，本番のテストと同様に，アメリカ・イギリス・カナダ・オーストラリア出身のナレーターにより音声を収録しています。ナレーター国籍については，アメリカ：米，イギリス：英，オーストラリア：豪，カナダ：カ のように表示しています。各国の発音の特徴に注意しながら音声を聞くようにすると効果的です。

## Chapter 1

# 学校英語を TOEIC に
# バージョンアップ

1-1 意外な意味
1-2 関連語

# Chapter 1-1 学校英語を TOEIC にバージョンアップ

学校英語 ▶▶▶ TOEIC® TEST  意外な意味

Chapter 1 では，すでに学んだ単語の意味を TOEIC ならではの意味に変換することで，効率よく頻出語をマスターできます。Ｔマークの語義が TOEIC でよく使われる意味，学マークの語義がこれまでに学んだ意味です。

また，必ずマスターしておきたい単語には必マーク，難易度が高くスコアに差がつく単語には難マークがついていますから，しっかり覚えましょう。

---

The Interior Ministry was found to have **abused** their relationships with the logging industry to get extra funding.
内務省が追加の資金を得るために伐採業者との関係を**悪用**していたことがわかった。

**1 abuse**
[動] [əbjúːz] [名] [əbjúːs]

Ｔ 他 を乱用〔悪用〕する　名（職権）乱用
学 他 を虐待する　名 虐待
abuse of human rights　人権侵害

---

There wasn't enough cash in the **account** to handle the draft that was requested.
**口座**には，必要な為替手形を処理するのに十分な現金がなかった。

**2 account**
[əkáunt]　必

Ｔ 名 預金口座；勘定書；会計簿　学 自 説明する
→ 160 accountant　161 accounting
account for ～　～を説明する

---

Until the board gets together and chooses a new CEO, Bob Stowe is the **acting** president.
委員会が集まって新しい CEO を決めるまでは，ボブ・ストウが**代理**の社長である。

**3 acting**
[ǽktiŋ]

Ｔ 形 代理の　学 名 行為
an acting mayor　市長代理

---

During the third quarter, the R&D department is going to **adopt** strict controls over the handling of radioactive materials.
第 3 四半期中に，研究・開発部では，放射性物質の扱いへの厳密な統制**を採用する**予定だ。

**4 adopt**
[ədɑ́pt]

Ｔ 他〈意見・方針〉を採用する；〈提案〉を認可する
学 他 を養子にする
adopt a new approach　新しい方法を採用する

The firm in question has asked for an advance on the balance of their loan.
問題の会社は，貸付残金の前払いを求めてきた。

**5 advance**
[ədvǽns]

🆃 名 前払い；昇進　目 昇進する　学 名 前進
⇒派 advancement 名 前進；昇進

in advance　前もって

---

Part of the agreement concerns the drilling and water rights along their mutual borders.
協定の一部は，互いの国境沿いの掘削権と水利権に関するものだ。

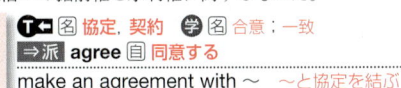

**6 agreement**
[əgríːmənt]

🆃 名 協定，契約　学 名 合意；一致
⇒派 agree 目 同意する

make an agreement with ～　～と協定を結ぶ

---

The candidate's application was missing any mention of nationality and that was the reason he wasn't hired.
その候補者の応募用紙には国籍に関する記述がなく，それが理由で彼は採用されなかった。

**7 application**
[æplikéiʃən]

🆃 名 出願；申込書　学 名 適用，応用　→409 apply

an application form　申し込み用紙

---

Please tell all of your colleagues in the sales department that we at B & Q, Inc. appreciate all your hard work.
販売部の同僚の皆さんに，我々B&Q株式会社は皆さんの勤勉に感謝していますとお伝えください。

**8 appreciate**
[əpríːʃièit, -si-]

🆃 他 に感謝する　学 他 を評価する；を鑑賞する
⇒派 appreciation 名 感謝；正しい評価

I would appreciate it if ...　…していただければ幸いです

---

The various policies that regulate the judicial branch of the U.S. government are in Article III of the Constitution.
合衆国政府司法府を統制するさまざまな方策は憲法第3条にある。

**9 article**
[áːrtikl]　必

🆃 名 物品；条項　学 名 記事

a newspaper article　新聞記事
domestic articles　家庭用品

The package said that the unit required no assembly, but it turned out we did have to put it together.

包装には，その装置は組み立て作業の必要がないと書かれていたが，実際には組み立てなければならないことがわかった。

**10 assembly**
[əsémbli] 難

🆃 图 組み立て；組み立て品　学 图 集会
⇒派 assemble 自 集まる

freedom of assembly　集会の自由

---

That lady in the blue suit is a reporter on assignment from a famous national publication.

青いスーツを着たその女性は有名な全国的出版物から任命を受けたレポーターだ。

**11 assignment**
[əsáinmənt] 難

🆃 图 任務，割り当て，任命　学 图 宿題

the assignment of chores　雑用の割り当て

---

Gene was in a lunch meeting with an associate yesterday when he was called by the head office.

ジーンは昨日提携会社との昼食会議に出ていたが，そのとき本部から呼ばれた。

**12 associate**
图 [əsóuʃiət, -si-]
動 [əsóuʃièit, -si-]

🆃 图 同僚，提携者　学 他 を連想する

be associated with ～　～と関連している

---

The condominium complex has a homeowner's association meeting on the first Tuesday night of the month at the recreation center.

集合住宅では，毎月，第1火曜日の夜に娯楽施設で住宅所有者組合の集まりがある。

**13 association**
[əsòusiéiʃən, -ʃi-]

🆃 图 協会，団体，組合　学 图 連想；交際

alumni association　同窓会

---

My printer isn't working, so let me e-mail the photo to you as an attachment.

私のプリンターが動かないので，写真をEメールの添付として送ります。

**14 attachment**
[ətǽtʃmənt] 必

🆃 图 添付ファイル；付属物　学 图 取り付け
→572 attach

send ～ as an attachment　～を添付ファイルで送る

Jill called and asked if Mr. Brown would be available to meet and discuss the contract tomorrow.
ジルが電話してきて，ブラウン氏には明日会って契約について話す時間があるかたずねた。

**15 available**
[əvéiləbl]

🆃 形 手があいている，会うことができる
🎓 形 利用できる　⇒派 availability 名 有効性
readily available　すぐに入手〔利用〕できる

---

We are going to have to make sure our account balance stays over $3,000,000 for two months to start a new branch.
新しい支店を開くには，うちの口座の残高が2か月間必ず300万ドル以上を保つようにしておかなければならない。

**16 balance**
[bæləns]

🆃 名 差引残高，差額　🎓 名 バランス
available balance　利用可能残高

---

Mr. Jones has informed us that his company will bear the expenses for training our new staff.
ジョーンズ氏は，彼の会社が当社の新しいスタッフの研修費を持つと知らせてくれた。

**17 bear**
[béər]

🆃 他 〈費用・責任など〉を負担する　🎓 他 に耐える
bear the cost　費用を負担する

---

Debbie was going to take the job, but she wanted to know whether or not the benefits applied to full-time employees.
デビーはその職に就くつもりだったが，諸手当が正社員だけに支給されるのかどうかを知りたいと思った。

**18 benefit**
[bénəfit]　難

🆃 名 [benefits] 給付金，手当　自 利益を得る
🎓 名 利益
benefit from ～　～から利益を得る

---

Last year was a difficult period, but this fiscal term has been relatively easy for paying the bills.
昨年は厳しい期間だったが，今期は請求書の支払いが比較的楽だ。

**19 bill**
[bíl]　必

🆃 名 請求書；為替手形；法案　🎓 名 紙幣
an outstanding bill　未払い勘定

From next month, the board has decided to give everyone merit-based bonuses on a quarterly basis.
来月から四半期ごとに能力に応じたボーナスを全員に支払うことを**役員会**が決めた。

**20 board** [bɔ́ːrd] 必
- T← 名 役員会, 会議　自他 (に)搭乗する　学 名 板
- the board of directors　取締役会, 役員会
- a boarding pass　搭乗券

For our company to expand our presence in the industry, we are going to have to find some more capital.
我が社が業界での存在を拡大するためには，もう少し**資本**を見つけなければならない。

**21 capital** [kǽpətl]
- T← 名 資本　学 名 首都　形 主要な
- invested capital　投資資本

Because of his experience with real estate, the vice president was asked to chair the new property search committee.
不動産会社での経験により，副社長は新設された不動産調査委員会**の議長を務める**よう打診された。

**22 chair** [tʃéər]
- T← 他 の議長を務める　名 議長職　学 名 いす
- take the chair at today's meeting　今日の会合で議長を務める

There is a good chance that the company will show a strong third quarter if their marketing campaign is successful.
販促キャンペーンが成功すれば，会社が好調な第3四半期を示す**見込み**は十分ある。

**23 chance** [tʃǽns]
- T← 名 見込み, 可能性　学 名 機会
- grab the chance　好機に飛びつく

Janet, we need you to get these products through the sales channels that you have developed in Asia.
ジャネット，この製品を君がアジアで開拓した販売**経路**に乗せてもらいたい。

**24 channel** [tʃǽnl] 必
- T← 名 経路, ルート　学 名 チャンネル；海峡
- a distribution channel　流通経路

We're going to have to go with your contact on this job, as the other company wants to **charge** too much.
もう一方の会社が多額の請求をしたがっているので，この仕事に関しては，あなたが紹介してくれた会社にしなくてはならないでしょう。

### 25 charge
[tʃɑ́ːrdʒ]

🅣 他〈代価〉を請求する 名 請求金額
🅢 他〈責任〉を負わせる 名 責任

be in charge of ～　～の担当である

---

These are duplicate **checks**, so press hard with the pen and an exact copy of everything you wrote will remain.
この伝票は二重なので，ペンで強く押して書けば，書いたものにはすべて正確な写しが残る。

### 26 check
[tʃék]

🅣 名 小切手；伝票　🅢 他 を調べる 名 点検

pay by check　小切手で支払う

---

The **claim** for the whole shipment lost in the last typhoon was paid in full by the insurance company.
保険会社は，この前の台風で紛失したすべての出荷品に対する支払い請求を全額支払った。

### 27 claim
[kléim]

🅣 名（権利としての）請求　他 を請求する
🅢 名 主張　他 を主張する

baggage claim　手荷物引渡所

---

Economic **climate** data has not been fully gathered, so we'll have to take an extra week to get our projection reports done.
経済環境データが十分集まっていないので，予測報告の完成にはもう1週間必要だろう。

### 28 climate
[kláimət]

🅣 名 環境，風潮　🅢 名 気候

climate condition　気候条件

---

This month's best employee, Laura, has earned a 25% increase in **commissions** over the previous month.
今月の最優秀従業員であるローラは，先月，歩合を25パーセント伸ばした。

### 29 commission
[kəmíʃən] 難

🅣 名 手数料，歩合　🅢 名 委任；委員会

a commission merchant　ブローカー，委託販売人
commission of experts　専門委員会

Our sales manager has committed himself to get this order out by the end of the week.
うちの営業部長は，今回の注文を今週末までに出すことを確約した。

**30 commit**
[kəmít]

- 🅣 他 を委託する；[commit oneself] 確約する
- 🅢 他 を犯す ⇒派 **commitment** 名 委託；約束

commit oneself to ～　～を確約する；～に専心する

---

The companies have similar products and pricing, but Royal Marketing has a better compensation plan.
それらの会社の製品と定価は似通っているが，ロイヤルマーケティングはよりよい報酬制度を持っている。

**31 compensation**
[kὰmpənséiʃən, -pen-]

- 🅣 名 補償金；報酬　🅢 名 埋め合わせ
- ⇒派 **compensate** 他 を補償する；を埋め合わせる

demand compensation　補償を要求する

---

Our laboratory is located in the industrial complex downtown, but our main office is near the lake.
当研究室は市の中心部にある産業複合ビルの中にあるが，本社は湖の近くにある。

**32 complex**
名 [kámpleks]
形 [-́-, -́-]

- 🅣 名 複合施設　🅢 形 複雑な

a shopping complex　複合ショッピングビル

---

They'll only sign the contract on the condition that we concede Articles 3 and 4.
彼らは，我々が第3条と第4条に譲歩するという条件でしか契約に署名しないつもりだ。

**33 condition**
[kəndíʃən]

- 🅣 名 条件，規定　🅢 名 状態

be in good [bad/poor] condition　健康である〔ない〕

---

My uncle is a retired judge who consults for a number of large corporations concerning legal issues both domestic and abroad.
叔父は引退した裁判官で，国内外の法律問題について多くの大企業の顧問を務めている。

**34 consult**
[kənsʌ́lt]
難

- 🅣 自 顧問を務める　🅢 他〈医者〉に診てもらう
- ⇒派 **consultation** 名 相談

consult one's doctor　医者に診てもらう

Our company's president has made a **contribution** of one of his favorite pieces of art to the local charity.
我が社の社長はお気に入りの美術品の1つを地元の慈善団体に寄付した。

**35 contribution**
[kὰntrəbjúːʃən]

🔵名 寄付(金) 学名 貢献 →contribute
make a contribution to [toward] ~　~に貢献〔寄付〕する

---

Kate helped us **correct** the influx in the generator after the storm that came through last month.
ケイトは先月の嵐のあと、発電機の流れを直すのを手伝ってくれた。

**36 correct**
[kərékt]

🔵他 を訂正する；を直す 学形 正しい
correct errors　誤りを正す

---

Most hotels have **courtesy** vans that leave regularly from the airport at all hours of the day.
ほとんどのホテルには特別送迎バンがあり、毎時間空港から定期的に出ている。

**37 courtesy**
[káːrtəsi]

🔵名 優遇措置, サービス 学名 礼儀
→courteous
courtesy card　優待カード

---

We need a lot of documents to make sure the product gets through the **customs** clearance point without any problems.
製品が税関の通関点を問題なく確実に通過するためには大量の書類が必要だ。

**38 custom**
[kʌ́stəm]
必

🔵名 [customs] 税関；愛顧 学名 習慣
clear customs　税関を通過する

---

While the industry is generally weak this quarter, Al was able to make a **deal** that brought us a great profit.
この四半期、当産業は全体的に弱いが、アルは我々に大きな利益をもたらす取引を成立させることができた。

**39 deal**
[díːl]

🔵名 取引 自 取引をする 学自 扱う
⇒派 dealer 名 業者
close a deal　商談をまとめる

The quality of traditional woodworking has **declined** as many of the older master craftsmen are passing away.
伝統的な木工細工の品質は，高齢の巨匠の多くが亡くなるにつれて**低下**してきた。

### 40 decline
[dikláin]

- ⓣ 自 衰退する，低下する　名 低下；衰退
- 学 自他 (を) 断る
- decline an offer　申し出を断る

---

Our statistics show that the devices sell much better if the salesperson actually **demonstrates** it in the store.
統計によると，販売員が実際に店内で**実演する**ほうがはるかに道具がよく売れるとわかる。

### 41 demonstrate
[démənstrèit]

- ⓣ 他 を**実演説明する**　学 他 を論証する
- →1146 **demonstration**
- demonstrate one's ability　自分の能力を証明する

---

The Accounting **department** has given us the go-ahead on our proposal to change over to environmentally safe energy.
経理**部**は環境上安全なエネルギーに変えるという我々の提案を承認した。

### 42 department
[dipá:rtmənt]　必

- ⓣ 名 **部門，〜部**　学 名 [department store] デパート
- ⇒派 **depart** 自 **出発する；はずれる**
- in every department of one's life　生活のあらゆる分野で

---

In a rare **departure** from his traditional role as adviser, our manager helped us put together the first model in the shop.
部長は，めったにないことだが，アドバイザーという彼の従来の役割から**離れて**，店頭で私たちが最初のモデルを組み立てるのを手伝ってくれた。

### 43 departure
[dipá:rtʃər]　難

- ⓣ 名 **逸脱**　学 名 出発　⇒派  **depart** 自 **出発する**
- departure from 〜　〜からの出発〔逸脱〕

---

The insurance form has a special entry for the number of **dependents** in your immediate family.
保険の申込書には肉親の中の**扶養家族**数を記入する特別な欄がある。

### 44 dependent
[dipéndənt]

- ⓣ 名 **扶養家族**　学 形 頼っている，依存している
- be dependent on one's parents　親に依存している

Do you have the receipts from last month's sales **deposits** entered into the database?
データベースに入力されている先月の販売手付金の領収書を持っていますか。

**45 deposit**
[dipázət]

📕 名 預金；手付金　他〈金など〉を預ける
🎓 他 を置く

security deposit　手付金, 保証金

---

It looks like the economy has stabilized and is going to come out of this **depression** into positive growth within the year.
経済は安定し，年内に不景気から抜け出してプラス成長に転じるようだ。

**46 depression**
[dipréʃən] 必

📕 名 不振；不景気　🎓 名 憂鬱

a depression in trade　不景気

---

Our course catalog offers a detailed **description** of each class and all the requirements for enrollment.
講座のカタログでは各講座の詳細説明と入学するための必要条件を提示している。

**47 description**
[diskrípʃən]

📕 名 説明書；解説　🎓 名 描写　→⁴²⁸ **describe**

a job description　職務記述書

---

Can you **detail** the necessary items for us to overcome this bottleneck in our production line?
当社の生産ラインのこの障害を克服するのに必要な項目を詳しく説明してくれますか。

**48 detail**
[díːteil, ditéil]

📕 他 を詳しく説明する　🎓 名 詳細

go into (the) details about ～　～について詳しく述べる

---

The European branch hasn't been able to **distribute** our summer line of dresses evenly amongst the sales outlets.
欧州支店は夏服のラインナップを販売店に均等に配送することができていない。

**49 distribute**
[distríbjət] 難

📕 他〈商品など〉を配送する　🎓 他 を分配する
⇒派 **distribution** 名 流通　**distributor** 配達業者

distribute the agenda　議事日程表を配布する

In order to calculate how well people are reacting to our charity campaign you must **divide** the total proceeds by the number of contributors.

我々の慈善運動への反応頻度を計測するには，寄付者の数で全収益**を割る**必要がある。

50 **divide**
[diváid]

🅣 他 〈数〉を割る　🅢 他 を分ける，配分する
→ 51 division

divide ~ in [into] ...　~を…に分ける

---

Paul now works in the new Materials **division** that has its headquarters in the southern part of the industrial park.

ポールは今は，工業団地の南部に本部がある新しい資材**部**で働いている。

51 **division**
[divíʒən]

🅣 名 (官庁・会社などの)部門，課　🅢 名 分割
→ 50 divide

personnel division　人事課

---

While our **domestic** sales have been steadily increasing, our international production and sales seem to be weakening.

当社の**国内**販売が着実に増えている一方，海外生産と販売は減退しているようだ。

52 **domestic**
[dəméstik]　必

🅣 形 国内の　🅢 形 家庭の

domestic affairs　家事

---

According to the tabloids, the launch of their new cosmetic line is **due** any day now.

タブロイド紙によれば，彼らの新たな化粧品は今すぐにでも**発売予定**である。

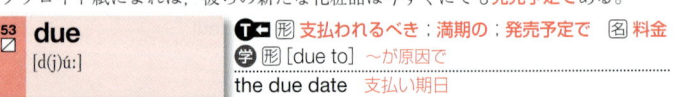

53 **due**
[d(j)úː]

🅣 形 支払われるべき；満期の；発売予定で　名 料金
🅢 形 [due to] ~が原因で

the due date　支払い期日

---

The **duties** that we are going to have to pay on these items in the Indonesian region are quite different than we assumed.

インドネシア地域でこれらの品物に対して払わなければならない**関税**は，我々が想定していたものとはかなり違う。

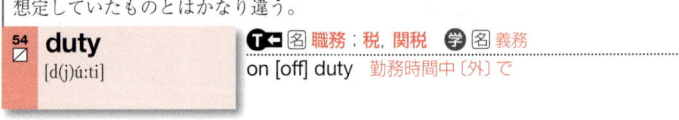

54 **duty**
[d(j)úːti]

🅣 名 職務；税，関税　🅢 名 義務

on [off] duty　勤務時間中〔外〕で

We told Bruce to go to a doctor and have him **examine** that bruise that seems to keep getting bigger.

私たちはブルースに，医者に行って，どんどん腫れてくるように見える傷を診てもらうように言った。

**55 examine**
[iɡzǽmin, eɡz-] 難

🇹 他 を診察する　学 他 を調査する；を吟味する

examine whether ...　…かどうか吟味〔考察〕する

---

Ken is getting today's stock **exchange** closing prices and charts for the chemical and industrial sectors.

ケンは化学部門と産業部門に関する今日の株式取引の終値とグラフを収集中だ。

**56 exchange**
[ikstʃéindʒ, eks-]

🇹 名 取引；両替；為替　学 他 を交換する

exchange contracts　契約書を取り交わす

---

Did you know that Thor's motor company is considering **expanding** into the body paint area?

トールの自動車会社が車体塗装分野に事業拡張をしようとしていると知っていましたか。

**57 expand**
[ikspǽnd, eks-]

🇹 自 〈会社・事業などが〉発展する　学 他 を広げる
自 広がる　⇒派 expansion 名 拡大；発展

expand one's knowledge　知識を広げる

---

Between 10:00 and 12:00 I'll be in a meeting, but you can reach me at **extension** 5022 throughout the afternoon.

10時から12時までは会議に出ていますが，午後はずっと内線5022で私に連絡がつきます。

**58 extension**
[iksténʃən] 必

🇹 名 (電話の)内線；増築
学 名 広げること，拡張；伸び　→436 extend

an extension of one's business　事業の拡大

---

If you want 24-hour access to stock market information during the cruise, you will have to pay a little **extra** when you purchase your tickets.

船旅の間，株価情報に24時間アクセスしたい場合は，チケットを購入する際に少し割増料金を払わなければなりません。

**59 extra**
[ékstrə]

🇹 名 [extras] 割増料金　形 追加料金の；臨時の
学 形 余分の

at no extra cost　追加費用なしで

This new car that we are offering this spring **features** a radical new steering function and three headlights.
我々がこの春提供するこの新車は，新しく急進的なハンドル操作機能とヘッドライト3つを備えている。

**60 feature**
[fíːtʃər]

- 他 を呼び物にする，含む　名 目玉商品，呼び物
- 学 名 特徴；顔立ち

a notable feature　顕著な特徴

---

Emily asked me to send along the latest sales **figures** for our new line of electric clocks.
エミリーから，当社の電気時計の新製品に関する最新の販売数値を送るように頼まれた。

**61 figure**
[fígjər]　必

- 名 数字　学 名 形；姿；図(案)；〜な人

a public figure　よく知られた人

---

Susan is going to **file** a claim for the shipping costs that were added on to our last transaction.
スーザンは我々の最近の取引に上乗せされた配送料の支払い請求を申し立てるつもりだ。

**62 file**
[fáil]

- 他 〈申請書など〉を提出する　自 申請する
- 学 名 ファイル　他 を整理保存する

file a lawsuit against 〜　〜を告訴する

---

Our factory is going to have to pay some heavy **fines** if we don't repair our air filters.
当工場は，空気ろ過器を修理しなければ重い罰金を払わなければならなくなる。

**63 fine**
[fáin]　必

- 名 罰金　学 形 すばらしい；晴れた

impose a fine　罰金を科す

---

Recent reductions in investment are going to cause about 100 people to be **fired** in the entertainment sector.
最近の投資削減により，娯楽部門で約100人が解雇されることになるだろう。

**64 fire**
[fáiər]　必

- 他 を解雇する　学 名 火；火事

fire extinguisher　消火器

Leslie works for a **firm** that deals in investments and retail development throughout the Midwest region.
レスリーは中西部全域で投資と小売店開発を扱う会社に勤めている。

**65 firm**
[fə́ːrm] 必

🅣 名 会社　🅢 形 堅い；断固たる
an advertising firm　広告会社
a firm commitment　確約

---

The local government is proposing a **flat** monthly rate for energy expenses for all the firms.
地方自治体は、すべての会社に対して、光熱費として一律の月額を提案している。

**66 flat**
[flǽt]

🅣 形 〈価格が〉均一の
🅢 形 平らな；〈タイヤが〉空気の抜けた
have a flat tire　タイヤの空気が抜けた

---

Our new contractor told us that building costs are in a **fluid** state now and we may have a better price in a month.
新しい請負業者は、今、建設費用が変わりやすい状況だから、1か月先にはもっとよい値段になるかもしれないと言ってきた。

**67 fluid**
[flúːid]

🅣 形 〈意見・状況などが〉変わりやすい
🅢 名 流体　形 流動体の
a cleaning fluid　洗浄液

---

Jane told me that she would **forward** the e-mail and the attached document to you tomorrow.
ジェーンは明日、あなたにEメールと添付ファイルを転送すると言っていました。

**68 forward**
[fɔ́ːrwərd] 必

🅣 他 〈手紙など〉を転送する
🅢 形 前方の　副 前方へ
look forward to ～　～を楽しみにする

---

Next week we have a meeting with the directors of the new art **foundation** that has been formed in the county area.
来週我々は、郡部にできた新しい芸術基金の重役たちと会合する。

**69 foundation**
[faundéiʃən] 難

🅣 名 基金；財団　🅢 名 創設；基礎；根拠
without foundation　根拠なく

This golf shirt has been designed to work well with a person who has a strong **frame**.
このゴルフシャツはがっしりした**体格**の人に合うようにデザインされている。

| 70 | **frame** [fréim] | **T←** 名 体格；構造；体制　学 名 骨組；枠<br>the frame of a building　建物の骨組 |

---

The warm **front** and low pressure areas resulted in a record number of hurricanes and major tropical storms.
温暖**前線**と低気圧領域は，記録的な数のハリケーンと大型熱帯性低気圧を生み出す結果となった。

| 71 | **front** [fránt] | **T←** 名 (気象) 前線　学 名 前部；正面　形 前部の<br>a cold [warm] front　寒冷〔温暖〕前線 |

---

Many of our employees are **graduates** from local trade schools and community colleges.
当社の社員の多くは地元の職業訓練校とコミュニティ・カレッジの**卒業生**だ。

| 72 | **graduate** 名 [grǽdʒuət] 動 [grǽdʒuèit] | **T←** 名 (大学の) 卒業生　学 自 (大学を) 卒業する<br>graduate from college　大学を卒業する |

---

Stan was helped in his doctoral studies by a **grant** from a local foundation that gave him two years of field work time.
スタンの博士課程の研究は，2年間の実地調査を可能にしてくれた地元財団法人からの**助成金**によって援助された。

| 73 | **grant** [grǽnt] | **T←** 名 助成金　学 他 を認める<br>take ~ for granted　~を当然のことと思う |

---

The Conference Center in Chicago has **hosted** a variety of international symposiums as well as local fundraisers.
シカゴの会議場は地元の募金イベントのみならず，さまざまな国際シンポジウム**を主催して**きた。

| 74 | **host** [hóust] | **T←** 他 を主催する　学 名 主人<br>host a reception　歓迎会を主催する |

Even though he only stayed for seven months, the college sent him a bill for a full year's tuition and **incidentals**.

たった7か月しか在学していなかったにもかかわらず，大学は彼に丸1年分の授業料と雑費の請求書を送ってきた。

| 75 | **incidental** [ìnsədéntl] | **T←** 名 [incidentals] 雑費，臨時費<br>**学** 形 付随的な，偶然の |
|---|---|---|

the duties incidental to a job　仕事に付随する義務

---

The ability of factories to prosper in non-traditional areas has made the steel **industry** much more competitive.

非伝統的な地域で工場が成功することができ，鉄鋼業界にはさらに競争力がついた。

| 76 | **industry** [índəstri] 難 | **T←** 名 業界，…業　**学** 名 産業<br>⇒派 **industrial** 形 産業の |
|---|---|---|

a growth industry　成長産業

---

Our **initial** date for moving the factory had to be moved back by six months due to material shortages overseas.

工場移転の当初の予定日を，海外の原料不足のために6か月延期しなければならなかった。

| 77 | **initial** [iníʃl] | **T←** 形 初期の　**学** 名 イニシャル，頭文字<br>⇒派 **initially** 副 最初は |
|---|---|---|

the initial stage of a disease　病気の初期段階

---

One of the parts needed to **install** this machine in the new warehouse has been damaged in shipping.

新しい倉庫にこの機械を設置するのに必要な部品の1つが，運搬中に破損した。

| 78 | **install** [instɔ́ːl] | **T←** 他 を設置する　**学** 他 をインストールする<br>⇒派 **installation** 名 取り付け；設備 |
|---|---|---|

have ~ installed　~を設置する

---

Pamela has asked me to **interview** the initial 25 applicants next Monday over at the main office complex.

パメラは私に，来週の月曜日本社ビルで，応募者の最初の25人を面接するよう頼んだ。

| 79 | **interview** [íntərvjùː] 必 | **T←** 他 自 (と)面接する　名 面接　**学** 他 自 (に)インタビューする　⇒派 **interviewer** 名 面接する人<br>**interviewee** 名 面接を受ける人 |
|---|---|---|

I ordered some more forms so that we can **issue** all the paychecks next month.
来月すべての支払い明細書<u>を発行する</u>ことができるように，用紙をいくらか発注した。

80 **issue**
[íʃuː]

T← 自 発行される　他 を発行する
名 (新聞・雑誌の)号　学 名 論点
the current issue　最新号

---

I called the company for service because almost every time I used the copy machine it had a paper **jam**.
そのコピー機は使うとほぼ毎回紙<u>詰まり</u>を起こすので，その会社に電話して修理を頼んだ。

81 **jam**
[dʒǽm]　

T← 名 詰まること；故障　自 〈機械などが〉詰まって動かなくなる　学 名 渋滞；ジャム
traffic jam　交通渋滞

---

Even though there is a growing number of workers in the unemployment pool, skilled **labor** is increasingly difficult to find.
失業者の増加にもかかわらず，熟練した<u>労働者</u>を見つけるのはますます難しくなっている。

82 **labor**
[léibər]

T← 名 労働力, 労働者　学 名 労働；骨折り
labor force　労働力
labor costs　人件費

---

The **launch** date of our new software has been shifted back by one month due to coding errors.
当社の新しいソフトウェアの<u>発売</u>日は，コードエラーのために1か月遅くなった。

83 **launch**
[lɔ́ːntʃ]

T← 名 新発売　他 〈新製品〉を売り出す；〈事業など〉を始める　学 他 を発射する
launch a scheme　計画を始める

---

Even though inflation has **leveled** off for the past two quarters, the price of gasoline has increased by 18%.
過去2四半期でインフレは<u>収まって</u>きたにもかかわらず，ガソリンの値段は18パーセント上がった。

84 **level**
[lév l]　

T← 自 平均化する；平らになる　形 平らな　名 階
学 名 水準
on the upper level　上の階に

Quincy took on a heavy **load** when he agreed to be the director and manager of the Research department.

クインシーは調査部の取締役兼部長になることに同意して，相当な仕事量を引き受けた。

### 85 load
[lóud]

🅣 名 負担；仕事量　学 名 積荷　他 に荷を積む

a reasonable load of work　妥当な仕事量

---

Could you see if you can **locate** the nearest supplier of frozen foods in this area?

この地域で最も近い冷凍食品の供給業者が見つかるか調べてくれますか。

### 86 locate
[lóukeit, -́-]

🅣 他 を探し出す　学 他 [be located] 位置する
→ location

be located in the suburbs　郊外に位置する

---

Make sure that you check the supply **log** of the laboratory before you leave every Friday.

毎週金曜日，退室前に必ず研究室の備品記録をチェックしてください。

### 87 log
[lɔ́(:)g]

🅣 名 経過記録；交信記録　学 名 丸太，薪

log-on password　ログオンパスワード

---

Wellington has **maintained** that his data is correct despite the reaction at the home office.

ウェリントンは，本社の反発にもかかわらず，自分のデータは正しいと主張している。

### 88 maintain
[meintéin, men-, mən-]

🅣 他 を主張する　学 他 を維持する
⇒派 maintenance 名 メンテナンス，整備

maintain good health　健康を保つ

---

It looks like you're going to end up with a 5% profit **margin** on these cooking goods.

最終的に，あなたはこの調理用具で5パーセントの利幅を得ることになりそうだ。

### 89 margin
[mɑ́:rdʒin]

🅣 名 利ざや　学 名 縁；余白

leave a margin　余白を残す

With a projected loss coming up in the travel sector, we are going to **marry** the tourism and the finance bureaus next year.

旅行部門で損失が出る見込みであるため，我々は来年，観光局と財務局と**を合併する**ことになっている。

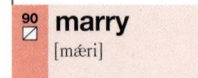

| 90 | **marry** [mǽri] | **T**← 他 を結合させる　学 他 自 (と)結婚する<br>get married to ～　～と結婚する |

I'd like you to **monitor** the sales of fishing goods versus camping goods over the early summer months.

初夏の何か月間か，つり道具とキャンプ道具を対比させた販売**を監視**してほしい。

| 91 | **monitor** [mάnətər] 難 | **T**← 他 を監視する　学 名 スクリーン，モニター<br>monitor performance　仕事ぶりを監視する |

The factory has cut energy costs by 40% by **mounting** solar panels onto the rooftops of every building in the complex.

工場は，施設内の全社屋の屋根にソーラーパネル**を取り付け**，光熱費を 40 パーセント削減した。

| 92 | **mount** [máunt] 難 | **T**← 他 を取り付ける　学 他 を登る〔上る〕<br>mount a massive campaign　大規模なキャンペーンを開始する |

The company's gross loss percentage **narrowed** to 8% in the March quarter, versus 59% a year ago.

その会社の総損失率は 1 年前の 59 パーセントに対して，3 月期には 8 パーセントに**減少した**。

| 93 | **narrow** [nǽrou] | **T**← 他 を狭める：を縮小する　自 狭くなる；減る<br>学 形 狭い<br>a narrow path　狭い道 |

The boss put a **notice** up over the water cooler to remind everyone that lunch times have changed.

上司は，昼食時間が変更になったことを皆に念押しするために，ウォータークーラーの上に**張り紙**を掲示した。

| 94 | **notice** [nóutəs] 必 | **T**← 名 通知，警告；掲示文　学 他 に気づく<br>notice a mistake　間違いに気づく |

Safety regulations and procedures are to be **observed** at all times when in the operating area.
運転区域では安全規則や手順は常に遵守されなければならない。

**95 observe** [əbzə́:rv]
- 他 を遵守する　学 他 を観察する
- ⇒派 observation 名 観察
- observe that ...　…であることに気づく

---

She gathered **odd** bits of information to enable the company to foresee competitor investments.
彼女は，競合企業の投資を予測できるよう，半端なちょっとした情報を集めた。

**96 odd** [ád]
- 形 半端な；余分の　学 形 奇妙な
- an odd choice　意外な選択

---

It's going to be easier to send the payments by money **order** in this case than it is to use an electronic transfer.
この場合は支払金を電信振替するよりも郵便為替で送るほうが簡単だろう。

**97 order** [ɔ́:rdər] 難
- 名 為替；注文(品)　学 名 命令；順序
- place an order for ～　～を注文する

---

George is the director of the **panel** that is going to pick out the new construction site for the factory.
ジョージは工場の新しい建設用地を選ぶ委員会の委員長だ。

**98 panel** [pǽnl]
- 名 (専門)委員団　学 名 パネル
- ⇒派 panelist 名 討論者
- a panel of experts　専門家委員会

---

All the **parties** concerned in the negotiations met at the hotel downtown to work out their differences.
意見の不一致を解決するために，交渉に関係しているすべての当事者が中心街のホテルに集まった。

**99 party** [pá:rti]
- 名 当事者；一行；政党　学 名 パーティ
- a third party　第三者

Samantha was praised for her **performance** as leader upon the successful conclusion of the project.
サマンサは，プロジェクトを成功に導いたリーダーとしての<u>功績</u>を賞賛された。

**100 performance**
[pərfɔ́ːrməns]

🆃← 名 仕事の出来；遂行；性能　学 名 上演, 演奏
⇒派 **perform** 他 を行う；を上演する
good [poor] performance　好成績〔成績不振〕

---

In order to work in the Electrical department, you have to receive a **permit** from the city to allow you on-site.
電気部門で働くためには，現場に入る<u>許可証</u>を市からもらわなければならない。

**101 permit**
名 [pə́ːrmit]
動 [pərmít]

🆃← 名 許可証　学 他 を許可する
⇒派 **permission** 名 許可
grant an immigration permit　移民許可証を交付する

---

The boss's **philosophy** for sales is to push hard, but for marketing is to research everything thoroughly.
社長の<u>考え方</u>は，販売については押しを強くするが，マーケティングについてはすべてを徹底的に調査するということだ。

**102 philosophy**
[fəlásəfi]

🆃← 名 見解, 考え方　学 名 哲学
a philosophy of living　処世法

---

They've had to hire extra workers at the packaging **plant** to keep up with demand.
需要に追いつくため，包装<u>工場</u>では臨時雇いの労働者を雇わなければならなかった。

**103 plant**
[plǽnt]　必

🆃← 名 施設, 設備；工場　学 名 植物
a manufacturing plant　製造工場

---

Roger has just gotten a new **position** as manager in the biochemical division at MIO, Inc.
ロジャーは MIO 社の生化学部門で新しく部長の<u>職位</u>を得たところだ。

**104 position**
[pəzíʃən]　必

🆃← 名 職位；職, 勤め口　学 名 位置
a social position　社会的地位

---

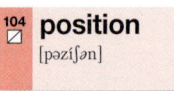

30

After giving us so many peaches, the farmer suggested that we use any leftover fruit to make peach **preserves**.
その農夫は大量の桃をくれ，残りを使って桃の<u>ジャム</u>を作ることを提案した。

**105 preserve**
[prizə́:rv] 必

🅣← 名 保存食品, <u>ジャム</u>　学 他 を保存する
preserve historical monuments　歴史的記念物を保存する

---

Do you prefer us to list your title as **president** of the company, or CEO?
あなたの肩書きは<u>社長</u>と CEO のどちらで名簿に載せるのがよいですか。

**106 president**
[prézədənt] 必

🅣← 名 <u>社長</u>, 頭取　学 名 大統領；学長
the incoming president　後任の社長

---

Helene heard that a new car stereo product will be announced at the **press** conference today.
ヘレンは新しいカーステレオ製品が今日の<u>記者</u>会見で発表されると聞いた。

**107 press**
[prés] 必

🅣← 名 報道機関, マスコミ；出版物
学 他 自 (を)押す
press the accelerator pedal　アクセルを踏み込む

---

The **proceeds** from the ticket sales will go to help victims of the recent floods.
チケットの売上からの<u>収益</u>は，この間の洪水の犠牲者を支援するために使われます。

**108 proceed**
名 [próusi:d]
動 [prəsí:d] 難

🅣← 名 [proceeds] <u>収益</u>；売上高
学 自 前進する；手続きをとる
proceed (along) with one's work　仕事を続ける

---

I was the research assistant for three years before I was **promoted** to investment manager.
投資マネージャーに<u>昇進する</u>までの3年間，私は研究助手だった。

**109 promote**
[prəmóut] 必

🅣← 他 を<u>昇進させる</u>　学 他 を促進する
⇒派 promotion 名 昇進；販売促進
promote a project　計画を推進する

I'm not sure who left the bucket here, but it says **Property** of Mayfield School on it.
だれがここにバケツを放置したのか知らないが「メイフィールド校所有物」と書いてある。

### 110 property
[prápərti]

🅣 名 不動産；所有物　🅢 名 特性
fixed property　固定資産
a property developer　土地開発業者

---

The auditor wants to see a profit and loss statement for the last **quarter** of 2004.
監査役は2004年の最終四半期の損益計算書を見たがっている。

### 111 quarter
[kwɔ́ːrtər]　必

🅣 名 四半期　🅢 名 4分の1
compared with the previous quarter　前期比で

---

Theresa got a pay **raise** as well as a better office when her company restructured itself.
会社が再建したとき，テレサはよりよいオフィスを得ただけでなく，昇給した。

### 112 raise
[réiz]

🅣 名 賃上げ，昇給
🅢 他 を上げる；を増す；を育てる
raise a price　価格を上げる

---

We've been considering moving our factory over to the next township where the gas **rates** are better.
我々は工場を，ガス代の安い隣の郡区に移すことを考えている。

### 113 rate
[réit]

🅣 名 (サービスなどの) 料金　🅢 名 レート，割合
interest rate　金利，利率
postal rate　郵便料金

---

Luckily, only half of the cars in our sales fleet are affected by the manufacturer's **recall** on engine parts.
幸運なことに，メーカーによるエンジン部品の回収の影響を受けるのは，当社が販売している全車両の半分だけだ。

### 114 recall
名 [ríːkɔːl, -kɑ̀ːl]
動 [rikɔ́ːl]　必

🅣 名 (欠陥商品の) 回収　他 を回収する
🅢 他 を思い出す
recall a product because of defects　欠陥商品を回収する

The company recognized the retiring chairman for his many years of service with a cash bonus and a gold watch.
会社は，退職する会長の長年の勤労を表彰して，現金のボーナスと金の時計を与えた。

## 115 recognize
[rékəgnàiz]

**T** 他 〈人〉の功労を表彰する　**学** 他 に見覚えがある；を認める　⇒派 recognition 名 認識

recognize ~ as one's equal　~を対等な存在と認める

---

Are there any manuals that I should refer to when I make out the insurance claim?
保険金請求をするときに参照すべき手引書が何かありますか。

## 116 refer
[rifə́ːr]

**T** 自 問い合わせる；参照する　**学** 自 言及する
→ reference

refer to ~　~に言及する；~を参照する

---

We've contracted with the municipal government for refuse collection and product recycling.
我々は，廃棄物の収集と製品のリサイクルに関して市役所と契約した。

## 117 refuse
名 [réfjuːs]
動 [rifjúːz]

**T** 名 廃棄物　**学** 他 を拒む

collect the refuse　廃棄物を収集する

---

The new tooling on our production line has allowed us to cut our reject rate in half.
生産ラインに新しい工作機械を入れたので，不合格品の率が半分になった。

## 118 reject
名 [ríːdʒekt]
動 [ridʒékt]

**T** 名 不合格品，きずもの　**学** 他 を拒絶する

reject an offer　申し出を拒絶する

---

The press release stated that there won't be any final decisions made on the new regulations until Monday.
報道発表によると新しい規則に関しては月曜日まで最終決定はないとのことだった。

## 119 release
[rilíːs]

**T** 名 公表，公開；発売　他 を公表〔公開〕する；を発売する　**学** 名 解放　他 を解放する

recently released films　最近封切られた映画

Herbert has been working with a **relief** organization that provides aid and housing for victims of major floods.
ハーバートは大洪水の被害者に援助と住居を提供する**救援**組織で働いてきた。

**120 relief**
[rilíːf]

🅣 名 救済, 救援  🅢 名 (苦痛などの) 除去；安堵
a relief fund　救済基金

---

Nikola invented a boat that was wirelessly **remote**-controlled and displayed it in Madison Square Garden.
ニコラは無線で**遠隔**操作されるボートを発明し，それをマジソン・スクエア・ガーデンに展示した。

**121 remote**
[rimóut]

🅣 形 遠隔操作による  🅢 形 遠く離れた；へんぴな
by remote control　リモコンで

---

The **rent** on our retail outlet downtown is almost the same as both of our sales offices combined.
繁華街にある当社の小売店の**賃貸料**は2つの営業所を合わせた額とほぼ同じだ。

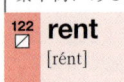

**122 rent**
[rént]

🅣 名 賃貸料  🅢 他自 (を) 賃借りする
pay high [low] rent　高い〔安い〕家賃を払う

---

The factory equipment has been under **repair** now for the past month, and production has suffered a 30% decrease.
工場の設備がこの1か月**修理**中だったので，生産は30パーセント低下した。

**123 repair**
[ripéər]

🅣 名 手入れ, 修理；[repairs] 修繕作業
🅢 他 を修理する
repair a deficiency　不足を補う

---

Jim is **representing** the engineering department at the annual sales and development conference this year.
ジムは今年，年1回の販売開発会議で技術部**を代表する**。

**124 represent**
[rèprizént]

🅣 他 を代表する  🅢 他 を表す, 象徴する
→ 247 **representative**
represents a group　ある集団を代表する

In a piece of great news, the return on our green-tech investments is up to 15% from 2% a year ago.
あるよいニュースによると，環境技術の投資の利益は，昨年の2パーセントから15パーセントまで上がった。

**125 return**
[ritə́ːrn] 難
🅣 名 利益，収益；報酬；納税申告書
🅢 自 戻る 名 戻ること
a tax return  所得税申告

---

The dog's owner is offering a $500 reward for the safe return of the French Poodle.
犬の飼い主は，フレンチプードルが無事戻れば500ドルの謝礼金を払うつもりである。

**126 reward**
[riwɔ́ːrd]
🅣 名 謝礼金 🅢 名 報酬 他 に報いる
reward and punishment  賞罰

---

He forgot to calculate the royalties due to Dynagroup Corp. into their final product cost.
彼はダイナグループ社に支払うべき特許権使用料を最終製品原価の計算に入れ忘れた。

**127 royalty**
[rɔ́iəlti] 必
🅣 名 特許権使用料；印税 🅢 名 王族
⇒派 royal 形 王室の
royalties on one's book  印税

---

We have to save two seats at the conference for representatives from the coal industry.
石炭産業の代表者のために，会議の席を2つ確保しなければならない。

**128 save**
[séiv]
🅣 他 自 (を)たくわえる，を確保する
🅢 他 自 (を)救う
save ～ for ...  ～を…のためにとっておく

---

I decided to give our proposal to the senior management for comments before we make the prototype.
試作品を作る前に，意見を求めて提案を上層部に上げることにした。

**129 senior**
[síːnjər]
🅣 形 上司の 名 上司 🅢 形 年長の
a senior partner  幹部社員

35

The new package offered a **sensible** reduction in cost and led to a noticeable improvement in customer satisfaction.
新しい容器はコスト面での<u>目立った低下</u>を提供したので，顧客満足度の著しい改良につながった。

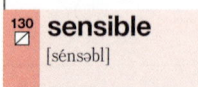

| 130 | **sensible** [sénsəbl] | T← 形 目立つほどの  学 形 分別のある<br>a sensible decision  賢明な決定 |

---

If you target your movie at teenagers, you are more likely to get a better **share** of box office sales.
あなたの映画の対象を10代にすれば，興行収入でもっと<u>市場占有率</u>を取れる可能性が高い。

| 131 | **share** [ʃéər] | T← 名 市場占有率；株式<br>学 名 分け前  他 を共有する<br>share one's opinion  〜と同意見だ |

---

Let's **ship** these big packages by truck tomorrow and send the fragile pieces by parcel delivery service later.
この大きな荷物は明日トラックで<u>出荷し</u>，壊れやすい部品はあとで宅配サービスで送ろう。

| 132 | **ship** [ʃíp] 必 | T← 他 を出荷する  学 名 船舶  →253 shipment<br>ship an order  注文品を発送する |

---

In order to install a second **sink** in the kitchen, we need to get a permit from the county.
台所に<u>流し台</u>をもう1つ設置するためには，郡の許可を得る必要がある。

| 133 | **sink** [síŋk] | T← 名 (台所の)流し  学 自 沈む  他 を沈める<br>sunk cost  埋没原価 |

---

It's important that we maintain our **solid** reputation as a high-quality provider of goods and services.
高品質の商品とサービスの提供者であるという<u>揺るぎない</u>評価を保つことが重要だ。

| 134 | **solid** [sɑ́ləd] | T← 形 しっかりした；堅実な  学 形 固体の  名 固体<br>solid evidence  確たる証拠 |

I agree with Janice that the flat-screen televisions should be the **special** for next month.
フラットテレビを来月の特売品にするというジャニスの意見に賛成です。

**135 special**
[spéʃl]

T← 名 特売品　学 形 特別な；専門の
⇒派 specialize 他 を専門にする
a special case　特例

---

Before I go back and make an offer, I'd like to have all the **specifics** available in chart form.
戻って提議する前に，すべての詳細を表の形で見られるようにしてほしい。

**136 specific**
[spəsífik]

T← 名 [specifics] 詳細；明細書　学 形 明確な
⇒派 specifically 副 明確に，特に
state one's specific purpose　目的をはっきり述べる

---

In the old days, young people gathered to socialize in the town **square**, but that rarely happens today.
昔は若者たちは街の広場に集まって交流したが，今日ではめったにそういうことはない。

**137 square**
[skwéər] 必

T← 名 (四角の) 広場　学 名 四角　形 四角の
a tiny square of glass　四角い小さなガラス

---

The summer brochure needs to **state** clearly that we provide air-conditioning at all of our hotels.
夏のパンフレットでは，当社の全ホテルにエアコンがあることを明確に記す必要がある。

**138 state**
[stéit]

T← 他 を述べる，申し立てる　学 名 状態；州
in the present state of things　現状では

---

Last week's board meeting concluded after reviewing the fiscal **statements** for the previous three years.
先週の重役会は，過去3年間の事業報告書を再検討して終了した。

**139 statement**
[stéitmənt]

T← 名 事業報告書　学 名 声明；陳述　→138 state
financial statements　財務諸表

There's enough syrup in stock to make three more batches, but we'll need to order some more flavorings.
あと3回分のシロップの在庫は十分あるが，香味料はいくらか注文する必要がある。

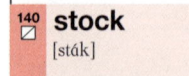

**140 stock**
[sták]

T← 名 在庫；株式　学 名 蓄え
dispose of stock　在庫を処分する

---

The company is using that closet to store bottled water and emergency supplies in case of a storm or disaster.
会社はその収納室を，嵐や災害のときに備えて水と防災用品を貯蔵するのに使っている。

**141 store**
[stɔ́:r]

T← 他 を貯蔵する；〈データ〉を保存しておく
学 名 店

---

Fred submitted a request for his vacation time once he know what the production schedule would be.
製造のスケジュールがわかると，フレッドは休暇願いを提出した。

**142 submit**
[səbmít]
必

T← 他 を提出する　学 他 を服従させる
⇒派 submission 名 提出；服従
submit an application　申請書を提出する

---

When they can't find common ground on a proposal, the managers send it on to their superiors for further action.
提案に見解の一致を見出せないとき，課長はさらなる行動を求めてそれを上司に送る。

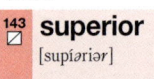

**143 superior**
[supíəriər]

T← 名 上司　形 上司の　学 形 優れた
be superior to 〜　〜よりもまさっている

---

Eugene has assured us that we have a three-month supply of paper in the warehouse.
ユージンは倉庫に3か月分の紙の在庫があると請け合った。

**144 supply**
[səplái]
難

T← 名 在庫；用品　学 他 を供給する　→261 supplier
office supplies　事務用品

It is possible to save about $30 if you send the package by **surface** mail instead of by air.

航空便でなく船便で小包を送れば，約30ドルの節約ができます。

### 145 surface
[sə́ːrfəs]

🇹 形 陸上〔海上〕輸送の　学 名 表面

surface mail　船便，陸上輸送便

---

Without a steady **surplus** of funds, the research for this new product is never going to happen.

資金に安定した余剰金がないと，この新製品の研究は決して実行されないだろう。

### 146 surplus
[sə́ːrpləs, -pləs]

🇹 名 余剰金　学 名 余り　形 余分な

accumulate a surplus　余剰を蓄積する

---

It's amazing that they already have a **suspect** in that jewelry store break-in this morning.

今朝の宝石店強盗の容疑者がすでにいるとは驚きだ。

### 147 suspect
名 [sʌ́spekt]
動 [səspékt]

🇹 名 容疑者　学 他 をあやしむ；…ではないかと思う

a suspected person　容疑者

---

We are **targeting** the single, 18-35-year-old male audience for this new television station.

我々はこの新しいテレビ局では18歳から35歳の独身男性視聴者を対象としている。

### 148 target
[tɑ́ːrgət]

🇹 他 〈商品が〉を対象にする　学 名 標的

reach the target　目標に到達する

---

In addition to the normal work force, **temporary** laborers were employed to meet the deadline for the renovation of our headquarters downtown.

商業地区の本社の修繕の期限に間に合うように，通常の労働力に加えて，臨時の労働者が雇われた。

### 149 temporary
[témpərèri]

🇹 形 臨時の　名 臨時職員　学 形 一時的な

a temporary decision　一時的な決定

One of the **terms** and conditions for being vice president is to keep track of futures market fluctuations on a daily basis.
副社長であるための条件と規定の1つは日々将来の市場変動を追っていくことである。

**150 term** [tə́ːrm]
- 🅣 名 [terms]（支払い・契約などの）条件
- 🅢 名 期間；学期；言葉
- in terms of 〜　〜の観点からすると

---

I'd like to propose a **toast** to Malcolm Granger, the best CEO this company has ever known!
この会社史上最高のCEO、マルコム・グレンジャーに乾杯したいと思います。

**151 toast** [tóust] 難
- 🅣 名 乾杯　自 乾杯する　🅢 名 トーストパン
- toast to 〜　〈人〉の健康を祝して乾杯する

---

He told me that I would never survive in management if I couldn't tackle the **tough** issues.
彼は、私が困難な問題に取り組めないのなら、経営者として絶対に生き残れないと言った。

**152 tough** [tʌ́f]
- 🅣 形 骨の折れる、困難な　🅢 形 じょうぶな
- a tough question　厄介な質問

---

The director said she would **value** input from the team, but was unhappy when they actually offered feedback.
重役はチームからの意見を尊重すると言ったが、実際に感想が出されたときは不満だった。

**153 value** [vǽljuː]
- 🅣 他 の値段を見積もる；を尊重する　🅢 名 価値
- ⇒派 **valuable** 形 価値のある
- market value　市場価値

---

That charity receives a lot of donations, because they have a good reputation and high **visibility**.
その慈善団体は、よい評判と注目度の高さで多額の寄付金を受け取っている。

**154 visibility** [vìzəbíləti]
- 🅣 名 注目度　🅢 名 目に見えること；視界
- ⇒派 **visible** 形 目に見える
- good [poor] visibility　よい〔悪い〕視界

There is a new technology that was developed on the East Coast that can turn **waste** into fuel.
東海岸で開発された新しい技術で、ごみを燃料に変えることができるものがある。

### 155 waste
[wéist]

- 名 廃棄物　形 廃棄物の
- 他 を浪費する　形 荒れ果てた

waste disposal　廃棄物処理

---

With online banking, I can **withdraw** money from my savings and put it into my checking account with a few clicks.
オンラインバンキングでは、何回かクリックするだけで、自分の貯蓄預金からお金を下ろして、当座預金に入れることができる。

### 156 withdraw
[wiðdrɔ́ː, wiθ-]　難

- 他〈貯金〉を下ろす　他 を引っ込める
- ⇒派 **withdrawal** 名 撤回；預金の引き出し

withdraw a deposit　預金を引き出す

---

Mr. Patterson decided to invest in the overseas fund when he found out how high the **yield** was.
パターソン氏は、利回りがいかに高いかを知って、海外ファンドへの投資を決意した。

### 157 yield
[jíːld]

- 名 収益；産出(高)　他〈利益など〉をもたらす
- 自 [yield to] に屈服する

a yield on investments　投資の利回り

# Chapter 1-2 学校英語を TOEIC にバージョンアップ

学校英語 ▶▶▶ TOEIC® TEST 関連語

Chapter 1-2 では，学校ですでに学んだ単語を記憶のキーとして見出し語を覚えましょう。♂マークの単語が学校英語で学んだ関連語です。

---

Joe meant to reply just to the sender; however, by clicking the wrong tab, he accidentally sent the message to all the managers.
ジョーは送信者だけに返信するつもりだったが，間違ったタブをクリックしたために誤って全部長にメッセージを送ってしまった。

**158 accidentally**
[æksədéntəli]
♂ accident

副 誤って；偶然に　⇒派 accidental 形 偶然の
accidentally on purpose　偶然を装い

---

There was a fruit basket in the hotel suite and the manager called to ask how we found the accommodation.
そのホテルのスイートルームには果物のかごが置いてあり，支配人がそのサービスはいかがでしたかと電話で聞いてきた。

**159 accommodation**
[əkàmədéiʃən]
♂ 564 accommodate

名 順応, 適応；宿泊設備 (部屋・食事・サービス料など)
receive free accommodation　無料の宿泊サービスを受ける

---

The accountant told us that we should purchase some additional office equipment to use as a write-off on our taxes.
会計士は追加でいくつかの社用備品を税金控除のために買わねばならないと言った。

**160 accountant**
[əkáuntənt]
♂ account

名 会計士
a certified public accountant　公認会計士；C.P.A.

---

He has degrees in both accounting and business administration, so he would be an excellent addition to your staff.
彼は会計学と経営学の両方の学位を持っているので，すばらしい人員が加わることになる。

**161 accounting**
[əkáuntiŋ]
♂ account

名 会計, 経理；会計学
an accounting period　会計期間

The manager was pleased when he realized that such a competent assistant had answered the classified **ad** we placed.
部長は，当社が出した求人**広告**にこれほど有能なアシスタントが応募したと知り喜んだ。

**162 ad**
[ǽd]
♂ ²⁷⁷ advertisement

名 広告 (advertisement の略)
a classified ad　部門別案内広告

---

The revenue from refreshments at a movie theater is much higher than what they bring in from **admissions**.
映画館では飲食物による収入が**入場料**収入よりもずっと大きい。

**163 admission**
[ədmíʃən, æd-]
♂ ⁵⁶⁷ admit

名 入場許可；入場料
admission fee　入場料

---

After reviewing the company budget, the committee selected a more **affordable** health insurance program for its employees.
委員会は，会社予算の検討後，社員のためにより**手ごろな**健康保険プログラムを選んだ。

**164 affordable**
[əfɔ́ːrdəbl]
♂ afford

形 手ごろな；購入しやすい
an affordable price　手ごろな値段

---

For overnight trips, the company offers an overnight bonus in addition to a daily **allowance** for food and lodging.
前泊出張に対し，会社は食事と宿泊に対する**日当**に加えて一泊用特別支給金を支払う。

**165 allowance**
[əláuəns]
♂ allow

名 割当量〔額〕；手当；値引
an overtime allowance　残業手当

---

Fill in your mobile telephone number next to where the form says **Alternate** Phone Number.
用紙の「**代替**電話番号」と書かれた横にあなたの携帯電話番号を記入してください。

**166 alternate**
[ɔ́ːltərnət, áːl-, ǽl-]
♂ ⁶⁹⁵ alter

形 交互の；代わりの　名 代替物〔案〕
alternate use　代替使用

The president doesn't want to have the banquet at the usual restaurant but nobody has suggested a reasonable alternative.
社長はいつものレストランで晩餐会を開きたくないが、だれも適当な代案を出していない。

### 167 alternative
[ɔːltə́ːrnətiv]
alter

名 選択肢；代案　形 二者択一の；代替の

alternative medicine　代替医療

---

After the lawyers amend the document, it needs to be signed by officers of both companies.
弁護士が書類を修正したあと、双方の会社の役員によって署名されなければならない。

### 168 amend
[əménd]
mend

他 〈憲法・法律など〉を修正する、改正する
≒類 revise 〜を改正する
amend rules　規則を改正する

---

Residents of Texas and Florida need to add the taxes applicable to the price of the product.
テキサス州とフロリダ州の住民は、製品の値段に応じた税金を加えなければならない。

### 169 applicable
[ǽplikəbl, əplíkəbl]
apply

形 適用できる；該当する、適切な
if applicable　該当する場合

---

Every applicant was advised that there were over 1,000 people interviewing for the three positions that were available.
応募者のだれもが、3つの空きポストに1,000人を超える人が面接を受けていると忠告された。

### 170 applicant
[ǽplikənt]
apply

名 出願者、応募者
an applicant for 〜　〜への応募者
a job applicant　求職者

---

At fancy restaurants and hotels you can usually give your keys to a parking attendant and let him park the car.
高級レストランやホテルではたいてい、車のキーを駐車係に渡して車を停めてもらえる。

### 171 attendant
[əténdənt]
attend

名 係員、接客係　形 付き添いの；出席の
a gas-station attendant　ガソリンスタンドの店員

In order to raise awareness, many schools are now offering programs that teach children the dangers of drugs.
多くの学校では，生徒の意識を高めるため，生徒に薬物の危険性を教えるプログラムを提供している。

**172 awareness**
[əwéərnəs]
🔑 aware

名 意識；気づいていること

raise awareness　意識を高める

---

If you are a hotel club member, you can contact the front desk and request late checkout.
ホテルクラブの会員なら，フロントに連絡して遅い時間のチェックアウトを要求できる。

**173 checkout**
[tʃékàut]
🔑 check

名 精算，チェックアウト

checkout counter　（スーパーなどの）レジ；精算台

---

Even though he does not suspect problems, the surgeon insisted on doing several checkups after the operation.
その外科医は，問題があるとは思わないが手術後にいくつか検査をすべきだと主張した。

**174 checkup**
[tʃékʌ̀p]
🔑 check

名 健康診断，検査

a medical checkup　健康診断

---

There were several good bargains at the clearance corner in the home improvement store.
そのホームセンターの在庫一掃コーナーには，いくつかのお買い得品があった。

**175 clearance**
[klíərəns]
🔑 clear

名 一掃；通関手続き

clearance sale　在庫一掃セール

---

The economic situation was given as the main reason for the closure of so many factories in the area.
その地域の非常に多くの工場の閉鎖の主な原因として経済状況が挙げられた。

**176 closure**
[klóuʒər]
🔑 close

名 閉鎖

temporary closure　一時的な閉鎖

Someone in the PR department should be sure to follow the advertising campaigns of all your **competitors**.
宣伝部の者なら，必ず全競合他社の広告キャンペーンを見守っておくべきだ。

### 177 competitor
[kəmpétətər]
⚥ compete

图 競争相手，競合他社

major competitors　主な競争相手

---

The Federal Aviation Administration is now negotiating to avoid another air-traffic **controller** strike.
現在，連邦航空局は航空管制官によるストの再発を避けるために交渉を行っている。

### 178 controller
[kəntróulər]
⚥ ³⁰⁸ control

图 経理担当役員；会計監査官；(航空機の)管制官

the controller of the company　企業の経理部長〔監査役〕

---

Choosing to outsource your support staff is usually cheaper, but if you choose the wrong partner it can end up being **costly**.
支援スタッフを外部調達すると通常は安くつくが，相手を間違えると結局は高くつく。

### 179 costly
[kɔ́(ː)stli]
⚥ ³¹² cost

形 値段の高い，高くついた

costly medical care　高価な医療

---

**Creditors** can request consumer credit information about a customer from credit bureaus and lower or raise a consumer's spending limits.
貸主は，客の消費者金融の情報を興信所から求め，利用限度額を上げ下げできる。

### 180 creditor
[kréditər]
⚥ credit

图 債権者，貸主

make a composition with one's creditors　債権者たちと示談にする

---

Not acting **decisive** during the negotiations will give the other side the impression that you are weak.
交渉中に断固とした行動をとらないと，相手側に自分が弱いという印象を与えてしまう。

### 181 decisive
[disáisiv]
⚥ decide

形 断固とした；決定的な
⇔反 indecisive 形 優柔不断な；決定的でない

a decisive vote　決選投票

The company had no choice but to **discharge** the bus driver because he tested positive for alcohol.
そのバス運転手はアルコール検査で陽性だったので，会社は彼を解雇せざるを得なかった。

**182 discharge**
動 [distʃáːrdʒ]
名 [́--, -́]
⚥ charge

他 を解放する；を降ろす；を解雇する；〈義務・責任〉を果たす 名 荷揚げ；解雇；解放

discharge one's duties　職務を果たす

---

If something happens to **disconnect** the power source, the backup battery will supply power immediately.
電源を断絶するようなことが起これば，予備のバッテリーが直ちに電力を供給する。

**183 disconnect**
[dìskənékt]
⚥ connect

他 との接続を断つ；から分離する

disconnect a phone cord　電話線を切る

---

If headaches or muscle aches occur from using this medication, please **discontinue** use and consult your physician.
この薬の使用で頭痛または筋肉痛が起きた場合には使用をやめ，医師に相談してください。

**184 discontinue**
[dìskəntínjuː]
⚥ continue

他 をやめる

discontinue business　廃業する

---

Joe's **dismissal** came as a surprise to no one; his unexplained absences had increased steadily over the last month.
ジョーの解雇にはだれも驚かなかった。無断欠勤が先月の間確実に増えていたのだ。

**185 dismissal**
[dismísl]
⚥ dismiss

名 解雇；退去

unfair dismissal　不当解雇

---

The local government was in such **disorder** after the disaster the national agency wasn't sure how to assist them.
その地方政府は災害のあと非常に混乱していたので，政府機関はどうやって彼らを援助したらよいかわからなかった。

**186 disorder**
[disɔ́ːrdər, diz-]
⚥ order

名 無秩序，混乱；異常

be in disorder　混乱している

The company cannot be held responsible for what happens if the consumer **disregards** the warnings on the label.
消費者がラベルの警告を無視すれば，企業は起こったことに責任を持てない。

**187 disregard**
[dìsrigáːrd]
♂ regard

他 を無視する；を軽視する 名 無関心
disregard for [of] ～  ～に対する無関心

---

A lot of customers explained which features of the product **dissatisfied** them in the comments section of the survey.
多くの顧客は調査のコメント欄で，その製品のどの特徴に不満があるかを説明した。

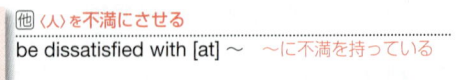

**188 dissatisfy**
[dissǽtisfài]
♂ satisfy

他 〈人〉を不満にさせる
be dissatisfied with [at] ～  ～に不満を持っている

---

Following the trend toward more healthy eating, the snack company has decided to **diversify** their product line.
より健康的な食生活が好まれる傾向を受けて，そのスナック会社は自社の製造ラインを多様化することに決めた。

**189 diversify**
[dəvə́ːrsəfài]
♂ diverse

他 を多様化〔多角化〕する 自 多様化〔多角化〕する
diversify away from ～  ～を脱却して多角化する

---

The boss has set the thermostat a bit lower in order to **economize** on heating costs.
上司は暖房費を節約するために，温度を少し低く設定した。

**190 economize**
[ikánəmàiz]
♂ economy

自 出費を切り詰める 他 を節約する
economize time  時間を節約する

---

Taking the tropical fish away and disturbing them are all illegal, but the government rarely **enforces** the restriction.
熱帯魚を持ち去り，その生態を乱すのはすべて違法だが，政府はめったに規制を強化しない。

**191 enforce**
[enfɔ́ːrs]
♂ force

他 〈法律・規則など〉を施行する；を強化する
⇒派 **enforcement** 名 施行
enforce a law  法律を施行する

The guest of honor was forced to leave the reception early because of another **engagement**.
ほかの約束のため，主賓は歓迎会を早々と退出することを余儀なくされた。

### 192 engagement
[engéidʒmənt]
♂ engage

图 約束；婚約；契約；雇用, 雇用期間
a prior engagement　先約
make an engagement with ～　～と約束〔契約〕を交わす

---

I suggest we **enlarge** handout number three and use it for our poster session at the symposium.
配布資料の3番を拡大して，シンポジウムのポスターセッションで使うことを提案します。

### 193 enlarge
[enláːrdʒ]
♂ large

他 を拡大する；を拡張する
enlarge an image 15 times　画像を15倍に拡大する

---

As an **entrepreneur** without a steady paycheck, Bob must fill out a stated income loan form, versus the regular form.
安定した稼ぎのない事業家なので，ボブは一般の用紙ではなく収入自己申告型ローン用紙に記入しなければならない。

### 194 entrepreneur
[àːntrəprənə́ːr]
♂ enterprise

图 起業家, 事業家
a business entrepreneur　企業経営者

---

These cleaning wipes are not commercially feasible because the solution tends to **evaporate** in a short time.
溶液は短時間で蒸発しやすいので，この掃除用ウェットシートは商業的に実現可能でない。

### 195 evaporate
[ivǽpərèit]
♂ vapor

自 蒸発する　他 を蒸発させる
evaporate from ～　～から消える

---

The management called in Wayne Sykes to consult, because Wayne has a lot of **expertise** in product placement.
経営陣は，意見を聞くためにウェイン・サイクスを呼び入れた。というのは，ウェインは商品配置に関して多くの専門知識を持っているからである。

### 196 expertise
[èkspəːrtíːz]
♂ expert

图 専門的技術〔知識〕
business expertise　事業の専門知識

In response to the **fitness** boom, many large companies have been building in-house gyms to help keep employees fit.
健康ブームに応え，社員の体調維持に役立つよう，多くの大企業が社内ジムを設けている。

### 197 fitness
[fítnəs]
♂ ⁴³⁷ fit

名 健康, 体力；適合；適性

one's fitness for the job　仕事に対する適性

---

It was obvious that the speaker was a master of public speaking, as his delivery was **flawless**.
話しぶりが完璧だったので，講演者は人前で話をする達人であることは明白だった。

### 198 flawless
[flɔ́ːləs]
♂ ⁶⁶³ flaw

形 完璧な

flawless technique　完璧な技術

---

Mr. Rosen prints out documents from his computer for everything, because he claims nobody else can read his **handwriting**.
ローゼン氏は，自分の手書きの文字は彼以外だれも読めないと主張して，何でもかんでもコンピュータから文書をプリントアウトする。

### 199 handwriting
[hǽndràitiŋ]
♂ hand + writing

名 手書き, 筆跡

neat handwriting　きれいな筆跡

---

With an e-ticket, you make the reservation and produce **identification**, when picking up the ticket.
電子チケットについては，予約をして，チケットを受け取るときに身分証明書を提示する。

### 200 identification
[aidèntəfikéiʃən]
♂ ⁵⁸⁷ identify

名 身分証明(書)；同一であることの証明（略：ID）

identification papers　身分証明書類

---

The client took their time getting back to us, but now they are **impatient** and pushing for a revised proposal.
その取引先は返事をしてくるのに時間をかけたのに，今度は我々が提案を修正するのを待ちきれずに執拗に求めている。

### 201 impatient
[impéiʃənt]
♂ ¹⁰²⁹ patient

形 我慢できない；待ち遠しく思う

be impatient for ～　～が待ち遠しい

After finalizing the transaction the art consultant noticed an **imperfection** in the print and ordered the customer a different copy.
取引が最終的に成立したあと，その美術コンサルタントは印刷の不備を見つけて，取引先に別の刷りものを注文した。

### 202 imperfection
[ìmpərfékʃən]
⚥ perfection

名 不完全, 欠点
reduce product imperfections　製品の欠陥を減らす

If you act nervous during the presentation, the **implication** is that you aren't really that well informed.
発表中に不安そうにすると，情報をあまりきちんと把握していないのを暗に示すことになる。

### 203 implication
[ìmplikéiʃən]
⚥ 588 imply

名 言外の意味, 含意；密接な関係, 関与
by (way of) implication　それとなく, 暗に

I didn't realize our report was **incomplete** until I counted the pages and noticed we had skipped the third section.
ページを数えて第3部を飛ばしたことに気づくまで，報告書が不完全だと気づかなかった。

### 204 incomplete
[ìnkəmplí:t]
⚥ 1058 complete

形 不完全な, 不十分な
an incomplete application　不備のある願書

The **inconvenience** of parking at the shopping mall and walking to the stadium was much worse in the August heat.
商店街に車を停めて競技場まで歩いていく不便さは，8月の暑さでさらにひどくなった。

### 205 inconvenience
[ìnkənví:njəns]
⚥ 309 convenience

名 不便, 不都合, 迷惑
if it's no inconvenience to you　ご迷惑でなければ
apologize for the inconvenience　迷惑を謝罪する

Our agents need to listen carefully on the phone, as several customers have complained that their address labels were **incorrect**.
何人かの顧客が住所のラベルが間違っていたと苦情を言ってきたので，代理店は注意して電話を聞く必要がある。

### 206 incorrect
[ìnkərékt]
⚥ 36 correct

形 間違った, 不正確な；適切でない
an incorrect statement　不正確な陳述

The online auction company has predetermined **increments** at which your bid will increase if another bidder matches you.

オンラインオークションの会社は，もしほかの入札者があなたと対等であった場合に，あなたの入札額がいくら上がるかという増加額をあらかじめ決めている。

**207 increment**
[íŋkrəmənt, ín-]
⚥ increase

名 増大，増加；増加量

special increment of salary　給料の特別増額

---

The flashing of the red **indicator** light means that the electronic pressure cooker is still building up pressure.

赤い表示灯の点滅は，電気圧力鍋がまだ圧力をかけている最中であることを示す。

**208 indicator**
[índikèitər]
⚥ indicate

名 指示者；表示器；指標

an indicator of economic growth　経済成長の指標

---

Even though the country is at war, most citizens are **indifferent** to politics and international policy.

国が戦争中にもかかわらず，ほとんどの市民は政治や国際政策に無関心だ。

**209 indifferent**
[indífərnt, -dífərənt]
⚥ different

形 無関心な；よくも悪くもない

be indifferent to ～　～に無関心である

---

We interviewed several financial officers and found Greta to be the most **informative** of those we talked to.

私たちは何人かの財務官に面接調査をし，話をした中でグレタが一番情報をたくさん持っていることがわかった。

**210 informative**
[infɔ́:rmətiv]
⚥ information

形 有用な情報の多い　→ inform

an informative book　有益な本

---

The bank was unable to cash the check written on the account due to **insufficient** funds.

資金が不十分だったので，銀行は明細に書かれた小切手を現金化することができなかった。

**211 insufficient**
[ìnsəfíʃənt]
⚥ sufficient

形 不足の，不十分な

an insufficient supply of food　不十分な食糧供給

We can only **insure** your safety if you follow the rules and wear a hardhat around the construction site.
規則を守り，建設現場付近ではヘルメットをかぶらなければ，安全は保証できない。

### 212 insure
[inʃúər]
♂ ³⁴⁶ insurance

他 を保証する；を保険に入れる　自 保険に入る

insure one's house against fire　家に火災保険をかける

---

Doug is taking an **intensive** Chinese class before his business trip to Shanghai in the fall.
ダグは秋に上海に出張する前に中国語の集中講義を受けている。

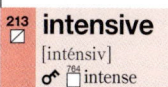

### 213 intensive
[inténsiv]
♂ ⁷⁰⁴ intense

形 短期間に集中した；徹底的な

intensive instruction　集中教育

---

We are calling this a **joint** venture, rather than a merger, as each company will retain its individual identity.
それぞれの会社が個々の独自性を保持することになるので，私たちはこれを合併というよりは共同事業と呼ぶのです。

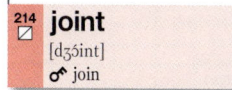

### 214 joint
[dʒɔ́int]
♂ join

形 共同の　名 関節；継ぎ目　他 を継ぎ合わせる

out of joint　脱臼して

---

Hosting a major international sporting event was a **landmark** event for the small skiing village.
主要な国際的スポーツイベントを主催することは，その小さなスキーの村にとって画期的な出来事だった。

### 215 landmark
[lǽndmɑ̀ːrk]
♂ land + mark

名 目印になる建物；歴史的建造物；画期的な出来事

a landmark visible from miles away　数マイル先から見える目印

---

**Lawmakers** proposed severe penalties on companies handling industrial waste in an irresponsible manner.
立法家たちは産業廃棄物の無責任な処分をしている会社に対する厳しい罰則を提案した。

### 216 lawmaker
[lɔ́ːmèikər]
♂ law + maker

名 (立法府の)議員，法制定者

a lawmaker from New York　ニューヨーク州選出の議員

Since they decided to **lengthen** the presentation, the chairman moved it up to come after the lunch break.
プレゼンの時間を長くすることに決めたので, 議長は開始を昼休み後に動かした。

### 217 lengthen
[léŋkθn]
o⁷ length

他 を(長さ・時間の面で)長くする
lengthen a holiday　休暇を延ばす

---

Unfortunately, spam blockers don't filter out all of the unwanted advertisements and other **misuse** of e-mail.
残念ながら, スパムを阻止するプログラムは, 迷惑広告やその他のメールの誤用をすべて除去してくれるわけではない。

### 218 misuse
名[mìsjúːs] 動[mìsjúːz]
o⁷ use

名 誤用, 悪用　他 を誤用する
misuse of funds　資金の悪用

---

It was called a **multinational** gathering, so we were disappointed to learn we were all from Singapore and Taiwan only.
それは多国籍集会と呼ばれていたので, 全員, シンガポールと台湾出身者だけだとわかって私たちはがっかりした。

### 219 multinational
[mʌ̀ltinǽʃənl]
o⁷ national

形 多国籍(企業)の
a multinational corporation　多国籍企業

---

The New York agency deals with famous performers, **namely** the actors in Broadway plays.
ニューヨークの代理店は有名な役者, つまりブロードウェー演劇の俳優と取引している。

### 220 namely
[néimli]
o⁷ name

副 すなわち
≒類 that is to say ...　すなわち…

---

We placed ads **nationwide** and still could not find an engineer with all of the necessary qualifications.
全国規模で広告を出したが, それでも必要な資格をすべて持った技師は見つからなかった。

### 221 nationwide
[nèiʃənwáid]
o⁷ nation + wide

形 全国規模の　副 全国規模で
arouse nationwide interest　全国民の関心を呼び起こす

Among his many **notable** accomplishments, Dr. Mitchell spent four years in Africa volunteering his medical services.
ミッチェル博士の多くの注目すべき偉業の1つに，アフリカで4年間，自ら進んで医療に従事したことが挙げられる。

**222 notable**
[nóutəbl]
⚥ note

形 注目すべき；著名な
a notable scholar　著名な学者

---

The new manager has asked that we skip the **obligatory** welcome party and instead take turns eating lunch with him.
新しい部長は，義務的な歓迎会はやめて，代わりに順番に自分と昼食をとるように求めた。

**223 obligatory**
[əblígətɔ̀ːri]
⚥ oblige

形 義務的な，強制的な；必須の　→ obligation
an obligatory subject　必修科目

---

The judge explained to him that the sentence would be more severe as he was a repeat **offender**.
判事は，彼は常習の犯罪者なので，判決はより厳しくなると説明した。

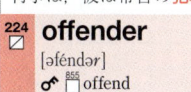

**224 offender**
[əféndər]
⚥ offend

名 犯罪者，違反者
a first offender　初犯者

---

The sale price wasn't in the store computer, so they **overcharged** me for the toaster that I purchased.
セールの価格が店のコンピュータに保存されていなかったので，私は買ったトースターに余分なお金を請求された。

**225 overcharge**
動 [òuvərtʃáːrdʒ]
名 [´-`]
⚥ charge

他 に高い値段を請求する　名 不当請求
the overcharged amount　過剰請求額

---

The daily commute on the **overcrowded** commuter train always makes me feel irritated and exhausted.
混雑した通勤電車で毎日通勤すると，いらいらしてひどく疲れる。

**226 overcrowded**
[òuvərkráudid]
⚥ crowded

形 込み合った，超満員の
an overcrowded room　人でいっぱいの部屋

You should take the car to the dealer; we're **overdue** for an oil change and tire rotation.

君は車をディーラーに持っていかなければならない。オイル交換とタイヤのローテーションの**期限が切れている**から。

**227 overdue**
[òuvərd(j)úː]
⚥ due

形 期限の過ぎた

an overdue check　期限経過小切手

---

The best way to get to the island is to take an **overnight** ferry from Wilson's Pier.

その島に行く一番よい方法は、ウィルソン埠頭から**夜行**フェリーに乗ることだ。

**228 overnight**
形 [óuvərnàit] 副 [- - -]
⚥ night

形 一泊の；夜行の；翌日配達の　副 一晩中；夜の間に

overnight mail　翌日配達便

---

If you check in with me **periodically**, I can let you know if we get more stock on that item.

**定期的に**私におたずねいただければ、その商品の在庫が増えたときにお知らせできます。

**229 periodically**
[pìəriádikəli]
⚥ period

副 定期的に

check ~ periodically　~を定期的に点検する

---

The movie **portrayed** the 19th century railroad company boss as a cold and ruthless businessman.

その映画は、冷酷で無情な事業家としてその19世紀の鉄道王**を描いていた**。

**230 portray**
[pɔːrtréi]
⚥ portrait

他 〈物・人〉を表現する

portray ~ as ...　~〈人〉を…であると描写する

---

When I have to catch more than one flight, I always carry a change of clothes as a **precaution**.

2つ以上飛行機に乗らなければならないときには、いつも**万一の備え**として着替えを持っていくことにしている。

**231 precaution**
[prikɔ́ːʃən]
⚥ caution

名 用心、備え；予防策

take precautions against ~　~を警戒〔用心〕する

Mr. Lane seems to have quite a **preoccupation** with how young the computer consultant is.
レイン氏はそのコンピュータコンサルタントが非常に若いことについて，かなり懸念を抱いているようだ。

**232 preoccupation**
[priàkjəpéiʃən]
⚬ occupation (641)

名 没頭，夢中；気がかりな状態
a preoccupation with 〜　〜への没頭

---

The need for that type of business is strong, but the question is whether or not it would be **profitable**.
その種の商売の必要性は高いが，問題はそれがもうかるかどうかだ。

**233 profitable**
[práfətəbl]
⚬ profit (274)

形 もうかる，利益を生む；役に立つ
a profitable market　もうかる市場

---

Company recruiters visited many university campuses in search of **promising** future employees.
会社の雇用担当者は，前途有望な未来の社員を求め，多くの大学キャンパスを訪れた。

**234 promising**
[prámәsiŋ]
⚬ promise

形 前途有望な，期待の持てる
a promising market　将来有望な市場

---

The company thought Rolf was embezzling, but they were never able to find sufficient **proof**.
会社はロルフが横領していると思ったが，結局十分な証拠を見つけられなかった。

**235 proof**
[prú:f]
⚬ prove (693)

名 証拠；証明　形〈水・火などに〉耐えられる
proof against fire　耐火性の

---

Milford Wireless is a new **provider** that is attempting to capture a market share with lower rates and nicer phones.
ミルフォード無線はより低い料金とより魅力的な電話機で市場でのシェアを獲得しようとしている新しい供給業者だ。

**236 provider**
[prəváidər]
⚬ provide (451)

名 供給業者
service provider　サービス業者；インターネット接続業者

We need a **provision** in the contract for non-delivery due to disasters such as earthquakes.

私たちは，地震のような災害による不着損害に対する条項を契約に含める必要がある。

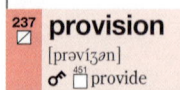

**237 provision**
[prəvíʒən]
provide

名 供給；準備，備え；条項
make provision for the future　将来に備える

---

The memo said that we should not make any large purchases until after the release of the **quarterly** income statement.

規約には，四半期の損益計算書の公開まで，大口の購入をしてはいけないとあった。

**238 quarterly**
[kwɔ́:rtərli, kɔ́:r-]
quarter

形 年4回の，四半期の　副 年4回　名 季刊誌
a quarterly report　四半期ごとの報告

---

The surgeon followed up on his patients' progress by having them fill out six-month and one-year post-operative **questionnaires**.

その外科医は，患者に手術後半年および1年のアンケートに記入してもらうことによって，患者の回復状況を追跡調査した。

**239 questionnaire**
[kwèstʃənéər]
question

名 質問票，アンケート
fill in a questionnaire　アンケートに記入する

---

The recipe calls for the spice sumac, which is rare here, but **readily** available in the Middle East.

レシピによると，この辺では珍しいが中近東では簡単に手に入るウルシという香辛料が要る。

**240 readily**
[rédili]
ready

副 難なく；快く
a readily accessible library　たやすく利用できる図書館

---

Mort Jaffe of Mort's Auto Repair is this year's **recipient** of the city's Best Car Mechanic award.

モート自動車修理のモート・ジャフィーは今年の市内「ベスト・カー・メカニック」賞受賞者だ。

**241 recipient**
[risípiənt]
receive, receipt

名 受取人，受領者
the recipient of a prize　受賞者

Mr. Wolf's secretary called the airline to **reconfirm** his reservation and get his seat assignment.
ウルフ氏の秘書は航空会社に電話して予約を再確認し、座席の指定をした。

**242 reconfirm**
[rèkənfə́ːrm]
o— 420 confirm

他〈予約など〉を再確認する

reconfirm the flight 搭乗便を再確認する

---

If you are willing to **relocate**, you could probably find a higher paying job in a bigger city.
引っ越してもいいのなら、たぶんもっと大きな街でもっと収入のよい仕事が見つかるよ。

**243 relocate**
[rìːlóukeit]
o— 86 locate

自 新しい場所に移る 他 を新しい場所に移す
⇒派 relocation 名 移転

relocate ~ to ... ~を…に移転する

---

After he paid off his credit card debt, he used the **remainder** of the loan to redecorate his home.
彼はクレジットカードによる借金を払い終えると、ローンの残りを家の改装に使った。

**244 remainder**
[riméindər]
o— 456 remain

名 残り

the remainder of the day その日の残りの時間

---

If the gym doesn't put in some better equipment, I won't **renew** my membership.
もしそのスポーツクラブがもっとよい設備を導入しないなら、私は会員契約を更新しない。

**245 renew**
[rin(j)úː]
o— new

他 を更新する；を再開する ⇒派 renewal 名 更新

renew a lease 賃貸借契約書を更新する

---

The Burkes live on the second floor and they use their first floor space as a **rental** unit.
バーク夫妻は2階に住んでおり、1階のスペースは賃貸物件として使っている。

**246 rental**
[réntl]
o— 122 rent

形 賃貸借のできる 名 賃貸料；賃貸物件

a rental fee 賃貸〔貸借〕料

Each department must select a **representative** to attend next week's Safety in the Workplace seminar.

それぞれの部署では，来週の「職場での安全」に関するセミナーに出席する**代表者**を選ばなければならない。

**247 representative**
[rèprizéntətiv]
represent

名 代表者；代議士　形 代表する
a legal representative　法定代理人

---

If you use your car for company business, it is a **requirement** that you have both accident and liability insurance.

車を会社の仕事で使う場合，損害保険と責任保険の両方に入ることが**条件**となります。

**248 requirement**
[rikwáiərmənt]
require

名 必要条件；必需品
travel requirements　旅行に必要な品々

---

Mr. Evans is away on a family emergency and has asked me to **reschedule** all of his appointments.

エヴァンズ氏は家庭の急用で出かけていて，すべての約束**を再調整する**ように私に頼んだ。

**249 reschedule**
[riskédʒu:l]
schedule

他 〈日程〉を再調整する；〈債務〉の繰延べをする
reschedule debts　（貸付金などの）償還期限を延ばす

---

Our high school class **reunion** was held at a hotel in July with parties on both Friday and Saturday evening.

私たちの高校のクラスの**同窓会**が7月にあるホテルで開かれ，金曜日と土曜日の両方の夜にパーティがあった。

**250 reunion**
[rì:jú:njən]
union

名 再会；同窓会
a class reunion　同窓会

---

If office assignments were based on **seniority** instead of performance, Bill would have the corner office with a view.

もし会社の配属が業績ではなく**年功**に基づいたものであれば，ビルは景色のよい角部屋の執務室を与えられるだろうに。

**251 seniority**
[si:njɔ́:rəti]
senior

名 先輩であること；勤続年数の長さ，年功
a seniority allowance　勤続手当

The details of the murders resemble one another, so the police are looking for a serial killer.

殺人事件の細部が互いに似通っているため，警察は連続殺人犯を捜している。

**252 serial**
[síəriəl]
○ series

形 連続して起こる；ひと続きの
名 (テレビ・ラジオ・新聞・雑誌の) 連続物

in serial order　連続して　　a serial number　通し番号

---

My order arrived in two different shipments, but the company only charged me a single shipping charge.

注文品は2つの積み荷に分かれて届いたが，その会社は1つ分の配送料しか請求しなかった。

**253 shipment**
[ʃípmənt]
○ ship

名 出荷；貨物，積み荷

delayed shipment　積み遅れ

---

The shutdown of the system is a safety feature that keeps the circuits from getting overheated and causing a fire.

システムの停止は，回路が過熱して火事を引き起こすことを防ぐための安全措置の1つだ。

**254 shutdown**
[ʃʌ́tdàun]
○ shut

名 運転停止，活動停止

shutdown of the plant　工場閉鎖

---

Excuse me, Ms. Wilson; I need your signature on this document that we received from General Affairs.

ウィルソンさん，すみません。総務部から受け取ったこの書類にあなたの署名が要ります。

**255 signature**
[sígnətʃər]
○ sign

名 自筆署名；痕跡

write one's signature　サインする

---

Overall, the hotel suite was quite spacious, but we were a bit disappointed that the bathroom was so small.

そのホテルのスイート全体はかなり広かったが，浴室がとても狭くて少しがっかりした。

**256 spacious**
[spéiʃəs]
○ space

形 広大な

a spacious car　車内が広々とした車

I understand it's the chef's **specialty**, so I think we should order the goat cheese souffl.

ヤギのチーズのスフレはシェフの**名物料理**だと思うので，それを注文すべきだ。

### 257 specialty
[spéʃəlti]
○ special

图 専門, 得意分野；名物料理

make a specialty of ～　～を専門にする

---

Automating that one process should **streamline** their operations to the point where they can reduce labor.

その1つの工程を自動化することにより，彼らの作業は労働力を削減できるほどに**能率化**されるはずだ。

### 258 streamline
[stríːmlàin]
○ stream + line

他 を合理化する；を流線型にする

streamline the lawmaking process　立法手続きを合理化する

---

He could offer us a **substantial** savings if we could buy the copper in quantity up front.

前払いで大量に銅を買うことができれば，彼は**かなりの**値引きを申し出てくれるのだが。

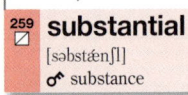

### 259 substantial
[səbstǽnʃl]
○ substance

形 かなりの, 相当な

a substantial progress　かなりの進歩

---

Hundreds of people are working to restore the town and conditions improve with each **succeeding** day.

何百という人々が街を復旧するために働いており，**次の**日になるにつれ状況は改善している。

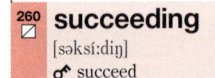

### 260 succeeding
[səksíːdiŋ]
○ succeed

形 続いて起こる, 次の

succeeding generations　あとの世代

---

It wasn't the price; it was the unfavorable terms of the contract that made us seek out a new **supplier**.

新しい**供給業者**を探すことになったのは，値段ではなく契約の不利な条件のためだった。

### 261 supplier
[səpláiər]
○ supply

图 (商品などの) 供給業者

a domestic [an overseas] supplier　国内〔海外〕の供給業者

I'm not asking you to do anything except to be **supportive** about our decision to use Frank's facility.
私はあなたに，フランクの施設を利用するという私たちの決定を支持してほしいということしか頼んでいない。

**262 supportive**
[səpɔ́ːrtiv]
♂ support

形 協力的な；支持する

be strongly supportive　強力に支持する

---

When I asked about the **surcharge** at the front desk, she explained that there's a state hotel tax of 11%.
フロントで追加料金についてたずねると，彼女は州のホテル税が11パーセントかかると説明してくれた。

**263 surcharge**
[sɔ́ːrtʃɑ̀ːrdʒ]
♂ charge

名 追加料金

a surcharge for late payment　延滞金

---

The article says the U.S. **Treasury** is going to issue two new coins in the next several months.
その記事には，アメリカ財務省が今後数か月以内に新しい硬貨を2種類発行すると書かれている。

**264 treasury**
[tréʒəri]
♂ treasure

名 財務省，大蔵省；国庫

a Treasury bond　財務省債券

---

Many fields offer few positions for those who only have an **undergraduate** degree in the subject.
その学科で学士号しか持たない者に職を提供する分野はほとんどない。

**265 undergraduate**
[ʌ̀ndərgrǽdʒuət]
♂ graduate

形 学部在学生の　名 学部在学生

undergraduate courses　学部学生用の科目

---

It doesn't really matter that the local **unemployment** rate is low when most jobs here pay so poorly.
この地域の仕事の給料は非常に低いので，ここの失業率が低いといってもあまり関係ない。

**266 unemployment**
[ʌ̀nimplɔ́imənt]
♂ employment

名 失業状態；失業率

keep unemployment low　失業者数を低く抑える

The public's overwhelming response to the product was **unparalleled** in the history of the industry.
その製品に対する大衆の圧倒的な反応は、この業界の歴史上例を見ないものだった。

### 267 unparalleled
[ʌnpǽrəleld]
○⁺ ▢parallel (824)

形 並ぶもののない, 無比の
unparalleled in modern history　近代史上並ぶもののない

---

We decided to hire an outside company to **update** our Web site and improve its appearance and functionality.
自社のサイトを更新して見た目と機能性を高めるために、外部の会社を雇うことに決めた。

### 268 update
動 [ʌpdéit] 名 [ʌ́pdeit]
○⁺ date

他 を更新する, 最新のものにする　名 更新, 最新情報
update a list of available documents　入手可能な書類のリストを更新する

---

There was an **urgent** message for you to call Cindy at your office.
あなたの事務所のシンディーさんに電話をするようにとの緊急のメッセージが届きました。

### 269 urgent
[ə́ːrdʒənt]
○⁺ ▢urge (747)

形 緊急の
in urgent need of ～　～を緊急に必要として

---

A parking ticket is less damaging to your record, because it is not a moving **violation**.
走行中の違反ではないため、駐車違反の切符による運転記録へのダメージは少ない。

### 270 violation
[vàiəléiʃən]
○⁺ violate

名 (法律などの)違反, 侵害
in violation of ～　～に違反して

---

I thought we couldn't make the sandwiches on that budget until I learned how cheap the meat would be **wholesale**.
私はその予算でサンドイッチを作るのは無理だと思ったが、その後卸売りで肉がどれだけ安いかを知った。

### 271 wholesale
[hóulsèil]
○⁺ whole + sale

形 卸売りの
a wholesale price　卸売価格

The school's idea of dealing with less revenue is to give the instructors heavier **workloads** for the same pay.

学校がもっと低い資金でやり繰りすると考えているということは，教師に同じ給料でより多い**仕事量**をこなしてもらうということになる。

**272 workload**
[wə́:rklòud]
⚥ work + load

图 仕事量，作業負荷

a heavy workload　大量の仕事

---

I thought the shortage of vanilla beans was just in this country, but I now understand that it is **worldwide**.

バニラビーンズ不足はこの国だけだと思っていたが，今は**世界的規模**だと理解している。

**273 worldwide**
[wə́:rldwáid]
⚥ world + wide

形 全世界に広がる

worldwide demand　全世界の需要

---

The bonus is 10% of your **yearly** income, so that is just a little more than one month's pay.

ボーナスは**年**収の 10 パーセントだから，1 か月分の給料より少しだけ多いということだ。

**274 yearly**
[jíərli]
⚥ year

形 副 年1回(の)；毎年(の)
≒類 annual 形 毎年の

a yearly revenue of 〜　〜の年収

## Chapter 2

# 使える学校英語を総ざらい

- 2-1 頻度★★★
- 2-2 頻度★★
- 2-3 頻度★

# Chapter 2-1 使える学校英語を総ざらい

**学校英語 ▶▶▶ TOEIC® TEST**　**頻度★★★**

　Chapter 2 では，学校英語でも頻出だった重要単語を TOEIC でよく出る話題にそった英文の中で覚えます。

　各英文の空欄に当てはまる単語を下の枠内から選び，適切な形に直して補いましょう。また，隣のページで解答，語義を確認しましょう。

> advertisement　　audience　　appliance　　amount
> 　　attraction　　ability　　advantage

(1) When considering candidates for the position, the committee was interested in each applicant's (　) to handle conflict.
その職への志願者を検討する際，委員会は各人の対立を処理する能力に興味を示した。

(2) Living abroad as a child gave Tsuyoshi a major (　) when he later had to do business with English-speaking companies.
少年時代に海外で暮らしたことは，ツヨシが後に英語圏の会社と取引を行わなければならなくなったとき，大きな強みとなった。

(3) They recommended we take out an (　) in their bulletin, but their readers are not appropriate for our product.
彼らは会報への広告の掲載を勧めてきたが，彼らの読者は我々の製品にふさわしくない。

(4) The tip can be calculated on the (　) of the food only, rather than on the final total including tax.
チップは税込みの最終合計からよりはむしろ，食べ物だけの金額から計算できる。

(5) During the (　) sale, we were able to get a free microwave oven with the purchase of a refrigerator and range.
電化製品のセールで冷蔵庫と調理用レンジを買ったので，電子レンジを無料でもらえた。

(6) When the designer revealed the plans for the new office, nobody felt (　) for the track lighting.
設計者が新事務所の図面を示したとき，だれも移動照明に魅力を感じなかった。

(7) When he saw that there were so many seniors in the (　), he switched the focus of his speech slightly.
聴衆の中に大勢の高齢者を見かけ，彼はスピーチの焦点を少し切り換えた。

## 275 ability
[əbíləti]

名 能力  ⇒派 able 形 能力がある

ability to do  …できること

## 276 advantage
[ədvǽntidʒ]

名 有利；利点，強み

take advantage of ~  ~を利用する
have an advantage over ~  ~より有利である

## 277 advertisement
[ædvərtáizmənt, ədvə́ːrtəs-, -təz-]

名 広告  ⇒派 advertise 他 を広告する

answer an advertisement  広告に応募する

## 278 amount
[əmáunt]

名 量；金額  自 合計（~と）なる

a large [small] amount of money  多額〔小額〕の金

## 279 appliance
[əpláiəns]

名 （電気）器具，設備

an electronic appliance  電気器具

## 280 attraction
[ətrǽkʃən]

名 呼び物；引きつける力，魅力  ⇒派 attract 他 を引きつける  attractive 形 魅力的な

a tourist attraction  観光名所

## 281 audience
[ɔ́ːdiəns]

名 聴衆

a large [small] audience  多数〔少数〕の聴衆

解答 (1) ability (2) advantage (3) advertisement (4) amount (5) appliance (6) attraction (7) audience

| author | candidate | career | cabinet |
| campaign | cash | catalog | budget |

(1) If you go to the bookstore to buy it tomorrow at 3:00, you'll have a chance to meet the (　　).
もしそれを買いに明日の3時に本屋に行けば，著者に会える可能性がある。

(2) While the (　　) allows for thirty people to attend, we anticipate some cash will be left over, as not everyone will be free.
予算は30人の出席を可能としているが，全員が空いているわけではないので，私たちはいくらか現金が残ると見込んでいる。

(3) Employees provide their own coffee mugs which are stored in the (　　) above the coffeemaker.
従業員は自分専用のコーヒーカップを用意していて，それはコーヒーメーカーの上の戸棚に置いてある。

(4) Many potential rivals are shocked to hear that she is starting her (　　) three years before the election.
彼女が選挙の3年前に運動を始めていると聞くと，多くの対抗馬になりそうな人々はショックを受けた。

(5) You must make a $500 donation in order to attend the luncheon to meet the (　　).
候補者に会いに昼食会に出席するには，500ドル寄付しなければならない。

(6) Oscar began his (　　) in engineering in Massachusetts, but before that he spent many years in Asia.
オスカーはエンジニアとしての経歴をマサチューセッツ州で開始したが，その前はアジアに何年もいた。

(7) Sometimes vendors at the market will offer customers a discount for paying in (　　).
市場の商人は，時には現金で買う客に値引きをしてくれるだろう。

(8) The company charges $5.00 for a color (　　), but it can be viewed for free online.
企業はカラーのカタログに5ドルの値をつけているが，ネットなら無料で見られる。

## 282 author
[ɔ́:θər]

名 著者　他 を著す

an authoring tool　オーサリングツール（画像，音声，動画などのファイルを作成するソフトウェア）

## 283 budget
[bʌ́dʒət]

名 予算

balance the budget　予算を均衡させる
budget management　予算管理

## 284 cabinet
[kǽbənət]

名 戸棚；内閣

a medicine cabinet　薬品棚
a cabinet council　閣議

## 285 campaign
[kæmpéin]

名 運動，キャンペーン；選挙戦

a sales campaign　販売促進活動

## 286 candidate
[kǽndədéit, -dət]

名 候補者，志願者

a successful candidate　当選者，合格者

## 287 career
[kəríər]

名 職業；職歴

pursue one's career goals　職業における目標を追い求める

## 288 cash
[kǽʃ]

名 現金　他 を現金に換える

pay cash = pay in cash　現金で支払う

## 289 catalog
[kǽtəlɔ́(:)g]

名 商品目録，カタログ　他 の目録を作る

a mail-order catalog　通販カタログ

---

解答　(1) author　(2) budget　(3) cabinet　(4) campaign
(5) candidate　(6) career　(7) cash　(8) catalog

| clerk | cause | challenge | class |
| chart | choice | chairman | client |

(1) It appears that his body is filling with fluid, but the doctors are not really sure of the (    ).
彼の体は水分でいっぱいになっているようだが，医者には原因がよくわかっていない。

(2) Even though the company is run by a woman, she uses the title "(    ) of the Board" on her business card.
その会社はある女性が経営しているが，彼女の名刺には「取締役会長」という肩書きが使われている。

(3) There is no (    ) in making the same, predictable kind of presentation to the group every year.
毎年そのグループに，同じありきたりの類のプレゼンをしても何のやりがいもない。

(4) On page five, it might have more impact to replace this (    ) with a bar or a pie graph.
5ページでは，この図を棒グラフか円グラフに置き換えるとより効果があるかもしれない。

(5) The entrees are between $20 and $25 and come with your (    ) of soup of the day or tossed salad.
メインコースは20ドルから25ドルの間で，それに本日のスープかドレッシングであえたサラダのうちからお選びいただいたものがつきます。

(6) Based on the price quoted, the buyer was afraid that the (    ) of materials would not meet the company's standards.
仕入れ係は，見積もり価格に基づくと，その材料のランクが会社の水準に見合わないのではと懸念した。

(7) Although he is considered a diplomat as far as his visa status, he is basically a (    ) at the Canadian embassy.
彼は在留資格に関する限り外交官と見なされるが，基本的にはカナダ大使館の事務官である。

(8) Let the (    ) know not to worry, because his account will be handled by the CEO himself.
お客様に心配しないよう知らせてください。請求書はCEO自身が取り扱いますから。

| 290 | **cause** [kɔ́:z] | 名 原因, 根拠　他 を引き起こす |
|---|---|---|
| | | be caused by ～　～に起因する |

| 291 | **chairman** [tʃéərmən] | 名 議長；会長　→ chair |
|---|---|---|
| | | be elected chairman　議長に選出される |

| 292 | **challenge** [tʃǽlindʒ] | 名 やりがいのある仕事；難題<br>他 に挑む；に異議を唱える |
|---|---|---|
| | | face a challenge　難題に取り組む |

| 293 | **chart** [tʃɑ́:rt] | 名 図表 |
|---|---|---|
| | | an organizational chart　組織図 |

| 294 | **choice** [tʃɔ́is] | 名 選択；選択された物　⇒派 choose 他 を選ぶ |
|---|---|---|
| | | make a choice among [from/out of] ～　～から選択する |

| 295 | **class** [klǽs] | 名 等級；階級；授業　他 を分類する<br>→ classify |
|---|---|---|
| | | first-aid classes　応急手当の講習 |

| 296 | **clerk** [klə́:rk] | 名 事務員；窓口係, 店員 |
|---|---|---|
| | | a desk clerk　ホテルのフロント係 |

| 297 | **client** [kláiənt] | 名 顧客 |
|---|---|---|
| | | a valued client　大切な顧客 |

解答　(1) cause　(2) chairman　(3) challenge　(4) chart
(5) choice　(6) class　(7) clerk　(8) client

> company   comment   committee   code
> consumer   colleague   complaint   concern

(1) The security company advised us to change the security (　　) on our system every month.
   警備会社は私たちに，システムの警備用の暗号を毎月変えるよう忠告した。

(2) Fran was a (　　) of mine at my former firm, so I know her quite well.
   フランは，以前勤めていた会社での同僚だったので，私は彼女をとてもよく知っている。

(3) If you'd like to make any (　　) about today's presentation, please use the card inside your folder.
   今日の発表に何かコメントなさりたい場合は，フォルダの中のカードをご利用ください。

(4) Candidates for manager must meet with the selection (　　) and then go before the board of directors.
   部長候補者は，人選委員会を通過し，次に取締役会にかけられる必要がある。

(5) Doug is friends with several corrupt government officials, so I can't help judging him by the (　　) he keeps.
   ダグは何人かの汚職官僚と友達なので，私は彼を付き合う仲間で判断せざるをえない。

(6) The problem began when the ex-employee took his (　　) about the organization to the state government.
   その問題は，その元従業員が組織の不満を州政府に持ち込んだことに端を発した。

(7) I am feeling much better now, but I appreciate your get-well card and your (　　).
   今はずいぶん気分がよくなりましたが，お見舞いカードとお心遣いには感謝しています。

(8) Others in the industry think of that company as amateurish, but they have a large following among (　　).
   業界のほかの会社は，その会社を素人と考えているが，消費者に多くの支持者を得ている。

## 298 code
[kóud]

名 規範, 規約；コード；暗号

a code of conduct　行動規範
a customer code　顧客コード

## 299 colleague
[káli:g]

名 同僚　≒類 co-worker 名 同僚

one's colleagues at work　職場での同僚

## 300 comment
[káment]

名 論評, 解説, コメント
自 他 (…だと) 論評する, 見解を述べる

receive a comment　コメントをもらう

## 301 committee
[kəmíti]

名 委員会

be in committee　委員会で審議中である
a steering committee　運営委員会

## 302 company
[kʌ́mpəni]

名 会社；同席 (行) すること；仲間

a company brochure　会社概要冊子
enjoy one's company　〜の同行を楽しむ

## 303 complaint
[kəmpléint]

名 不満, 苦情, 抗議　⇒派 complain 自 不平を言う

a letter of complaint　苦情の手紙

## 304 concern
[kənsə́:rn]

名 関心, 心配；関心事　他 に関係する；を心配させる

To whom it may concern　関係各位

## 305 consumer
[kəns(j)ú:mər]

名 消費者　⇒派 consume 他 を消費する
consumption 名 消費

consumer research　市場調査

---

解答 (1) code (2) colleague (3) comments (4) committee (5) company (6) complaint (7) concern (8) consumers

| convention | convenience | control | contract |
| crew | contact | corporation | cost |

(1) So many companies with an online presence do not include extensive ( ) information, thereby losing sales.
オンラインに進出する非常に多くの企業が，多くの連絡情報を表示していないために，売上を減らしている。

(2) The other party refuses to sign a ( ) until they can inspect the inventory personally.
相手方は，在庫を個人的に点検できるようになるまで，契約への署名を拒否している。

(3) Unless McPherson is able to get 51% of the shares, he will be unable to maintain ( ) of the company.
マクファーソンが株式の51パーセントを得られなければ，彼は会社の支配を維持できないだろう。

(4) Please look over the proposal and get back to us about it at your ( ).
提案に目を通し，ご都合のよいときに，それについてご連絡ください。

(5) The facility is primarily used for trade fairs and industry ( ), but occasionally non-profit groups rent it.
その施設は主として見本市と産業会議に使われているが，時たま非営利団体が借りる。

(6) According to the brochure, the ( ) has more than doubled in size since it was founded 20 years ago.
会社案内によると，会社は20年前の創立以来，倍以上の大きさになっている。

(7) In the initial stages of the negotiations, the issue was more about mutual trust than ( ).
交渉の最初の段階では，争点はコスト以上に相互の信頼だった。

(8) When you choose a cruise, look for a company with a reputation for a hardworking, friendly and reliable ( ).
船旅を選ぶときは，勤勉，親切で信頼できる船員で評判の会社を探しなさい。

| 306 | **contact** 名[kántækt] 動[kántækt, kəntækt] | 名 連絡  他 に連絡する |
|---|---|---|
| | | contact information　連絡先 |

| 307 | **contract** 名[kántrækt] 動[kəntrækt] | 名 契約；契約書  他自 (を)契約する |
|---|---|---|
| | | a breach of contract　契約違反 |
| | | sign a contract　契約書に署名する |

| 308 | **control** [kəntróul] | 名 規制；管理；支配  他 を統制する；を制限する |
|---|---|---|
| | | out of control　制御不能な |

| 309 | **convenience** [kənví:niəns] | 名 便利, 便宜　⇒派 convenient 形 都合のよい |
|---|---|---|
| | | at one's convenience　都合のよいときに |

| 310 | **convention** [kənvénʃən] | 名 集会, 会議；慣習；国際協定 |
|---|---|---|
| | | an annual convention　年次総会 |

| 311 | **corporation** [kɔ̀:rpəréiʃən] | 名 会社, 法人 |
|---|---|---|
| | | corporation taxes　法人税 |

| 312 | **cost** [kɔ́(:)st] | 名 経費  他 〈費用〉がかかる　→179 costly |
|---|---|---|
| | | repair costs　修理費 |

| 313 | **crew** [krú:] | 名 乗組員, 乗務員；一団 |
|---|---|---|
| | | a wrecking crew　救援作業隊 |

解答　(1) contact　(2) contract　(3) control　(4) convenience　(5) conventions　(6) corporation　(7) cost　(8) crew

> customer    director    degree    demand
> destination    delivery    decision    damage

(1) The technology on the Web site allows a returning ( ) to sign in and accrue frequent shopper points.
ウェブサイトの技術のおかげで，再訪する**顧客**がサインインして顧客特典ポイントを蓄積することができる。

(2) The tornado did a lot of ( ) to houses in the towns of Troy and Riverdale.
竜巻がトロイとリバーデイルの町の家々に甚大な**被害**を与えた。

(3) The client is waiting for a response, so you will need to make a ( ) in the next day or two.
クライアントが返事を待っているので，あなたは明日かあさってには**決断**する必要がある。

(4) We have a new employee who has advanced ( ) in both business administration and accounting.
ここには経営学と会計学の両方で大学院の**学位**を持った新入社員がいる。

(5) By including ( ) and installation in the purchase price, customers feel they are saving money.
**配送**と設置を販売価格に含めることによって，客は得していると感じる。

(6) ( ) for that commodity is up in Asia, but the only affordable source seems to be in South America.
アジアでのその商品への**需要**は上昇しているが，可能な供給地は南米だけのようだ。

(7) We suggest that you retain your boarding pass until you arrive at your final ( ).
最終**目的地**に到着するまで，搭乗券をお持ちになるようお勧めします。

(8) While I sympathize with your problems, you'll have to speak to the ( ) himself to get them resolved.
私はあなたの問題に同情するが，解決するためには**管理者**本人と話さねばならないだろう。

## 314 customer
[kʌ́stəmər]

名 顧客

a regular customer　常連客

## 315 damage
[dǽmidʒ]

名 損害, 被害；損害賠償金　他 に損害を与える

cause ~ damage　~に損害を与える

## 316 decision
[disíʒən]

名 決定　⇒派 decide 他 を決定する

decision-making　意思決定
a final decision　最終決定

## 317 degree
[digríː]

名 程度；(測定単位の)度；学位

have a degree in ~　~の学位を持つ
15 degrees Fahrenheit　華氏15度

## 318 delivery
[dilívəri]

名 配達；出産　⇒派 deliver 他 を配達する

special delivery　速達

## 319 demand
[dimǽnd]

名 要求；需要　他 を要求する
⇔反 supply 名 供給

demand ~ of [from] ...　〈人〉に〈物事〉を要求する

## 320 destination
[dèstənéiʃən]

名 目的地, 行先

arrive at one's destination　目的地に着く

## 321 director
[dəréktər]

名 指導者, 管理者；重役, 取締役；映画監督

in the capacity of director　取締役として
a director of marketing　マーケティング責任者

---

解答　(1) customer　(2) damage　(3) decision　(4) degrees
(5) delivery　(6) Demand　(7) destination　(8) director

| engineer | entertainment | discount | effect |
| document | employee | entry | entrance |

(1) The consumer base for ( ) department stores is the largest in the country and it should be courted.
ディスカウントストアの消費者基盤は国内最大なので，この支持を取り付けるべきだ。

(2) The ( ) includes a glossary of terms in the preface so you can reference the difficult terminology throughout.
その文書には序文に用語解説が入っており，難しい専門用語を終始参照できる。

(3) The memo says the new pay scale does not take ( ) until the first of next year.
来年の初めまでは新しい給与表は効力を持たないと通達には書かれている。

(4) The new trend in car sale promotions in the U.S. is to offer regular consumers the car company's "( ) discount."
アメリカでの自動車販売促進の新しい動向は，常連客にその自動車会社の「社員割引」を提供することである。

(5) Kara is the new ( ) who transferred to the Chicago office from Denver a month ago.
カーラは1か月前，デンバー事務所からシカゴ事務所に異動した新しい技術者だ。

(6) As chairperson of the conference, you will also need to hire the ( ) for the big dinner party.
会議の議長として，あなたは大晩餐会に余興となるものも用意しなければならないだろう。

(7) After the bomb threat, the ( ) to the building is being manned with armed guards.
爆破の脅迫後，そのビルの入口は武装した警備員に守られている。

(8) They put up fences and created a special border patrol between the two countries to stop illegal ( ).
不法入国阻止のため，防壁が立てられて，2国間に特別国境監視隊が創設された。

| 322 | **discount** 名 [dískaunt] 動 [ˊ--, --ˊ] | 名 割引, ディスカウント 他 を割り引く<br>make [allow/give] a discount 割引を行う ≒ mark down 値下げする |
|---|---|---|
| 323 | **document** 名 [dákjəmənt] 動 [dákjəmènt] | 名 文書；コンピュータのファイル<br>他 を文書に記録する<br>a public document 公文書 |
| 324 | **effect** [ifékt, ə-] | 名 効果, 効力 ⇒派 **effective** 形 効果のある<br>have an effect on ～ ～に影響を及ぼす |
| 325 | **employee** [emplɔ́iiː, ˊ--ˊ] | 名 従業員<br>a permanent employee 正社員 |
| 326 | **engineer** [èndʒəníər] | 名 技師 ⇒派 **engineering** 名 工学<br>a construction engineer 建築技師 |
| 327 | **entertainment** [èntərtéinmənt] | 名 娯楽；楽しませるもの；接待<br>⇒派 **entertain** 他〈人〉を楽しませる<br>an entertainment allowance 接待費 |
| 328 | **entrance** [éntrəns] | 名 入口；入ること；入る権利<br>⇒派 **enter** 自 他 (に)入る<br>at the entrance 玄関で<br>gain entrance to ～ ～に入るのを認められる |
| 329 | **entry** [éntri] | 名 入場；記載事項 ≒類 328 **entrance** 名 入場<br>an entry visa 入国査証 |

解答 (1) discount (2) document (3) effect (4) employee (5) engineer (6) entertainment (7) entrance (8) entry

| expert | excuse | flood | experience |
| estimate | expense | fax | estate |

(1) The law requires a certain waiting period before final settlement of the ( ) of a person who has passed away.
故人の遺産が最終決着するまでに法律は一定の待機期間を要求する。

(2) If you are able to provide these services, please submit an ( ) for the job described on this sheet.
これらのサービスを提供できるなら，この用紙に記されている作業の見積もりを提出してください。

(3) There is simply no ( ) for careless work habits and irresponsible behavior, and none will be accepted.
軽率な仕事の仕方と無責任な行動に弁解の余地はまったくなく，何も受け入れられない。

(4) The price of gasoline has made the business ( ) of our sales department almost too high to continue.
ガソリンの値段のせいで，存続できないほど我が営業部の運営経費が高くなった。

(5) The hotel is committed to creating the most comfortable ( ) possible for its business travelers.
そのホテルは，出張者が得られる最も好ましい体験を作り出すことに全力を傾けている。

(6) Even if your taxes are simple, you can often pinpoint more deductions if you hire an ( ).
たとえ税金がシンプルなものであっても，専門家を雇うとより多くの控除を正確に指摘できることがしばしばある。

(7) With widespread Internet use, the ( ) machine has become less essential to many businesses than it once was.
インターネットの普及で，多くの企業にとってファックスはかつてほど重要でなくなった。

(8) With so much rain in such a short period of time, there are bound to be ( ) all over the area.
こんなに短時間にこれほど大量の雨が降ると，この地域一帯で洪水が起こるにちがいない。

## 330 estate
[istéit, es-]

名 地所, 財産

a real estate agent　不動産業者

## 331 estimate
名 [éstəmət]
動 [éstəmèit]

名 見積もり, 概算；判断　他 を見積もる

a rough estimate　概算

## 332 excuse
名 [ikskjúːs]
動 [ikskjúːz, eks-]

名 理由；弁解, 言い訳　他 を許す

in excuse of one's late arrival　遅刻の弁解として

## 333 expense
[ikspéns, eks-]

名 費用, 必要経費；損失　≒類 312 cost 名 費用

unexpected expense　予定外の出費

## 334 experience
[ikspíəriəns, eks-]

名 経験　他 を経験する

business experience　実務経験

## 335 expert
[ékspəːrt]

名 熟練者, 専門家　形 巧みな, 熟達した
→ 196 expertise

expert on [in/with] 〜　〜の専門家

## 336 fax
[fæks]

名 ファックス；複製
他 をファックスで送る（facsimile の略）

fax an application form　応募用紙をファックスする

## 337 flood
[flʌd]

名 洪水；殺到　他 を水浸しにする；に殺到する

be flooded with 〜　〜が殺到して

---

解答　(1) estate　(2) estimate　(3) excuse　(4) expenses　(5) experience　(6) expert　(7) fax　(8) floods

| impact | influence | fuel | government |
| income | human | illness | increase |

(1) It is interesting to note that the cost of ( ) has almost doubled in this country over the past two years.
興味深いことには，過去2年間でこの国では，燃料の価格がほぼ倍になっている。

(2) He's made a fortune selling a reference book that explains how to get grants and other money from the ( ).
彼は政府の助成金やその他の金を獲得する方法を解説した参考書を販売し，財を成した。

(3) Not only do they do questionable drug testing on animals, but they release drugs too quickly, which means testing on ( ).
問題の多い薬物検査を動物に行うだけでなく，彼らは薬物を早く販売しすぎる。つまり人間に対して検査をしているということだ。

(4) Until we got word that the accountant had passed away, we had no idea that his ( ) was so serious.
その会計士の訃報を受けるまで，私たちは彼の病気がそんなに深刻だとは知らなかった。

(5) Even three years later, the community is still feeling the ( ) of the unfortunate bus accident.
3年経っても，その自治体は不幸なバス事故の衝撃をいまだに感じている。

(6) The tax office considers benefits such as a housing allowance part of the employee's taxable ( ).
税務署は，住宅手当のような諸手当は従業員の課税所得の一部と見なす。

(7) The company may be famous as a success story, but the employees have not seen a pay ( ) in years.
その会社は成功談で有名かもしれないが，従業員の昇給は何年もない。

(8) When it seemed impossible to schedule a meeting, we asked a politician friend to use his ( ) to get us in.
面会の予約は不可能に思えたので，私たちは政治家の友人に，彼の影響力を使って私たちが入れるようにしてくれるよう頼んだ。

## 338 fuel
[fjúːəl]

名 燃料　自他 (に) 燃料を補給する

adequate fuel　十分な燃料

## 339 government
[gÁvərnmənt]

名 政府

municipal government　市政

## 340 human
[hjúːmən]

名 人間　形 人間の；人間的な
⇒派 **humanity** 名 人類；人間性

human resources　人材, 人事課

## 341 illness
[ílnəs]

名 病気の状態　⇒派 **ill** 形 病気の

a serious illness　重病

## 342 impact
名 [ímpækt]
動 [ímpækt]

名 刺激, 衝撃, 影響　他 に影響〔衝撃〕を与える
自 衝突する

a great impact on [upon] ～　～に対する大きな影響

## 343 income
[ínkʌm]

名 所得, 収入

income tax　所得税

## 344 increase
名 [ínkriːs, -´-, íŋ-]
動 [-´-, -´-]

名 増加, 上昇　他 を増やす　自 増える, 増大する
⇔反 **decrease** 名 減少　他 を減らす　自 減少する

increase in number [amount]　数〔量〕が増す

## 345 influence
[ínfluəns]

名 影響, 作用；影響力　他 に影響を与える；を左右する

a man of influence　実力者

---

解答 (1) fuel (2) government (3) humans (4) illness (5) impact (6) income (7) increase (8) influence

> | loan | limit | lobby | laboratory |
> | item | invitation | lack | insurance |

(1) The company's ( ) policy will cover you in that rental car, so you don't need to buy the extra insurance.
あのレンタカーについては，会社の保険約款があなたを保障するので追加保険は不要だ。

(2) The CEO received an ( ) to the grand opening of the company that will be his largest competitor.
そのCEOは，最大の競合先となるであろう企業の設立記念式への招待を受けた。

(3) Did you see the ( ) about kite surfing in the sports section of today's newspaper?
今日の新聞のスポーツ欄でカイトサーフィンの項目を見ましたか。

(4) The business headquarters are located in Los Angeles, whereas the ( ) is in rural Oregon.
事業本部はロサンゼルスに位置するのに対し，研究所はオレゴンの田舎にある。

(5) We used to have a company chorus, but it was disbanded for ( ) of enthusiasm.
我が社にはかつて企業合唱部があったが，熱意不足のため解散した。

(6) The message says that you've reached your ( ), so you will be charged extra for any additional time.
通達には限度に達したとあるので，余分にかかった時間には割増料金がかかる。

(7) Even though my job pays well, I still had to take out a six figure ( ) to help pay for my new home.
私の稼ぎはよいが，それでも新居の支払いのために6桁のローンを組まねばならなかった。

(8) We'll wait for you in the ( ) tomorrow at 9:30 and accompany you to the meeting.
私たちは明日9:30にロビーであなたをお待ちし，会議にお連れします。

| 346 | **insurance** [inʃúərəns] | 名 保険 |
|---|---|---|
| | | buy insurance　保険に入る |
| | | insurance contract　保険契約 |

| 347 | **invitation** [ìnvitéiʃən] | 名 招待, 招待状；誘因　⇒派 invite 他 を招く |
|---|---|---|
| | | send out invitations　招待状を出す |

| 348 | **item** [áitəm] | 名 項目, 品目 |
|---|---|---|
| | | items on the agenda　協議事項 |

| 349 | **laboratory** [lǽbərətɔ̀:ri] | 名 実験室, 研究所 |
|---|---|---|
| | | a laboratory experiment　研究室での実験 |

| 350 | **lack** [lǽk] | 名 不足, 不足しているもの　他 を欠いている 自 不足している |
|---|---|---|
| | | lack common sense　常識に欠ける |

| 351 | **limit** [límit] | 名 限度；境界　他 を限定する |
|---|---|---|
| | | to the limit　極端に |

| 352 | **loan** [lóun] | 名 融資, ローン　他 を貸し付ける, 貸す |
|---|---|---|
| | | get a bank loan　銀行の融資を受ける |

| 353 | **lobby** [lábi] | 名 ロビー　自他 〈議案の〉通過運動をする |
|---|---|---|
| | | lobby a bill through Congress　圧力をかけ議会で議案を通過させる |

解答　(1) insurance　(2) invitation　(3) item　(4) laboratory
(5) lack　(6) limit　(7) loan　(8) lobby

```
          marketing    manual    operation    offer
          loss    material    method    location
```

(1) We believe that the highest point on the eastern side of the island is the best (     ) to shoot the commercial.
   島の東側の一番高い地点がコマーシャルの撮影に一番よい場所だと思う。

(2) After you figure out the totals on the profit and (     ) statement, make copies for each one of the department heads.
   損益計算書の総計を計算したら，各部門長用にコピーをしなさい。

(3) We followed the instructions in the (     ) exactly, but still could not start up the computer.
   説明書の指示に正確に従ったが，それでもコンピュータを立ち上げられなかった。

(4) It sometimes seems like the guys in (     ) could even make water seem attractive to a well.
   マーケティング部の連中は井戸の水を魅力的に見せることすらできるように思えることがある。

(5) I don't have time to discuss that now, but send me some (     ) and I'll take a look at it.
   今その件を話す時間はありませんが，いくつか資料を送ってくだされば，目を通します。

(6) Dr. Bricker's revolutionary new surgical (     ) has been praised by surgeons all over the globe.
   ブリッカー博士の革命的な新しい手術法は，全世界の外科医の賞賛を浴びてきた。

(7) Before I can get a letter of intent from the buyer, I need you to draft a formal corporate (     ).
   私がバイヤーから同意書をもらう前に，正式な会社の申し込みを書いてください。

(8) The surgeon would like to meet with the patient and his family and explain the (     ) in detail.
   外科医は患者とその家族に会って，手術の詳細を説明したいと思っている。

| 354 | **location** [loukéiʃən] | 名 場所, 立地 → 86 locate<br>a good location for 〜　〜に好適の場所 |
|---|---|---|
| 355 | **loss** [lɔ́(:)s] | 名 喪失；損失；死　⇒派 lose 他 を失う<br>equate profit and loss　損益をならす |
| 356 | **manual** [mǽnjuəl] | 名 手引き, 説明書　形 手動の；手先の<br>an instruction manual　取扱説明書<br>a manual gearshift　手動ギアシフト |
| 357 | **marketing** [má:rkitiŋ] | 名 マーケティング；市場での売買<br>direct marketing　直接販売 |
| 358 | **material** [mətíəriəl] | 名 材料；資料　形 物質的な<br>building material　建築資材 |
| 359 | **method** [méθəd] | 名 方法；秩序<br>an effective method　効果的な方法 |
| 360 | **offer** [ɔ́(:)fər] | 名 申し込み, 付け値　他 を申し出る, 提供する<br>自 援助を申し出る<br>an offer of help　援助の申し入れ |
| 361 | **operation** [àpəréiʃən] | 名 作動；作業；事業；手術　⇒派 operate 自 作動する；仕事をする；操業する；手術をする<br>operation division　事業部 |

解答　(1) location　(2) loss　(3) manual　(4) marketing　(5) material　(6) method　(7) offer　(8) operation

> package　plan　participant　organization
> opinion　passenger　plate　physician

(1) It was impossible to reach a consensus with such clear differences of (　) among the board members on the subject.
その議題について役員の間でこのような明らかな意見の相違があったので，意見の一致に至るのは不可能だった。

(2) Janice joined the (　) right out of college in 1985 and has worked in various departments throughout her career.
ジャニスは1985年に大学を卒業するとすぐにその組織に加わり，勤めている間はさまざまな部署で働いた。

(3) According to the courier company, we can send the (　) to the client "overnight" for just $5 more.
その宅配会社によれば，たった5ドルの追加で小包を「翌日配達」で顧客に送れる。

(4) There are students passing out handouts to each of the (　) when they enter the room.
参加者が部屋に入るときに，一人一人にチラシを手渡している学生たちがいる。

(5) According to the list, there were 175 (　) on the airplane when it took off from Las Vegas.
リストによると，ラスベガスを離陸したとき175人の乗客がその飛行機に乗っていた。

(6) After a routine physical by the company (　), Rhoda was told that she needed further tests.
社医による定期健康診断のあと，ローダは追加検査が必要だと言われた。

(7) The new CEO's (　) included a possible merger with our second largest competitor.
新しいCEOの計画には，2番目に大きい競合企業との合併の可能性も含まれていた。

(8) After you put the batteries back in, you need to insert this (　) into the opening.
電池を入れ直したら，開口部にこの厚板を差し込む必要があります。

| 362 | **opinion** [əpínjən] | 名 意見；世論<br>opinion poll 世論調査 |
|---|---|---|
| 363 | **organization** [ɔ̀ːrɡənəzéiʃən] | 名 組織, 団体；構成<br>a charitable organization チャリティ団体 |
| 364 | **package** [pǽkidʒ] | 名 小包, 束；包装；(商品の)セット<br>他 を梱包する；を(客の目を引くように)提示する<br>benefits package 福利厚生制度 |
| 365 | **participant** [pɑːrtísəpənt] | 名 参加者, 関係者 →448 participate<br>a participant in the event その事件の当事者 |
| 366 | **passenger** [pǽsəndʒər] | 名 乗客<br>a first-class passenger ファーストクラスの乗客 |
| 367 | **physician** [fizíʃən] | 名 医者, 内科医<br>consult [see] a physician 医者に診察してもらう |
| 368 | **plan** [plǽn] | 名 計画 他 の計画を立てる 自 計画する<br>put one's plan into action 計画を実行する |
| 369 | **plate** [pléit] | 名 皿；1皿分の料理；(金属などの)板<br>clean one's plate 皿の料理を平らげる<br>a license plate (自動車の)ナンバープレート |

解答 (1) opinion (2) organization (3) package (4) participants (5) passengers (6) physician (7) plan (8) plate

| publication | proposal | process | procedure |
| project | product | profit | production |

(1) If the fire alarm sounds, the ( ) is to stop whatever you are doing and proceed to the nearest fire exit.
   火災警報器が鳴った場合の手順は，とにかく作業を中断し最寄りの非常口へ進むことだ。

(2) Making coffee ready to drink involves a lengthy picking, pulping, drying and roasting ( ).
   飲用のコーヒー豆を作るには，採取，果肉除去，乾燥，焙煎の長期にわたる工程がある。

(3) When the package arrived, I could tell immediately that it was not the same ( ) I saw in the catalog.
   その包みが届いたとき，カタログで見た製品と同じではないことがすぐにわかった。

(4) The decision to change some materials after the safety test put final ( ) off for several months.
   安全テストのあといくつかの材料を変更するという決定が下され，最終的な生産は数か月後に延期となった。

(5) Spending a little bit extra to make the product safer will not cut into our ( ) that much.
   その製品をより安全にするため，少々余分な費用を使うことは，私たちの利益をそれほど減らすことにはならない。

(6) When people have many problems, finding little ( ) to do will help take their minds off of them.
   多くの問題を抱える人には，小さな課題を見つけてやることが，気を紛らわす助けになる。

(7) Let's get together tomorrow and go over all the ( ) we've had and then choose someone for the project.
   明日集まって，私たちが出した全提案を見直し，その上でプロジェクトの人選を行おう。

(8) University professors are usually required to have their work appear in various ( ) in order to keep their positions.
   大学教授は通常，地位を維持するため，多くの出版物に研究成果を載せねばならない。

| # | Word | Definition |
|---|---|---|
| 370 | **procedure** [prəsíːdʒər] | 名 手順；手続き；処置<br>follow procedures 手順を踏む<br>emergency procedures 緊急時の対応手段 |
| 371 | **process** [práses, -əs] | 名 過程, 工程；作用　他 を処理する　形 処理加工された<br>the process of organizing labor 労働者を組織する手順 |
| 372 | **product** [prádəkt, -ʌkt] | 名 製品；所産　→ **production**<br>domestic [home] products 国産品 |
| 373 | **production** [prədʌ́kʃən] | 名 生産　⇒派 **produce** 他 を生産する<br>mass production 大量生産 |
| 374 | **profit** [práfət] | 名 利益　自 利益を得る　他 の利益になる<br>maintain a steady profit margin 安定した利益率を維持する |
| 375 | **project** 名 [prádʒekt] 動 [prədʒékt, prou-] | 名 計画；事業；課題<br>他 を計画する；を映写する；を見積もる<br>carry out a project into execution 計画を実行する |
| 376 | **proposal** [prəpóuzl] | 名 提案（書）, 申し込み　⇒派 **propose** 他 を申し込む<br>accept a proposal 申し込みを受け入れる |
| 377 | **publication** [pʌ̀blikéiʃən] | 名 出版；出版物<br>a trade publication 業界誌 |

解答 (1) procedure (2) process (3) product (4) production (5) profits (6) projects (7) proposals (8) publications

| | | | |
|---|---|---|---|
| reply | salary | receipt | purpose |
| report | research | retirement | resource |

(1) To receive a stamp in your passport, you need to explain the (　) of your visit to the country.
パスポートにスタンプをもらうには，入国目的を説明する必要がある。

(2) Employees are expected to keep the (　) of all expenditures charged to the company expense account.
社員は，会社の経費になる出費はすべて領収書を取っておくことになっている。

(3) I want to draft a (　) to the Paris office while my thoughts are fresh, so I'll be late getting home.
思い付きが新鮮なうちにパリの事務所への返事を書きたいので，帰宅は遅くなるだろう。

(4) Lori was asked to give us a (　) on recent activities in the Kansas City office.
ローリは，カンザスシティ支社の最近の活動について報告書を我々に出すよう求められた。

(5) Could you make copies of the (　) you found online and distribute it to all of the participants?
あなたがインターネットで見つけた調査をコピーして，参加者全員に配ってください。

(6) Living in a big city, you probably have (　) available to get legal advice from a legal aid center.
大都市に住んでいれば，おそらく法律相談センターから法的助言を受ける手段がある。

(7) If your company doesn't have a good (　) plan, you can create your own fund with the bank.
自社によい退職金積立制度がなければ，銀行で自分の基金を作ることができる。

(8) Mr. Smith threatened to leave the company and join a competitor if his (　) was not raised.
スミス氏は給料が上がらなければ会社を辞めて競争相手の会社に入ると脅した。

|  |  |  |
|---|---|---|
| 378 | **purpose** [pə́ːrpəs] | 名 目的；意図<br>the purpose for the survey　調査の目的<br>on purpose　わざと, 故意に |
| 379 | **receipt** [risíːt] | 名 受領；領収書, レシート；収益<br>⇒派 **receive** 他 を受け取る<br>upon receipt of ～　～の受領をもって |
| 380 | **reply** [riplái] | 名 返事　自 返事をする<br>reply to a question　質問に答える |
| 381 | **report** [ripɔ́ːrt] | 名 報告（書）；報道　他 自 (を) 報告 〔報道〕 する<br>sales report　売上報告書 |
| 382 | **research** 名 [ríːsəːrtʃ, risə́ːrtʃ] 動 [-́-] | 名 調査　自 研究する, 調査する<br>research and development　研究開発 (略：R&D) |
| 383 | **resource** [ríːsɔːrs, -zɔːrs] | 名 資源；財源；手段, 頼みの綱<br>human resources　人材, 人事課 |
| 384 | **retirement** [ritáiərmənt] | 名 退職, 引退（時期）　⇒派 **retire** 自 退職する<br>raise the retirement age to ～　定年を～に引き上げる |
| 385 | **salary** [sǽləri] | 名 給料<br>a high [low] salary　高い〔安い〕給料 |

解答　(1) purpose　(2) receipts　(3) reply　(4) report　(5) research　(6) resources　(7) retirement　(8) salary

| task | strategy | standard | source |
| session | subject | stress | seminar |

(1) The ( ) is mandatory for all employees who were hired within the last six months.
そのセミナーは，ここ半年以内に雇用された社員全員の受講が必須である。

(2) The first ( ) of the advertisement design workshop begins today after lunch.
広告デザイン研究会の第1回の会合は今日の昼食後に始まる。

(3) Next year we will diversify our business so that we have more than one ( ) of revenue.
来年我々は事業を多様化させて，収入源を2つ以上にする。

(4) We will have to redesign the connectors to be compatible with local ( ) and regulations.
我々は，地元の基準と規則に適うようにコネクターを再設計しなければならない。

(5) The public relations ( ) is to release progress reports and hold press conferences at regular intervals.
広報活動戦略は，定期的に進展状況の報告書を出し，記者会見を開くことだ。

(6) Regular exercise and the occasional vacation can help reduce the ( ) of a busy job.
定期的な運動と時々の休暇は，忙しい仕事からくるストレスを軽減する助けとなりうる。

(7) The main ( ) of discussion at the next board meeting will be how we can improve our efficiency.
次の重役会で論じる主な議題は，どうすれば効率を上げられるかということだ。

(8) I was given the unwanted ( ) of informing a co-worker that the firm was letting him go.
会社が解雇することを同僚に伝えるという嫌な任務を与えられた。

| # | 見出し語 | 意味 | 用例 |
|---|---|---|---|
| 386 | **seminar** [sémənɑ̀ːr, ーーー] | 名 (大学の)ゼミ；セミナー，研究会 | attend a seminar　セミナーに出席する |
| 387 | **session** [séʃən] | 名 会議，会合；開会；会期 | an opening session　開会式<br>in session　開会〔会議〕中 |
| 388 | **source** [sɔ́ːrs] | 名 供給源；原因；情報源 | a source of anxiety　心配のもと |
| 389 | **standard** [stǽndərd] | 名 水準，標準；規範　形 一般的な；標準の | set a high standard for ～　～に高い水準を設ける |
| 390 | **strategy** [strǽtədʒi] | 名 戦術，戦略；計略 | an effective strategy　有効な戦略 |
| 391 | **stress** [strés] | 名 緊張；圧力；強調；ストレス<br>他 を強調する；に圧力を加える | put (a) stress on ～　～に重点を置く |
| 392 | **subject** 名形 [sʌ́bdʒekt, -dʒikt] 動 [səbdʒékt] | 名 主題；議題；科目　形 影響を受けやすい；服従する<br>他 を服従させる | be subject to change　変更する場合がある |
| 393 | **task** [tǽsk] | 名 仕事，任務 | assign a task to ～　〈人〉に仕事を課する |

解答　(1) seminar　(2) session　(3) source　(4) standards　(5) strategy　(6) stress　(7) subject　(8) task

| | | | |
|---|---|---|---|
| temperature | ticket | technology | |
| track | technique | traffic | |

(1) The engineers were confident that the new manufacturing (　) would improve the quality of the products.
技術者たちは，新しい製造技術が製品の質を向上させるだろうと確信していた。

(2) The new video game console is crammed full of the latest in virtual reality (　).
新しいテレビゲーム端末には最新のバーチャル・リアリティ技術が詰まっている。

(3) The high (　) outside makes it unpleasant to step out of the office during the summer.
夏の間は外の気温が高いので，会社から出るのが嫌になる。

(4) You must have a (　) to enter the exposition hall; and it's in the packet waiting for you at your hotel.
展示場に入るにはチケットが必要です。ホテルに準備してある小包の中にあります。

(5) Keeping (　) of the orders, the inventory and the sales all at once is a stressful task.
注文と在庫と売上の経過をすべて同時に把握しておくのはストレスの多い仕事だ。

(6) Ever since the redesign of our online store's Web site, we've been getting twice as much (　).
我が社のオンラインストアのウェブサイトを一新して以来，アクセス量が倍になった。

| 394 | **technique** [tekníːk] | 名 (専門)技術；技巧, テクニック |
|---|---|---|
| | | manufacturing techniques 製造技術 |
| | | problem-solving techniques 問題解決のテクニック |

| 395 | **technology** [teknάlədʒi] | 名 科学技術　⇒派 **technological** 形 科学技術の |
|---|---|---|
| | | a highly developed technology 高度に発達した技術 |

| 396 | **temperature** [témpərtʃər, -pərə-, -tʃùər] | 名 温度；気温, 体温 |
|---|---|---|
| | | a rise [drop] in temperature 温度の上昇〔下降〕 |

| 397 | **ticket** [tíkət] | 名 切符；荷札；チケット |
|---|---|---|
| | | a speeding ticket = a ticket for speeding スピード違反の反則切符 |

| 398 | **track** [træk] | 名 跡；筋道, 経過；道　他 をたどる |
|---|---|---|
| | | a track record 履歴 |

| 399 | **traffic** [trǽfik] | 名 交通量, 通行；データの流通量, 通信量 |
|---|---|---|
| | | a bad [heavy] traffic jam 交通の大渋滞 |

解答　(1) techniques　(2) technology　(3) temperature　(4) ticket　(5) track　(6) traffic

> transportation   warning   wage
> tray   variety

(1) Having reliable and cost-efficient (　) is necessary to make sure products get to the stores on time.
製品が時間通りに確実に店舗に届くようにするためには，信頼できてコスト効率の高い輸送方法を押さえておくことが必要だ。

(2) The personnel director's assistant will bring a (　) of refreshments into the meeting at around ten o'clock.
人事部長のアシスタントが10時前後に軽食をのせた皿を会議に持ってくる。

(3) The next generation of voice-activated mobile phones will come in a wider (　) of colors.
次世代の音声起動携帯電話は，もっと多様な色で発売される。

(4) Our company is well-respected in the industry for the high (　) it pays all of its workers.
我が社は全労働者に支払う給料の高さで，業界では一目置かれている。

(5) My superior believes in the two (　) system; third time and you're out of a job.
私の上司は2回警告システムを信奉している。3回目で失業だ。

## 400 transportation
[trænspərtéiʃən]

名 交通機関；運送；輸送手段
⇒派 transport 他 を輸送する

means of transportation　交通〔輸送〕機関

## 401 tray
[tréi]

名 盆；トレイ, 盛り皿

a serving tray　飲食物をよそう盆

## 402 variety
[vəráiəti]

名 種類；多様性

a variety of ～　さまざまな種類の～

## 403 wage
[wéidʒ]

名 賃金

a minimum wage　最低賃金

## 404 warning
[wɔ́ːrniŋ]

名 警告　⇒派 warn 自他 (に) 警告する

without warning　何の通知もなく

---

解答　(1) transportation　(2) tray　(3) variety
(4) wages　(5) warning

| announce | arrange | accompany | argue |
| apply | address | affect | approach |

(1) He will meet you in the hotel lobby at 9:15 and ( ) you to the 10:30 meeting.
   彼はあなたとホテルのロビーで9時15分に落ち合い，10時半の会議には**一緒に行く**。

(2) The president of the company is very casual and would prefer that you ( ) him by his first name.
   その会社の社長はとてもくだけているので，下の名前で**呼びかけら**れるほうを好む。

(3) In the United States just having a lender check on a person's credit can negatively ( ) the credit score.
   アメリカでは，個人の信用借りで貸付小切手を持っているだけで，信用格付け**に悪影響を及ぼす**ことがある。

(4) The actors, directors and others in the industry get up very early on the morning they ( ) the Academy Award nominations.
   俳優，監督，その他の業界関係者はアカデミー賞候補**が発表**される朝は非常に早く起きる。

(5) Ted Shaw told us he was going to ( ) for the position that will be opening up in the London office.
   テッド・ショーはロンドン事業所で空きが出る地位に**応募する**つもりだと述べた。

(6) Since they didn't accept our proposal, it is obvious that we need to change our focus and ( ) them once again.
   提案が承諾されなかったので，焦点を変えて再度彼ら**にもちかけ**ねばならないのは明白だ。

(7) We wanted to send out a repairperson, but the customer ( ) that a defective machine should be replaced, not serviced.
   私たちは修理人を派遣したかったが，顧客は欠陥品の修理ではなく交換**を主張した**。

(8) The client said they would ( ) for a limousine to meet us at the airport when we arrive.
   取引先は私たちの到着の際，空港で出迎えのリムジン**を手配する**とおっしゃった。

| 405 | **accompany** [əkʌ́mpəni] | 他 に同行する；に伴う<br>snow accompanied by high winds　激しい風を伴う雪 |
|---|---|---|
| 406 | **address** [ədrés] | 他 に宛てる；に呼びかける；に取り組む<br>名 あいさつ、演説；宛先<br>deliver [give] an address　あいさつをする |
| 407 | **affect** [əfékt] | 他 に作用する、影響を及ぼす<br>affect one's life　～の生活に影響を与える |
| 408 | **announce** [ənáuns] | 他 を公表する、告知する<br>⇒派 announcer 名 アナウンサー<br>announce (that) ...　…であると公表する |
| 409 | **apply** [əplái] | 自 応募する 他 を応用する；〈資金など〉を充当する<br>→ applicant　application<br>apply for a job　仕事に応募する |
| 410 | **approach** [əpróutʃ] | 自他 (に)近づく；(に)話をもちかける 名 接近(方法)<br>adopt a ～ approach　～な方法を採用する |
| 411 | **argue** [ɑ́ːrgjuː] | 他 …だと主張する 自 議論する<br>argue for [against] ～　～に賛成〔反対〕論を唱える |
| 412 | **arrange** [əréindʒ] | 他 を配置する；を取り決める；を手配する<br>⇒派 arrangement 名 配置；取り決め；手配<br>arrange for ～ to do　～が…するように手配する |

解答　(1) accompany　(2) address　(3) affect　(4) announce
(5) apply　(6) approach　(7) argued　(8) arrange

| attend | compare | cancel | confirm |
| classify | assist | conduct | avoid |

(1) If you can't afford a lawyer, the state will (　) you in finding some sort of legal representation
弁護士を雇う余裕がなければ，州が法的な代理人を見つける援助をしてくれる。

(2) It isn't mandatory for you to (　) the session, but your manager is almost always at these functions.
会に出席するのは強制ではないものの，課長はほぼ常にこうした行事に出ている。

(3) We did everything we could to (　) mentioning the scandal in her division, but she brought it up herself.
彼女の部署でスキャンダルについて触れるのは避けようとできる限りのことをしたが，彼女は自分で言い出してしまった。

(4) If the reservation is (　) fewer than 60 days prior to the arrival date, the customer loses the deposit.
予約が到着日の60日前以降に取り消された場合は，客は頭金を失うことになる。

(5) We can (　) any piece of equipment that was repaired and rebuilt by our factory in Mexico as "refurbished."
メキシコ工場で修理，再生された機器は，どの部品であれ「新装された」と分類できる。

(6) The auditor asked for the profit and loss statements from the past two quarters in order to (　) them.
会計監査役は過去2四半期の損益計算書を比較するためにそれらを求めた。

(7) The marketing company suggested we (　) a survey of current subscribers to get ideas for attracting new ones.
マーケティング会社は，現在の購読者の調査を実行し，新たな購読者を引きつけるアイデアを得るよう提案した。

(8) (　) this reservation directly with the airlines at least 72 hours prior to the departure date.
出発日の最低72時間前までに，航空会社に直接この予約の確認をしなさい。

### 413 assist
[əsíst]

他 を手助けする
⇒派 **assistance** 名 援助　**assistant** 名 助手

assist ~ in ...ing　~が…するのを手伝う

### 414 attend
[əténd]

他 に出席する　→171 **attendant**

attend a meeting　会議に出席する

### 415 avoid
[əvɔ́id]

他 を避ける

avoid ...ing　…するのを避ける

### 416 cancel
[kǽnsl]

他 を取り消す　⇒派 **cancellation** 名 取り消し

cancel a booking　予約を取り消す

### 417 classify
[klǽsəfài]

他 を分類する　→295 **class**

classify ~ as ...　~を…として分類する

### 418 compare
[kəmpéər]

他 を比較する　→1090 **comparison**

compare ~ with [to] ...　~と…を比較する
compared to [with] ~　~と比較すると

### 419 conduct
動 [kəndʌ́kt]
名 [kándʌkt]

他 を管理する；を指導する；〈調査〉を行う　名 行い；管理

conduct a business　業務を遂行する

### 420 confirm
[kənfə́ːrm]

他 を確かめる；を確認する　→242 **reconfirm**

confirm a booking　予約を確認する

---

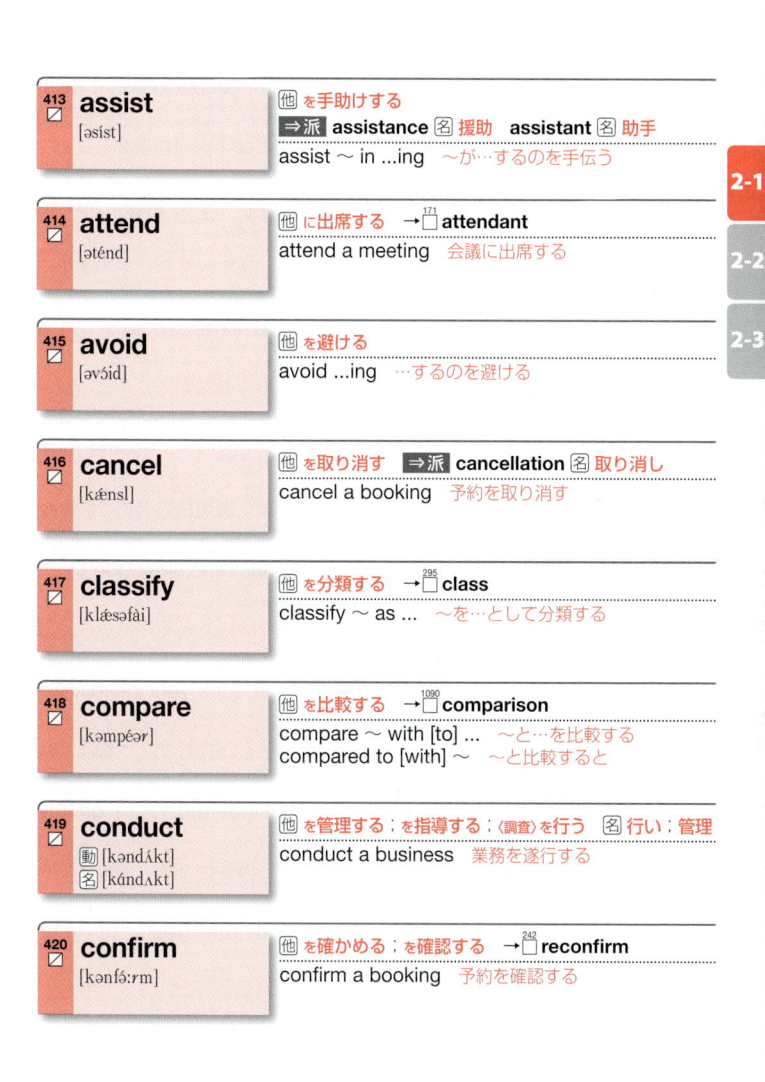

解答　(1) assist　(2) attend　(3) avoid　(4) canceled
(5) classify　(6) compare　(7) conduct　(8) Confirm

> contain　counter　create　describe
> depend　connect　consider　confuse

(1) When we had three men named "Bill" in this department, it used to really (　) our customers.
この課にビルという名の社員が3人いたときには，本当に顧客を混乱させたものだった。

(2) You're on Flight 893 to Las Vegas, which (　) to Flight 561 to Los Angeles.
お客様はロサンゼルス行き561便に接続する，ラスベガス行き893便にご搭乗中です。

(3) The other day the manager asked Kevin if he would (　) a transfer to the Baltimore office.
先日，部長はケビンにボルチモアの事務所への転勤を考えてみないかとたずねた。

(4) In order to enter a recipe in the contest it must (　) some form of chicken that is not barbecued.
コンテストにレシピを出すには，直火焼きでない調理法の鶏肉を含めなければならない。

(5) Rather than just walk away from the negotiations, why don't you try to (　) their offer and see what happens.
交渉をただ放り出さないで，彼らの申し出に反論しようとしてから，出方を見たらどうですか。

(6) If you don't have a database program that suits your needs, we can (　) a custom program for you.
もしご自身の要望に適したデータベースソフトをお持ちでなければ，私どもがオーダーメイドのソフトをお作りできます。

(7) Whether or not we'll be able to go on that trip (　) on my partner's busy schedule.
その旅行に行けるかどうかは，私のパートナーの多忙なスケジュール次第だ。

(8) How would you (　) the focus and the goals of your "Community Outreach Program?"
どのようにあなたの「地域福祉プログラム」の焦点とゴールを説明しますか。

| 421 | **confuse** [kənfjúːz] | 他 を困惑させる；を混同する<br>⇒派 confusion 名 混乱<br>confuse ~ with ...　~を…と混同する |
|---|---|---|
| 422 | **connect** [kənékt] | 自〈交通機関が〉連絡する　他 をつなぐ<br>connect ~ with ...　（電話で）~を…につなぐ |
| 423 | **consider** [kənsídər] | 他 を考慮する；を（~と）見なす<br>⇒派 consideration 名 考慮<br>consider ~ to be [as] ...　~を…だと見なす |
| 424 | **contain** [kəntéin] | 他 を含む；を収容する<br>contain the customer's data　顧客のデータを含む |
| 425 | **counter** [káuntər] | 他 に対抗する　名 台, カウンター；反対〔逆〕のもの<br>a check-in counter　チェックインカウンター<br>a counter-proposal　反対提案, 代案 |
| 426 | **create** [kriéit, kriː-] | 他 を創造する<br>create a disturbance　騒動を引き起こす |
| 427 | **depend** [dipénd] | 自 依存する；（~）次第である　→44 dependent<br>depending on conditions　条件次第で |
| 428 | **describe** [diskráib] | 他 の特徴を描写する；を説明する　→47 description<br>describe ~ as ...　~を…と評する |

解答　(1) confuse　(2) connects　(3) consider　(4) contain　(5) counter　(6) create　(7) depends　(8) describe

> explain   earn   discuss   extend
> export   eliminate   encourage   engage

(1) When you come to pick up the inventory, we can (　) payment methods and terms.
あなたが在庫表を取りに来るときに，支払い方と取引条件について話し合えますね。

(2) Thirty years ago, to (　) one thousand dollars as an annual salary was considered successful.
30年前，年俸として1,000ドルを稼ぐと，成功していると見なされた。

(3) Let's (　) the necessity of getting the middle manager's signature on papers like this to speed up the process.
手続きの時間短縮のため，このような書類に中間管理職のサインをもらう必要をなくそう。

(4) If his superiors had not (　) Cal when he first started, he never would have stuck with the job.
開始時に上司がキャルを励まさなかったら，彼は決して仕事をやり通さなかっただろう。

(5) Although the company is incorporated in Japan, they are (　) in various aspects of processing metal in China.
その企業は日本の法人組織だが，中国での金属加工のさまざまな面に携わっている。

(6) Let's wait until everyone gets here and gets settled before Hannah (　) the revised plan.
ハンナが変更プランの説明をする前に，全員がそろって場が落ち着くまで待とう。

(7) A growing number of local farmers have joined an organization through which they can (　) produce.
そこを通して生産品を輸出することができる団体に参加する地元の農家が増えてきた。

(8) If you (　) your stay a few days, that will give you time to visit the factories.
数日間滞在を延長すると，工場を訪問する時間ができるでしょう。

## 429 discuss
[diskʌ́s]

他 について話し合う　⇒派 discussion 名 討議

discuss a problem　問題について討論する

## 430 earn
[ə́ːrn]

他 を稼ぐ

earn a good monthly income　かなりの月収を稼ぐ

## 431 eliminate
[ilímənèit]

他 を排除する；を殺す　≒類 exclude 他 を除外する

eliminate risks　危険を除く

## 432 encourage
[enkə́ːridʒ]

他 を励ます；を促進する；を奨励する

encourage ~ to do　~が…するよう励ます〔促進する〕
encourage consumption　消費を促す

## 433 engage
[engéidʒ]

他 [be engaged]（仕事などに）従事している；(~で)忙しい

be engaged in ~　~に携わる

## 434 explain
[ikspléin, eks-]

他 を説明する　⇒派 explanation 名 説明

explain how to do the work　仕事の方法を説明する

## 435 export
動 [ikspɔ́ːrt, ékspɔːrt]
名 [ékspɔːrt]

他 自 (を)輸出する　名 輸出（品）
⇔反 import 自 他 (を)輸入する　名 輸入（品）

an article for export　輸出用の製品

## 436 extend
[iksténd, eks-]

他 を拡張する；を延長する
自 及ぶ, 広がる；延びる　→ 58 extension

extend one's hotel reservations　ホテルの予約を延長する

---

解答　(1) discuss　(2) earn　(3) eliminate　(4) encouraged
(5) engaged　(6) explains　(7) export　(8) extend

| | | | |
|---|---|---|---|
| hire | indicate | note | fix |
| measure | found | fit | obtain |

(1) Heinrich decided to leave the company, because he felt his ideas didn't ( ) with the direction the board was taking.
ハインリッヒは会社を辞めることに決めた。なぜなら自分の考え方が役員のとる方向と一致しないと感じたからだ。

(2) The editor said that they would accept the article if you just ( ) the typographical and spelling errors.
編集者は，ちょっとタイプミスとスペルミスを直せば，その記事は受け入れられるだろうと言った。

(3) For a country ( ) on freedom from religious oppression, there is an inordinate amount of religious intolerance.
宗教的抑圧からの自由の下に建国された国にしては，宗教的不寛容が過度に多い。

(4) I am happy to report that the company is finally going to let us ( ) five new people this year.
会社がついに今年5人の新人を採用させてくれることを報告できてうれしい。

(5) If you have experience in a foreign country, please ( ) that in the comments box of your application.
外国生活の経験があれば，申請書のコメント欄でその旨を述べなさい。

(6) He considers himself to be quite wealthy spiritually and says he doesn't ( ) success by money.
彼は自分を精神的にとても豊かだと考えており，金で成功を測らないと言っている。

(7) ( ) that the author is not specific about this point, but most analysts agree that that is what he means here.
留意すべきは，著者がこの点について明確ではないが，大方のアナリストがそれがここで著者が言わんとすることだと意見を一致させていることだ。

(8) If you get a signed release, you can ( ) all the records that you are looking for without a problem.
同意書を手に入れれば，問題なくあなたが探しているすべての記録を入手できる。

## 437 fit
[fít]

自 一致する, 合う　他 に適合する；を取り付ける
形 適した；体調がよい　→197 fitness

feel fit　体の具合がよい

## 438 fix
[fíks]

他 を固定する；を修理する, 直す；〈日時・場所〉を設定する　≒類 123 repair 他 を修理する

fix a place for the meeting　会合の場所を決める

## 439 found
[fáund]

他 を設立する；に根拠を与える

found a new publishing company　新しい出版社を設立する

## 440 hire
[háiər]

他 を雇う；を賃借する

hire ～ for a position　ある職に～を雇用する
hire new employees　新しい従業員を雇う

## 441 indicate
[índikèit]

他 を示す, 指し示す；を簡単に述べる　→208 indicator

indicate one's agreement to ～　～に同意の気持ちを伝える

## 442 measure
[méʒər]

他 を測る；を評価する　名 測定, 計量；尺度

be a good measure of ～　～を測る正しい尺度である

## 443 note
[nóut]

他 に注意する；を書き留める
名 メモ；短い手紙, 通告；注釈

a thank-you note　手短な礼状

## 444 obtain
[əbtéin]

他 を入手する

obtain permission　許可を得る

解答　(1) fit　(2) fix　(3) founded　(4) hire
(5) indicate　(6) measure　(7) Note　(8) obtain

> organize    provide    quit    postpone
> predict    occur    participate    overcome

(1) If the crime (    ) in another state, our police force does not have jurisdiction.
もし犯罪が別の州で起こると，我々警察には権限がない。

(2) Since you have experience with charity work, I wonder if you could (    ) this fundraiser.
あなたには慈善活動の経験があるので，この資金集めのイベントを取り仕切ってもらえないかと考えています。

(3) The owner of the company (    ) many hardships as a young man, so he supports many youth organizations.
その会社のオーナーは若いころ多くの困難を克服したので，多数の青年団体を援助している。

(4) Leave a message for me at extension 5401, if you decide you want to (    ) in the focus group.
フォーカス・グループに参加するのを決めたら，内線5401で私に伝言を残してください。

(5) When the chairman fell ill, they decided to (    ) the board meeting for a week.
会長が病気で倒れたとき，彼らは重役会を1週間延期することに決定した。

(6) Economists (    ) that interest rates will rise in the coming months, so now is the time to get a loan.
経済学者は，金利は来月には上がるだろうと予測している。だから今が借り入れ時だ。

(7) Unlike American hotels, Japanese hotels will often (    ) guests with amenities like a throw-away toothbrush.
アメリカのホテルとは異なり，日本のホテルは使い捨て歯ブラシのようなアメニティを宿泊客に提供することが多い。

(8) Please don't (    ) before you talk to the chairman about your concerns about the committee.
委員会について懸念していることを委員長に話す前に辞めないでください。

## 445 occur
[əkə́ːr]

自 起こる, 発生する；〈考えなどが〉浮かぶ

it occurred to me that ...　…ということが心に浮かんだ

## 446 organize
[ɔ́ːrɡənàiz]

他 を組織する；をまとめ上げる

organize facts　いろいろな事実を系統立ててまとめる

## 447 overcome
[òuvərkʌ́m]

他 を克服する；を打ち負かす　自 勝つ

overcome a difficulty　困難を乗り越える

## 448 participate
[pɑːrtísəpèit]

自 参加〔関係〕する　≒類 take part in 他 に参加する
→365 participant

participate in profits　利益の分け前にあずかる

## 449 postpone
[poustpóun]

他 を延期する

postpone one's departure for a week　出発を1週間延期する

## 450 predict
[pridíkt]

他 を予測〔予言〕する　⇒派 prediction 名 予測

predict rain for tomorrow　明日は雨と予報する

## 451 provide
[prəváid]

他 に〔を〕提供する　自 準備を整える　→236 provider

provide employees with various benefits　従業員にさまざまな恩典を与える

## 452 quit
[kwít]

自 中止する；辞職する
他 を放棄する；を辞職する；を中止する；を返済する

notice to quit　立ち退き通知；辞職勧告

解答　(1) occurs　(2) organize　(3) overcame　(4) participate
(5) postpone　(6) predict　(7) provide　(8) quit

> remain　remind　regret　require
> respond　rush　recommend　register

(1) Since I've never been to this restaurant before, I'll have to ask you what you (　　).
このレストランには今まで来たことがないので，あなたが何を勧めてくれるか聞かないとね。

(2) If you want to go to the developer's conference next month, you have to (　　) for it by the 9th.
来月の開発者会議に出席したいのなら，9日までにその登録をしなければなりません。

(3) I (　　) having a headache and not getting to see the old town of Jerusalem on our last day in Israel.
イスラエルの最終日に，頭痛でエルサレムの古い街並を見に行けなかったことが残念だ。

(4) We had 5,000 tiles at the beginning of the project and now that stack there is all that (　　).
計画の初期には5,000枚のタイルがあったが，そこの山が今残っているすべてだ。

(5) When I'm working I often forget about time, so I told my assistant to (　　) me right before the cyber conference.
仕事中は時間をよく忘れるので，助手にネット会議の直前に思い出させてくれるよう頼んだ。

(6) Even though it is a part-time position, it (　　) a training course that takes twenty hours to complete.
パートタイムの職種であっても，修了するのに20時間かかる研修が義務づけられている。

(7) I waited for him to (　　) to the e-mail message, but since he didn't, I called on the phone.
彼がそのEメールに返信してくれるのを待ったが，来なかったので私から電話をかけた。

(8) Wendy had to (　　) the paperwork through by noon to get the order out on the 2:00 truck.
2時のトラックに注文品を載せるため，ウェンディは事務処理を正午までに急いで終えなければならなかった。

## 453 recommend
[rèkəménd]

他 を勧める，推薦する
⇒派 recommendation 名 推薦

recommend a course to be followed　取るべき道を勧める

## 454 register
[rédʒistər]

自 登録する　他 に登録する；を記録する
名 記録（簿）；レジ　⇒派 registration 名 登録

register for [with] ～　～に登録する

## 455 regret
[rigrét]

他 を後悔する；を残念に思う　名 後悔；哀悼

express regret for ～　～をわびる

## 456 remain
[riméin]

自 (～の)ままである；残っている　→244 remainder

remain calm during the disturbance　混乱の中で平静を保つ

## 457 remind
[rimáind]

他 〈人〉に思い出させる

remind ～ of ...　～に…のことを思い出させる

## 458 require
[rikwáiər]

他 を必要とする　→248 requirement

a required subject　必修科目

## 459 respond
[rispánd]

自 返答する；反応する　⇒派 response 名 応答

respond briefly to a question　質問に手短に答える

## 460 rush
[ráʃ]

自 突進する；急いで…する　他 を急いでする；をせきたてる　名 勢いよく流れること；忙しさ

in a rush　大急ぎで

---

解答 (1) recommended (2) register (3) regret (4) remains (5) remind (6) requires (7) respond (8) rush

| | | |
|---|---|---|
| support | suit | solve |
| suggest | satisfy | suppose |

(1) Students who are not interested in biology, physics or chemistry may choose anthropology to (　　) the university science requirement.
生物学，物理学，化学に興味のない学生は，大学の科学の単位**を満たす**ために人類学を取ってもよい。

(2) It's important to not only (　　) problems as they happen, but also to think ahead before they happen.
問題が起きたときにそれ**を解決する**だけでなく，起きる前に考えておくことも大切だ。

(3) The client (　　) that we go back to the drawing board and rethink our entire concept.
依頼主は我々が製図板に戻ってコンセプト全体を考え直すよう**に提案した**。

(4) His quick math skills and careful nature made him well (　　) for the accounting job.
すばやい計算処理能力と慎重な性格のおかげで，彼は会計の仕事に本当**に向いていた**。

(5) If your business proposal is good, I will (　　) you at the next strategy meeting.
もしあなたのビジネスの提案書がよければ，次の戦略会議であなた**を支援します**。

(6) He was smart to (　　) that the fashion trends would change quickly in the teen market.
彼は賢明にも，10代の若者の市場ではファッション傾向はすぐに変わるだろう**と推測した**。

## 461 satisfy
[sǽtisfài]

他 を満足させる, 喜ばせる；を満たす
⇒派 **satisfaction** 名 満足　**satisfying** 形 満足のいく

be satisfied with ~　~に満足している

## 462 solve
[sάlv]

他 を解決する

solve a case　事件を解決する

## 463 suggest
[sʌgdʒést]

他 を提案する；を推薦する；…と示唆する
⇒派 **suggestion** 名 提案

suggest a solution　解決策を提案する

## 464 suit
[súːt]

他 に最適である；に似合う　名 スーツ；民事訴訟

go to suit　起訴する

## 465 support
[səpɔ́ːrt]

他 を支持する；を養う　名 支持；裏づけ
→ 262 **supportive**

support oneself by writing　文筆で暮らしを立てる

## 466 suppose
[səpóuz]

他 と考える；と推測する

be supposed to do　…することになっている

---

解答　(1) satisfy　(2) solve　(3) suggested　(4) suited　(5) support　(6) suppose

> actually   commercial   average   efficient
> despite   entire   downtown   comfortable

(1) ( ), I was astonished to learn that Personnel was not going to offer the position to someone on the inside.
実のところ，人事課が内部の人材に地位を提供するつもりがないと知って私は驚いた。

(2) Suzie has a job in the shipping department with an ( ) salary but great retirement benefits.
スージーは出荷部で働いている。そこは給料は平均的だが，退職金が非常によい。

(3) Since my husband started his own small company, we are much less ( ) financially.
夫が自分で小さな会社を始めたので，私たちは財政的にはずっと楽ではなくなっている。

(4) The area we are looking at is not designated for ( ) use, but we may get special permission to use it.
私たちが注視している地区は商業利用に指定されていないが，それを利用する特別な許可を得られるかもしれない。

(5) I interviewed that young movie star and ( ) her fame, she is kind and down-to-earth.
その若い映画スターにインタビューしたが，その名声にもかかわらず彼女は親切で堅実だ。

(6) The ( ) area has been revitalized in the last decade which has greatly increased the value of the property there.
商業地区一帯は過去10年間で活性化され，それによりそこの不動産の価値が大幅に上がった。

(7) Scanning prices is much more ( ) than punching in numbers at a cash register.
値段をスキャンするのは，レジに数字を打ち込むよりずっと効率的だ。

(8) She planned to look at her notes during the speech, but she practiced so much she had the ( ) piece memorized.
彼女はスピーチ中にメモを見るつもりでいたが，かなり練習したので全文を暗記していた。

| 467 | **actually** [ǽktʃuəli, ǽktʃəli] | 副 実際に, 実は, 本当に<br>⇒派 actual 形 実際の |
|---|---|---|

| 468 | **average** [ǽvəridʒ] | 形 平均の 名 平均(値)<br>on (the) average 平均して |
|---|---|---|

| 469 | **comfortable** [kʌ́mftəbl, -fərt-] | 形 快適な；心地よく感じる；くつろいだ<br>→1091 comfort ⇒派 comfortably 副 快適に<br>a comfortable chair 座り心地のよいいす |
|---|---|---|

| 470 | **commercial** [kəmə́ːrʃl] | 形 商業(上)の, 営利の 名 コマーシャル<br>⇒派 commerce 名 商業<br>commercial use 商業利用 |
|---|---|---|

| 471 | **despite** [dispáit] | 前 にもかかわらず<br>≒類 in spite of ～ ～にもかかわらず<br>despite the fact that ... …という事実にもかかわらず |
|---|---|---|

| 472 | **downtown** [dáuntáun] | 形 商業地区〔中心部〕の 副 商業地区〔中心部〕へ〔で〕<br>名 商業地区〔中心部〕<br>go downtown 町に出る |
|---|---|---|

| 473 | **efficient** [ifíʃənt] | 形 能率のよい；有能な ⇒派 efficiency 名 能率<br>be efficient at one's work 仕事において有能である |
|---|---|---|

| 474 | **entire** [entáiər] | 形 すべての<br>the entire population of ～ ～の全人口 |
|---|---|---|

解答 (1) Actually (2) average (3) comfortable (4) commercial (5) despite (6) downtown (7) efficient (8) entire

| excess | further | general | financial |
| helpful | independent | extremely | highly |

(1) Hydrotherapy involves using hot or cold water to dampen a towel and then getting rid of the (　) water.
水治療法は，湯か冷水を用いてタオルを湿らせ，余分な水分をふき取ることを必要とする。

(2) It's (　) easy to find administrative assistants these days, but not all of them can handle such a workload well.
最近は経営のアシスタントを見つけるのはきわめて簡単だが，全員がそんな仕事量をうまくこなせるわけではない。

(3) If we successfully sell this patent to a large company, it will guarantee our (　) freedom.
もしこの特許が首尾よく大企業に売れたら，それにより金銭的な自由が保証されるだろう。

(4) If you have the time, may I suggest we discuss this (　) over lunch tomorrow?
もしお時間があれば，明日，昼食を取りながらこの件についてさらに検討しませんか。

(5) While everyone understood the (　) idea, most of us were unclear on the specifics.
だれもがだいたいの概念は理解したのだが，ほとんどの人にとって詳細は不明確だった。

(6) Eric is new, but he has experience with that type of fund and he may be (　) to you.
エリックは新人だが，そのタイプの基金管理機関での経験があるので，助けになるかもしれない。

(7) I wasn't sure about this brand of office supplies, but the clerk (　) recommended it.
私はこの銘柄の事務用品についてはよく知らなかったが，店員はこれを強く薦めた。

(8) They asked that we have the books reviewed by an (　) auditor before rendering a decision on the merger.
彼らは合併の決断を言い渡す前に，私たちに社外監査人に帳簿を閲覧させるよう要求した。

| # | Word | Meaning | Example |
|---|---|---|---|
| 475 | **excess** [iksés, ek-] | 形 過度の、余分な 名 超過、過剰 ⇒派 excessive 形 過度な | an excess fare 乗り越し料金 |
| 476 | **extremely** [ikstríːmli, eks-] | 副 極度に ⇒派 extreme 形 極端な | extremely important きわめて重要な |
| 477 | **financial** [fənǽnʃl] | 形 財務の、金銭上の ⇒派 finance 名 財政；財源 | financial statements 財務報告書 |
| 478 | **further** [fə́ːrðər] | 副 さらに遠くへ；さらに 形 さらに遠い；それ以上の 他 を促進する | further instructions さらなる指示 |
| 479 | **general** [dʒénərəl] | 形 一般的な；概略の ⇒派 generally 副 一般的に | a general contractor 一般請負業者、ゼネコン |
| 480 | **helpful** [hélpfl] | 形 有用な、助けになる ⇒派 help 他 を助ける | helpful information 有用な情報 |
| 481 | **highly** [háili] | 副 非常に；高度に；高く評価して ⇒派 high 形 高い | speak highly of ～ ～を激賞する |
| 482 | **independent** [ìndipéndənt] | 形 独立した；関係がない ⇒派 independence 名 独立 | be independent of ～ ～から独立している |

解答 (1) excess (2) extremely (3) financial (4) further (5) general (6) helpful (7) highly (8) independent

| minimum | likely | medical | legal |
| local | otherwise | novel | lean |

(1) The company made a small profit, but it was a ( ) year compared to the last few.
会社はわずかな利益を上げたが、過去数年と比べて不況の年だった。

(2) Tom doesn't have very good social skills, but everyone says he has an excellent ( ) mind.
トムはそれほど優れた社交術を持っていないが、すばらしい法律的思考力があると皆言う。

(3) Criminals often have patterns, so similar crimes are ( ) to occur in similar situations at the same time of day.
犯罪者にはしばしば類型があり、似た犯罪が同時刻に似た状況で起こる可能性が高い。

(4) Rather than have the usual hotel food for our banquet, we rented out a ( ) restaurant.
私たちはパーティにいつものホテルの料理を頼まず、地元のレストランを借り切った。

(5) Her assistant said that Lily had to postpone her business trip to Rome for ( ) reasons.
リリーは医療上の理由でローマ出張を延期せねばならないと彼女の助手は言った。

(6) We can't make a profit if our customers keep only making the ( ) order.
顧客が最小限の注文しかしないままなら、我々は利益を得られない。

(7) Having a quiet juice bar and reading room connected by a soundproof wall to a loud sports bar is a ( ) idea.
騒々しいスポーツバーと防音壁を隔てて隣り合う静かなジュースバーと読書室を作ることは、新しい発想だ。

(8) I have to run errands and stop at my brother's house, ( ) I'd be happy to offer you a ride home.
いくつか用件を済ませ、兄の家に寄らなくてはなりません。そうでなければ喜んであなたを車でご自宅までお送りするのですが。

| 483 **lean** [líːn] | 形 細い；乏しい 自 傾く，もたれる |
|---|---|
| | lean against ～ 〜に寄り掛かる |

| 484 **legal** [líːgl] | 形 適法の，合法的な；法定の；法律の ⇔反 illegal 形 違法の |
|---|---|
| | the legal profession 法律関係の職業，法曹 |

| 485 **likely** [láikli] | 形 ありそうな，起こりそうな 副 おそらく，たぶん |
|---|---|
| | be likely to do …しそうだ |

| 486 **local** [lóukl] | 形 地元の；当地の；各駅停車の 名 地元の住民 |
|---|---|
| | a local train 普通列車 |

| 487 **medical** [médikl] | 形 医学の，医療の |
|---|---|
| | medical care 医療 |

| 488 **minimum** [mínimǝm] | 形 最小の，最低限の 名 最低限，最小量 ⇔反 maximum 形 最大限の 名 最大限 |
|---|---|
| | a minimum rate 最も低い率 |

| 489 **novel** [návl] | 形 新奇な 名 小説 |
|---|---|
| | the movie version of the novel その小説の映画版 |

| 490 **otherwise** [ʌ́ðǝrwàiz] | 副 さもないと；ほかのすべての点では；違ったふうに |
|---|---|
| | his otherwise equals ほかの点では彼に匹敵する人々 |

解答 (1) lean (2) legal (3) likely (4) local (5) medical (6) minimum (7) novel (8) otherwise

> regional　physical　private
> regular　previous

(1) The doctor said that Edgar's troubles were most likely more psychological than (　).
エドガーの問題はおそらく肉体的なものより精神的なものであると医師は言った。

(2) The (　) owners had a cat, so we have found lots of scratch marks on the floors and walls.
前の家主が猫を飼っていたので，私たちは床や壁に引っかき傷の跡をたくさん見つけた。

(3) We chartered a (　) jet to take the VIP from New York to our Chicago office.
要人をニューヨークから当社のシカゴ支社まで移動させるため私用ジェット機をチャーターした。

(4) Ernie has been promoted to (　) manager and is taking us out to celebrate.
アーニーは地域担当部長に昇進したので，私たちをお祝いに連れ出してくれる。

(5) Since being diagnosed with a heart condition the boss has been trying to eat and sleep on a (　) schedule.
心臓が悪いと診断されて以来，上司は規則正しい時間に寝食するように心がけている。

| 491 | **physical** [fízikl] | 形 体の, 肉体の；物質の；自然法則の 名 健康診断 ⇒派 **physically** 副 物理的に；肉体的に |
|---|---|---|
| | | a physical characteristic 身体的特徴 |

| 492 | **previous** [príːviəs] | 形 以前の, 先の ⇒派 **previously** 副 以前に |
|---|---|---|
| | | previous to ～ ～より前に, ～以前に |

| 493 | **private** [práivət] | 形 私的な, 私有の；内密の；民間の |
|---|---|---|
| | | by private contract or arrangement 内々の契約ないしは協定により |

| 494 | **regional** [ríːdʒənl] | 形 地域の ⇒派 **region** 名 地域 |
|---|---|---|
| | | a regional dialect 地域方言 |

| 495 | **regular** [régjələr] | 形 正規の；通常通りの 名 常連；(衣服の)通常サイズ |
|---|---|---|
| | | a regular audit 定期的な会計検査 |

解答 (1) physical (2) previous (3) private (4) regional (5) regular

> similar   responsible   steady
> total   successful

(1) I'd like to speak to the person who was ( ) for placing this ad in yesterday's newspaper.
昨日の新聞にこの広告を載せた責任者の方とお話したいのですが。

(2) The products are ( ); the difference is that our brand has better name recognition.
製品は似たようなものだ。違いは、我々のブランド名のほうがよく知られていることだ。

(3) We have seen a ( ) rise in our sales numbers over the last six months.
ここ6か月の間、当社の売上の数字は安定した伸びを見せている。

(4) The most ( ) businessman I ever met came from a single parent home and only had a junior high school education.
私が今までに会った中で最も成功している実業家はひとり親の家庭出身で中卒だった。

(5) His ( ) sales last year was more than the rest of the entire sales team combined.
昨年の彼の売上総額は、残りの販売チーム全員の分を合わせたものより多かった。

| 496 | **responsible** [rispánsəbl] | 形 責任がある；信頼できる<br>⇒派 responsibility 名 責任<br>make oneself responsible for ～　～の責任を取る |
|---|---|---|
| 497 | **similar** [símələr] | 形 類似した；相似の　⇔反 different 形 異なる<br>⇒派 similarity 名 類似(点)<br>similar to ～　～に類似した |
| 498 | **steady** [stédi] | 形 着実な；固定された；安定した；一定の<br>⇒派 steadily 副 着実に<br>walk with steady steps　しっかりとした足取りで歩く |
| 499 | **successful** [səksésfl] | 形 成功した, うまくいった　⇒派 success 名 成功<br>a successful applicant　合格者<br>be successful in ～　～で成功する |
| 500 | **total** [tóutl] | 形 完全な；全体の　名 合計, 総額　他 総計で～になる<br>自 合計する　⇒派 totally 副 完全に<br>a grand total　総計 |

解答 (1) responsible (2) similar (3) steady (4) successful (5) total

# Chapter 2-2 使える学校英語を総ざらい

学校英語 ▶▶▶ TOEIC® TEST　頻度★★

> aspect　appearance　attitude　atmosphere
> background　administration　aid　athlete

(1) He was rather disorganized as a sales representative, but he changed dramatically when he got a position in (　).
彼は営業部員としてはやや手際が悪かったが、管理部に職を得て劇的に変わった。

(2) The company says that the product is simply a study (　), but many students read it instead of the textbook.
会社はその製品は単なる勉強の補助であると言っているが、大勢の学生が教科書代わりにそれを読んでいる。

(3) I thought the CEO was going to speak at the reception, but she just made a brief (　) and left.
私はCEOが歓迎会で話をするだろうと思ったが、彼女は少し姿を見せただけで退出した。

(4) You don't seem to be interested in accounting, so I was wondering what (　) of this job you find attractive.
会計に興味がなさそうなので、この仕事のどの面に魅力を見出すだろうかと思っています。

(5) We learned that Frank is quite an (　) and he will be participating in a triathlon next month.
我々は、フランクはかなりの運動選手であり、彼が来月のトライアスロンに参加する予定であることを知った。

(6) Since Carol quit, everyone has said that the (　) in the office is much more pleasant.
キャロルが辞めて以来、だれもがオフィスの雰囲気がはるかに明るくなったと言っている。

(7) The news from the doctor was not very encouraging, but Bud was determined to maintain a positive (　).
医者からの知らせはあまり望みあるものでなかったが、バッドは前向きな姿勢を維持することにした。

(8) We could certainly use someone with a (　) in Chinese culture to be involved in this project.
このプロジェクトに参画するために、中国文化を背景に持つ人をきっと起用するだろう。

| 501 | **administration** [ədmìnəstréiʃən] | 名 管理；管理責任者, 執行部；行政<br>business administration　経営管理学<br>administration bureau　行政局, 管理局 |
|---|---|---|
| 502 | **aid** [éid] | 名 救助；援助；補助物　他 を助ける<br>first aid　応急手当<br>financial aid　財政的援助 |
| 503 | **appearance** [əpíərəns] | 名 姿を現すこと, 出現；出席；外見<br>⇒派 **appear** 自 現れる<br>one's public appearance　公衆の前に姿を現すこと |
| 504 | **aspect** [æspekt] | 名 側面<br>consider ~ in all its aspects　~をあらゆる面から考える |
| 505 | **athlete** [æθli:t] | 名 運動選手<br>⇒派 **athletic** 形 運動競技の |
| 506 | **atmosphere** [ætməsfìər] | 名 空気, 大気；雰囲気<br>relaxed atmosphere　くつろいだ雰囲気 |
| 507 | **attitude** [ǽtət(j)ù:d] | 名 態度, 姿勢<br>a positive [negative] attitude　肯定的〔否定的〕な態度 |
| 508 | **background** [bǽkgràund] | 名 背景, 履歴<br>background information　予備知識, 背景事情 |

解答 (1) administration (2) aid (3) appearance (4) aspect (5) athlete (6) atmosphere (7) attitude (8) background

> burden   caution   bond   conclusion
> content   circumstance   capacity   boundary

(1) Venture capitalism can be risky, but some investors prefer it to the stock and (　) markets.
ベンチャービジネス投資はリスクが高いが，投資家には株や債券市場より好む人がいる。

(2) It is important to retain professional distance and be conscious of interpersonal (　) when giving advice to employees.
社員に忠告するときは，職務上の距離を維持し，人間関係の境界を意識するのが重要だ。

(3) The (　) of proof is on the prosecution and they don't seem to have much evidence against my client.
立証責任は検察側にあるが，私の依頼人に対抗する証拠をそう持っているようには見えない。

(4) We can't use that room for the keynote speech, because the seating (　) is only 350 and we have 400.
基調演説にあの部屋は使えない。350席の収容能力しかないのに，我々は400人だからだ。

(5) The word "hot" is printed out on the hot water dispenser so that employees will use it with (　).
従業員が注意して利用するよう，その湯沸かし器には「熱い」という言葉が貼られている。

(6) Under the (　), we can understand why so many employees are afraid of losing their jobs to downsizing.
その状況ならば，なぜ多くの従業員が規模縮小による失業を懸念するのか理解できる。

(7) The only (　) I can draw from your careless work is that you really don't want this job.
あなたの軽率な仕事から引き出せる結論は，あなたは特にこの仕事をしたくないということだけだ。

(8) Jose likes this program the best because he says it's easy to change Web (　) using it.
ホセはこのソフトを使うと簡単にウェブコンテンツを変えられると言い，一番気に入っている。

| 509 | **bond** [bánd] | 名 公債, 債券；きずな；接着剤<br>a public bond　公債<br>a government bond　国債 |
|---|---|---|
| 510 | **boundary** [báund(ə)ri] | 名 境界線<br>mark the boundary　境界を区切る |
| 511 | **burden** [bə́:rdn] | 名 荷, 重荷；負担　他 を負わせる<br>be a burden to ～　～の負担となる<br>tax burden　税負担 |
| 512 | **capacity** [kəpǽsəti] | 名 収容能力；容量<br>at full capacity　フル操業で |
| 513 | **caution** [kɔ́:ʃən] | 名 注意；警告　⇒派 cautious 形 注意深い<br>cautiously 副 注意深く<br>with caution　用心して |
| 514 | **circumstance** [sə́:rkəmstæns] | 名 状況, 事情；境遇<br>under no circumstances　どんなことがあっても…ない |
| 515 | **conclusion** [kənklú:ʒən] | 名 結論　⇒派 conclude 他 と結論を下す<br>come to the conclusion that ...　…という結論に達する |
| 516 | **content** 名 [kántent] 形 [kəntént] | 名 内容物, 中身, コンテンツ；容量<br>形 (～に) 満足している<br>table of contents　目次 |

解答 (1) bond (2) boundaries (3) burden (4) capacity (5) caution (6) circumstances (7) conclusion (8) content

> decade    disaster    employer    desire
> debate    currency    experiment    counterpart

(1) I'd like to introduce you to Gilbert, my (　　) in our London office.
ロンドン事務所で私と同じ地位にいる人物である，ギルバートを紹介させてください。

(2) I need to stop at the (　　) exchange and put some of these euros into pounds for the U.K. trip.
イギリス旅行のため，通貨交換所に寄って，このユーロの一部をポンドに換える必要がある。

(3) There was quite a (　　) about which subcontractor to put work out to because two were close in price.
2社は価格が接近していたため，いずれの下請け業者に外注すべきかについてかなりの討論があった。

(4) You will probably get permission, because your office hasn't been remodeled or even repainted in at least a (　　).
あなたはたぶん許可を得られるでしょう。なぜならあなたのオフィスは少なくとも10年間改装しておらず，再塗装すらしていないのですから。

(5) Every restaurant in that location has been worse than the last, so I have no (　　) to try the new one.
その地のレストランはどれもこの前より悪くなってきているので，私には新しいレストランを試したいという希望はまったくない。

(6) If you'd like to make a donation, you can easily find the local (　　) relief fund information online.
寄付をなさりたいなら，ネットで地元の災害救援基金情報を簡単に見つけられますよ。

(7) To qualify for government childcare assistance, you must provide various documents from your (　　).
政府の子育て援助の資格を得るには，雇用主からのさまざまな書類を提出せねばならない。

(8) We're going to try flexible working hours as an (　　) from the first of the year.
私たちは，年始から実験としてフレックスタイムを試行するつもりだ。

| 517 | **counterpart** [káuntərpàːrt] | 名 対応するもの〔人〕；異なる組織で同等の位置にある人〔立場〕 |
| --- | --- | --- |
| | | export counterpart　輸出国 |

| 518 | **currency** [káːrənsi] | 名 通貨；流通 |
| --- | --- | --- |
| | | currency of payment　支払通貨 |

| 519 | **debate** [dibéit] | 名 討論　他 自 (について) 討論する |
| --- | --- | --- |
| | | hold a debate on ～　～について議論する |

| 520 | **decade** [dékeid, -´-, di-] | 名 10年間 |
| --- | --- | --- |
| | | in the last decade　この10年の間に |

| 521 | **desire** [dizáiər] | 名 希望　他 を望む |
| --- | --- | --- |
| | | desire to do　…することを望む |

| 522 | **disaster** [dizǽstər] | 名 天災, 災害；大失敗　⇒派 disastrous 形 悲惨な |
| --- | --- | --- |
| | | a natural disaster　天災 |

| 523 | **employer** [emplɔ́iər] | 名 雇用主 |
| --- | --- | --- |
| | | one's former employer　前の雇用主 |

| 524 | **experiment** 名[ikspérəmənt, eks-] 動[ikspérəmènt] | 名 実験　自 実験する |
| --- | --- | --- |
| | | a chemical experiment　化学実験 |

解答　(1) counterpart (2) currency (3) debate (4) decade (5) desire (6) disaster (7) employer (8) experiment

| | | | |
|---|---|---|---|
| instrument | institute | harvest | flavor |
| flexibility | interior | failure | extent |

(1) If you cannot understand the information, we will provide it in another format to the ( ) that is possible.
その情報を理解できないのでしたら，できる限り別のフォーマットで提示いたします。

(2) The lawsuit could be dropped based on the other side's ( ) to appear for the court date.
相手側が公判日の出頭を履行しなかったことに基づくと，訴訟は中断されうる。

(3) Many are surprised to find out that the most popular ice cream ( ) is vanilla.
最も人気のあるアイスクリームの味がバニラだと知って驚く人は多い。

(4) People with health problems often have far less ( ) in their daily routine than healthy people.
健康に問題を抱える人々は，健康な人よりはるかに日常業務の柔軟性を欠くことが多い。

(5) The supplement manufacturer emphasizes that they grow the herbs in rich soil to guarantee a rich ( ).
サプリメントの製造者は，豊かな土壌でハーブを育てることで豊かな収穫が保証されることを強調している。

(6) Blondell ( ) is a non-profit research organization that is sponsored and funded by Blondell Industries.
ブロンデル研究所はブロンデル工業によって後援と資金を受ける非営利研究組織だ。

(7) Until his father bought him a guitar, Josh had never really been interested in a musical ( ).
父親にギターを買ってもらうまで，ジョシュは本当に楽器に興味を持ったことはなかった。

(8) The ( ) of the building suffered tremendous damage from the fire, but the structure is still sound.
その建物の内部は火事で甚大な被害を受けたが，構造的にはなお問題ない。

| # | 見出し | 意味・例 |
|---|---|---|
| 525 | **extent** [ikstént, eks-] | 名 程度, 限界<br>to the extent that ...  …という程度まで |
| 526 | **failure** [féiljər] | 名 失敗；故障；…しないこと<br>power failure  停電 |
| 527 | **flavor** [fléivər] | 名 風味, 味<br>give flavor to food  食べ物に味をつける |
| 528 | **flexibility** [flèksəbíləti] | 名 柔軟性 ⇒派 flexible 形 柔軟な<br>have the flexibility to adapt to change  変化に適合する柔軟性がある |
| 529 | **harvest** [háːrvist] | 名 収穫；結果<br>a good [poor] harvest  豊作〔凶作〕 |
| 530 | **institute** [ínstət(j)ùːt] | 名 (学術・教育の) 機関, 研究所；(理工系の) 大学<br>an institute of technology  工科大学 |
| 531 | **instrument** [ínstrəmənt] | 名 楽器；精密機器, 器具<br>drawing instruments  製図器械 |
| 532 | **interior** [intíəriər] | 名 内部；内政 形 内部の；国内の<br>the interior of a car  車の内装 |

解答 (1) extent (2) failure (3) flavor (4) flexibility (5) harvest (6) institute (7) instrument (8) interior

| | | | |
|---|---|---|---|
| machinery | judge | landscape | label |
| investigation | native | mechanic | medicine |

(1) The ( ) into insider trading is at a standstill because so many people have refused to cooperate.
インサイダー取引の捜査は，捜査協力を拒んだ者がとても多いため行き詰まっている。

(2) Our case is going up before the ( ) in a month, so I'll need all the reports in by Friday.
我々の申し立ては1か月後に判事に届くので，金曜日までにすべての報告書が届いている必要がある。

(3) We are required to put ( ) on our products marking them as inedible.
我々は，製品に食べられないことを示すラベルをつけるよう求められている。

(4) One would think an office building in such a luxurious setting would have better ( ) surrounding it.
こんな豪華な構えのオフィスビルなら，もっとよい景色に囲まれていると思われるだろう。

(5) Until the construction is over, we'll have to put up with sounds of heavy ( ) outside the office.
工事が終わるまで，事務所の外の重機の騒音を我慢しなければならないだろう。

(6) The ( ) suggested we ask the dealer to do some computer testing on the car.
その機械工は我々に，ディーラーに頼んで車のコンピュータ検査をするよう提案した。

(7) If this ( ) doesn't give you some relief, you might consider contacting an acupuncturist.
この薬が苦痛軽減にならないなら，鍼灸師にかかることを考えるのもよいでしょう。

(8) Because he spoke so quickly, I mistakenly assumed that Doug was a ( ) of New York.
ダグがあまりに速く話したため，私は誤って彼はニューヨーク生まれの人だと思い込んだ。

| 533 | **investigation** [invèstəgéiʃən] | 名 調査；調査する行為；調査報告書 ⇒派 **investigate** 自他 (を)調査する |
|---|---|---|
| | | on further investigation　さらに調査してみると |

| 534 | **judge** [dʒʌ́dʒ] | 名 裁判官, 判事；鑑定家　他 を判断する |
|---|---|---|
| | | to judge by appearances　外見で判断すると |

| 535 | **label** [léibl] | 名 ラベル；表示　他 にラベルをつける |
|---|---|---|
| | | put labels on one's luggage　荷物に荷札を張りつける |

| 536 | **landscape** [lǽndskèip] | 名 風景, 景観 |
|---|---|---|
| | | a rural landscape　田舎の風景<br>landscape architecture　景観設計, 造園 |

| 537 | **machinery** [məʃíːnəri] | 名 機械装置, 機械設備　⇒派 **machine** 名 機械 |
|---|---|---|
| | | install, operate and maintain machinery　機械の取り付け, 運転, 整備を行う |

| 538 | **mechanic** [məkǽnik, mi-] | 名 機械工, 修理工 |
|---|---|---|
| | | a garage mechanic　自動車修理工 |

| 539 | **medicine** [médəsn] | 名 薬；医学, 医療 |
|---|---|---|
| | | a specific medicine　特効薬 |

| 540 | **native** [néitiv] | 名 (〜の)出身者　形 出生地の；(土地に)固有の |
|---|---|---|
| | | native to North Europe　北ヨーロッパ原産の |

解答 (1) investigation (2) judge (3) labels (4) landscape (5) machinery (6) mechanic (7) medicine (8) native

> privilege outline path patience
> pursuit profession reaction occupation

(1) He must have a very private or special job because he wouldn't tell anybody anything about his ( ).
彼は自分の職業についてだれにも何も語らないので非常に私的か特殊な仕事にちがいない。

(2) One way to take notes is to try to make an ( ) of what you are reading or listening to.
メモを取る1つの方法は，読んだり聞いたりしていることの概要を書いてみることだ。

(3) The company originally sold rubber fittings, but they took a new ( ) and got into the tire business.
その会社は当初はゴム製付属品を販売していたが，新方針をとりタイヤ産業に参入した。

(4) If you think you have the ( ) to explain the procedure to amateurs, why don't you take over the group?
素人に手順を説明する忍耐力があると思うなら，そのグループを引き継ぎませんか。

(5) Tom Ferris, Ms. Carter; I consider it an honor and a ( ) to meet you.
トム・フェリスです，カーターさん。お目にかかれて光栄で名誉に思います。

(6) Ivan has been working in marketing for years, but this was not his original ( ).
イワンは何年もマーケティングの仕事をしているが，これは彼の本来の専門ではなかった。

(7) The police cruiser got into an accident in ( ) of a speeding driver attempting to escape.
そのパトカーは，逃げようとしたスピード違反のドライバーを追跡していて事故にあった。

(8) Reports indicate that the ( ) to the change in policy has been positive for the most part.
報告書は，政策の転換に対する反応はおおむね肯定的であったと示唆している。

| 541 | **occupation** [àkjəpéiʃən] | 名 職業, 活動；占有 →591 occupy<br>people of various occupations さまざまな職業の人たち |
|---|---|---|
| 542 | **outline** [áutlàin] | 名 概略；輪郭 他 の要点を述べる<br>give an outline 概略を述べる |
| 543 | **path** [pǽθ] | 名 小道；進路；方針<br>the path of a hurricane ハリケーンの進路 |
| 544 | **patience** [péiʃəns] | 名 忍耐力 →1029 patient<br>have the patience to do 辛抱強く…する |
| 545 | **privilege** [prívəlidʒ] | 名 特権；特権階級；名誉<br>privilege of free transportation 交通費免除の特典 |
| 546 | **profession** [prəféʃən] | 名 職業, 専門職；同業者集団<br>⇒派 professional 形 専門職の, プロの<br>go into a profession 専門職につく |
| 547 | **pursuit** [pərs(j)úːt] | 名 追跡；追求 ⇒派 pursue 他 を追い求める<br>in pursuit of ～ ～を追って, ～を得ようとして |
| 548 | **reaction** [ri(ː)ǽkʃən] | 名 反応, 反響；反発 ⇒派 react 自 反応する<br>a chemical reaction 化学反応 |

解答 (1) occupation (2) outline (3) path (4) patience (5) privilege (6) profession (7) pursuit (8) reaction

|         |           |            |          |
|---------|-----------|------------|----------|
| snack   | risk      | reputation | routine  |
| solution| reference | row        | shortage |

(1) This article from *Computing Today* magazine was cited as one of the (　) in his presentation.
この『コンピューティング・トゥデイ』誌の記事は，彼の発表で参考文献の１つとして挙げられていた。

(2) We had never eaten the chef's food, but we chose her for the luncheon based on her (　).
そのシェフの料理を食べたことはなかったが，評判をもとにその昼食会には彼女を選んだ。

(3) Making the investment is a big (　), but the potential gain is also quite phenomenal.
投資することは大きなリスクだが，その潜在的利益もまたかなり驚異的である。

(4) When the call came from overseas, the assistant knew her boss's (　) and located him immediately.
その電話が海外からかかってきたとき，アシスタントは彼女の上司の日課を知っていたので，すぐに彼の所在を突き止めた。

(5) There have been three sales calls in a (　), so let's let the answering machine pick up this one.
立て続けに３本もセールス電話がかかってきたから，この電話は留守番電話にしよう。

(6) We have decided to increase the number of suppliers in order to avoid another (　) of materials like last year.
昨年のような材料不足の再発を防ぐために，供給会社の数を増やすことに決めた。

(7) The employee's lounge has a refrigerator, a coffee maker and vending machines for (　) and soft drinks.
社員用のラウンジには冷蔵庫とコーヒーメーカー，軽食とソフトドリンクの自動販売機がある。

(8) With hard work and patience I am sure a (　) to our problems will eventually appear.
努力と忍耐によって，我々の問題の解決法がきっと最終的には見つかると思う。

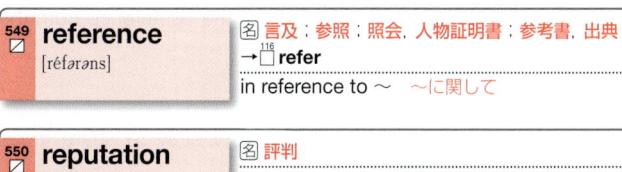

|  |  |  |
|---|------|---------|
| 549 | **reference** [réfərəns] | 名 言及；参照；照会，人物証明書；参考書，出典 →116 refer<br>in reference to 〜　〜に関して |
| 550 | **reputation** [rèpjətéiʃən] | 名 評判<br>have a good reputation　評判がよい |
| 551 | **risk** [rísk] | 名 危険；危険な事柄，リスク<br>run the risk of 〜　〜の危険を冒す |
| 552 | **routine** [ru:tí:n] | 名 いつもする仕事，日課　形 いつもの；決まりきった<br>take up one's daily routine　日課に取り掛かる |
| 553 | **row** [róu] | 名 (横の)列；座席の列<br>in a row　続けて，連続して |
| 554 | **shortage** [ʃɔ́:rtidʒ] | 名 不足<br>shortage of commodities　物不足<br>a power shortage　電力不足 |
| 555 | **snack** [snǽk] | 名 軽食，スナック　自 軽食を取る<br>a quick snack　すぐ済ませられる軽い食事 |
| 556 | **solution** [səlú:ʃən] | 名 解決(策)，解答；溶液　→462 solve<br>a solution to [for] 〜　〜の解決策 |

解答　(1) references　(2) reputation　(3) risk　(4) routine　(5) row　(6) shortage　(7) snacks　(8) solution

> substitute    tool    venture    wildlife
> stage    treatment    structure

(1) The CEO will give the opening speech of the conference from the (     ) in the main conference room.
CEO は大会議室の壇上から会議の開会演説をする。

(2) The (     ) of our company makes it very easy to share ideas between different departments.
我が社は違う部署同士でアイデアを分かち合うのがとても容易な構造になっている。

(3) Using plastic as a (     ) for the metal parts was cheaper, but it wasn't good for quality.
プラスチックを金属部品の代わりに使うとより安くついたが，品質はよくなかった。

(4) No matter how clever or skilled you are, you have to have the right (     ) in order to finish the job.
どんなに器用で技術のある人でも，仕事を仕上げるには適切な道具が必要だ。

(5) A history of bad (     ) left the factory floor workers bitter and resentful towards the management.
昔から待遇がひどかったために，工場の労働者は経営側に苦い思いと怒りを抱いていた。

(6) I'm leaving my job of 15 years to start a new business (     ) with my best friend.
私は親友と新しいベンチャー事業を始めるために，15 年来の仕事を辞める。

(7) Before building the new factory we studied to see if it would negatively affect the nearby (     ).
新工場の建設前に我々はそれが近隣の野生生物に悪い影響を与えるかどうか調査した。

|  |  |  |  |
|---|---|---|---|
| 557 | **stage** [stéidʒ] | 名 段階；舞台　他 を上演する；を企画する | at the present stage　目下のところ |
| 558 | **structure** [strʌ́ktʃər] | 名 構造, 組み立て；建造物；組織 | be complicated in structure　構造が複雑である |
| 559 | **substitute** [sʌ́bstət(j)ùːt] | 名 代用品　他 を代用する　自 代理を務める | substitute margarine for butter　マーガリンをバターの代わりにする |
| 560 | **tool** [túːl] | 名 道具；手段 | tools of the trade　商売道具 |
| 561 | **treatment** [tríːtmənt] | 名 治療法；取り扱い | take medical treatment　治療を受ける |
| 562 | **venture** [véntʃər] | 名 投機的事業, ベンチャー | a joint venture　合弁事業<br>venture capital　ベンチャーキャピタル, ベンチャー投資資金 |
| 563 | **wildlife** [wáildlàif] | 名 野生生物 | a wildlife preserve　野生動物保護地区 |

解答　(1) stage　(2) structure　(3) substitute　(4) tools　(5) treatment　(6) venture　(7) wildlife

> assign   accommodate   appeal   admit
> acquire   arise   assume   accomplish

(1) Although the restaurant is quite full tonight, Oswald is an excellent customer, so let's try to (　) their request for reservations.
今晩レストランは大変込んでいるが，オズワルドは上得意なので，予約のリクエストのために便宜を図りましょう。

(2) If I can (　) a lot today, I should be able to begin the new project tomorrow or Monday.
もし今日多くを達成できたら，明日か月曜日には新しい企画を始められるはずです。

(3) We represent a client who is looking to (　) an existing distribution firm in your area.
我々はあなたの地区で既存の販売会社を取得しようとしている依頼人の代理を務めている。

(4) After the client wrote a letter praising Jacob's efforts, the boss had to (　) he had done an excellent job.
取引先がヤコブの努力を讃える手紙を書いたあとは，上司は彼がすばらしい仕事をしたことを認めざるを得なかった。

(5) While the performer seems to (　) to certain audiences, many people don't understand his political humor.
その俳優は特定の聴衆には訴えているようだが，多くの人たちは彼の政治的なユーモアが理解できない。

(6) If any disputes (　) from this agreement, the court system in the country of the disputing party shall have jurisdiction.
当契約からいかなる論争が生じた際も，争う当事者の国の法廷が裁判権を持つものとする。

(7) If you're not at work on Tuesday, you'll miss the day the boss (　) our roles in the presentation.
火曜日に仕事を休むと，上司が我々のプレゼンでの任務を割り当てる日を逃しますよ。

(8) Don't (　) that the job is ours just because the client agreed to take a meeting with us.
クライアントが会合に同意したとはいえ，仕事がものにできたと決め込んではいけない。

| 564 | **accommodate** [əkámədèit] | 他 のために便宜を図る, に対応する；を収容できる<br>→ accommodation<br>accommodate a change　変更に対応する |
|---|---|---|
| 565 | **accomplish** [əkámpliʃ] | 他 を達成する　⇒派 accomplishment 名 達成, 成果<br>accomplish one's mission　使命を果たす |
| 566 | **acquire** [əkwáiər] | 他 を手に入れる；を身につける<br>acquire education　教養を身につける |
| 567 | **admit** [ədmít, æd-] | 他 を（〜に）入ることを許す；を通す；を認める<br>→ admission<br>admit 〜 to ...　〜を…に入ることを許す |
| 568 | **appeal** [əpí:l] | 自 他 (に)訴える　名 魅力；嘆願；上訴<br>make an appeal to 〜　〜に訴える |
| 569 | **arise** [əráiz] | 自 起こる, 発生する<br>arise from 〜　〜から生じる |
| 570 | **assign** [əsáin] | 他 を（〜に）割り当てる；を（地位・部署に）任命する<br>→ assignment<br>assign 〜 a task　〜に仕事を割り振る |
| 571 | **assume** [əs(j)ú:m] | 他 と想定する, 決め込む；を引き受ける<br>assume (that) ...　…と想定する |

解答 (1) accommodate (2) accomplish (3) acquire (4) admit (5) appeal (6) arise (7) assigns (8) assume

> blame　calculate　attempt　attach
> combine　compose　beat　bother

(1) Many e-mail programs display a paper clip for you to click to (　) a file to a message.
多くのEメールソフトは，メッセージにファイル**を添付する**ためにクリックすることを示してペーパークリップを表示する。

(2) We made several (　) to call Margaret in the hospital, but something was wrong with the telephone in her room.
私たちは病院のマーガレットに数回電話**を試み**たが，病室の電話は故障していた。

(3) We (　) out the other agency for the account because we charge less.
私たちの課す料金のほうが安いため，その取引でもう一方の代理店**を打ち負かした**。

(4) Psychologists say that children of divorce often (　) themselves for the situation, even though it is never their fault.
心理学者は，離婚した親の子どもたちは，それが決して自らの責任でなくても，しばしばその状況にある自分自身**を責める**と言う。

(5) We've had a change of heart, so if you haven't started to fill our order yet, please don't (　).
気が変わったので，もしこちらの注文に応じ始めていませんでしたら，どうぞお**構い**なく。

(6) I (　) the savings to be $120 a year to switch from cable broadband to DSL, but DSL is slower.
有線ブロードバンドからDSLに切り換えると節約額は年120ドルだと**算出した**が，DSLのほうが遅い。

(7) The new technology (　) the processing power of the human left brain hemisphere with the creative qualities of the right.
新技術は，人の左脳半球が持つ処理能力を，右脳半球が持つ創造的資質と**結合させる**。

(8) When I want to (　) an important business e-mail, I usually compose it in the word processing program first.
重要な業務上のEメール**を作成し**たいときは，通常，最初にワープロソフトで作成する。

## 572 attach
[ətǽtʃ]

他 をくっつける；を添付する →¹⁴attachment

attached form  添付の用紙

## 573 attempt
[ətémpt]

他 を試みる　名 企て

in attempt to do  …することを試みて

## 574 beat
[bíːt]

他 を打つ，打ち負かす；に先んじる
名 打つこと；巡回区域

be on the beat  巡回中である

## 575 blame
[bléim]

他 〈人〉を（〜のことで）とがめる；〈人〉のせいにする
名 責任；非難

be to blame for 〜  〜の責めを負うべきである

## 576 bother
[báðər]

他 に面倒をかける；わざわざ…する

bother to do  わざわざ…する

## 577 calculate
[kǽlkjəlèit]

他 を計算する　⇒派 calculation 名 計算

calculate the cost  費用を算出する

## 578 combine
[kəmbáin]

他 を結合させる。

a combined statement of income and surplus
損益・剰余金結合明細

## 579 compose
[kəmpóuz]

他 を作る；を構成する；を作曲する

be composed of 〜  〜から成り立つ

---

解答 (1) attach (2) attempts (3) beat (4) blame (5) bother (6) calculated (7) combines (8) compose

| gather | explore | declare | count |
| feed | identify | define | exhaust |

(1) Sorry, we're running late because I didn't ( ) on such bad traffic when I chose this route.
すみません，この道路を選んだときは，これほどひどい交通渋滞とは思わず，遅れています。

(2) After assessing the situation after the storm, the governor had no choice but to ( ) it a disaster area.
嵐のあとの状況を調査し，知事はそこを災害地区と宣言せざるを得なかった。

(3) After the CEO said that this had been a successful year, several unhappy shareholders asked him to ( ) "successful."
CEO が今年は上出来の1年だったと述べると，数人の不満を持つ株主たちが「上出来な」の意味を明確にするよう求めた。

(4) We'd prefer that you ( ) every possibility for promoting someone inside the company before looking elsewhere.
ほかを探す前に，社内でだれかを昇格させるあらゆる可能性を尽くしてもらいたい。

(5) Mr. Hiller said we were going to ( ) the idea of my getting a raise, so it didn't sound definite.
ヒラー氏は私の昇給案を検討するつもりだと言ったため，それはあまり確定的に聞こえなかった。

(6) With a page that size, you'll have to use the manual paper feeder to ( ) it into the printer.
その大きさのページだと，プリンターに紙を送り込むのに手動の給紙機を使わなければならないだろう。

(7) The group going to Paris will ( ) at the airport at two tomorrow afternoon.
そのパリに行くグループは，明日の午後2時に空港に集合する予定だ。

(8) A professional chef was able to ( ) 15 of the 18 spices used in the top secret recipe.
プロの料理人は，極秘レシピに使われる18種のスパイスのうち15種を特定できた。

| 580 | **count** [káunt] | 自 計算する 他 を数え上げる；を考慮する ⇒派 **countless** 形 数え切れない |
| --- | --- | --- |
| | | count on ~　~を当てにする；~を期待する，予期する |

| 581 | **declare** [dikléər] | 他 を公に宣言する　⇒派 **declaration** 名 宣言 |
| --- | --- | --- |
| | | declare a ban on ~　~の禁止を布告する |

| 582 | **define** [difáin] | 他 を明らかにする，明確に説明する；を定義する |
| --- | --- | --- |
| | | define one's responsibilities　自己の責任を明確にする |

| 583 | **exhaust** [igzɔ́:st, egz-] | 他 を使い尽くす；を疲れさせる　名 排気管；排気ガス；排出　⇒派 **exhausted** 形 疲れ果てた |
| --- | --- | --- |
| | | exhaust oneself by [with] ~　~で疲れきる |

| 584 | **explore** [iksplɔ́:r, eks-] | 他 を探検する；を調査する；を検討する；を診察する ⇒派 **exploration** 名 探検 |
| --- | --- | --- |
| | | explore the idea further　その考えをさらに検討する |

| 585 | **feed** [fí:d] | 他 に食事〔えさ〕を与える；を送る 名 えさ，食事；（燃料・原料などの）供給 |
| --- | --- | --- |
| | | be fed up with ~　~にうんざりしている |

| 586 | **gather** [gǽðər] | 自 集まる　他 を集める；と推論する |
| --- | --- | --- |
| | | gather volume　増大する，大きくなる |

| 587 | **identify** [aidéntəfài, idén-] | 他 がだれ〔何〕かを特定する |
| --- | --- | --- |
| | | identify oneself　（話などで）名乗る |

解答 (1) count (2) declare (3) define (4) exhaust (5) explore (6) feed (7) gather (8) identify

| | | | |
|---|---|---|---|
| occupy | object | prove | lag |
| prevent | reflect | recover | imply |

(1) Just tell them we're not interested, because if you say we'll think about it you ( ) we want further dialogue.
彼らに私たちが関心がないとだけ伝えてください。検討すると伝えると，私たちがさらなる対話を望んでいる**という含みになる**からです。

(2) If our team continues to ( ) behind the others, we'll all be reassigned to other work.
もしうちのチームがほかのチームより**遅れ**続ければ，全員ほかの仕事に回される。

(3) When Kathy brought up asking Central Semiconductor to be our supplier, I had to ( ).
キャシーがセントラル・セミコンダクターを我々の供給業者にするという要求を持ち出したとき，私は**反対せ**ざるを得なかった。

(4) While waiting to change planes in Detroit, I found an interesting business magazine to ( ) my time.
デトロイトでの飛行機の乗り換え待ちの間に，時間**を埋める**おもしろい業界誌を見つけた。

(5) Putting a traffic light on that corner would surely ( ) some of the numerous accidents that occur there.
その角に信号機を設置すれば，そこで多発する事故のいくつか**を防ぐ**ことは確実だろう。

(6) The fact that Angus was at the scene of the crime doesn't ( ) that he committed it.
アンガスがその犯行現場にいたというだけでは，彼が犯人だという**証明にはならない**。

(7) If we follow the budget precisely, we should be able to ( ) our investment in less than a year.
その予算に正確に従えば，1年もしないうちに投資**を回収する**ことができるはずだ。

(8) The decision to cancel that service directly ( ) on the manager's plan to economize.
そのサービスを中止するという決定は，経営者の節減計画**を直接反映する**。

## 588 imply
[implái]

他 をそれとなく示す；を含意する →203 implication

imply that ... …ということを匂わせる

## 589 lag
[lǽg]

自他 (より)遅れる 名 遅延, 時間の隔たり

lag behind ～ ～に遅れる
a six-month lag 6か月の隔たり

## 590 object
動 [əbdʒékt]
名 [ábdʒikt]

自 反対する 他 …だと言って反対する
名 物体；対象；目的

an object of study 研究の対象

## 591 occupy
[ákjəpài]

他 〈場所〉に滞在する；を占有する, 〈時間〉を費やす

occupy oneself in [with] ～ ～で忙しい

## 592 prevent
[privént]

他 が(…するのを)妨げる；を防ぐ

prevent ～ from ...ing ～が…するのを防ぐ

## 593 prove
[prú:v]

他 を証明する 自 (～であると)判明する →235 proof

prove productive 生産性が高いとわかる

## 594 recover
[rikʌ́vər]

他 を取り戻す, 回収する 自 回復する
⇒派 recovery 名 回復

recover a loss 損失を取り戻す

## 595 reflect
[riflékt]

自他 (を)反射する；(を)反映する；(を)熟考する
→684 reflection

reflect on one's attitude 自分がとった態度を反省する

---

解答 (1) imply (2) lag (3) object (4) occupy
(5) prevent (6) prove (7) recover (8) reflects

> retain    search    stimulate    reveal    spread

(1) After the meeting and discussion of contracts, I called a law firm and made arrangements to (     ) an attorney.
契約に関する会議と討議のあと、私は法律事務所に電話し、弁護士を雇うよう調整した。

(2) The mystery was well-crafted in that the author did not (     ) the true murderer until the end of the story.
作家が結末まで殺人の真犯人を明かさなかったという点で、そのミステリーはとても精巧だった。

(3) The human resources department is (     ) for someone who speaks Japanese and English fluently.
人事部では日本語と英語を流暢に話す人を探している。

(4) Even with the workload (     ) out over several months we still have a difficult task ahead of us.
仕事量を数か月間に分散させたにもかかわらず、まだ目の前には困難な仕事がある。

(5) Everyone hopes the new advertising campaign will help (     ) sales in what has been a sluggish market.
新しい広告キャンペーンが、不活発な市場での売上を刺激する助けになることを全員が望んでいる。

## 596 retain
[ritéin]

他 を保持する；を雇う

retain one's right　権利を保有する

## 597 reveal
[rivíːl]

他 を明らかにする；〈秘密など〉を明かす

reveal oneself　身分を明かす，名乗る

## 598 search
[sə́ːrtʃ]

自 探し求める　他 〈場所・物〉を探す；の身体検査をする
名 捜索，探求；検索

in search of ～　～を探して
search for ～　～を探す

## 599 spread
[spréd]

他 を広げる；を広める；を分散させる
自 広がる；覆う　spread-spread-spread

spread rapidly　急速に広まる

## 600 stimulate
[stímjəlèit]

他 を刺激する

stimulate ～ to work harder　～を励ましてより懸命に働かせる

解答 (1) retain (2) reveal (3) searching (4) spread (5) stimulate

> weigh   vary   sweep   vote

(1) The typhoon ( ) away the entire crop just a couple of weeks before the harvesting season.
台風は収穫期までちょうど 2 週間というときに全農作物を一掃してしまった。

(2) Depending on the custom options a customer adds, the price of the car may ( ) from reasonable to expensive.
顧客が付け加えるカスタムオプションによって，車の価格は手ごろなものから高いものまで変わるだろう。

(3) The owners of the company ( ) unanimously to make the 35-year-old business woman the new CEO.
会社のオーナーが投票した結果，満場一致で 35 歳の女性実業家を新しい CEO にすることにした。

(4) Every piece of cargo must be inspected and ( ) before we can send it overseas by ship.
貨物はすべて，海外に船便で出荷する前に検査し，重量を測定しなければならない。

## 601 sweep
[swíːp]

他 を掃く；を一掃する　自 掃き掃除をする
名 一振り；一掃

sweep away dust　ほこりを払う

## 602 vary
[véəri]

自 さまざまである；変化がある　他 を変える

vary in size [price, opinion]　大きさ〔値段, 意見〕がさまざまである

## 603 vote
[vóut]

自 投票する　名 投票

a secret vote　無記名投票

## 604 weigh
[wéi]

他 の重さを量る　自 (〜の)重さがある
⇒派 **weight** 名 重さ；体重

weigh oneself　自分の体重を量る

---

解答　(1) swept　(2) vary　(3) voted　(4) weighed

| absolutely | bound | complicated | consequently |
| considerable | absent | boring | brief |

(1) With five people ( absent ) from the meeting, it was impossible for the board members to vote on any critical issues.
５人が会議を欠席したので，取締役会はいかなる重要案件についての投票も不可能だった。

(2) The boss made it ( absolutely ) clear that he would not allow us to hold a private gathering in the suite.
上司は，私たちが特別室で個人的な集まりを持つのを認めないと完全に明言した。

(3) If the president didn't have to repeat each point three times, the meetings wouldn't be so ( boring ).
社長が要点をいちいち３回も繰り返さなければ，会議はそれほど退屈ではないだろうに。

(4) An attorney is ( bound ) to keep information provided by a client confidential, especially if the information is sensitive.
弁護士は，特にそれが慎重な注意を要するものである場合，依頼人から提供された情報を秘密にしておかねばならない。

(5) You're on a direct flight, but you do have a ( brief ) stopover in Denver on your way there.
あなたは直行便にご搭乗中ですが，そこに行く途中でデンバーに短時間立ち寄ります。

(6) Your idea for a children's game might be commercially viable if it were not quite so ( complicated ).
子どものゲームについてのあなたのアイデアは，これほど複雑でなければ商業的に見込みがあるかもしれないのだが。

(7) I volunteered to help with mailing whereupon they ( consequently ) put me in charge of the entire newsletter.
私は発送を手伝おうと自主的に申し出たため，結果的に会報全体の責任者にされた。

(8) It turned out that switching to solar heating did not offer them the ( considerable ) savings they had anticipated.
太陽熱システムへ切り換えても，期待していたような相当の節約を生まないと判明した。

## 605 absent
[ǽbsənt]

形 欠席の；不在の　⇒派 **absence** 名 不在

be absent from ～　～を欠席する

## 606 absolutely
[ǽbsəlùːtli, ˌ-ˈ--]

副 完全に　⇒派 **absolute** 形 完全な

absolutely not　全然違う（強い否定の表現）

## 607 boring
[bɔ́ːriŋ]

形 退屈な　⇒派 **bore** 他 をうんざりさせる

a boring discussion　退屈な議論

## 608 bound
[báund]

形 ～行きの；…しなければならない；拘束された

be bound to do　…する義務がある；きっと…する

## 609 brief
[bríːf]

形 簡潔な，短い　⇒派 **briefly** 副 手短に（言えば）

in brief　手短に，要するに

## 610 complicated
[kámpləkèitəd]

形 複雑な，入り組んだ

a complicated process　複雑な手順

## 611 consequently
[kánsəkwèntli]

副 結果的に
⇒派 **consequent** 形 結果として起こる

as a result　その結果

## 612 considerable
[kənsídərəbl]

形 かなりの，相当な

a considerable delay　かなりの遅れ

---

解答　(1) absent　(2) absolutely　(3) boring　(4) bound
(5) brief　(6) complicated　(7) consequently　(8) considerable

| essential | exact | mechanical | illegal |
| eager | dental | net | hardly |

(1) A decent health insurance plan will include (　　), as well as cover alternative treatments such as acupuncture.
ちゃんとした健康保険プランは，歯の治療のほかに，針治療などの代替治療も補償する。

(2) I thought I would enjoy a leisurely vacation, but I am actually (　　) to get back to work tomorrow.
私はのんびり休暇を楽しもうと思っていたが，実は明日仕事に戻りたくてたまらない。

(3) The health practitioner I see believes that a daily helping of olive oil is (　　) for me.
かかりつけの健康管理医は，毎日１杯のオリーブオイルが私に不可欠だと信じている。

(4) If you have the satellite help service on your car, they can find your (　　) location after an accident.
もし車に衛星によるヘルプサービスを搭載していれば，事故後，正確な居場所がわかる。

(5) I was sure we had enough in our travel fund for a cruise, but this is (　　) enough for a car trip.
船旅の旅行資金として十分なのは確かだったが，車の旅にはほとんど十分とは言えない。

(6) Those goods are not (　　), but they were not obtained from reputable sources.
それらの商品は非合法ではないが，信頼できる供給源から調達されていない。

(7) Gordon figured out that it wasn't an electronic problem but something more (　　) in how the parts fit together.
ゴードンは，それは電子的な問題ではなく，部品の組み合わせ方というもっと機械的な問題だとわかった。

(8) I missed part of the report and was not sure what he said our (　　) profits from the venture came out to.
報告の一部を聞き逃したので，彼がベンチャーからの純利益がいくらになったと言ったかわからなかった。

## 613 dental
[déntl]

形 歯の, 歯科の

a dental implant　差し歯；人工歯根

## 614 eager
[í:gər]

形 熱心な；熱望して

be eager to do　…したがる

## 615 essential
[isénʃl, es-]

形 必要不可欠で；根本的な

It is essential for ～ to do　～には…することが不可欠だ

## 616 exact
[igzǽkt, egz-]

形 正確な, ぴったりの　⇒派 exactly 副 正確に
≒類 correct　accurate　precise 形 正確な

the exact sum　正確な額

## 617 hardly
[háːrdli]

副 ほとんど…ない

hardly ever ...　ほとんど…しない

## 618 illegal
[ilíːgl]

形 違法の, 非合法の　⇔反 legal 形 適法の

an illegal act　不法行為

## 619 mechanical
[məkǽnikl]

形 機械の　→ mechanic

a mechanical failure　機械の故障

## 620 net
[nét]

形 正味の, 純～　名 網；通信ネットワーク

net earnings　純利益

解答　(1) dental　(2) eager　(3) essential　(4) exact　(5) hardly　(6) illegal　(7) mechanical　(8) net

| practical | portable | numerous | primary |
| precise | online | parallel | nevertheless |

(1) He had already donated to the cause, but ( ), he bought some candy from my daughter.
彼はすでにその運動に寄付をしていたが，**それでも**私の娘からキャンディを買ってくれた。

(2) There are ( ) qualified candidates, so narrowing it down to just one is quite a challenge.
適任の候補者が**多数**いるので，それをたった1人にまで絞り込むのは相当困難だ。

(3) Spyware invades the user's privacy by tracking the person's ( ) activity.
スパイウェアはユーザーの**オンライン上の**活動を追跡して，プライバシーを侵害する。

(4) Let's move this plank so that it's completely ( ) with the other one.
この厚板をもう1枚の厚板と完全に**平行**になるよう動かそう。

(5) I am confident that our company's new ( ) video player is the best on the market.
私は，我が社の新しい**ポータブル**ビデオプレーヤーが市場で最高だと確信している。

(6) If Joe is still so sick, it isn't ( ) for him to think about coming back to work next week.
ジョーがまだかなり不調なら，来週仕事に戻ることを考えるのは彼には**現実的で**ない。

(7) The clock in my computer is not very ( ), as it seems to lose a minute or two every month.
私のコンピュータの時計は1か月に1，2分遅れるようなので，**正確で**はない。

(8) You may be enjoying this new part-time job, but don't get so tired that you ignore your ( ) job.
この新しいパートタイムの仕事を楽しんでいるかもしれないが，疲れすぎて**本**業をないがしろにしないようにしなさい。

| 621 | **nevertheless** [nèvərðəlés] | 副 それにもかかわらず<br>≒類 **nonetheless** 副 それにもかかわらず<br>**however** 副 しかしながら |
|---|---|---|
| 622 | **numerous** [n(j)úːmərəs] | 形 多数の<br>a numerous collection of books　おびただしい蔵書 |
| 623 | **online** [ánláin] | 形 オンラインの　副 オンラインで<br>online advertising　オンライン広告 |
| 624 | **parallel** [pǽrəlèl] | 形 類似の；平行の　名 類似点；平行線<br>parallel lines　平行線 |
| 625 | **portable** [pɔ́ːrtəbl] | 形 持ち運びのできる，ポータブルの<br>a portable apparatus　持ち運びができる器具 |
| 626 | **practical** [prǽktikl] | 形 実際の；事実上の；実現可能な；実用的な<br>⇒派 **practice** 名 習慣　他 を練習する<br>practical experience　実地の経験 |
| 627 | **precise** [prisáis] | 形 正確な，精密な；ちょうどの，厳格な<br>⇒派 **precisely** 副 正確に<br>precise directions　正確な指示 |
| 628 | **primary** [práimèri, -məri] | 形 最も重要な，第一の，主要な<br>⇒派 **primarily** 副 まず第一に<br>a question of primary importance　最重要問題 |

解答 (1) nevertheless (2) numerous (3) online (4) parallel (5) portable (6) practical (7) precise (8) primary

| proper | productive | select | significant |
| separate | raw | rural | |

(1) Studies have found that workers are more ( ) when they are happy and can listen to music.
研究により，労働者は幸せで音楽が聞けるときに，より**生産力が高く**なるとわかった。

(2) Not reading the instructions means you will never understand the ( ) way of operating the equipment.
取扱説明書を読まなければ，その器具の**正しい**操作方法を決して理解できない。

(3) "Seared ahi," found on many menus, is Hawaiian tuna that is cooked on the outside and ( ) on the inside.
多くのメニューにある「シアードアヒ」は，外側を焼いて内側は**生の**ハワイのマグロのことだ。

(4) This post office services the entire ( ) area, so the mail carriers have to cover a lot of ground.
この郵便局は**農村**部全域にサービスを提供しているので，郵便配達員は多くの地域を担当しなければならない。

(5) Only a few ( ) managers will go on to become top executives in this firm.
この会社ではごくわずかな**選ばれた**部長だけがトップ重役に昇進する。

(6) For long-term success it's important to keep your work and your personal life ( ).
長期的な成功を収めるには，仕事と私生活を**分けて**おくことが大切だ。

(7) A new CEO is a ( ) change for a company that has had the same leadership for 20 years.
新しい CEO は，20 年間同じ指導者でやってきた会社にとって**重大な**変化だ。

## 629 productive
[prədʌ́ktiv]

形 生産的な、生産力のある
⇒派 **produce** 他 を生産する

productive enterprises　利益の上がる企業

## 630 proper
[prɑ́pər]

形 適切な、正しい；妥当な
⇒派 **properly** 副 適切に、きちんと

a proper prescription　正しい処方

## 631 raw
[rɔ́ː]

形 生の、未加工の

a raw oyster　生のカキ

## 632 rural
[rúərəl]

形 田舎の、農村の；農業の　⇔反 641 **urban** 形 都会の

lead a rural life　田園生活をする

## 633 select
[səlékt]

形 選ばれた　他 を選ぶ
⇒派 **selective** 形 えり抜きの

select ~ over ...　…よりも~を選ぶ

## 634 separate
形 [sépərət]
動 [sépərèit]

形 離れた；別個の　他 を切り離す、分ける
⇒派 **separation** 名 別離；解雇　**separately** 副 別々に

separate ~ from ...　~を…から分離する

## 635 significant
[signífikənt]

形 重大な；大きな；特別な意味を持った
⇒派 **significance** 名 意義

a significant change in ~　~における大きな変化

解答　(1) productive　(2) proper　(3) raw　(4) rural　(5) select　(6) separate　(7) significant

> sophisticated　slightly　unique
> suitable　stable　urban

(1) Although I still work in the same department, my job has changed ( ) since the merger.

私はまだ同じ部署で働いてはいるが，私の仕事は合併以来**わずかに**変化してきた。

(2) The technology in our new product is not the most ( ), but it has a track record for reliability.

我々の新製品の技術は最も**洗練された**ものではないが，信頼性には実績がある。

(3) The prototype software will need further development before it becomes ( ) enough to be released to the public.

そのソフトウェアの試作品は世に発売できる**安定した**ものになるまでさらに開発が必要だ。

(4) The packaging and marketing strategy we used in the U.S. is not ( ) for the Japanese market.

我々が合衆国で用いた売り込みとマーケティングの戦略は日本の市場には不**適当だ**。

(5) The approach of our new quality control officer is ( ), but I also think it's effective.

我々の新しい品質管理委員のアプローチは**独特だ**が，効果的だとも思う。

(6) If we keep focusing our marketing campaign on the suburbs we'll lose the ( ) youth.

もし販促キャンペーンの焦点をずっと郊外に合わせるなら，**都市の**若者を逃してしまう。

## 636 slightly
[sláitli]

副 わずかに　⇒派 slight 形 わずかな

be slightly wounded　軽傷を負った

## 637 sophisticated
[səfístikèitid]

形 洗練された；〈機械・装置などが〉精巧な

a sophisticated audience　洗練された観客
sophisticated equipment　精巧な装置

## 638 stable
[stéibl]

形 安定した，固定した　⇒派 stability 名 安定

a stable foundation　がっちりした基盤

## 639 suitable
[sú:təbl]

形 適した　→464 suit

a suitable book for children　子どもにうってつけの本

## 640 unique
[ju:ní:k]

形 独特の；並ぶもののない；特有の

a plant unique to that country　その国特有の植物

## 641 urban
[ə́:rbn]

形 都市の；都市特有の　⇔反 632 rural 形 田舎の

an urban area　都市圏

解答 (1) slightly (2) sophisticated (3) stable (4) suitable (5) unique (6) urban

# Chapter 2-3 使える学校英語を総ざらい

**学校英語 ▶▶▶ TOEIC® TEST** **頻度★**

> affection  compromise  abstract  collapse
> clue  column  characteristic  ban

(1) When you submit the paper to the journal, they will ask for an ( ) summarizing the piece in one paragraph.
雑誌に論文を投稿すると，作品を1段落にまとめた要約を求められるだろう。

(2) Steve knew his uncle had had a great deal of ( ) for him, but he was surprised to receive an inheritance from him.
スティーブは伯父が大いに愛情を注いでくれたのは知っていたが，伯父から遺産を受け取ることには驚いた。

(3) Until we find out why those patients developed skin problems, we have imposed a ( ) on using that medicine.
患者がなぜ皮膚の問題を悪化させたかがわかるまで，その薬の使用禁止を課した。

(4) The selection committee didn't think Ned had ( ) they were looking for in a new personnel manager.
選考委員会は，新しい人事課長に求めている特性をネッドが備えているとは考えなかった。

(5) I don't have a ( ) why nobody volunteered to write the press releases for the new product.
なぜだれも新製品のプレスリリースを書くのを買って出ないのか，手がかりがつかめない。

(6) The ( ) of the economy in the country where we produce our product has actually made labor cheaper.
我々が製品を作っている国での経済崩壊は，実際は労働力をより安価にしている。

(7) There is a ( ) on home improvement and home repairs in almost every newspaper in the country.
その国ではほぼすべての新聞に住宅の修繕やリフォームを扱った欄がある。

(8) One group wanted to ski and the others chose a cruise, so it's hard to find a reasonable ( ).
1つのグループはスキーを，その他のグループはクルーズを希望しているので，ほどよい妥協案を見つけるのは難しい。

### 642 abstract
[ǽbstrækt]

名 要約　形 抽象的な

abstract thought　抽象的思考

### 643 affection
[əfékʃən]

名 愛情

with affection　愛情を持って

### 644 ban
[bǽn]

名 禁止(令)　他 を禁止する
≒類 forbid 他 を禁じる

ban ~ from ...ing　～が…するのを禁じる

### 645 characteristic
[kæ̀rəktərístik, kæ̀rik-]

名 特質　形 特徴的な

it is characteristic of ~ to do　…するのは～の特徴である

### 646 clue
[klúː]

名 手がかり；糸口

get a clue to a question　問題解決の手がかりを見つける

### 647 collapse
[kəlǽps]

名 崩壊, 倒産　自 崩壊する

economic collapse　経済的崩壊
collapsed buildings　崩壊した建物

### 648 column
[káləm]

名 柱；コラム, 欄

an ad column　広告欄

### 649 compromise
[kámprəmàiz]

名 妥協(案)　自 妥協する

make a compromise with ~　～と妥協する

解答 (1) abstract (2) affection (3) ban (4) characteristics (5) clue (6) collapse (7) column (8) compromise

> element   controversy   conservation
> ecology   disease   crack   discipline

(1) The International Union for ( ) of Nature and Natural Resources assists societies around the globe with methods of preserving nature and conserving resources.
国際自然保護連合は，自然を守り資源を保全する方法により，世界中の社会を支援している。

(2) During the ( ) about the safety of the device, we stopped producing the product in question.
その装置の安全性についての論争の間，我々は問題の製品の製造を停止した。

(3) Right after the workmen left, I noticed a big ( ) in the ceiling and had to call them back.
作業員が帰った直後に，私は天井の大きな割れ目に気がついて彼らを呼び戻さなければならなかった。

(4) The reason the company started a computer skills class is that many people can't find the ( ) to study alone.
その会社がコンピュータ技能クラスを始めた理由は，多くの人々が1人で勉強する学習法を見出せないからだ。

(5) The doctor informed his patient that the ( ) had spread from his lungs to other parts of his body.
医師は患者に，病気が肺から身体のほかの部分に転移したことを知らせた。

(6) The city office has produced several pamphlets for those who wish to learn more about ( ) and environmental care.
市役所はエコロジーや環境への配慮について詳しく知りたい人々のために数種類のパンフレットを作成している。

(7) Not only was the romantic comedy aspect of the film enjoyable, but there was also an ( ) of surprise.
その映画は，ロマンチックコメディの面が楽しかっただけでなく，驚きの要素も備えていた。

| 650 | **conservation** [kὰnsərvéiʃən] | 名 天然資源の保護, 保全<br>⇒派 **conserve** 他 を保全する<br>conservation of wildlife　野生生物の保護 |
|---|---|---|
| 651 | **controversy** [kάntrəvə̀:rsi] | 名 論争, 議論<br>⇒派 **controversial** 形 議論の余地のある<br>the controversy over [about] 〜　〜をめぐる議論 |
| 652 | **crack** [krǽk] | 名 割れ目, ひび　自 ひびが入る<br>他 を割る, にひびを入れる<br>a crack in the window　窓のひび |
| 653 | **discipline** [dísəplin] | 名 訓練；学習法；懲罰；規律<br>a rigid discipline　厳しい規律 |
| 654 | **disease** [dizí:z] | 名 病気<br>convey a disease to 〜　〜に病気を移す |
| 655 | **ecology** [ikάlədʒi] | 名 エコロジー, 環境保護；生態学；生態系<br>ecology movement　環境保護運動 |
| 656 | **element** [éləmənt] | 名 要素；基本<br>an essential element　本質的な要素 |

解答　(1) Conservation　(2) controversy　(3) crack
(4) discipline　(5) disease　(6) ecology　(7) element

| | | | |
|---|---|---|---|
| enthusiasm | finding | extinction | function |
| emission | flaw | exception | fame |

(1) Concern about the negative effects of ( ) on the environment has spurred interest in electric and hybrid cars.
排出物の環境への悪影響についての懸念は，電気自動車やハイブリッド・カーへの興味に拍車をかけている。

(2) I thought he might have questions about the proposal, but his overwhelming lack of ( ) surprised me.
私は，彼はその提案に質問があるだろうと思ったが，そのあまりの熱意のなさに驚いた。

(3) Committee meetings are usually held on Mondays, but we made an ( ) due to the national holiday yesterday.
委員会の会合は通常月曜に開かれるが，昨日は祝日だったため例外とした。

(4) While buffalos were headed for ( ) forty years ago, they are back to being a food source now in the U.S.
バッファローは40年前絶滅に向かったが，アメリカでは今，食料源として復活している。

(5) Dr. Olsen stated in the article that he had not conducted his research with the goals of ( ) and fortune.
オルセン博士はその記事で，名声や富を目的として研究をしたのではないと述べた。

(6) After the research project is completed, the team will publish their ( ) in an academic journal.
研究プロジェクトが完了したら，チームはその研究結果を学術雑誌に発表するつもりだ。

(7) Although a ( ) was discovered in the program, it was easily corrected before any damage was done.
プログラム内に欠陥が発見されたものの，それは損害が生じる前に簡単に修正された。

(8) The device has an auto shutoff ( ) to prevent accidental overheating that can lead to fire.
その装置には火災を招く恐れのある偶発的過熱を防ぐための自動遮断機能がついている。

|  |  |  |
|---|---|---|
| 657 | **emission** [imíʃən] | 名 放出；放出物, 排気物　⇒派 **emit** 他 を放出する<br>emissions control　排気ガス規制 |
| 658 | **enthusiasm** [enθ(j)úːziæzm] | 名 熱狂, 熱中；熱意<br>with enthusiasm　熱心に |
| 659 | **exception** [iksépʃən, ek-] | 名 例外　⇒派 **except** 前接 ～以外は<br>with the exception of ～　～を除いて |
| 660 | **extinction** [ikstíŋkʃən, eks-] | 名 消すこと；絶滅<br>⇒派 **extinct** 形 消えた；絶滅した<br>be threatened with [by] extinction　絶滅に瀕する |
| 661 | **fame** [féim] | 名 名声, 有名<br>come to fame　有名になる |
| 662 | **finding** [fáindiŋ] | 名 発見；発見物；調査結果<br>findings of an audit　監査の結果 |
| 663 | **flaw** [flɔ́ː] | 名 欠陥, 不備　他 を損なう　→ **flawless**<br>a structural flaw　構造上の欠陥 |
| 664 | **function** [fʌ́ŋkʃən] | 名 機能；職務　自 機能する<br>discharge one's functions　職務を遂行する |

解答　(1) emissions　(2) enthusiasm　(3) exception　(4) extinction　(5) fame　(6) findings　(7) flaw　(8) function

> obligation  merit  initiative  grade
> innovation  layout  objective  glance

(1) After being in the antique business for twenty years, Isaac could tell at a (　) if something was worth appraising.
骨董業に20年携わっているので，アイザックは一目で鑑定に値する物か判別できた。

(2) This steak is not as tender as what I bought last time, so I wonder if the (　) is the same.
このステーキ肉はこの前買ったものほど柔らかくないので，等級が同じかどうかあやしい。

(3) Roger does routine tasks fairly well, but he shows no (　) when he isn't given specific instructions.
ロジャーは日常業務は非常に優秀だが，具体的な指示がないときは自発性を発揮しない。

(4) You would barely recognize it, because the new owners have instituted lots of (　) in the store.
新オーナーがその店で大幅な刷新を始めたので，ほとんどその店とはわからないだろう。

(5) We've hired a new Web designer to work on the (　) of our online store.
当社のオンラインストアの設計を手がけてもらうために新しいウェブデザイナーを雇った。

(6) They said our proposal had (　), but they still chose to do it the way they always have.
彼らは我々の提案は価値があると言ったが，それでもいつもの方法をとることを選んだ。

(7) Your research will make more sense if you constantly check and make sure you are meeting your own (　).
常にチェックして自分自身の目的に合っているかを確かめれば，あなたの調査はもっと妥当なものになる。

(8) You agreed to listen to my presentation, but you are under no (　) to purchase the product unless it appeals to you.
私のプレゼンを聞くことを承諾していただきましたが，お気に召さない限りは，その製品を買う義務は一切ありません。

| 665 | **glance** [glǽns] | 名 ちらりと見ること 自 ちらりと見る |
|---|---|---|
| | | at first glance 一目見ただけで |

| 666 | **grade** [gréid] | 名 等級 他 に等級をつける |
|---|---|---|
| | | be graded according to ～ ～によって等級がつけられている |

| 667 | **initiative** [iníʃətiv, -ʃiə-] | 名 自ら行動する力, 進取の気性；計画；主導権 |
|---|---|---|
| | | lack initiative 自発性に欠ける |

| 668 | **innovation** [ìnəvéiʃən] | 名 革新；新しい手法 |
|---|---|---|
| | | technical innovations 技術革新 |

| 669 | **layout** [léiàut] | 名 配置, 設計 |
|---|---|---|
| | | an expert in layout 設計の専門家 |

| 670 | **merit** [mérət] | 名 長所, 価値 他 に値する |
|---|---|---|
| | | a man of merit 優秀な人 |

| 671 | **objective** [əbdʒéktiv] | 名 目標, 目的 形 目標の；事実に基づく, 客観的な |
|---|---|---|
| | | an objective opinion 客観的な意見 |

| 672 | **obligation** [ὰbligéiʃən] | 名 義務, 責務；責任；義理 ⇒派 **oblige** 他 を強制する |
|---|---|---|
| | | fulfill one's obligations 義務を果たす |

解答 (1) glance (2) grade (3) initiative (4) innovations (5) layout (6) merit (7) objectives (8) obligation

> phase　　proportion　　preparation　　principle
> perspective　　pile　　outcome　　opponent

(1) My ( ) wants to distract you with rumors about my personal life, while I would prefer to discuss real issues.
敵は私の私生活のうわさであなたを混乱させたがっているが，私は真の問題を議論したい。

(2) We ran the experiment at least a dozen times and the ( ) was more or less the same each time.
私たちはその実験を少なくとも 12 回行い，その都度結果はだいたい同じだった。

(3) Whether you consider Chester a business genius or just a lucky man depends upon your ( ).
チェスターをビジネスの天才と見るか，ただの幸運な男と見るかは考え方次第だ。

(4) During the first ( ) of the reconstruction our offices will have to be temporarily relocated to another building.
事務所改築の第 1 段階の間は，一時的に別のビルに移転しなければならないだろう。

(5) We're sorting research documents; put everything that mentions "artificial intelligence" in that ( ) over there.
私たちは調査資料を分類しているところです。「人工知能」に言及しているものすべてを，向こうのあの書類の山に置いてください。

(6) In ( ) for the proficiency test, students are advised to review major grammar points and vocabulary.
検定試験の準備に，学生は主な文法事項と語彙を復習するようアドバイスを受けている。

(7) It isn't necessary to memorize the entire set of rules as long as you understand the ( ) behind them.
その背後にある原則を理解している限り，公式を一式覚える必要はない。

(8) The ( ) of the characters must remain constant when the calligrapher creates the final written version.
書道家が清書をするときは，文字の釣り合いを一定に保たねばならない。

| # | 見出し | 発音 | 意味・例 |
|---|---|---|---|
| 673 | **opponent** | [əpóunənt] | 名 相手, ライバル, 敵対者<br>defeat one's opponent　ライバルを打ち負かす |
| 674 | **outcome** | [áutkʌm] | 名 結果<br>an eventual outcome　最終結果 |
| 675 | **perspective** | [pərspéktiv] | 名 観点, 視点；距離感；遠近法<br>from my perspective　私の見るところでは |
| 676 | **phase** | [féiz] | 名 段階, 局面；面；相　他 を段階的に導入する<br>enter upon a new phase　新段階に入る |
| 677 | **pile** | [páil] | 名 積み重ね, 山積み　自 積もる<br>a pile of papers　書類の山<br>pile up　積み重なる |
| 678 | **preparation** | [prèpəréiʃən] | 名 準備　⇒派 prepare 自 準備する<br>tax preparation　確定申告書類作成 |
| 679 | **principle** | [prínsəpl, -səbl] | 名 主義；方針；原理；原則<br>a basic principle　基本原則 |
| 680 | **proportion** | [prəpɔ́ːrʃən] | 名 割合；釣り合い；割当　他 を適合させる<br>in the proportion of 3 to 1　3対1の割合で |

解答 (1) opponent (2) outcome (3) perspective (4) phase (5) pile (6) preparation (7) principles (8) proportions

| quote | prospect | reflection |
| province | statistics | remark |

(1) The reason Professor Robbins has so many job (　) is that she has a Ph.D. in engineering and 15 years experience.
ロビンス教授が就職先の可能性を非常にたくさん持っている訳は，彼女が工学博士号を持ち，15年の経験があるからだ。

(2) Research shows that most non-Canadians can only name one or two of the Canadian (　).
調査によると，ほとんどの非カナダ人が，カナダの州名を1つか2つしか挙げられない。

(3) I can't recall the exact (　), but Confucius has a saying that means anyone you meet can be your teacher.
正確な引用句は思い出せないが，孔子には，会う人のだれもが師となりうるという格言がある。

(4) Our three gold stars for excellent service are a good (　) on our company in the local community.
すばらしいサービスに対する金の3つ星は，地域社会における当社の姿のよい現れである。

(5) You'll probably get more data if you add a space on this feedback sheet for additional (　).
この評価用紙に追加の意見を書く欄を加えれば，おそらくより多くのデータが取れるだろう。

(6) (　) are important, but they don't tell the whole story behind the success or failure of a product.
統計は大切だが，それだけでは製品の成功や失敗の裏にある，話の一部始終はわからない。

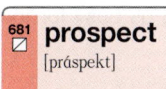

| 681 | **prospect** [práspekt] | 名 見込み, 可能性；(将来の) 見通し ⇒派 prospective 形 将来の；見込みのある |
|---|---|---|
| | | a long-term prospect  長期の見通し |

| 682 | **province** [právins] | 名 (行政区画の) 州, 省；地方；専門分野 |
|---|---|---|
| | | in the provinces  地方で, 田舎で |

| 683 | **quote** [kwóut] | 名 引用文 他 を引用する；に値段をつける ⇒派 quotation 名 引用；見積もり額 |
|---|---|---|
| | | quote a commodity at ～  商品に～の値段をつける |

| 684 | **reflection** [riflékʃən] | 名 熟考；反射；反映, 現れ →595 reflect |
|---|---|---|
| | | on [upon] reflection  よく考えてみると |

| 685 | **remark** [rimá:rk] | 名 発言, 論評 他 …と述べる |
|---|---|---|
| | | as remarked above  上述の通り |

| 686 | **statistics** [stətístiks] | 名 統計 (の数字)；統計学 ⇒派 statistic 名 統計値 |
|---|---|---|
| | | statistics show (that) …  統計によれば… |

解答 (1) prospects (2) provinces (3) quote (4) reflection (5) remarks (6) Statistics

> tendency　welfare　stream
> suburb　symptom　tension

(1) The constant (　) of orders has been keeping us busy for the last three or four weeks.
ここ3〜4週間，私たちは絶え間ない注文の連続で忙しい。

(2) The life in the (　) is great, but the one hour and a half commute each way is killing me.
郊外での生活はすばらしいが，片道1時間半の通勤には本当にうんざりだ。

(3) The doctor said the typical (　) of a flu are a high fever, a sick stomach, and excessive sweating.
医師はインフルエンザの典型的な症状は高熱，胃のむかつき，過度の発汗であると述べた。

(4) Tom has good ideas but he has a (　) to keep quiet and let others speak.
トムはよいアイデアを持っているが，黙っていてほかの人に意見を言わせる傾向がある。

(5) The (　) between the two vice presidents competing for the top job was obvious to all of us.
頂点をねらって競い合う2人の部長の間の緊張は，我々のだれが見ても明らかだった。

(6) As their superior I feel personally responsible for the (　) of those who work under me.
私は上司として，自分の部下の幸福に個人的に責任を感じている。

## 687 stream
[stríːm]

名 流れ；連続；小川　自 流れる；移動する　他 を流す

on stream 〈工場などが〉操業中で

## 688 suburb
[sʌ́bəːrb]

名 郊外

a typical middle-class suburb　中流階級の住む典型的な郊外住宅地

## 689 symptom
[símptəm]

名 徴候；症状

symptoms of an ordinary cold　普通のかぜの症状

## 690 tendency
[téndənsi]

名 傾向　⇒派 tend 自 …する傾向がある

a tendency to decline　減少傾向

## 691 tension
[ténʃən]

名 緊張

release the tension　緊張を解く

## 692 welfare
[wélfèər]

名 幸福，福利；社会福祉

welfare work　福祉事業

---

解答　(1) stream　(2) suburb　(3) symptoms
(4) tendency　(5) tension　(6) welfare

|  |  |  |  |
|---|---|---|---|
| assure | adapt | alter | accumulate |
| annoy | attain | anticipate | cast |

(1) We used to put old equipment in the storeroom but it would (　　), so now we donate it to charity immediately.
古い機器は物置にしまう習慣だったが，**たまる**ので今はすぐにチャリティに寄付している。

(2) The company told Brazil conference participants to arrive a few days early to (　　) to the climate and time changes.
会社は，気候と時間差に**順応する**ため数日早く到着するようにと，ブラジルでの会議参加者に伝えた。

(3) If you decide you need to (　　) the contract, you should make the changes and initial each change.
契約**を変更する**必要があると判断したら，変更を加えて，それぞれの変更箇所にイニシャルで署名しなければならない。

(4) After a few days the sound of the construction from the building across the street began to (　　) us to no end.
数日後，道の反対側のビルの建設の騒音は，果てしなく私たち**をいらいらさせ**始めた。

(5) If he had been able to (　　) the popularity of that technology, the broker could have earned his clients a fortune.
もし仲買人があの技術の流行**を予想**できていたら，顧客に一財産もうけさせられたのに。

(6) Having the magazine's endorsement of the product (　　) us that someone tasted and tested it.
その雑誌で製品の推薦があることは，それが試食・検査されたことを我々**に保証する**。

(7) I am certain that if I continue to work at it, I will be able to (　　) my goal quickly.
もし私がその仕事に取り組み続ければ，すぐに目標**を達成**できることは確かだ。

(8) The company was happy to be able to recycle the outer rings that are (　　) off the product they make.
自社で出している製品から**廃棄**される外側のリングを再利用でき，会社は満足だった。

| 693 | **accumulate** [əkjúːməlèit] | 自 たまる；積もる 他 をためる；を積み上げる ⇒派 accumulation 名 蓄積；蓄財 accumulate a fund 資金をためる |
|---|---|---|
| 694 | **adapt** [ədǽpt] | 自 順応する 他 を適応させる adapt oneself to ~ ~に順応する |
| 695 | **alter** [ɔ́ːltər] | 他 を変える，改める ⇒派 alteration 名 変更 ≒類 change 他 を変える alter one's policy 方針を変更する |
| 696 | **annoy** [ənɔ́i] | 他 〈人〉を悩ます，いらいらさせる annoy ~ with ... ~を…のことで悩ませる |
| 697 | **anticipate** [æntísəpèit] | 他 を予想する ⇒派 anticipation 名 予想 it is anticipated (that) ... …と予想される |
| 698 | **assure** [əʃúər, əʃɔ́ːr] | 他 に (~のことを) 請け合う；に保証する ⇒派 assurance 名 保証，確信 assure ~ of ... ~に…を保証する |
| 699 | **attain** [ətéin] | 他 を達成する attain one's goal 目標を達成する |
| 700 | **cast** [kǽst] | 他 を投げる；を投じる；を投げ捨てる 名 投げること cast doubts on ~ ~を疑う cast a ballot 投票する |

解答 (1) accumulate (2) adapt (3) alter (4) annoy (5) anticipate (6) assures (7) attain (8) cast

| dig | confront | convey | constitute |
| depress | deny | contribute | consist |

(1) After the auditing company found the discrepancy, we decided to ( confront ) the accountant about the matter.
監査事務所が矛盾を発見したあと，その事柄について会計士と対決することを決めた。

(2) You must realize that the entire committee ( consists ) of Peter, Nancy, Fred and me, the four department heads.
あなたは，委員会全体がピーター，ナンシー，フレッド，そして私の4人の部門長で構成されていることを理解しなければならない。

(3) Since he continually criticized my reasoning, I asked him what he thought ( constituted ) a reasonable analysis.
彼が絶えず私の論法を批判したので，私は何が道理にかなった分析を構成すると考えるのかたずねた。

(4) The envelope on your seats has information about how you can ( contribute ) further to this worthy cause.
あなたの席にある封筒には，この価値ある目標にさらにどう貢献することができるかについての情報が入っています。

(5) We heard about your boss's daughter's tragic accident; please ( convey ) our sympathies to the family.
あなたの上司のお嬢さんの悲惨な事故についてお聞きしました。どうぞご遺族に私どもの弔意をお伝えください。

(6) When you receive a request to join the e-mail list, you have the option to approve or ( deny ) the membership.
Eメール配信リストに加わるよう要請を受けたときは，その会員になることに同意または拒否する選択権を持っている。

(7) The chairman of the Federal Reserve says that raising interest rates would ( depress ) our economy.
連邦準備金制度議長は，利率の引き上げは経済を不振にするだろうと言う。

(8) I had to ( dig ) through my desk drawer, but I finally found the stapler I was looking for.
私は机の引き出しを探らざるを得なかったが，最後に探していたホチキスを見つけた。

| 701 | **confront** [kənfrʌ́nt] | 他 に立ち向かう；〈困難などが〉の前に立ちはだかる<br>⇒派 confrontation 名 直面；対立<br>confront a problem 問題に立ち向かう |

| 702 | **consist** [kənsíst] | 自 成り立つ；構成される<br>consist of ～ ～から成り立っている |

| 703 | **constitute** [kánstət(j)ùːt] | 他 を構成する；を設立する<br>⇒派 constitution 名 憲法, 規約<br>constitute the majority of ～ ～の大多数を構成する |

| 704 | **contribute** [kəntríbjuːt] | 自他 (に)寄付する, 貢献する<br>contribute to the project プロジェクトに貢献する |

| 705 | **convey** [kənvéi] | 他 を(～に)伝える；を運ぶ<br>convey a message メッセージを伝える |

| 706 | **deny** [dinái] | 他 を否定する；を拒む ⇒派 denial 名 否定<br>deny an accusation 非難を受けるいわれはないと言う |

| 707 | **depress** [diprés] | 他 を気落ちさせる；を不振にする →46 depression<br>be depressed by [about/over] ～ ～のことで気落ちする |

| 708 | **dig** [díg] | 自他 (を)掘る；(を)探求する dig-dug-dug<br>dig up information 情報を見つけ出す |

解答 (1) confront (2) consists (3) constituted (4) contribute (5) convey (6) deny (7) depress (8) dig

| | | | |
|---|---|---|---|
| encounter | dismiss | diminish | dispose |
| emerge | expose | equal | evolve |

(1) Some people believe that laws that seek to respect human rights have (　) the effectiveness of the police.
人権の尊重を求める法律は警察の有効性**を減退させ**たと信じている人もいる。

(2) After the story appeared in the newspaper the company decided to (　) all the employees involved in the incident.
その話が新聞に載ったあと，会社は事件にかかわった全従業員**を解雇する**ことに決めた。

(3) The hospital uses a special service that (　) of their used blood products and other hazardous medical waste.
その病院は，使用済みの血液製剤やその他の有害医療廃棄物**を処理して**くれる特別なサービスを利用している。

(4) Mostly a supporting actress in the 1980s, she has (　) as a leading lady in the past ten years.
彼女は，1980年代にはほとんどで助演女優をしていたが，ここ10年間は主演女優として**登場して**いる。

(5) You can always call the helpline if you (　) a problem when installing our program.
当ソフトのインストール中に問題**に出くわし**たら，いつでもヘルプラインに電話できます。

(6) Even though the criminal got a heavy sentence in court, the victim feels the punishment does not (　) his suffering.
犯人が法廷で重い判決を受けても，被害者はその刑は自分の苦しみ**には及ば**ないと感じる。

(7) What started out as a hobby for Richard (　) into a successful international business.
リチャードが趣味として始めたことが，立派な国際事業に**発展した**。

(8) The journalists wrote the article in order to (　) the secret agreements and corruption in the government.
ジャーナリストたちは政府における秘密協定と汚職**を暴露する**ために記事を書いた。

| 709 | **diminish** [dimíniʃ] | 他 を減少させる 自 減少する ≒類 decrease 自 減少する<br>diminish chances 可能性を少なくする |
|---|---|---|
| 710 | **dismiss** [dismís] | 他 を解雇〔免職〕する →185 dismissal<br>dismiss a worker 労働者を解雇する |
| 711 | **dispose** [dispóuz] | 自 処理する ⇒派 disposal 名 処理；ごみ処理<br>dispose of ～ ～を始末する |
| 712 | **emerge** [imə́ːrdʒ] | 自 出現する<br>emerge from [out of] ～ ～から現れ出る |
| 713 | **encounter** [enkáuntər] | 他 に出会う 自 出くわす 名 出会い<br>have an encounter with ～ ～と偶然出会う |
| 714 | **equal** [íːkwəl] | 他 と同じである 形 等しい<br>be equal to ～ ～と等しい |
| 715 | **evolve** [iválv] | 自 進化する，発達する 他 を進化させる，発達させる ⇒派 evolution 名 進化<br>evolve from [out of] ～ ～から進化する |
| 716 | **expose** [ikspóuz, eks-] | 他 をさらす；を暴露する ⇒派 exposure 名 さらされること；暴露<br>expose ～ to ... ～を…にさらす |

解答 (1) diminished (2) dismiss (3) disposes (4) emerged (5) encounter (6) equal (7) evolved (8) expose

> impose    frustrate    instruct    generate
> insist    float    fulfill    impress

(1) In order to avoid insect problems, the owners of the inn (　) the wood for their building in seawater before construction.
虫の問題の発生を防ぐため，宿の主は，建設前に海水に建物用の材木を浮かべた。

(2) It (　) me that you have come to me for advice and I really have none to offer.
あなたが私に助言を求めて来たのに何もしてあげられないのはやるせない。

(3) The company has gone out of business, but they recommended someone else who could (　) the order.
その会社は倒産したが，注文を実現することができる別の人を推薦してくれた。

(4) It's not my favorite area of the business, but last year it (　) more than 60% of our income.
それは私の好きな分野の仕事ではないが，去年はそれが私の収入の6割以上を生み出した。

(5) Employers are afraid to (　) strict service standards on their low-paid, part-time employees, but in the end bad service hurts their reputation.
雇用者は低賃金のパートタイム従業員に厳格なサービス水準を課すことを遠慮してできないが，結局，ひどいサービスは彼らの評判を傷つける。

(6) It's not your fancy suit that will (　) them; they are much more interested in what you say.
彼らに印象を与えるのはすてきな衣装ではない。言葉のほうにずっと関心が集まるだろう。

(7) I had planned to treat the client, but she (　) on picking up the check.
私は顧客にご馳走するつもりだったが，彼女が勘定を持つと言い張った。

(8) We ask that you (　) your client to speak only when the court addresses him.
裁判官が彼に呼びかけたときだけ話をするよう，あなたの依頼人に指示してください。

| 717 | **float** [flóut] | 他 を浮かべる　自 浮かぶ, 漂う；変動相場制である<br>the floating exchange rate　変動為替相場 |
|---|---|---|
| 718 | **frustrate** [frÁstreit] | 他 を欲求不満にさせる；を妨害する<br>be frustrated in the attempt　企てに失敗する |
| 719 | **fulfill** [fulfíl] | 他 を実現する；を果たす　⇒派 **fulfillment** 名 達成<br>fulfill an engagement　約束を果たす |
| 720 | **generate** [dʒénərèit] | 他 を作り出す；を引き起こす；を発生させる<br>→□ **generator**<br>generate electricity　発電する |
| 721 | **impose** [impóuz] | 他 を課す；を押し付ける<br>impose taxes　課税する |
| 722 | **impress** [imprés] | 他 に感動を与える；を理解させる, 印象づける<br>⇒派 **impression** 名 感動<br>be impressed by [at/with] 〜　〜に感動する |
| 723 | **insist** [insíst] | 自 強く請求する, 言い張る　他 …だと主張する<br>insist on 〜　〜を強く要求する |
| 724 | **instruct** [instrÁkt] | 他 に指示を与える；に教える<br>⇒派 **instruction** 名 指示<br>instruct 〜 on [about] ...　〜に…について指図する |

解答　(1) floated　(2) frustrates　(3) fulfill　(4) generated　(5) impose　(6) impress　(7) insisted　(8) instruct

| modify | perceive | neglect | pour |
| lower | possess | interrupt | justify |

(1) I'm sorry to ( interrupt ) the meeting, but it's the hospital calling about Mr. Daniel's pregnant wife.
会議を中断してすみませんが，ダニエルの妊娠中の奥様のことで病院からお電話です。

(2) One little mistake does not ( justify ) the boss wanting to change advertising agencies altogether.
1つの小さなミスは，上司が広告代理店をすべて替えたがることの正当な理由にならない。

(3) We are hoping that our cable modem provider will decide to ( lower ) their rates to be competitive.
我々のモデムプロバイダーが競争力をつけるために価格を下げる決定をすればよいと思う。

(4) Art used the "Revise" function to indicate in red letters all the places he would like you to ( modify ).
アートは「修正」機能を使い，あなたに修正してほしい箇所をすべて赤字で示した。

(5) No matter how good you are at your main job, if you ( neglect ) your paperwork, they won't keep you here.
本業でどんなに優秀でも，事務処理をさぼるなら，ここに置いてもらえないでしょう。

(6) What do you ( perceive ) to be the key difference between the two versions of the manuscript?
この2つのバージョンの原稿間の鍵となる違いは何と考えますか。

(7) If you ( possess ) all of the qualities described here, you would be an excellent candidate for the training program.
ここに書いてあるすべての資質を持っていれば，研修制度の優秀な候補者になるでしょう。

(8) If you ( pour ) the cream over a spoon into the coffee, the cream sits in a neat ring at the top.
コーヒーにスプーンでクリームを注ぐと，クリームは表面できれいな輪になる。

### 725 interrupt
[íntərʌ́pt]

他 をさえぎる，中断する ⇒派 **interruption** 名 中断

interrupt the view 視界をさえぎる

### 726 justify
[dʒʌ́stəfài]

他 を正当化する；の正当な理由である

be justified in ...ing …するのは正当だ

### 727 lower
[lóuər]

他 を下ろす；を下げる ⇒派 **low** 形 低い

lower the rate of interest 利率を下げる

### 728 modify
[mάdəfài]

他 を変える，修正する

modify a contract 契約を一部改める

### 729 neglect
[niglékt]

他 を軽視する；をしないでおく 名 放置
⇔反 **attention** 名 注意

neglect a person's advice 人の忠告を無視する

### 730 perceive
[pərsíːv]

他 を理解する；を知覚する，に気づく
⇒派 **perception** 名 知覚

perceive that ... …であることに気づく

### 731 possess
[pəzés]

他 を所有する；をとらえる

possess a house and a car 家と車を持つ

### 732 pour
[pɔ́ːr]

他 を注ぐ，流し込む 自 どっと出る

pour water out of a jug into a glass 水差しからコップに水をつぐ

---

解答 (1) interrupt (2) justify (3) lower (4) modify (5) neglect (6) perceive (7) possess (8) pour

| | | | |
|---|---|---|---|
| restrict | regard | restore | praise |
| prolong | reinforce | resemble | prevail |

(1) Joshua was ( praised ) repeatedly by the company president for his splendid idea before the impossibility of it was realized.
ジョシュアは自分のすばらしいアイデアが不可能だとわかる前は，社長からそれを何度も**ほめられた**。

(2) I decided to keep calling the company and complaining about the problem, hoping that I would eventually ( prevail ).
最後には**勝つ**ことを願って，その会社に電話して問題の苦情を言い続けることに決めた。

(3) The doctors think that having this operation will ( prolong ) Sadie's life and make her more comfortable.
医師たちは，この手術を行うことで，セイディの寿命**を延ばし**，彼女をより楽にさせることができると考えている。

(4) Most experts ( regard ) Dr. Epstein's research on nutrition as groundless, but his patients feel better on the diet.
大方の専門家は，エプスタイン医師の栄養に関する調査には根拠がない**と見なしている**が，彼の患者たちは食事療法中に調子がよくなっている。

(5) Adding some extra brackets would ( reinforce ) the shelf and let you store heavier items on it.
いくつか追加の腕木を付け加えれば，その棚は**補強され**，そこにより重いものを載せられるようになるだろう。

(6) It is amazing that people really do begin to ( resemble ) their dogs; or do dogs begin to resemble their masters?
人が本当に飼い犬**に似**てくるのは驚くべきことだ。それとも，犬が飼い主に似てくるのか。

(7) If you have severe software conflicts, ( restore ) the operating system to an earlier point in time using the "tools" menu.
深刻なソフトウェアの競合がある場合は，「ツール」メニューを使ってOSをもとの段階に**戻して**ください。

(8) The hospital ( restricts ) access to the Intensive Care Unit to immediate family and medical personnel.
その病院は集中治療室への出入**を**肉親と医療関係者に**制限している**。

| 733 | **praise** [préiz] | 他 を賞賛する, ほめる 名 賞賛<br>in praise of 〜　〜をたたえて |
|---|---|---|
| 734 | **prevail** [privéil] | 自 広く普及している；打ち勝つ<br>prevail in 〜　〜に蔓延する, 広がる |
| 735 | **prolong** [prəlɔ́(ː)ŋ] | 他 を引き伸ばす；を延長する<br>prolong one's stay abroad　外国での滞在期間を延ばす |
| 736 | **regard** [rigɑ́ːrd] | 他 を(〜と)見なす；に注意を払う 名 敬意；配慮<br>⇔反 disregard 他 を無視する<br>regard the situation as serious　事態を重大視している |
| 737 | **reinforce** [rìːinfɔ́ːrs] | 他 を補強する, 強化する<br>⇒派 reinforcement 名 強化<br>reinforce security　警備を強化する |
| 738 | **resemble** [rizémbl] | 他 に似ている<br>resemble each other closely　互いによく似ている |
| 739 | **restore** [ristɔ́ːr] | 他 を戻す；を復帰させる；を回復する<br>restore activity　機能を回復する |
| 740 | **restrict** [ristríkt] | 他 を制限する ⇒派 restriction 名 制限<br>restrict the use of 〜　〜の使用を制限する |

解答　(1) praised　(2) prevail　(3) prolong　(4) regard　(5) reinforce　(6) resemble　(7) restore　(8) restricts

> ruin    surround    reverse    suffer
> struggle    urge    undertake

(1) When an older woman answered, he realized he had ( ) two of the numbers when dialing the company.
年配の女性が電話に出たので，彼は会社に電話をするときに電話番号の2つの数字を逆にしていたことに気がついた。

(2) If you walk out in the rain with your new suede shoes, you will surely ( ) them.
もし新しいスエードの靴で雨の中を外出したら，間違いなくその靴をだめにするだろう。

(3) At my last company I ( ) frequently with my superior over our different approaches towards problem solving.
前の会社では私はしばしば問題解決に対するアプローチの違いで上司ともめた。

(4) Some people seem to think that you have to ( ) greatly in order to achieve happiness.
幸せを得るにはものすごく苦労しなければならないと考えている人がいるようだ。

(5) At my new job I'm very lucky to be ( ) by kind, talented, and hardworking co-workers.
新しい職場では，親切で才能があり，勤勉な同僚たちに囲まれていて，私はとても幸運だ。

(6) The order from the Japanese electronics giant is the largest project we've ever ( ).
その日本の大手電子企業からの注文は，これまで請け負った中で最大のプロジェクトだ。

(7) My supervisor ( ) me to apply for the manager position at our Asian headquarters in Shanghai.
上司は私に上海にあるアジア本社で部長の職に志願するよう促した。

## 741 reverse
[rivə́ːrs]

他 を反対〔逆〕にする　形 反対〔逆〕の
名 逆, 反対；裏側

reverse oneself about ～　～のことで態度を変える

## 742 ruin
[rú(ː)in]

他 を台無しにする　名 荒廃；破滅；廃墟

ruin one's reputation　評判を台無しにする

## 743 struggle
[strʌ́gl]

自 奮闘する；苦闘する　名 闘争

struggle against adversity　逆境と戦う

## 744 suffer
[sʌ́fər]

自 苦しむ；損害を受ける　他〈肉体的・精神的苦痛〉を経験する；〈損害など〉を受ける

suffer from poverty　貧乏に苦しむ

## 745 surround
[səráund]

他 を取り囲む；を固める；を包囲する　名 飾り縁

be surrounded by ～　～に取り囲まれる

## 746 undertake
[ʌ̀ndərtéik]

他 を引き受ける, を請け負う；に着手する

undertake a task　任務を引き受ける

## 747 urge
[ə́ːrdʒ]

他 をせきたてる, 促す　自 刺激する, 駆り立てる
名 衝動；推進力

urge ～ to a task　～に仕事を強制する

---

解答 (1) reversed (2) ruin (3) struggled (4) suffer (5) surrounded (6) undertaken (7) urged

> conscious   contemporary   adequate   ancient
> concerning   contrary   critical   delicate

(1) We thought that the number of units we ordered would be (     ) for the project, but it turns out we need 100 more.
私たちが注文した機器の数量は，そのプロジェクトに対して十分であると考えたが，さらに 100 台必要だということが判明している。

(2) Professor Smythe is the only scholar of (     ) languages such as Hebrew that I know personally.
スマイス教授は私が個人的に知っている，ヘブライ語などの古代語の唯一の学者だ。

(3) I am contacting you (     ) the letter you sent us dated April 13th.
弊社にお送りくださった 4 月 13 日付けのお手紙の件でお電話を差し上げました。

(4) After the management training seminar, our boss made a (     ) effort to be more pleasant to all of us.
管理者研修セミナーのあと，上司は我々全員をもっと喜ばせるよう意識的な努力をした。

(5) Many people consider that popular (     ) play a remake of a classic work by Shakespeare.
多くの人がその人気の現代劇を，シェイクスピアの古典劇のリメークだと見なしている。

(6) (     ) to popular belief, people often gain more weight from using artificial sweeteners than sugar.
一般に信じられているのとは反対に，人が砂糖ではなく人工甘味料を使うことでより体重が増えることがよくある。

(7) Earl seems to be doing much better, but his doctor says the next few hours are (     ).
アールはだいぶよくなっているように見えるが，医者は今後数時間が重大だと言っている。

(8) I don't feel that I know Keith well enough to discuss as (     ) a matter as his wife's illness.
私はキースの妻の病気という微妙な話題を話し合うほどは彼をよく知らないと思う。

| 748 | **adequate** [ǽdəkwət] | 形 十分な；適切な |
|---|---|---|
| | | adequate to [for] ～　～のために十分な |

| 749 | **ancient** [éinʃənt] | 形 古代の |
|---|---|---|
| | | an ancient custom　古くからの慣習 |

| 750 | **concerning** [kənsə́ːrniŋ] | 前 ～について(の) |
|---|---|---|
| | | questions concerning the agreement　契約書に関する質問 |

| 751 | **conscious** [kánʃəs] | 形 自覚〔意識〕している；意識のある |
|---|---|---|
| | | be conscious of ～　～を意識している |

| 752 | **contemporary** [kəntémpərèri] | 形 同時代の；現代の |
|---|---|---|
| | | be contemporary with ～　～と同時代である |

| 753 | **contrary** [kántrèri] | 形 反対の　名 反対のもの |
|---|---|---|
| | | on the contrary　それどころか |

| 754 | **critical** [krítikl] | 形 重大な；批判的な, 批評の　⇒派 **critic** 名 批評家 |
|---|---|---|
| | | a critical moment　決定的な瞬間 |

| 755 | **delicate** [délikət] | 形 優美な；微妙な；細心の注意を要する |
|---|---|---|
| | | preserve a delicate balance　微妙なバランスを保つ |

解答　(1) adequate　(2) ancient　(3) concerning　(4) conscious　(5) contemporary　(6) contrary　(7) critical　(8) delicate

> informal    delighted    genuine    diverse
> ideal    elegant    enormous    incredible

(1) Post-purchasing surveys have indicated that consumers are (　) with the introductory package.
購入後の調査により，入門パッケージを消費者が喜んでいることがわかった。

(2) Especially in the international division, our company seeks job applicants with rich and (　) backgrounds.
特に国際部門で，我が社は豊かで多様な経歴を持つ求職者を求めている。

(3) The new model was praised for its (　) lines and roomy interior, as well as its fuel efficiency.
新しいモデルの上品な輪郭と広い車内が，燃料効率と同様に賞賛の対象となった。

(4) Did you see that (　) new flat screen TV they have in the employees' lounge on the sixth floor?
6階の社員用ラウンジにある，あの新しい巨大なフラットテレビを見ましたか。

(5) These handbags are reasonably priced because they are not (　) leather, even though they look so smooth.
これらのハンドバッグはとてもなめらかに見えるが，本皮ではないので手ごろな価格だ。

(6) While you may have a different idea about the (　) temperature, we are keeping it low here to conserve energy.
あなたは理想的な気温について別の考えをお持ちかもしれませんが，私たちは省エネのためにここの温度を低く保っています。

(7) After all their demands and all the meetings, it is just (　) that they decided to go with another firm.
あれだけ要求と会議を重ねたあとで結局他社を選ぶことにしたとはまったく信じられない。

(8) At this point, we are not calling our frequent talks "negotiations," but rather "(　) meetings."
現時点では，私たちは頻繁な話し合いを「交渉」ではなく「非公式会談」と呼んでいる。

| 756 | **delighted** [diláitid] | 形 喜んでいる |
| --- | --- | --- |
| | | a delighted audience　大喜びの観客 |

| 757 | **diverse** [dəvə́ːrs] | 形 多様な；異なった |
| --- | --- | --- |
| | | at diverse times　時々 |

| 758 | **elegant** [éləgənt] | 形 優雅な, 品位がある |
| --- | --- | --- |
| | | be elegant in one's manners　身のこなしに気品がある |

| 759 | **enormous** [inɔ́ːrməs] | 形 巨大な　⇒派 **enormously** 副 非常に |
| --- | --- | --- |
| | | an enormous fortune　莫大な財産 |

| 760 | **genuine** [dʒénjuin] | 形 純粋な, 本物の |
| --- | --- | --- |
| | | a genuine signature　本人直筆の署名 |

| 761 | **ideal** [aidíːəl] | 形 理想的な　名 理想 |
| --- | --- | --- |
| | | attain an ideal　理想を実現する |

| 762 | **incredible** [inkrédəbl] | 形 信じられない；途方もない<br>⇒派 **incredibly** 副 信じられないほどに |
| --- | --- | --- |
| | | incredible speed　途方もない速度 |

| 763 | **informal** [infɔ́ːrml] | 形 くだけた；形式ばっていない, 非公式の<br>⇔反 **formal** 形 公式の |
| --- | --- | --- |
| | | informal proceedings　非公式の手続き |

解答 (1) delighted (2) diverse (3) elegant (4) enormous (5) genuine (6) ideal (7) incredible (8) informal

| prominent | multiple | moreover | internal |
| nervous | intense | logical | profound |

(1) The management training is so ( ) that a few people dropped out because they couldn't handle the pressure.
管理者研修はとても厳しいので，数人がプレッシャーに負けて脱落した。

(2) The shareholders don't know that McKinley is planning to resign because the information only appeared in an ( ) memo.
情報が内部通達で出ただけだったので，株主はマッキンレーが辞職予定だと知らない。

(3) Even though her criticism wasn't ( ), it still stung to hear all those angry words come out of her mouth.
彼女の批判が論理的でなくても，彼女の口からそんな怒りの言葉が出るのを聞くのはつらかった。

(4) ( ), we will review information from the morning session and examine various related topics.
さらに，我々は午前中のセッションからの情報を吟味し，さまざまな関連問題を検討します。

(5) The insurance premiums went up because Tim had been involved in ( ) accidents.
ティムは多数の事故に巻き込まれたことがあるので，保険料が高くなった。

(6) It makes me ( ) whenever the gardener tries to cut something down with a chainsaw.
庭師がチェーンソーを使って物を切り倒そうとするたびに私はいらいらする。

(7) After changing her eating habits, Ritsuko noticed a ( ) difference in the way she felt.
リツコは，食習慣を変えたら，感じ方に大きな違いが出てきたことに気づいた。

(8) They have been a ( ) family in the Boston area for more than 200 years.
彼らは200年以上も前から，ボストン地区における有名な一族である。

| 764 | **intense** [inténs] | 形 激しい, 猛烈な →213 intensive |
|---|---|---|
| | | with intense attention 真剣に注意して |

| 765 | **internal** [intə́ːrnl] | 形 内部の, 国内の ⇔反 external 形 外部の |
|---|---|---|
| | | internal markets 国内市場 |

| 766 | **logical** [ládʒikl] | 形 論理的な |
|---|---|---|
| | | logical thinking 論理的思考 |

| 767 | **moreover** [mɔːróuvər] | 副 その上, さらに ≒類 besides, furthermore 副 さらに |
|---|---|---|

| 768 | **multiple** [mʌ́ltəpl] | 形 多数の；倍数の |
|---|---|---|
| | | multiple debts 多重債務 |

| 769 | **nervous** [nə́ːrvəs] | 形 心配して, 不安で；神経質な, 神経の |
|---|---|---|
| | | get nervous あがる |

| 770 | **profound** [prəfáund, prou-] | 形 心からの；深い；深刻な |
|---|---|---|
| | | profound insight 深い洞察力 |

| 771 | **prominent** [prámənənt] | 形 卓越した, 有名な；重要な；目立つ |
|---|---|---|
| | | a prominent feature 際立った特色 |

解答 (1) intense (2) internal (3) logical (4) Moreover (5) multiple (6) nervous (7) profound (8) prominent

| remarkable | reasonable | talented | tremendous |
| reluctant | sufficient | rigid | punctual |

(1) It's unbelievable to think that some of my co-workers don't see the importance of being (　　).
私の同僚で，時間を守ることの大切さを理解しない者がいるのは信じがたいことだ。

(2) We were afraid that hotels in such a big city would cost a fortune, but we found several that were (　　).
このような大都市のホテルは非常に高いと思ったが，手ごろなホテルをいくつか見つけた。

(3) I'm (　　) to recommend that service since Alvin, my favorite employee, left two months ago.
私の気に入っていた従業員アルビンが2か月前に辞めてから，そのサービスを勧める気になれない。

(4) The committee awarded the former executive for his (　　) achievements in community service.
その委員会は，社会奉仕における前役員のすばらしい功績に対して，彼を表彰した。

(5) I thought that Mr. Lowell would make an exception to the rules, but he is far more (　　) than I imagined.
ローウェル氏はその規則に例外を作ると思ったが，彼は想像よりはるかに柔軟性がない。

(6) I hope that the inventory we ordered is (　　) for the rush of customers we'll get on opening day.
我々が注文した在庫が，開店の日に押し寄せるお客様に十分であることを願っている。

(7) There is no question that their programmer is (　　), but he is also very temperamental.
彼らのプログラマーに才能があることは間違いないのだが，彼は非常に気まぐれでもある。

(8) It was a (　　) honor to receive the award for Most Productive Worker of the Year at last night's banquet.
昨夜の晩餐会で「年間最高生産労働者賞」を受賞したことはとてつもない名誉だった。

| 772 | **punctual** [pʌ́ŋktʃuəl, pʌ́ŋkʃuəl, -tʃl] | 形 時間に正確な ⇒派 **punctuality** 名 時間を守ること  be punctual for an appointment 約束の時間を守る |
|---|---|---|
| 773 | **reasonable** [ríːznəbl] | 形 〈人が〉分別のある；〈言動などが〉道理にかなった；〈質・額が〉適切な  a reasonable theory 筋の通った理論 |
| 774 | **reluctant** [rilʌ́ktənt] | 形 …したがらない；いやいやながらの  give a reluctant answer しぶしぶ返事をする |
| 775 | **remarkable** [rimáːrkəbl] | 形 注目すべき，驚くべき →685 **remark**  a remarkable change 著しい変化 |
| 776 | **rigid** [rídʒid] | 形 厳しい，厳格な；堅い  rigid rules 厳格な規則 |
| 777 | **sufficient** [səfíʃənt] | 形 十分な，足りる ⇔反 211 **insufficient** 形 不十分な  sufficient to do …するのに十分な |
| 778 | **talented** [tǽləntid] | 形 才能ある，有能な  a talented youth 才能のある青年 |
| 779 | **tremendous** [triméndəs] | 形 とても大きな；とてもすばらしい  tremendous progress 途方もない進歩 |

解答 (1) punctual (2) reasonable (3) reluctant (4) remarkable (5) rigid (6) sufficient (7) talented (8) tremendous

## Chapter 3

# TOEIC 特有の頻出語を覚える

3-1 頻度★★★
3-2 頻度★★

# Chapter 3-1 TOEIC 特有の頻出語を覚える

学校英語 ▶▶▶ TOEIC® TEST　頻度★★★

---

If the client wants to use our supplier in Jordan, all agreements made will have to **abide** by Jordanian law.

もしその取引先が我々のヨルダンの供給業者を利用したいなら，すべての合意はヨルダンの法を遵守したものでなければならないだろう。

**780 abide**
[əbáid]

自 忠実に守る，遵守する

abide by ～　～に従う

---

Wendy is afraid to **accuse** her boss of harassment, but she has indicated that he has been inappropriate with her.

ウェンディは嫌がらせを受けたとして上司を訴えることをためらっているが，彼が自分に不適切な態度をとったことを暗に示した。

**781 accuse**
[əkjúːz]

他 を訴える；を責める　⇒派 accusable 形 非難されて当然の　accusation 名 告発；非難

accuse ～ of ...　～を…について非難する

---

The company has put a warning on the label that their product requires special handling at high **altitudes**.

その会社は，その製品は高所では特別な取り扱いが必要だという警告を表示した。

**782 altitude**
[ǽltət(j)ùːd]

名 高度；標高；高所

at an altitude of ～　～の高さで

---

Don't just go along with them, when they ask for discussion, get in there and **assert** your objections.

彼らにただ同調しないこと。話し合いを求められたら，それに応じ，反対意見を主張しなさい。

**783 assert**
[əsə́ːrt]

他 を主張する；を断言する

assert oneself　自己を主張する

---

The company owns several vacation units in Hawaii that have turned out to be valuable **assets**.

その会社はハワイに休暇用施設をいくつか所有しているが，それらは高価な資産であることがわかった。

**784 asset**
[ǽset]

名 資産；利点

fixed assets　固定資産

After the discrepancy in the figures was discovered, the board decided to have a third party conduct a complete **audit**.
数字の不一致の判明後, 役員会は第三者に全面的な会計検査を行わせることにした。

**785 audit**
[ɔ́ːdət]

名 会計検査　他 〈会計・帳簿〉を検査する
⇒派 auditor 名 会計検査官, 監査役
an internal audit　内部監査

---

Despite the fact that the restaurant chain went **bankrupt**, someone bailed them out and they are still in operation.
そのレストランチェーンは倒産したにもかかわらず, 救済してくれる人が現れ, まだ営業している。

**786 bankrupt**
[bǽŋkrʌpt, -rəpt]

形 倒産した　⇒派 bankruptcy 名 破産, 倒産
go bankrupt　破産する

---

Instead of having the conference **banquet** at the hotel, the committee decided on holding it at restaurant by the pier.
委員会は, そのホテルではなく, 埠頭近くのレストランで会議の祝宴を開くことにした。

**787 banquet**
[bǽŋkwət, -kwet]

名 宴会；ごちそう
attend a banquet　宴会に出席する

---

This house is unusual because it has a **basement**, unlike most others in the area.
その地域のほとんどの家とは違い, この家には珍しいことに地下室がある。

**788 basement**
[béismənt]

名 地下室
a basement apartment　地下にある部屋

---

Some flights don't serve food, but even short ones generally offer **beverages** to the passengers.
機内食の出ない便もあるが, 乗客に飲み物が出されることは短距離便でも一般的だ。

**789 beverage**
[bévəridʒ]

名 飲み物
an alcoholic beverage　アルコール飲料

When we **bid** for this contract, I suggest you quote the client the price of $205 per metric ton.

この契約の入札の際には，発注者側に1トン当たり205ドルの価格を提示するとよい。

**790 bid** [bíd]
- 自 (入札で)値をつける 名 入札；付け値；競売品
- ⇒派 bidder 名 入札者
- bid for ～　～に入札する

---

If your company wants to have a **booth** at the trade fair, you need to contact us by April 1st.

もし御社が展示会で展示スペース設置を希望されるなら，4月1日までにご連絡ください。

**791 booth** [búːθ]
- 名 小さく仕切った部屋；展示スペース
- ≒類 cubicle 名 小さく区切った部屋
- a telephone booth　電話ボックス

---

A minimum order is 30,000 metric tons, which will fit perfectly on the smallest **cargo** ship.

注文は最低でも3万トンであり，それは最も小さい貨物船にぴったり収まるだろう。

**792 cargo** [káːrgou]
- 名 貨物；船荷
- discharge the cargo　積荷を降ろす

---

This airline doesn't fly to Paris, but can arrange for a connection with another **carrier**.

この航空会社はパリ行きではないが，ほかの航空会社への乗り継ぎを調整してくれる。

**793 carrier** [kǽriər]
- 名 運搬する人；輸送会社，旅客会社
- a mail carrier　郵便配達員

---

Bringing in a **catering** service and having the party in the conference room was cheaper than going to a restaurant.

仕出しサービスを取り入れて会議室で宴会をすれば，レストランに行くより安く済んだ。

**794 catering** [kéitəriŋ]
- 名 仕出し屋；仕出し物
- a catering service　仕出し屋

Participants receive a **certificate** for completion of the seminar that they can take back and submit to their supervisors.
参加者は，持ち帰って上司に提出することができるセミナー修了証を受け取る。

### 795 certificate
[sərtífikət]

名 証明書

an insurance certificate　保険証明書

---

If it has a USDA label on the package, it means that the government **certifies** that the meat has passed inspection.
包装にUSDAのラベルが貼られている場合，それは政府がその肉の検査通過を証明しているという意味である。

### 796 certify
[sə́ːrtifài]

他 を証明する

this is to certify that ...　…であることを本状により証明する

---

It seems unfair that the author didn't **cite** the originator of the material in his credits and acknowledgments.
著者がクレジットでも謝辞でも素材の原作者に言及していないのは，公正ではないように思う。

### 797 cite
[sáit]

他 を引用する；を引き合いに出す

cite ～ as ...　～を…として引き合いに出す

---

Most of the population lives north of downtown, so it is less stressful to **commute** from the south.
人口の大半は中心部の北側に住んでいるので，南側から通勤するほうがストレスが少ない。

### 798 commute
[kəmjúːt]

自 通勤〔通学〕する　名 通勤（時間, 距離）
⇒派 commuter 名 通勤者

commute to ～　～に通勤する

---

Most software is backwards **compatible** and can handle files created for lower versions of the program.
大半のソフトウェアには過去のものと互換性があるので，プログラムの古いバージョン用に作成されたファイルも使うことができる。

### 799 compatible
[kəmpǽtəbl]

形 互換性のある；両立する

be compatible with ～　～と互換できる

The author had good ideas but weak writing skills, so the fact that the editor was **competent** saved the work.

著者にはよい着想はあったが，執筆力に乏しかったため，編集者が有能だったことが仕事の助けとなった。

### 800 competent
[kámpətnt]

形 有能な；要求にかなう，十分な

be competent to do　…する力量のある

---

The caterer suggested a dessert that would be a good **complement** to the food we ordered.

仕出し業者は我々が注文した食べ物を完全にするであろうデザートを提案した。

### 801 complement
名 [kámpləmənt]
動 [kámpləmènt]

名 補うもの；(必要な) 全数，定数　他 を補完する

complement ~ with　~を…で補完する

---

One **component** of the anti-virus software is an Internet security traffic blocker that is not compatible with the LAN.

そのウイルス対策ソフトの構成要素の1つは，インターネットセキュリティのための情報の行き来の遮断であり，それは LAN との互換性はない。

### 802 component
[kəmpóunənt]

名 構成要素，部品

an essential component　不可欠の要素

---

This dictionary is of much better value and is actually more **comprehensive** than the other one.

この辞書はもう1つの辞書よりもずっと質が高く，実に網羅的だ。

### 803 comprehensive
[kàmprihénsiv]

形 包括的な，網羅的な，総合的な

a comprehensive survey　包括的な調査
a comprehensive insurance　総合保険

---

Their negotiator was very outspoken, but of course stopped short of revealing any **confidential** data.

交渉者は非常に率直だったが，もちろん，機密のデータを明かすには至らなかった。

### 804 confidential
[kànfidénʃl]

形 秘密の，親展の

strictly confidential　極秘
confidential document　機密文書

Two authors may have written this report, because the styles are not **consistent** between the beginning and the end.
文体が始めと終わりで一貫していないので，このレポートは2人の書き手によるものだったのかもしれない。

### 805 consistent
[kənsístənt]

形 首尾一貫した
be consistent with ~　～と一貫している，矛盾がない

---

When those rival corporations get together for charity events, the atmosphere is always **cooperative** and friendly.
それらの競合会社が慈善事業で集まるときは，雰囲気は常に協力的で友好的なものである。

### 806 cooperative
[kouápərətiv]

形 協同の；協同組合の　⇒派 cooperation 名 協力
a cooperative business　協同事業

---

Another organization offered to **coordinate** their trade fair with ours to broaden the scope and attract more visitors.
別の団体が，対象範囲を広げてより多くの訪問客を呼ぶために，我々と見本市を共同運営することを打診してきた。

### 807 coordinate
動 [kouɔ́:rdənèit]
形 [kouɔ́:rdənit]

他 〈行動など〉を組織する，調整する；を同格にする
形 同格の
coordinate activities　活動を調整する

---

You are **cordially** invited to a reception welcoming all new employees on October 18th at the Ritz hotel.
10月18日，リッツホテルで全新入社員を歓迎して行われるレセプションに心よりご招待申し上げます。

### 808 cordially
[kɔ́:rdʒəli]

副 心を込めて　⇒派 cordial 形 心からの
Yours cordially [Cordially yours].　（手紙の末尾で）敬具

---

The **courier** company competing for corporate business gives volume business discounts that make them cheaper than the postal service.
法人向け事業で競うその宅配業者は量に応じた割引をしており，郵便より安い。

### 809 courier
[kúriər]

名 宅配業者；急使，外交特使
by courier service　宅配便で

The cultural and scenic spots are of great interest, but most travelers to Italy rave most about the **cuisine**.
その文化的で風光明媚な地はとても興味深いが，イタリアへの旅行者のほとんどが料理のことばかりほめる。

**810 cuisine**
[kwizíːn]
名 料理法；料理
French cuisine　フランス料理

---

The product has a full replacement guarantee for five years against any **defect** in material or workmanship.
その製品は素材，製品の出来に関するあらゆる欠陥に対し，5年間の完全交換が保証されている。

**811 defect**
[díːfekt, difékt]
名 欠点，欠陥
a defect in a machine　機械の欠陥

---

The Advertising department ran a **deficit** for three years, then was absorbed by the Marketing department.
宣伝部は3年間赤字を出し続け，その後マーケティング部に吸収された。

**812 deficit**
[défəsit]
名 不足(額)，赤字
a deficit of $1,000　1,000ドルの赤字

---

We **definitely** want to buy from your company, but you need to guarantee these commodities with a government inspection certificate.
私たちは絶対にあなたの会社から買いたいと思っているが，これらの商品には政府の検査証をつけて品質保証をしてもらわなければならない。

**813 definitely**
[défənətli]
副 確かに，はっきりと
⇒派 definite 形 確実な；明確な
refuse definitely　きっぱり断る

---

Representatives from both labor and management are expected to **deliberate** the rest of the day and possibly into the night.
労使双方の代表は，日中の残りの時間は慎重に協議を進める見込みであり，夜になる可能性もある。

**814 deliberate**
動 [dilíbərèit]
形 [-rət]
自 他 (を)熟慮する；(を)審議する　形 故意の；熟考された
⇒派 deliberately 副 故意に
a deliberate choice　慎重な選択

A telephone **directory** is an extremely useful resource, especially in small or medium-sized cities.
電話帳はきわめて便利な情報源である。中小規模の都市では特にそうだ。

**815 directory**
[dəréktəri]
图 名簿, 住所録；ディレクトリ（ファイルを管理するディスク上のリスト）
a classified telephone directory　職業別電話帳

---

Since the company has grown significantly in the past year, shareholders are expecting a substantial **dividend**.
その会社は前年顕著な成長を遂げたので，株主はかなりの配当金を期待している。

**816 dividend**
[dívidènd]
图 配当金
a regular dividend　定期配当

---

The media plays a **dominant** role in forming public opinion and furthering the popular culture.
メディアは，世論を形成し，大衆文化を促進するのに主要な役割を果たす。

**817 dominant**
[dάmənənt]
形 有力な；主要な
a dominant position　主要な地位

---

The first **draft** of the proposal was so complete that few changes were necessary before presenting it to the client.
提案の第一草案が完璧だったので，顧客への提出前に必要な修正はほとんどなかった。

**818 draft**
[drǽft]
图 下書き, 草稿；為替手形　他〈草案〉を書く
a rough draft for a speech　スピーチの下書き

---

High interest rates have reduced movement in the financial arena, which is a **drain** on the economy.
高い利率のために財界での動きが減少したが，これは経済を疲弊させるものだ。

**819 drain**
[dréin]
图 排水管；流出；消耗をもたらすもの
他〈水など〉を排出する　自〈水が〉流れ出る
a storm drain　雨水配水管

3-1

3-2

The treasurer keeps all of the bankbooks and records locked in a **drawer** in his home office.
財務担当者は，すべての通帳や記録を本社の引き出しに錠をかけて保管している。

### 820 drawer
[drɔ́ːr]

名 引き出し

open a drawer　引き出しを開ける

---

The price will be fixed for the **duration** of the contract as stated in the original proposal.
もとの提案書に明記されているように，契約の継続期間中は価格は一定である。

### 821 duration
[d(j)uəréiʃən]

名 持続期間

for the duration of the contract　契約期間中

---

The improvements made to the house, especially the bathrooms and kitchen, will greatly **enhance** the value of the property.
その家の特にバスルームと台所の改装は，この不動産の価値を非常に高めるだろう。

### 822 enhance
[enhǽns]

他 を高める

enhance one's reputation　評判を高める

---

The market for **exotic** fruits and vegetables has grown tremendously over the last ten years.
過去10年間にわたって，外国産の果物と野菜の市場は大きく成長した。

### 823 exotic
[igzɑ́tik, egz-]

形 珍しい；異国風の，外国(産)の

exotic animal　外来の動物

---

The government financed an **expedition** into the rain forest to collect plants that are known to have medicinal qualities.
政府は，薬効があることで知られている植物を集めるための熱帯雨林遠征の資金を出した。

### 824 expedition
[èkspədíʃən]

名 探検，遠征；探検隊

a shopping expedition　買い出し

Our contract with Debra's shoe company is due to **expire** at the end of this quarter unless we re-negotiate.
デブラ靴会社と当社との契約は，再交渉しない限りこの四半期末に**期限が切れる**予定だ。

**825 expire**
[ikspáiər, eks-]

⾃ 期限が切れる

expire on June 30th　6月30日で期限が切れる

---

If the company continues to grow at this rate, it will need a new production **facility** before the end of the year.
会社がこのペースで成長を続ければ，年末までに新しい生産**設備**が必要になるだろう。

**826 facility**
[fəsíləti]

名 設備，機関；便宜

transportation facilities　運輸機関

---

You can **fasten** the briefcase with the magnetic clasp and choose your own combination to lock it.
そのブリーフケースは，磁石の金具で**固定し**，自分で数字の組み合わせを選んで錠をかけられる。

**827 fasten**
[fæsn]

他 を固定する；を (くぎ・錠などで) 留める

fasten a latch of a door　ドアの掛け金をかける

---

The entrance **fee** seemed unusually high for such a small museum in such a small town.
そんな小さな町の小さな博物館にしては，入場**料**が異常に高いように思えた。

**828 fee**
[fiː]

名 報酬；料金

a cancellation fee　キャンセル料

---

The end of the **fiscal** year is preceded by the rush to complete spending of the existing budgets.
残っている予算の消化を終えるための駆け込みが**会計**年度の終わりの前に生じる。

**829 fiscal**
[fískl]

形 国家財政の；会計の

a fiscal year　会計年度

The towels must all be **folded** the same way in order for them all to fit in the linen closet.
全部のタオルをリネン用棚に収めるためには，タオルはすべて同様に**たたま**ねばならない。

**830 fold**
[fóuld]
他 を折りたたむ，〈手・腕など〉を組む　名 折り目
⇒派 folder 名 ファイルを収めるフォルダー
with one's arms folded　腕組みして

The shipper guaranteed that all **fragile** items would be packed carefully and arrive in perfect condition.
荷送り人はすべての**壊れやすい**品を慎重に梱包し，完璧な状態で届けると保証した。

**831 fragile**
[frǽdʒəl]
形 もろい，壊れやすい
as fragile as glass　ガラスのように壊れやすい

After being accused of **fraud**, Sandy found it necessary to move to another city and start a new career.
**詐欺**で告訴されたあとで，サンディは別の都市に移って新しい仕事を始めることが必要だと気づいた。

**832 fraud**
[frɔ́:d]
名 詐欺，詐欺師
practice fraud　詐欺を働く

In North America more than twice as much **freight** is shipped by trucks than by trains.
北米では，鉄道で輸送される貨物の2倍以上の量の**貨物**がトラックで輸送される。

**833 freight**
[fréit]
名 貨物輸送(料)；運送貨物
freight prepaid　運賃前払い

The treasurer didn't mention the precise amount of the contribution, but said it was a **generous** donation.
財務担当者は寄付金の正確な金額は述べなかったが，**惜しみない**寄付だと言った。

**834 generous**
[dʒénərəs]
形 気前のよい；惜しみない，寛大な；たくさんの
generous aid　惜しみない援助

High **humidity** will make a hot summer day feel much hotter that it actually is.
湿度が高いと、暑い夏の日が実際以上に暑く感じられるだろう。

### 835 humidity
[hju:mídəti]

名 湿度　⇒派 humid 形 湿気の多い
relative humidity　相対湿度

---

Since the millionaire's heirs were lavished with money and gifts, they had no **incentive** to get jobs.
大富豪の相続人は金品をあり余るほど得たので、職に就こうという発奮材料を喪失した。

### 836 incentive
[inséntiv]

名 刺激になるもの；報奨金　形 刺激的な；鼓舞する
incentive wages　能率給

---

If you do your job faithfully and work well with others, you're not likely to **incur** the boss's anger.
誠実に仕事をし、周囲ともうまくやれば、上司の激怒を招くことはないだろう。

### 837 incur
[inkə́:r]

他 〈損害・出費など〉を招く、負う
incur unexpected expenses　思わぬ出費となる

---

If anything can **induce** corporate headquarters to make changes in the way they do business, it's the bottom line.
ビジネスの仕方を変えるように企業の本社を仕向けられるものがあるとすれば、それは最終損益だろう。

### 838 induce
[ind(j)ú:s]

他 に勧めて…させる、…するように仕向ける
induce ～ to an action　～に行動を起こす気にさせる

---

It should be no problem to **insert** a clause in the contract addressing the client's concerns in that area.
顧客のその地域での利害関係に的を絞った条項を契約書に入れるのは、問題ないはずだ。

### 839 insert
動 [insə́:rt]
名 [ínsə:rt]

他 を挿入する；を書き込む、掲載する　名 挿入物
insert a key in [into] a lock　錠前に鍵を差し込む

Mr. Collins started as an **intern** at that law firm in Washington, D.C. where he later became a senior partner.

コリンズさんはワシントン DC のその法律事務所で研修生として仕事を始め，後にそこで上級弁護士となった。

**840 intern**
[íntəːrn]

名 インターン，実習〔研修〕生　自 実習する

serve as an intern　インターンとして勤務する

---

If you turn right at the **intersection** of Washington and First, you'll be headed into the financial district.

ワシントン通りと一番街の交差点を右折すると金融街に入ります。

**841 intersection**
[ìntərsékʃən]

名 交差；交差点

cross an intersection　交差点を渡る

---

Without the supervisor's **intervention** the situation would probably have escalated into a very ugly scene.

その上司の調停がなければ，おそらく状況はひどく険悪なものへ激化していただろう。

**842 intervention**
[ìntərvénʃən]

名 干渉，介入；調停　⇒派 intervene　自 干渉する

government intervention to regulate prices　物価を統制するための政府の介入

---

The **invoice** from the supply company doesn't accurately reflect the shipment received on Tuesday of last week.

その供給業者からの請求書は，先週火曜日に受け取った出荷品を正しく反映していない。

**843 invoice**
[ínvɔis]

名 送り状，請求明細書，インボイス

an invoice form　明細記入請求書；送り状用紙

---

The travel agent will fax copies of the **itinerary** for the Chicago trip first thing in the morning.

その旅行代理店は，朝一番でシカゴ旅行の旅程表のコピーをファックスしてくるだろう。

**844 itinerary**
[aitínərèri, itín-]

名 旅程；旅程表；旅行案内

be on the itinerary　旅程表に記載されている

The manager made it clear that anyone who **leaked** product information would be fired.
部長は，製品情報を漏らした者はだれでも解雇するということをはっきりさせた。

**845 leak**
[líːk]

他 を漏らす 自 漏れる 名 穴

stop a leak in the roof　屋根の雨漏り穴をふさぐ

---

We'll have to find a new office space after the **lease** on our current office expires.
現事務所の賃貸契約が切れたあとの新しい事務所用スペースを見つけなければならない。

**846 lease**
[líːs]

名 賃貸借契約(書)；賃貸期間　他 を賃借する

by [on] lease　賃貸借で
sign a lease contract　リース契約を結ぶ

---

When I travel on business, I try to limit what I take to a couple of bags of carry-on **luggage**.
私は出張するときは，持っていくものを機内持ち込み荷物2，3個に抑えようとすることにしている。

**847 luggage**
[lʌ́gidʒ]

名 手荷物，旅行かばん類
≒類 baggage 名 手荷物

carry one's luggage　手荷物を運ぶ

---

I'm not a big fan of business **luncheons** because I prefer not to talk shop over lunch.
私は昼食を食べながら仕事の話をしたくないので，ビジネス昼食会はあまり好きではない。

**848 luncheon**
[lʌ́ntʃən]

名 午餐，昼食会

hold a luncheon　午餐会を催す

---

The premise of the story was interesting, but overall the **manuscript** needed a lot of rewriting.
物語の前提は興味深かったが，全体的に原稿は大幅な手直しが必要だった。

**849 manuscript**
[mǽnjəskrìpt]

名 原稿；写本

manuscript fee　原稿料

The **medication** helps to control my sickness, but unfortunately it makes me sleepy.
薬物治療は私の病気を抑えるのに役立つが、残念ながら眠くなる。

**850 medication**
[mèdikéiʃən]

名 薬物治療；薬物
take medication　薬物治療を受ける

---

The change is **moderate** rather than drastic, but right now it is what the company needs.
変化は抜本的なものというより穏やかなものだが、現時点ではそれが会社に必要なものだ。

**851 moderate**
形 [mάdərət]
動 [mάdərèit]

形 適度な；穏健な　他 を和らげる
at moderate speed　適度なスピードで

---

I've been reading self-help books to learn how to **motivate** myself to do better work.
私はよりよい仕事をするように自分にやる気を起こさせる方法を学ぼうと、自己啓発書を読んでいる。

**852 motivate**
[móutəvèit]

他 に意欲を起こさせる　⇒派 motive 名 動機
motivate ~ to do　~に…する動機を与える

---

Applying for a business permit at the **municipal** office is a long and tiring process.
市役所に事業許可を申請するのは、長くて面倒な手続きだ。

**853 municipal**
[mju:nísəpl]

形 市の；市政の
municipal bond　地方債

---

I have serious **objections** to someone with less talent and experience being promoted over me.
私は、自分よりも才能も経験もない人が私より先に昇進することに対して、真剣に抗議する。

**854 objection**
[əbdʒékʃən]

名 抗議, 反対, 異議；反対理由
make [raise] an objection to [against] ~　~に異議を唱える

In international business meetings it's important to take extra care not to **offend** anyone.
国際的なビジネス会議では，だれの気分も害さないように特別な注意を払うことが大切だ。

**855 offend**
[əfénd]

他〈人〉の気分を害する　自犯罪を犯す
⇒派 offense 名犯罪　→224 offender
be offended at [by/with] ～　～に立腹する

---

Every article is checked and re-checked in order to make sure no mistakes are **overlooked**.
どんな間違いも見落とさないように，全記事がチェックされ，さらに再チェックされる。

**856 overlook**
[òuvərlúk]

他を見落とす；を見下ろす，見渡す
a restaurant overlooking the sea　海の見えるレストラン

---

At one point my job involved **overseeing** 80 employees in five offices, in three countries.
一時，私の仕事は3か国にわたって5つの事務所で働く80人の社員を監督することだった。

**857 oversee**
[òuvərsí:]

他を監視する
oversee the construction crews　建設作業員を監督する

---

Mobile phone data networks have been faster ever since providers started using **packets** for data transmission.
携帯電話のデータネットワークは，プロバイダーがデータ送信にパケットを使うようになって以来，速くなった。

**858 packet**
[pǽkət]

名パッケージ；小包；パケット（ネットワークで送るために分割されたデータの単位）
a postal packet　郵便小包

---

After a lengthy battle in the courts, our company was able to obtain a **patent** for the technology.
長期にわたる法廷での戦いのあと，我が社はその技術に対する特許を得ることができた。

**859 patent**
[pǽtnt]

名特許；特許品　形特許に関する　他の特許を取る
off patent　特許期限切れの

Constantly in search of the bigger **paycheck**, Mark was already at his fifth company when he joined us.

マークは常により高い給料を求めており，うちに来たときにはすでに5社目だった。

### 860 paycheck
[péitʃèk]

名 給料；給料支払小切手

cash one's paycheck　給料小切手を現金にする

---

Despite providing its executives with perks, the company does everything it can do to shrink its **payroll**.

重役には役職手当てを支給しているのに，会社は給与総額を減らすためにあらゆることをする。

### 861 payroll
[péiròul]

名 給料支払簿；従業員名簿；給与総額

on the payroll　就業して
off the payroll　失業して

---

I was surprised and happy to see five **pedestrians** last week walking and talking on our new mobile phones.

私は先週，5人の歩行者が歩きながら我が社の新しい携帯電話で話をしているのを見て驚き，そしてうれしかった。

### 862 pedestrian
[pədéstriən]

名 歩行者　形 歩行者専用の

a pedestrian bridge　歩道橋

---

**Pending** approval from the government, we'll not be able to sell our new medical products.

政府の承認を待つ間，我々は当社の新しい医療品を売ることができないだろう。

### 863 pending
[péndiŋ]

前 …まで，…の間　形 未決定の，懸案の

a pending matter　懸案

---

Residents successfully **petitioned** not to have the chemical plant built in their town.

住民たちは，自分たちの町に化学工場を建設しないように請願して，受け入れられた。

### 864 petition
[pətíʃən]

他 自 (に)請願する　名 請願(書)；申請(書)

a petition for aid　補助申請

The cargo ships carrying automotive parts will dock at **pier** seven tonight at 8:30.
自動車の部品を積んだ貨物船が今夜8時半に第7桟橋に停泊する。

### 865 pier
[píər]

图 桟橋, 埠頭

bring a ship alongside the pier　船を桟橋に横付けにする
pier warehouse　港湾倉庫

---

Every team member made a **pledge** to improve their sales numbers from previous quarter.
チームメンバー全員が、前の四半期よりも売上数値を伸ばすという誓約をした。

### 866 pledge
[plédʒ]

图 誓約；抵当, 担保　他 を誓う；に誓約させる

be in pledge　担保に入っている

---

The workers took a **poll** to decide the best place for a company trip.
労働者たちは社員旅行に最適な場所を決めるために投票を行った。

### 867 poll
[póul]

图 投票, 選挙；投票結果；投票所；世論調査

go to the polls　投票所に行く

---

My stockbroker may be young, but he has an impressive **portfolio**.
私の株式仲介人は若いかもしれないが、なかなか印象的なポートフォリオを持っている。

### 868 portfolio
[pɔːrtfóuliòu]

图 ポートフォリオ, 有価証券の一覧表

portfolio management　資産運用

---

Customers were angry that they had to pay **postage** to send in the registration cards.
顧客は、登録証を送るのに郵送料を払わなければならないことを怒っていた。

### 869 postage
[póustidʒ]

图 郵便料金

postage-paid　郵便料金支払い済みの

In my **prior** job I worked longer hours and had more responsibilities; yet was paid less.

私は前職で，今より長時間働き，もっと重い責任を負っていたが，給料は少なかった。

### 870 prior
[práiər]

形 前の，事前の；より重要な

prior to ～　～に先立って
prior consent　事前の同意

---

Non-employees, even family members of employees, are **prohibited** from entering our research labs.

社員以外は，社員の家族であっても我々の研究室に入ることを禁じられている。

### 871 prohibit
[prouhíbət]

他〈人〉が(…するのを)禁止する

prohibit ～ from ...ing　～が…するのを禁じる

---

The e-mail was marked urgent, so I read it immediately and sent a **prompt** reply.

そのEメールには緊急マークがついていたので，すぐに読んで即座に返答した。

### 872 prompt
[prámpt]

形 即座の；即時(払い)の　他 を刺激する；に促す

prompt payment　即時払い
prompt ～ to do　～に…するよう促す

---

Even though she was young, her **qualifications** were such that I had no hesitation in recommending her as my replacement.

彼女は若いにもかかわらず，私の後任に推薦するのをためらわないほどの資質を備えていた。

### 873 qualification
[kwàləfikéiʃən]

名 資格；資質；免許状

a job qualification　仕事に就く資格
a qualification certificate　資格証明

The woman who worked in **reception** for 30 years will retire next week.
30年間<u>受付</u>で働いてきたその女性は来週退職する。

### 874 reception
[risépʃən]

名 受け入れること；歓迎；祝賀会；受付
⇒派 **receptionist** 名 受付係

a cordial reception　心からの歓迎

---

In some aspects the **recession** was harder on the more established companies.
ある面では，<u>不景気</u>は安定した会社のほうにより痛手となった。

### 875 recession
[riséʃən]

名 景気後退，不況

aggravate recession　不況を悪化させる

---

In addition to the public sector, the government's **reform** program is also likely to affect the private sector.
政府の<u>改革</u>計画は，公共部門だけでなく，民間部門にも影響を与えそうだ。

### 876 reform
[rifɔ́ːrm]

名 改革　他 を改善〔改革〕する

a drastic reform　抜本的な改革

---

In addition to a full **refund**, the clerk gave the customers a 20% discount on a future purchase.
全額を<u>返金</u>した上に，その店員は客たちに，今後の購入に対して20パーセントの値引きを約束した。

### 877 refund
名 [ríːfʌnd]
動 [rifʌ́nd]

名 払戻金，払い戻し　他 を払い戻す

refund the balance　差額を払い戻す

Last year the company spent millions of dollars in order to lobby the government for favorable **regulations**.
昨年その社は，自己に有利な規則を作るよう政府に働きかけるのに何百万ドルも使った。

**878 regulation**
[règjəléiʃən]

名 規制；規則　⇒派 regulate 他 を規制する

traffic regulations　交通法規

---

The company **reimbursed** me for the hotel fee and air fare of my last business trip.
会社は先日の出張のホテル代と航空運賃を払い戻してくれた。

**879 reimburse**
[rìːimbə́ːrs]

他 を(に)払い戻す；に弁償する

be reimbursed in full　全額弁償される

---

A memo concerning safety will be sent to all **relevant** departments and sections.
安全に関するメモが関係部課すべてに送られるだろう。

**880 relevant**
[réləvənt]

形 関連した

relevant documents　関連書類

---

The obvious **remedy** for the company's cash flow problem is to increase the operating capital.
その会社のキャッシュフローの問題の明らかな改善法は，運用資金を増やすことだ。

**881 remedy**
[rémədi]

名 対策，改善法；治療；救済
他 を治療する；を修復する

have no remedy at law　法的には救済方法がない

Attempting to **renovate** an older building turned out to be more expensive than building a new one.
古い建物を修復しようとするのは，新しい建物を建てるよりも高くつくことが判明した。

### 882 renovate
[rénəvèit]

他 を刷新する；〈建物など〉を修繕〔改装〕する
⇒派 renovation 名 改装；刷新
renovate a building　建物を修復する

---

Multi-level marketing plans are dependent upon the fact that the products are not available in **retail** outlets.
マルチ商法計画は，小売販売店ではその商品が手に入らないという事実に頼っている。

### 883 retail
[ríːtèil]

名 小売　他 を売る　自 販売される
the retail price　小売価格

---

Independent farms seldom bring in enough **revenue** to support a family, so family members often take part-time or seasonal jobs.
私営農場では家族を養うほどの収入が得られないことがほとんどなので，家族のそれぞれはしばしばパートや季節労働をする。

### 884 revenue
[révən(j)ùː]

名 (総) 収入；歳入
an increase in revenue　増収
revenue and expenditure　収支

---

Birds make delightful pets, but they **scatter** their food and feathers all over their cages and can carry certain diseases.
小鳥はかわいいペットになるが，かご中に食べ物や羽をまき散らすし，ある種の病気を媒介する可能性がある。

### 885 scatter
[skǽtər]

他 をばらまく，まき散らす
scatter ~ with ...　〈場所〉に…をまき散らす

The institute had the yacht built to **specification** to accommodate their marine biology research program.
協会は海洋生物学の研究計画に適応させるために，ヨットを仕様書通りに作ってもらった。

**886 specification**
[spèsəfikéiʃən]

名 仕様書, 設計書；明細事項

specifications for a car　車の設計書

---

The client can **specify** the number and types of devices to be installed before delivery.
顧客は配達前に，設置される装置の数と型を具体的に挙げておくことができる。

**887 specify**
[spésəfài]

他 を詳細に述べる；…ということをはっきり述べる
→136 **specific**

specify two conditions　２つの条件を明示する

---

There is a warning printed on the cases that says not to **stack** them more than five feet high.
箱には，５フィート以上の高さにそれを積み上げないようにとの警告が印刷されている。

**888 stack**
[stǽk]

他 を積み上げる　名 積み重ね, 山
≒類 677 **pile** 名 積み重ね　他 を積み上げる

a neat stack of papers　きちんと積み重ねた書類

---

The new **stationery** has a mistake in the address so it will have to be sent back and replaced.
新しい便箋にある住所に誤りがあるので，返送して取り替えてもらわなければならない。

**889 stationery**
[stéiʃənèri]

名 文房具；便箋

hotel stationery　ホテルの便箋

The high school marching band is selling magazine **subscriptions** this year instead of their usual bake sale fundraiser.
高校の楽隊は，今年はいつもの焼き菓子販売による資金集めの代わりに雑誌の**予約購読**を売り込んでいる。

### 890 subscription
[səbskrípʃən]

名 **予約購読（料）；予約申し込み；会費**
⇒派 subscribe 自 **定期購読する** → 1102 subscriber
renew one's subscription 購読を更新する

---

Each month's statement includes a **summary** of account activity as well as a detailed report organized by type of transaction.
月々の計算書には，取引の種類によってまとめられた詳しい報告と同時に，口座の出入金の**要約**が含まれる。

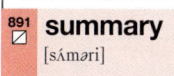

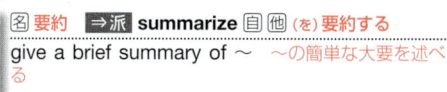

### 891 summary
[sʌ́məri]

名 **要約** ⇒派 summarize 自他 **(を)要約する**
give a brief summary of ～ ～の簡単な大要を述べる

---

There is a weekend magazine **supplement** in local newspapers that is very popular with high school current events teachers.
その地方紙には，高校の時事問題教師に人気のある週刊の**付録誌**が付いている。

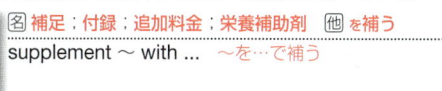

### 892 supplement
名 [sʌ́pləmənt]
動 [sʌ́pləmènt]

名 **補足；付録；追加料金；栄養補助剤** 他 **を補う**
supplement ～ with ... ～を…で補う

---

It looks as if the company's growth will **surpass** all expectations in the first year of business.
その会社の成長は初年度のあらゆる予想**を超える**ものになるようだ。

### 893 surpass
[sərpǽs]

他 **よりすぐれている；を超越する**
surpass all previous achievements すべての過去の業績を上回る

Even though the **tenant** refused to pay the rent increase, the owner was unable to get him out of the building.
賃借人は賃料の値上げ額の支払いを拒否したが，家主は立ち退きをさせられなかった。

**894 tenant**
[ténənt]
名 (家・土地・部屋などの) 賃借人
a prospective tenant　入居予定者

---

Either party can **terminate** the contract at any point after the first six months or after the sixth order.
いずれの当事者も，6か月あるいは6回発注後はいつでも契約を終了することができる。

**895 terminate**
[tə́ːrmənèit]
他 を終わらせる
terminate a lease　リースを解約する

---

The label clearly states that the cleaning agent is **toxic** and should be kept away from animals and children.
ラベルにはその掃除用洗剤は有毒で，動物や子どもに近づけてはいけないと明記してある。

**896 toxic**
[táksik]
形 毒性のある
toxic materials　毒性物質

---

Each **transaction** is recorded electronically and will be on the monthly statement; it can also be viewed online.
取引はそれぞれ電子的に記録され，毎月の計算書に掲載される。オンラインでも閲覧できる。

**897 transaction**
[trænsǽkʃən]
名 取引；(業務の) 処理
⇒派 transact 他〈取引〉を行う
bank transactions　銀行取引

The replacement parts are in transit; they can be tracked by logging on to the courier's Web site.

交換部品は輸送中だ。運送業者のウェブサイトにログオンすれば追跡調査ができる。

### 898 transit
[trǽnsət, -zət]

名 通過；輸送, 公共旅客輸送

a transit visa　通過ビザ
a transit route　公共輸送路

---

Cell phone transmissions are likely to break up in the mountains and in remote rural areas.

携帯電話の通信は山の中やへき地では切れることがある。

### 899 transmission
[trænsmíʃən, trænz-]

名 伝達；通信；送信　⇒派 transmit 他 を送信する

radio [television] transmission　ラジオ〔テレビ〕放送

---

In order to apply for the position, the applicant must have a valid driver's license and a clean driving record.

その職に応募するためには, 応募者には有効な運転免許証と, 違反のない運転歴が必要だ。

### 900 valid
[vǽlid]

形 〈契約・切符などが〉有効な
⇒派 validate 他 を有効にする
⇔反 invalid 形 無効の

a valid contract　法的に有効な契約

---

Ms. Preston and her staff have traveled around the country conducting workshops on building self-esteem.

プレストンさんと彼女の部下たちは, 全国を飛び回り, 自尊心を確立させるための講習会を実施してきた。

### 901 workshop
[wə́ːrkʃàp]

名 仕事場；研究会, 講習会

organize a workshop　研究会を主宰する

# Chapter 3-2 TOEIC特有の頻出語を覚える

学校英語 ▶▶▶ TOEIC® TEST　頻度★★

---

If you need your passport renewed quickly, you can pay an extra fee to have the government **accelerate** the process.
早急にパスポートの更新が必要なら，追加料金を払えば政府は手続き**を急い**でくれる。

**902 accelerate**
[əksélərèit, æk-]

他 を加速する；を早める　自 加速する

accelerate to ～　〈数値〉になるまで加速する
accelerated economic growth　加速する経済成長

---

On that SUV model, the screen that covers the back cargo area is considered an extra **accessory**.
そのSUV車モデルでは，後部の荷台を覆う仕切りは特別**付属品**と考えられている。

**903 accessory**
[əksésəri, æk-, ik-]

名 付属物，アクセサリー

a fashion accessory　アクセサリー

---

Personnel transferring in from headquarters are **accustomed** to much more sophisticated computer networking than we have.
本社から異動してきた社員は，我々よりずっと高度なコンピュータネットワークに**慣れ**ている。

**904 accustomed**
[əkʌ́stəmd]

形 慣れた　⇒派 accustom 他 を慣らす

be accustomed to ～　～に慣れている

---

The building **adjacent** to the main office is being redeveloped as an employee fitness center.
本社**隣の**ビルは，従業員用のフィットネスセンターとして再開発されている。

**905 adjacent**
[ədʒéisnt]

形 近くの；隣り合った

adjacent to ～　～に隣接した

---

Psychological statistics show that people who are **affluent** are not necessarily more content than other people.
心理学上の統計によると，**裕福な**人が必ずしも他人よりも満足感を感じているわけではない。

**906 affluent**
[ǽfluənt]

形 裕福な，豊かな

an affluent society　豊かな社会

The lawyer made a clear distinction between what the witness alleges happened and what can be proven.
その弁護士は，目撃者が事実だと主張する内容と，証明できる内容を明確に区別した。

**907 allege**
[əlédʒ]

他 を主張する
⇒派 **allegedly** 副 伝えられているところによると
be alleged to ...　…だと言われている

---

Many customers opt for our installment plan, as it alleviates the initial financial burden and makes purchases seem more affordable.
初期費用の負担が軽減され，購入しやすそうになるので，分割払い方式を選ぶ顧客が多い。

**908 alleviate**
[əlíːvièit]

他 をやわらげる，軽減する
alleviate suffering　苦しみを軽減する

---

The facilities chairman was concerned that he had not allocated enough booth space for the commercial display area.
施設の責任者は，商品展示ブースのスペースを十分確保しなかったことを懸念していた。

**909 allocate**
[æləkèit]

他 を(特別に)取っておく；を割り当てる
≒類 **allot** 他 を割り当てる
allocate ～ to ...　～を…に割り当てる

---

When passengers fly business class with our airlines, we give them an amenity kit with a tooth brush and razor to keep.
お客様が当社のビジネスクラスを利用される場合，歯ブラシとカミソリの入った便利用品セットを提供しております。

**910 amenity**
[əménəti, əmíːn-]

名 快適さ，アメニティ；生活を快適にするもの〔設備〕
shopping amenities　ショッピング施設

---

The authorities have placed the subject under arrest, but they can only hold him 24 hours with the evidence they have.
当局は本人を逮捕したが，当局が押さえている証拠では24時間しか拘留できない。

**911 arrest**
[ərést]

名 逮捕　他 を逮捕する
arrest a suspect　容疑者を逮捕する

If you are willing to work hard and have the ambition, you can surely **ascend** to the top of the company.
君に熱心に働く気があり大望があるなら，きっと会社のトップに上りつめられるだろう。

### 912 ascend
[əsénd]

自 登る；上昇する  他 に登る
⇔反 descend 自 降りる；減少する  他 を下る
ascend by the elevator　エレベーターで昇る

---

The price of oil is more than twice as much a **barrel** today as it was in 2001.
今日の1バレル当たりの原油の値段は，2001年当時の2倍以上だ。

### 913 barrel
[bǽrəl]

名 樽；バレル（容量の単位）
a barrel of beer　ビール1樽

---

The expense report says hotel expenses $1,450, but accounting needs a **breakdown** in terms of lodging, meals, etc.
その経費報告書ではホテル代が1,450ドルとなっているが，経理としては宿泊代，食事代などの内訳が必要だ。

### 914 breakdown
[bréikdàun]

名 故障；決裂；内訳，明細
a breakdown in negotiation　交渉の決裂

---

Our research was at a standstill for the longest time and then a scientist on the staff had a **breakthrough**.
研究は非常に長い間行き詰まっていたが，スタッフの1人の科学者が打開した。

### 915 breakthrough
[bréikθrù:]

名 （難問の）解決，打開；躍進
technological breakthrough　科学技術の大躍進

---

Even bringing a box of candy into that company to thank them for their business can be considered **bribery**.
仕事上のお礼でキャンディを1箱持っていくことすら，その会社では賄賂と見なされる。

### 916 bribery
[bráibəri]

名 贈賄，収賄
commit bribery　贈賄〔収賄〕する

Many organic seeds, grains, cereals and flours are available in **bulk** at the health food store.
その健康食品店では、多様な有機栽培の種や穀物、シリアル、小麦粉を**大量**に買える。

### 917 bulk
[bʌlk]

名 容積；かさ；**大量**
the bulk of ～　～の大部分

---

If anyone had **clarified** the assignment with the boss first, the team wouldn't have had to do the job twice.
もしだれかが上司と最初に割当て**を明確**にしていれば、チームは2度もその仕事をする必要はなかっただろう。

### 918 clarify
[klǽrəfài]

他 **を明らかにする**；を浄化する
clarify an issue　論争点をはっきりさせる

---

When the bill for February's electricity was four times higher than January's, it was clear there was a **clerical** error.
2月の電気代の請求が1月の4倍だったのは、明らかに**事務処理上**のミスだ。

### 919 clerical
[klérɪkl]

形 **事務の**
clerical work　事務の仕事

---

The classified ad states that pay is **commensurate** with ability and applicants with special experience will be compensated.
案内広告によると、給料は能力に**比例し**、専門の経験知識のある志願者には報酬が出る。

### 920 commensurate
[kəménsərət]

形 **釣り合った，同等の**；比例した
be commensurate with ～　～に釣り合っている

---

If the device was made before 1998, it does not **comply** with the new corporate standard and should be recycled.
その装置が1998年以前に作られていたら、新しい会社基準に**従って**いないため、再処理をする必要がある。

### 921 comply
[kəmplái]

自 〈規則・命令・要求などに〉**従う**
⇒派 compliance 名 従うこと，承諾
comply with ～　～に従う

Several of the volunteers have been unwilling to **conform** to the new director's rules and regulations.
ボランティアのうちの数人は，新しい理事のルールや規定に従う気がしなかった。

### 922 conform
[kənfɔ́ːrm]

自〈規則・慣習などに〉従う，順応する

conform to the rules　規則に従う

---

The editor-in-chief sent the reporter flowers to **congratulate** her for breaking the much sought-after story.
編集長は，大反響となった記事を報じたことでその記者を祝して花を贈った。

### 923 congratulate
[kəngrǽdʒəlèit, -grǽtʃə-]

他 を祝う　⇒派 congratulation 名 お祝いの言葉

congratulate ~ on [upon] ...　…のことで~にお祝いを言う

---

Reference books are located in two different rooms at the moment, but the librarian is attempting to **consolidate** them.
参考図書は現在別々の2部屋にあるが，図書館員はそれらを1つにしようとしている。

### 924 consolidate
[kənsάlidèit]

他 を合併する，統合する；を強固にする

a consolidated company　合同会社

---

After we **deduct** the cost of raw materials, labor and advertising, there is a very small profit margin.
原料費，人件費，広告費を差し引くと，利ざやはほとんど残らない。

### 925 deduct
[didʌ́kt]

他 を差し引く；を控除する

deduct ~ from ...　…から~を差し引く

---

In spite of the negotiator's best efforts, talks began to **deteriorate** in the late afternoon.
交渉人が最大限尽力したにもかかわらず，午後遅くに話し合いは悪化し始めた。

### 926 deteriorate
[ditíəriərèit]

自 悪くなる　他 を悪化させる

deteriorate into ~　~に悪化する

After trying to correct what we thought was a software problem, we finally got a **diagnosis** of faulty hardware.
ソフトの問題だと考えていたことの修正を試みたあとに，ついにハードに欠陥があるという分析を得た。

**927 diagnosis**
[dàiəgnóusis]
名 診断；分析
make a diagnosis　診断を行う

---

Matt is known to be a **diligent** worker and will be offered a promotion when his annual review comes up.
マットは勤勉な社員として知られ，年次評価書が出れば昇進を打診されるだろう。

**928 diligent**
[dílidʒənt]
形 勤勉な
be diligent in one's work　仕事に精励している

---

Because you will be working with confidential material, it's very important that you shred every document before you **discard** it.
あなたは機密資料を扱う仕事をするので，すべての書類を捨てる前にシュレッダーにかけることが非常に大切だ。

**929 discard**
動 [diská:rd]
名 [´- -]
他 を捨てる，処分する　名 捨てること，放棄
discard the data　データを破棄する

---

Applicants are not required to **disclose** any personal information, and you are not allowed to ask them any personal questions.
志願者はいかなる個人情報も明らかにする必要はなく，いかなる個人的な質問も志願者にしてはいけない。

**930 disclose**
[disklóuz]
他 を明らかにする，開示する
disclose a secret　秘密を暴露する

---

The size of the **down payment** will determine how much the monthly payments will be.
頭金の額で毎月の支払額がいくらになるかが決まることになる。

**931 down payment**
[dáun péimənt]
名 (分割払いの) 頭金
make a down payment on ～　～の頭金を支払う

The company hopes to **duplicate** the success it enjoyed with last year's line of product.

その企業は，前年の型の製品によって享受した成功を繰り返したいと望んでいる。

### 932 duplicate
動 [d(j)úːplikèit]
形名 [d(j)úːplikət]

他 を2倍にする；を複製する；を繰り返す　形 複製の　名 複製

in duplicate　正副2通で

---

The **durable** nature and superior quality of the product is what justifies its high price.

その製品の耐久性とすぐれた品質が，高価格を正当なものとしている。

### 933 durable
[d(j)úərəbl]

形 耐久性のある；永続する

durable goods　耐久財

---

It is the job of government to **embrace** the concerns of the people and help those people find solutions.

国民の懸念を受け止め，解決策を見出す手助けをするのが政府の責務である。

### 934 embrace
[embréis]

他 を受け入れる；を抱きしめる　名 抱擁

embrace an idea　ある案を採用する

---

The **eminent** Dr. Livingston was well respected for his dedication to his field and the contributions he made.

高名なリビングストン博士は，自らの分野への献身と貢献により，とても尊敬されていた。

### 935 eminent
[émənənt]

形 著名な，傑出した

be eminent for ～　～で有名である

---

Since Stephanie came to the job so highly qualified, she was given an **exemption** from the standard employee training program.

ステファニーは非常に高い技能を持ってその職に就いたため，標準的な従業員研修プログラムの免除を受けた。

### 936 exemption
[igzémpʃən, egz-]

名 課税控除（額）；免除

(a) tax exemption　免税

The craftsmanship has been described as **exquisite** in such magazines as *Fine Woodworking* and *Cabinetry International*.
その職人の技能は『ファイン・ウッドワーキング』や『キャビネトリー・インターナショナル』といった雑誌で見事だと評されている。

### 937 exquisite
[íkskwízit, ékskwizit]

形 この上なくすぐれた, 申し分のない；上品な

exquisite manners　優雅な振る舞い

---

The manufacturer has recalled all of the car seats manufactured between August and November due to inferior **fabric** quality.
その製造業者は布地の品質不良のために, 8月から11月の間に製造された車のシートをすべて回収した。

### 938 fabric
[fæbrik]

名 布地, 織物

weave a fabric　織物を織る

---

Even after more than 10 years of studying astronomy the subject continues to **fascinate** the researcher.
10年以上研究したあとでさえ, 天文学はその研究者を魅了し続ける。

### 939 fascinate
[fæsənèit]

他 を魅了する

be fascinated by [with] ～　～に引き付けられている

---

Employees are required to take breaks on a regular basis because **fatigue** is the greatest cause of industrial accidents.
疲労が業務災害の最大の原因であるため, 従業員は定期的な休憩が義務付けられている。

### 940 fatigue
[fətíːg]

名 疲労(感)　他 を疲れさせる

physical fatigue　肉体的な疲れ

---

Increasing the advertising budget is simply not **feasible** until we can be assured of the product's success.
製品の成功が確信できるまで, 広告費の予算増加はまったく実現可能ではない。

### 941 feasible
[fíːzəbl]

形 実現可能な

a feasible plan　実行可能な計画

Although some dog breeds have a reputation of being **fierce**, how they are trained is what really determines their behavior.
ある品種の犬は獰猛であると言われるが，実際にはどんな訓練を受けるかが習性を決める。

### 942 fierce
[fíərs]

形 荒々しい，獰猛な；激しい

fierce competition　激しい競争

---

We will be able to **finalize** the transaction after all parties have submitted the necessary documents.
すべての当事者が必要書類を提出したあと，取引を最終決定することができるだろう。

### 943 finalize
[fáinəlàiz]

他 を最終決定する；を仕上げる

finalize the agreement　契約を最終決定する

---

Company policy explicitly **forbids** people from the same family working in the same department.
会社の規則は，家族同士が同じ部署で働くことをはっきりと禁じている。

### 944 forbid
[fərbíd, fɔːr-]

他 を禁じる；を差し止める

forbid ～ from ...ing　～が…することを禁じる

---

Experts believe that the **garment** in this case here was worn by ancient religious leaders.
専門家は，この箱の中の衣服は古代の宗教指導者が着ていたものだと信じている。

### 945 garment
[gáːrmənt]

名 衣服 (特にメーカーの用語)
≒類 **apparel** 名 衣服

garment industry　服飾業

---

Market research firms help manufacturers **gauge** consumer reaction to new products before they are made available to the public.
市場調査会社は，新製品が一般に入手可能となる前に，製造業者がそれらへの消費者の反応を測る手助けをする。

### 946 gauge
[géidʒ]

他 を計測する；を判断する，見積もる　名 規格；計器

an oil pressure gauge　油圧計

Grab a notebook and come down to the storeroom where the person in charge will explain the inventory system.
ノートをつかんで，貯蔵室に降りて来なさい。担当者が在庫システムを説明します。

**947 grab** [grǽb]
他をつかむ；の注意を引き付ける，〈食事〉をさっと取る
grab a quick lunch　昼食をさっとすませる

---

The fare will be less if you hail a cab on the south side of the Union Street.
ユニオン通りの南側でタクシーを呼び止めれば，運賃は安くなります。

**948 hail** [héil]
他を呼び止める；を歓迎する　名ひょう，あられ
hail a taxi　タクシーを呼び止める
have hail　ひょうが降る

---

The company was forced to halt production when more than half of the workers walked off the job.
その会社は，半数以上の従業員が退社したとき，製造を停止せざるを得なかった。

**949 halt** [hɔ́:lt, hɑ́:lt]
他を止める　自止まる　名停止
bring ~ to a halt　~を止まらせる；~を中止させる

---

The telephone will make a loud beeping noise if you don't hang it up properly.
きちんと切らないと，その電話はビーという大きな音を出す。

**950 hang up**
他〈電話〉を切る；〈コートなど〉を掛ける
自電話を切る
hang up on ~　~の電話を一方的に切る

---

The harsh weather conditions made it impossible for the children to play outside on the weekend.
厳しい天候状況のせいで，子どもたちは週末屋外で遊ぶことができなかった。

**951 harsh** [hɑ́:rʃ]
形厳しい，過酷な
harsh realities　過酷な現実

The chemical spill on the highway was determined to be a **hazard** to the surrounding community.
幹線道路に流出した化学物質は，周辺地域に**危険を及ぼすもの**だと確定された。

### 952 hazard
[hǽzərd]

名 危険，危険要素

a health hazard　健康に有害な要因
fire hazard　火災の危険のあるもの

---

Thousands of people were hired in order to **implement** the new security measures at airports.
何千人という人が空港で新しい警備措置**を実施する**ために雇われた。

### 953 implement
動 [ímpləmènt]
名 [-mənt]

他 を実行する，実施する　名 道具；手段

agricultural implements　農機具

---

Some U.S. companies choose to **incorporate** in Nevada or Delaware, because the corporate tax structure is more favorable there.
ネバダ州かデラウェア州で**合併する**ことを選ぶアメリカの会社もある。なぜならそこでの法人税の体系がより望ましいものだからだ。

### 954 incorporate
[inkɔ́ːrpərèit]

自 合併する　他 を組み入れる；を合併する；を法人化する

become incorporated with ～　～と合併する
incorporate a firm　会社を法人組織にする

---

In this type of consumer-driven business, the information gained from good market research is **indispensable**.
この手の消費者主導の商売では，すぐれた市場調査から得られる情報が**欠かせない**。

### 955 indispensable
[ìndispénsəbl]

形 欠くことのできない；避けられない

things indispensable to life　生活必需品

---

It is reasonable to **infer** from the statements he made that management is seriously considering reorganizing the sales department.
彼の発言から，経営陣が販売部の再編を真剣に検討している**と推測する**のは妥当だ。

### 956 infer
[infə́ːr]

他 を推測する

infer (that) ...　…と推測する

The company truly needs an **injection** of capital, which is why they are approaching potential investors.
その企業は本当に資本注入が必要で、そのため彼らは可能性のある投資家に接触している。

### 957 injection
[indʒékʃən]

图 注射；注入（物）

administer [give] the drug by injection　注射で薬を投与する

---

The boss would never **jeopardize** his position in the firm by doing anything that would appear to be unethical.
上司は、倫理に反するようなことをして会社での地位を危うくすることは決してないだろう。

### 958 jeopardize
[dʒépərdàiz]

他 を危険にさらす

jeopardize one's fortune　財産を危険にさらす

---

The new environmental **legislation** is good for the trees, but bad for our business.
環境に関する新しい法律は、木にはよいが我々のビジネスには都合が悪い。

### 959 legislation
[lèdʒisléiʃən]

图 法律；法律の制定、立法

under current legislation　現行法の下では

---

The company could have **liability** for accidents that happened with its vehicles.
その企業の車に起きた事故に対する責任は企業自身にあったのかもしれない。

### 960 liability
[làiəbíləti]

图 責任、負担；負債；不都合なもの

the limit of liability　〈保険の〉最高責任額

---

The company created a **liaison** office to handle affairs with its business partners in China.
その会社は中国の提携先との業務をこなすために、連絡事務所を作った。

### 961 liaison
[liéizn]

图 連絡；連絡役

a liaison office　連絡事務所

Despite his intelligence and his achievements, his modest manner made him popular among the employees.
彼は知性と実績があるにもかかわらず，謙虚な態度なので社員に人気があった。

### 962 modest
[mɑ́dəst]

形 謙虚な，控えめな；質素な
a modest house　質素な住まい

---

We hoped our innovative new products would end the monopoly held by our competitor.
当社の革命的な新製品が，競合他社による独占状態を終わらせることを願っていた。

### 963 monopoly
[mənɑ́pəli]

名 独占(権)；専売会社，独占企業
⇒派 monopolize 他 を独占する
have a monopoly on ～　～の独占権を持っている

---

The recent setbacks had taken its toll on the morale of the workers in my department.
最近の後退は，当部署の社員の士気に大きな悪影響を及ぼした。

### 964 morale
[mərǽl]

名 士気，やる気
high [low] morale　高い〔低い〕士気

---

Technology that is obsolete here in the U.S. may still be useful in another country.
ここアメリカではすたれた技術も，ほかの国ではまだ役に立つかもしれない。

### 965 obsolete
[ɑ̀bsəlíːt, ́--́]

形 旧式の，すたれた　≒類 967 outdated 形 すたれた
obsolete equipment　老朽設備

---

A power outage at one of our factories brought production to a halt for an entire day.
我が社の工場の1つで起こった停電のせいで，丸1日生産が止まった。

### 966 outage
[áutidʒ]

名 (電気・ガス・水道などの)供給停止，停電
a power outage　停電

If we don't modernize our **outdated** inventory system, we're going to be in big trouble.
我が社の**時代遅れの**在庫管理システムを最新式にしなければ，大変なことになるだろう。

**967 outdated**
[àutdéitid]

形 すたれた；時代遅れの

outdated thinking　時代遅れの考え方

---

This time, not even his positive **outlook** was enough to lift the spirits of his co-workers.
今回は，彼の肯定的な**見解**ですら同僚たちの士気を高めるのに十分ではなかった。

**968 outlook**
[áutlùk]

名 見解，態度；見通し；見晴らし

one's positive outlook　積極的な態度

---

My foreign friend exclaimed that the costs of doing business in this country are **outrageous**.
私の外国人の友人は，この国で事業をするコストは**法外だ**と叫んだ。

**969 outrageous**
[àutréidʒəs]

形 許しがたい；法外な；突拍子もない

an outrageous remark　言語道断な言葉

---

Determining the **overhead** costs of a new business is not always an exact science.
新事業の**間接費**を決めることは，常に正確な科学だというわけではない。

**970 overhead**
名形 [óuvərhèd]
副 [´-´]

名 間接費　形 頭上の；一切を含めた；間接費としての
副 頭上に

reduce overhead costs　間接費を削減する

---

The billionaire CEO of the Internet startup was also an avid **patron** of the arts.
インターネット新興企業の億万長者のCEOは，熱心な芸術**後援者**でもあった。

**971 patron**
[péitrən]

名 常連客；後援者　⇒派 patronage 名 後援；愛顧

a patron of the arts　芸術の後援者

These days many people are reluctant to rely solely on government **pension** plans after retirement.

今日では、退職後に政府の年金制度だけに頼ることを渋る人が多い。

### 972 pension
[pénʃən]

名 年金

defined-benefit pension plan　確定給付年金制度

---

**Perishable** products require us to spend money on good refrigeration and quick delivery.

腐りやすい食品には、すぐれた冷蔵設備と迅速な配送に経費をかける必要がある。

### 973 perishable
[périʃəbl]

形 腐りやすい

perishable goods　腐りやすい商品

---

In the **preceding** two quarters we saw our profits increase by more than 50%.

これまでの半年間に、我々の利益は50パーセント以上増加した。

### 974 preceding
[prisí:diŋ]

形 前の；前述の　⇒派 **precede** 他 より先に起こる

the preceding page　前のページ

---

My **preferred** method of public transportation is the subway rather than the bus.

私の好みの公共交通機関はバスよりも地下鉄だ。

### 975 preferred
[prifə́:rd]

形 優先の；気に入った、好ましい
⇒派 **prefer** 他 のほうを好む

preferred stock　優先株

---

**Preliminary** tests show that the new batteries last twice as long as the previous model.

先行テストで、新しい電池は前のモデルの2倍長持ちすることがわかっている。

### 976 preliminary
[prilímənèri]

形 予備の；準備の；仮の；前置きの

a preliminary notice　予告
a preliminary application form　事前申込書

We believe people will pay a **premium** for something that is well-designed and reliable.
人々はすぐれた設計で信頼できるものには割増金を払うと我々は信じている。

### 977 premium
[príːmiəm]

名 保険料；割増料金；奨励金
give a premium for ～　～に対して報奨金を出す
insurance premiums　保険料

---

His failure was that he **presumed** that he was smarter than everyone around him.
彼の失敗は、自分が周囲のだれよりも利口だと決めてかかったことだ。

### 978 presume
[priz(j)úːm]

他 と想定する；厚かましくも…する；を前提とする
⇒派 presumable 形 ありそうな
presumably 副 おそらく

---

It's **probable**, but not likely, that the stock market bubble could burst tomorrow.
株式市場のバブルが明日はじけるということはあり得るが、ありそうではない。

### 979 probable
[prɑ́bəbl, prɑ́bl]

形 十分ありそうな、起こりそうな
⇒派 probably 副 たぶん、おそらく
a probable consequence　十分に考えられる結果

---

**Proximity** of the warehouses to the stores makes a big difference in how fast the products can be delivered.
店舗への倉庫の近さにより、商品がどれだけ速く配送されるかに大きな違いが出る。

### 980 proximity
[prɑksíməti]

名 近さ
in close proximity of ～　～のすぐ近くに

---

He was more than **qualified** on paper, but his temperament led us to believe he was not fit for the job.
彼は書類上は非常に適任だが、性格的にはその仕事に向いていないと考えさせられた。

### 981 qualified
[kwɑ́ləfaid]

形 有資格の；有能な、適任の
a fully-qualified doctor　資格を満たしている医師

Sometimes it seems like the production manager is on a mad **quest** to increase efficiency.

時々，生産部部長は効率を上げようという異常な追求に駆られているように見える。

**982 quest**
[kwést]

名 追求, 探求, 探索

a quest for efficiency　効率性の追求

---

Every sales person in the store has a sales **quota** he or she has to meet in order to get a raise.

その店の販売員全員が，昇給を得るのに必要な販売ノルマを与えられている。

**983 quota**
[kwóutə]

名 持分, 割当, ノルマ

exceed the quota　割当を超える
meet one's quarterly sales quota　四半期の売上ノルマを達成する

---

**Randomly** choosing which companies' stock to buy is probably not a good investment strategy.

どの会社の株を買うかを無作為に選ぶのは，おそらくうまい投資戦略ではないだろう。

**984 randomly**
[rǽndəmli]

副 無作為に, でたらめに　⇒派 random 形 任意の

choose a number randomly　無作為に数字を選ぶ

---

DigiPlay software is offering a $20 **rebate** if you purchase their software by the end of September.

9月末までにソフトを買えば，デジプレイソフトウェア社は20ドルの払い戻しをしている。

**985 rebate**
名 [ríːbeit]
動 [ribéit]

名 〈支払われた金額の〉一部払い戻し, 割り戻し
他 を払い戻す

a rebate for paying in cash　現金払いに対する割り戻し

---

I **recruited** the best people inside and outside of the company that I could find for the operation.

私はその事業のために，社内外から見つけられる限り最高の人材を新しく入れた。

**986 recruit**
[rikrúːt]

他 を新規に採用する

recruit ～ into ...　～を新たに…に入れる

After listening to four hours of lectures, everyone was ready for some **refreshments**.
4時間講義を聴き続けたあとで,みんな飲食物に飢えていた。

**987 refreshment**
[rifréʃmənt]

名 飲食物；休息,気分転換
⇒派 refresh 他 を爽快な気分にする

(a) between-meals refreshment 間食

---

**Regrettably** management has been forced to make severe cuts to our work force.
残念なことに,経営側は我が社の人員を厳しく削減せざるを得なかった。

**988 regrettably**
[rigrétəbli]

副 残念なくらい；遺憾ながら
⇒派 regret 他 を後悔する
≒類 unfortunately 副 残念ながら

---

Former U.S. president Jimmy Carter and his wife are **renowned** as human rights activists and peace negotiators.
合衆国の元大統領ジミー・カーターとその夫人は,人権活動家,そして平和交渉者として名高い。

**989 renowned**
[rináund]

形 名声ある ⇒派 renown 名 名声

renowned as ～　～として名高い

---

After the ground-breaking ceremony at the building site, everybody got in their **respective** cars and returned to work.
建築現場での起工式のあと,みんなはそれぞれの車に乗って仕事に戻った。

**990 respective**
[rispéktiv]

形 それぞれの　⇒派 respectively 副 それぞれ

according to one's respective abilities　それぞれの能力に応じて

---

It was clear that the lawyer could barely **restrain** himself from arguing with the judge over his ruling.
弁護士は,判事の判決に反論するのを抑えることがほとんど不可能なのは明らかだった。

**991 restrain**
[ristréin]

他 を制止する；を抑える

restrain oneself from ～　(自制して)～しない

It's a good idea to be **skeptical** of a business deal that sounds too good to be true.
信じがたいほど魅力のありそうなビジネス取引については疑い深くあるのが得策だ。

### 992 skeptical
[sképtikl]

形 疑い深い, 懐疑的な

be skeptical of ～　～を疑っている

---

For many years the Sears Tower in Chicago held the honor as the world's tallest **skyscraper**.
何年間も、シカゴのシアーズタワーは世界で最も高い高層ビルだという名誉を保っていた。

### 993 skyscraper
[skáiskrèipər]

名 超高層ビル, 摩天楼

a skyscraper hotel　超高層ホテル

---

As soon as the price of oil went up, prices at local gas pumps **soared**.
石油の価格が上がるとすぐに、地元の給油ポンプにおける価格も急に上昇した。

### 994 soar
[sɔ́ːr]

自 急に上昇する；舞い上がる

soar by 30%　30パーセントも急に上がる

---

The tourists from Mexico were amazed by the **spectacular** display that the northern lights presented.
メキシコからの旅行者たちは、オーロラが与える壮大なショーに驚いていた。

### 995 spectacular
[spektǽkjələr]

形 壮観な, めざましい　名 壮大なショー

a spectacular advertisement　はなばなしい広告

---

Mr. Jenkins has no interest in golf as a **spectator**, but he loves to play and does so often.
ジェンキンズ氏は観客としてはゴルフに関心がないが、自分がやるのは好きでよくやる。

### 996 spectator
[spékteitər, -–́–]

名 観客；傍観者, 目撃者

a mere spectator　単なる傍観者

What appeared to be a **stain** on the factory floor was actually an oil spill.
工場のフロアに**しみ**のように見えていた物は，実際はこぼれた油だった。

### 997 stain
[stéin]

图 汚れ, しみ　他 を汚す
an ink stain　インクのしみ
get a stain　しみをつける

---

The state's **stance** on illegal drug use is no tolerance, which means offenders are prosecuted fully.
その州の違法な薬物使用についての**姿勢**は「許容せず」である。すなわち，違反者は確実に起訴されるということだ。

### 998 stance
[stæns]

图 立場, 姿勢
take a cautious stance on ～　～に慎重な姿勢をとる

---

Scrap metal is a **staple** of the foundry and they are always shopping the international market for new sources.
くず鉄は鋳造業の**原料**であり，彼らは常に新しい資源を求めて国際市場を探している。

### 999 staple
[stéipl]

图 主要産物；原料；ホッチキスの針　形 主要な
他 をホッチキスで留める　⇒派 stapler 图 ホッチキス
a staple commodity　主要製品

---

Instead of installing **stationary** work stations, they will be built with heavy duty wheels that lock.
**常置の**ワークステーションを設置する代わりに，ロックできる重い車輪が取り付けられる。

### 1000 stationary
[stéiʃənèri]

形 静止した；常備の
a stationary bicycle　静止自転車，エアロバイク

---

There's a **stunning** view of the downtown area and the harbor from the new office building.
新しい社屋からは，町の中心街と港が**はっとするほど美しく**見える。

### 1001 stunning
[stÁniŋ]

形 とても魅力的な；驚くべき
a stunning success　実に見事な成功

The personnel director suggested that Mr. Kelly was more suitable for a subordinate position than management.

人事部長は，ケリー氏は経営者よりも部下としての地位のほうが向いていると示唆した。

**1002 subordinate**
[səbɔ́ːrdənət]

形 〈地位が〉下の；部下の　名 部下
a subordinate position　下位

---

The insurance investigator must substantiate the claim before the claims adjustor can begin calculating the payout.

保険の調査員は，請求の精算員が支払い計算を始める前に請求を実証せねばならない。

**1003 substantiate**
[səbstǽnʃièit]

他 を実証する；を具体化する
substantiate an idea through action　考えを行動で表す

---

By taking the tax credit option, the company can subtract any interest paid on property loans from their taxable income.

税額控除を選択することによって，会社は課税所得から資産ローンに支払ったあらゆる利子を引くことができる。

**1004 subtract**
[səbtrǽkt]

他 を引く，控除する　自 引き算する
subtract 2 from 5　5から2を引く

---

After a major disaster it's not unusual for the stock market to suspend trading for a short time.

大災害のあと，株式市場が短期間取引を中止するのは珍しくない。

**1005 suspend**
[səspénd]

他 を停止する；を停職〔停学〕処分にする；を吊り下げる
自 支払いを停止する
suspend payment　支払いを中止する

---

After systematically eliminating the obvious possibilities, the firm hired an investigator to determine the source of the security leak.

その会社は，自明の可能性を体系的な方法で排除したあと，情報漏洩のもとを特定するのに調査官を雇った。

**1006 systematically**
[sìstəmǽtikəli]

副 組織的に，体系的に
⇒派 systematic 形 系統立った，体系的な
survey ～ systematically　～を組織的に調査する

At this point only a **tentative** schedule is available; the dates should be confirmed by next week.
現時点では仮のスケジュールしかできていません。日程は来週までに確定します。

**1007 tentative**
[téntətiv]

形 仮の, 一時的な；ためらいがちな

reach a tentative agreement　仮の合意に達する

---

The witness's **testimony** contradicted statements made earlier, so it is up to the jury to decide what the truth is.
証人の証言はそれ以前の陳述と矛盾したので，何が真実かを決定するのは陪審員次第だ。

**1008 testimony**
[téstəmòuni]

名 証言；証拠

call ~ in testimony　~を証言に立たせる

---

The consulting firm guarantees that your business will **thrive** if you sign up for their services and follow their advice.
そのコンサルタント会社は，サービスに登録して助言に従えば事業が繁盛すると約束している。

**1009 thrive**
[θráiv]

自 成長する；繁栄する　⇔類 flourish 自 繁栄する

have a thriving business　事業がうまくいっている

---

The speaker is famous for blazing a **trail** into the computer industry at a very young age.
講演者は，非常に若いときにコンピュータ産業に道を開いたことで有名だ。

**1010 trail**
[tréil]

名 道；跡　他 のあとを追う
⇒派 trailer 名 トレーラー

leave a trail　痕跡を残す

---

A **transcript** of the meeting will be sent to all board members that were unable to attend.
会議記録は出席できなかった重役全員に送られる。

**1011 transcript**
[trænskript]

名 音声言語を書き取ったもの；記録；写し；謄本

a transcript of a lecture　講義録

During the **transition** period, the new owners of the company required old employees to take retraining seminars.

移行期間中，会社の新しいオーナーは以前からいた社員たちに再訓練セミナーを受講するように要請した。

### 1012 transition
[trænzíʃən, -síʃən]

名 移り変わり，推移；過渡期

transition into a market economy　市場経済への移行
be in transition　過渡期にある

---

The company credits its low employee **turnover** to flex time and on site day care for employees' children.

その会社は，従業員の離職率の低さはフレックスタイムと，社員の子ども用の職場託児所のおかげだとしている。

### 1013 turnover
[tə́ːrnòuvər]

名 回転率；離職率

make a quick turnover　商品の回転を速くする

---

The vote was **unanimous** to renew the CEO's contract at the end of the year.

投票は，そのCEOの契約を年末に更新することで全員一致だった。

### 1014 unanimous
[ju(ː)nǽnəməs]

形 満場一致の；同意見の

a unanimous conclusion　全員一致でまとまった結論

---

In an **unprecedented** move the president hired a consulting company to evaluate and reorganize the firm.

先例のない動きだが，社長は会社を評価し立て直すためにコンサルタント会社を雇った。

### 1015 unprecedented
[ʌnprésidəntid]

形 先例のない；空前の

on unprecedented scale　史上最大規模で

---

This year's conference is expected to be well attended because the **venue** is a resort hotel in Florida.

今年の会議は開催地がフロリダのリゾートホテルなので，多くの参加者が見込まれる。

### 1016 venue
[vénjuː]

名 開催地，会場；裁判地

a suitable venue　適当な開催地

The operator will **verify** that the customer is calling from a registered line and then begin the transaction.
オペレーターは顧客が登録された電話からかけていること**を確認**してから処理を始める。

**1017 verify**
[vérəfài]
他 を実証する；が正しいかどうかを確かめる
⇒派 **verification** 名 立証
verify calculations　計算結果を確かめる

---

Meetings between the director of sales and the director of customer service are usually **volatile**.
営業部長と顧客サービス部長の会議はいつも**一触即発**である。

**1018 volatile**
[vάlətl]
形 変わりやすい；揮発性の；一触即発の
a volatile situation　不安定な情勢

---

Without the proper insurance coverage the company would be **vulnerable** to lawsuits that could destroy them.
適正な保険補償がなかったら，会社は壊滅させられかねない訴訟に対して**弱い**だろう。

**1019 vulnerable**
[vÁlnərəbl]
形 傷つきやすい，脆弱な
be vulnerable to ～　～に対して傷つきやすい

---

The manufacturer will **waive** the repair fees because the product was damaged when it was delivered.
製品が配送されたときにすでに壊れていたため，製造業者は修理代金**を取らない**だろう。

**1020 waive**
[wéiv]
他 を放棄する；を延期する
waive one's right　権利を放棄する

---

The company will **withhold** state and federal taxes, health insurance and pension payments from each paycheck.
会社は各人の給料から州税および国税と健康保険，年金の支払い**を天引きする**。

**1021 withhold**
[wiðhóuld, wiθ-]
他 (税金など)を源泉徴収する，天引きする
a withholding tax　源泉徴収税

## Chapter 4

# TOEIC 形式の長文で覚える

4-1 Part 4 形式
4-2 Part 7 形式

# Chapter 4-1　TOEIC 形式の長文で覚える

**学校英語 ▶▶▶ TOEIC® TEST　　Part 4 形式**

Chapter 4 では，実際の TOEIC（Part 4, Part 7）形式の英文の中で単語を覚えます。単語学習をしながら，TOEIC 頻出の話題にも慣れておきましょう。

各英文には，TOEIC でも出題される類義語を問う語彙問題がついています。学んだ単語がしっかり身についているか，確認しましょう。

## 1　Announcement 1　院内放送

May I have your **attention**, please?　Visiting hours will end in **approximately** thirty minutes, at 8:30.　We would like to take this **opportunity** to remind you not to use cell phones in the **hallways**, on the Intensive Care floor or anywhere on floor B1, as your phone may **interfere** with hospital **equipment** or **disturb patients**.　You may use cell phones in the rooms of patients who are not on **vital** support systems or in the **designated** area on the lobby floor.　Thank you.　　　　　　　　　　　　　　　　　　　　　　(83 words)

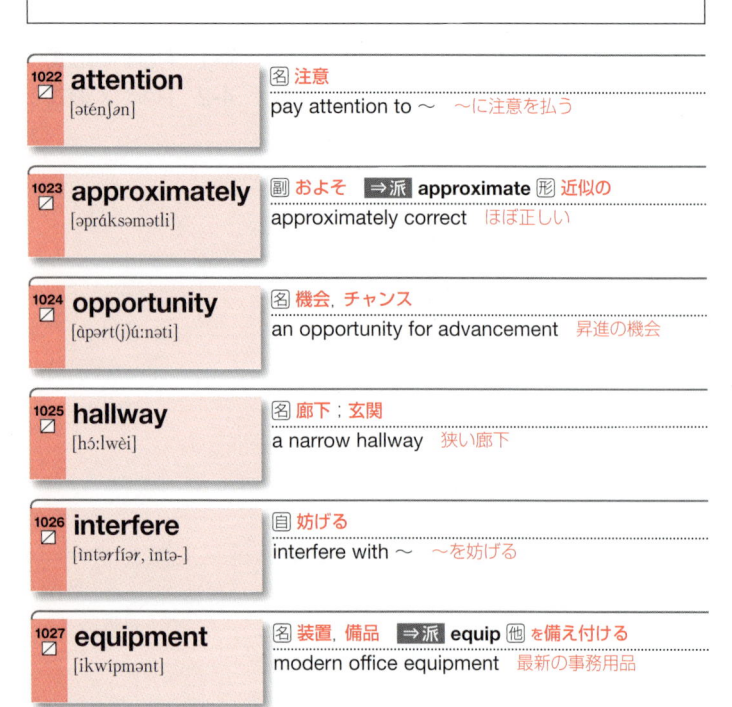

---

**1022　attention**
[əténʃən]

名 注意

pay attention to ～　～に注意を払う

---

**1023　approximately**
[əpráksəmətli]

副 およそ　⇒派 approximate 形 近似の

approximately correct　ほぼ正しい

---

**1024　opportunity**
[ὰpərt(j)ú:nəti]

名 機会，チャンス

an opportunity for advancement　昇進の機会

---

**1025　hallway**
[hɔ́:lwèi]

名 廊下；玄関

a narrow hallway　狭い廊下

---

**1026　interfere**
[ìntərfíər, ìntə-]

自 妨げる

interfere with ～　～を妨げる

---

**1027　equipment**
[ikwípmənt]

名 装置，備品　⇒派 equip 他 を備え付ける

modern office equipment　最新の事務用品

ご案内申し上げます（＝注目していただけますでしょうか）。面会時間はおよそ30分後の8時半に終了します。この機会に，再度お願い申し上げます。携帯電話は院内の機器の障害となったり，患者様にご迷惑をおかけすることがございますので，廊下，集中治療室の階，地下1階全域においてご使用をお控えください。生命維持装置を使用されていない患者様の病室と，ロビー階の所定の場所では携帯電話をご使用いただけます。よろしくお願い申し上げます。

---

**1028 disturb**
[distə́:rb]

他 を乱す；に迷惑をかける；を不安にする
⇒派 **disturbance** 名 不安；混乱
be disturbed at [by] ～　～で心配する

**1029 patient**
[péiʃənt]

名 患者　形 忍耐強い
⇔反 ²⁰¹ **impatient** 形 我慢できない
be patient with ～　〈人〉に我慢する

**1030 vital**
[váitl]

形 生命の；必要不可欠な
⇒派 **vitally** 副 生命上；絶対に
a vital part　生命にかかわる急所

**1031 designate**
[dézignèit]

他 を指し示す；を（～に）指名する，指定する
designate a chairperson　議長を指名する

---

**Q** The word "designated" in line 7 is closest in meaning to
(A) specified
(B) nominated
(C) elected
(D) scheduled

解答は p. 336

## 2 Announcement 2　店内放送

Good afternoon ladies and gentlemen. Thank you for shopping with us at Dooley's Discount Emporium today. There is a gray Toyota Corolla, license plate HAV 430, **blocking** the **emergency** exit. Please move your **vehicle** immediately. We are running an in-store special on **detergent**. All **brands** of **laundry** detergent, including Natural Wonder, our latest **environmentally**-friendly product, are as much as 50% off! All of our **household** cleaning products are at the back of the store on **aisles** 23 and 24. Thank you. (81 words)

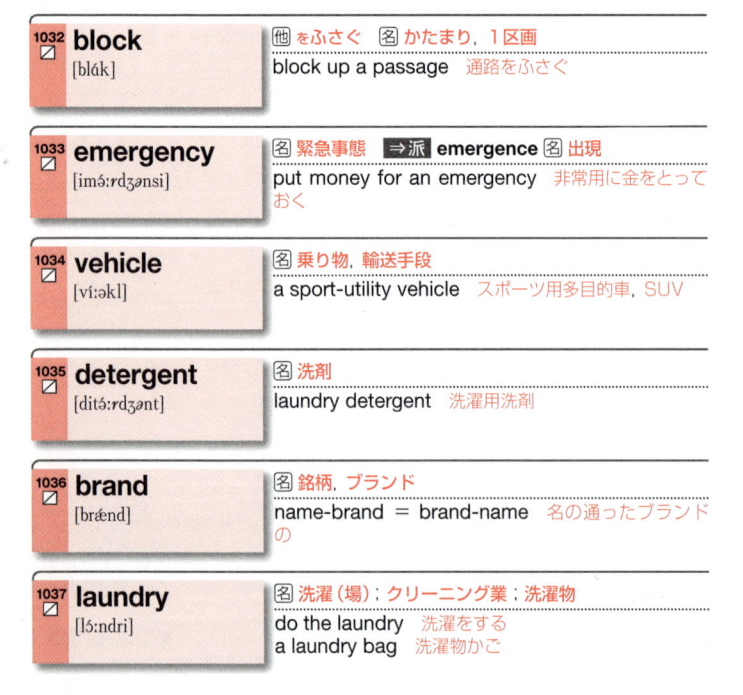

---

**1032 block** [blák]
他 をふさぐ　名 かたまり，1区画
block up a passage　通路をふさぐ

**1033 emergency** [imə́ːrdʒənsi]
名 緊急事態　⇒派 emergence 名 出現
put money for an emergency　非常用に金をとっておく

**1034 vehicle** [víːəkl]
名 乗り物，輸送手段
a sport-utility vehicle　スポーツ用多目的車，SUV

**1035 detergent** [ditə́ːrdʒənt]
名 洗剤
laundry detergent　洗濯用洗剤

**1036 brand** [brǽnd]
名 銘柄，ブランド
name-brand = brand-name　名の通ったブランドの

**1037 laundry** [lɔ́ːndri]
名 洗濯（場）；クリーニング業；洗濯物
do the laundry　洗濯をする
a laundry bag　洗濯物かご

皆様，こんにちは。本日はドゥーリーのディスカウント商店でお買い物くださいまして，ありがとうございます。グレーのトヨタカローラ，ナンバープレート HAV430 が**非常口をふさいでいます**。ただちにお**車**の移動をお願いいたします。当店では，店内にて**洗剤**の特別セールを行っております。当店の最新の**環境に**やさしい製品，ナチュラルワンダーを含むすべての**銘柄**の**洗濯**洗剤が 50 パーセントもお得！**家庭**洗剤類はすべて店内奥の 23 番と 24 番**通路**にございます。ありがとうございます。

---

### 1038 environmentally
[envài*r*nméntli]

副 環境保護に関して　⇒派 **environment** 名 環境
**environmental** 形 環境（保護）の
environmental preservation　環境保全

### 1039 household
[háushòuld, háusòuld]

名 世帯　形 家庭の
a large household　大所帯

### 1040 aisle
[áil]

名 通路
an aisle seat　通路側の席
on the aisle　〈座席が〉通路側の

---

**Q** The word "blocking" in line 3 is closest in meaning to
(A) shaping
(B) joining
(C) obstructing
(D) collecting

解答は p. 336

## 3 Speech 1　退職のあいさつ

As I stand here today announcing my retirement, I am filled with **vivid** memories of the past fifty years at the company. I will **refrain** from boring you with all my stories, but I will remind you that even if you see a very young person's face **staring** back at you in the mirror today, in due course you will be standing up here yourself one day. I am **grateful** to have had the opportunity to **collaborate** with some of the best talent in our industry. Although the market tends to **fluctuate**, I am **optimistic** that through its strong vision this organization will continue to enjoy success and **prosperity**. Thank you.　　　　　　　　　　　　　　　　　　　　　　(111 words)

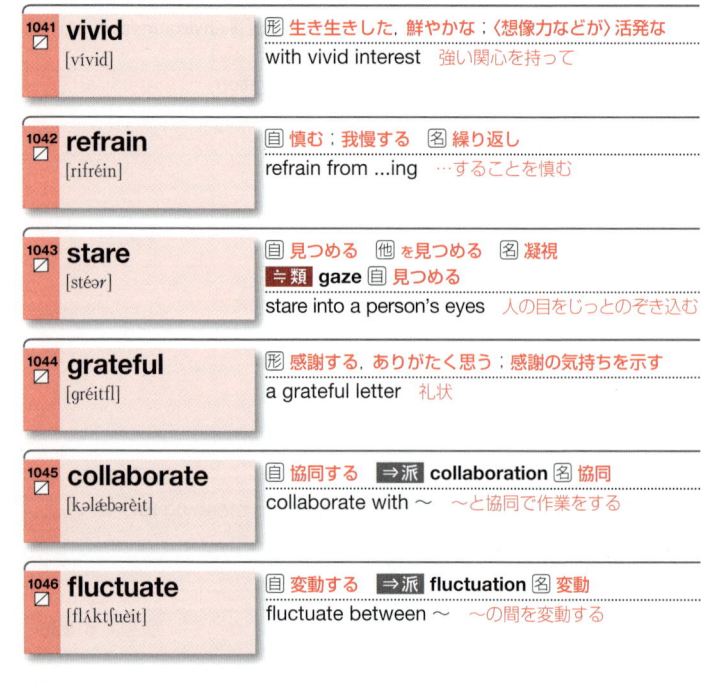

---

**1041 vivid**
[vívid]
形 生き生きした，鮮やかな；〈想像力などが〉活発な
with vivid interest　強い関心を持って

**1042 refrain**
[rifréin]
自 慎む；我慢する　名 繰り返し
refrain from ...ing　…することを慎む

**1043 stare**
[stéər]
自 見つめる　他 を見つめる　名 凝視
≒類 **gaze** 自 見つめる
stare into a person's eyes　人の目をじっとのぞき込む

**1044 grateful**
[gréitfl]
形 感謝する，ありがたく思う；感謝の気持ちを示す
a grateful letter　礼状

**1045 collaborate**
[kəlǽbərèit]
自 協同する　⇒派 **collaboration** 名 協同
collaborate with ～　～と協同で作業をする

**1046 fluctuate**
[flʌ́ktʃuèit]
自 変動する　⇒派 **fluctuation** 名 変動
fluctuate between ～　～の間を変動する

本日，退職のごあいさつにここに立っておりますと，会社でのこの50年間の鮮やかな思い出で胸がいっぱいになります。私の思い出話で皆さんを退屈させることは控えますが，たとえ現在は鏡を見ると非常に若い顔があなたを見つめ返しているとしても，いずれは皆さんもここに立つ日が来るのだということを心にとめておいていただきたいと思います。私は，この業界で最も優秀な人たちの何人かとともに働く機会を与えられたことに感謝しています。市場は変動する傾向にありますが，この会社は確固たるビジョンによって，成功と繁栄を享受し続けるものと楽観視しております。ありがとうございました。

---

**1047 optimistic**
[ὰptəmístik]

形 楽観的な　⇒派 optimism 名 楽天主義
⇔反 pessimistic 形 悲観的な
an optimistic plan　見通しの甘い計画

**1048 prosperity**
[prɑspérəti]

名 繁栄, 成功；好況
bring prosperity to 〜　〜に繁栄をもたらす

---

**Q** The word "refrain" in line 2 is closest in meaning to
(A) stop myself
(B) interrupt
(C) constrain
(D) repeat

解答は p. 336

## 4  Speech 2  人事部長からのお知らせ

My name is Margaret Fitch and, if I have not made your **acquaintance**, I am the head of personnel. Periodically, we **revise** policy and our quarterly focus this time is **aimed** at **achieving** a 20% **reduction** in **overtime** costs across the board. For this reason, we have called all the managers here today. We ask that you not **authorize** overtime **expenditures** unless you have a **compelling** reason to believe that the tasks in question cannot be **completed** during regular working hours.　　　　　(81 words)

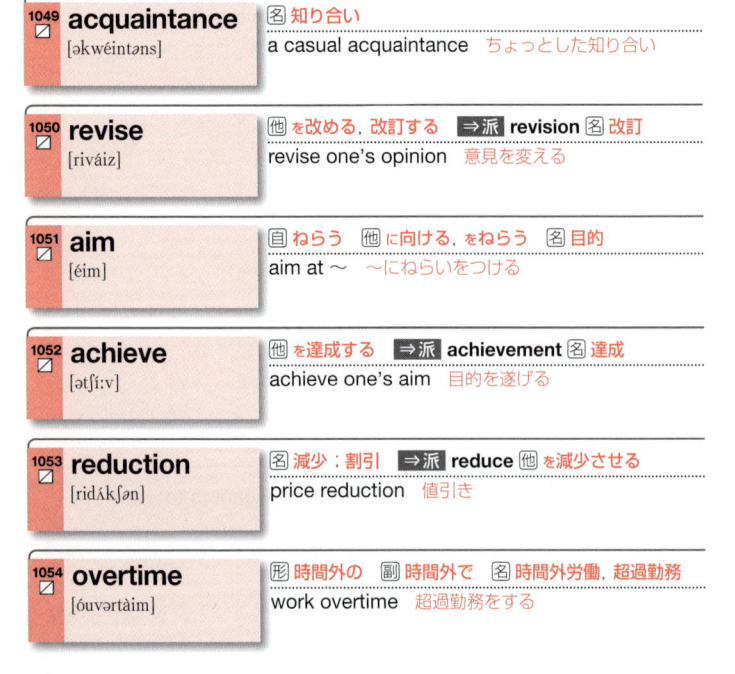

---

**1049 acquaintance** [əkwéintəns]
名 知り合い
a casual acquaintance　ちょっとした知り合い

**1050 revise** [riváiz]
他 を改める, 改訂する　⇒派 revision 名 改訂
revise one's opinion　意見を変える

**1051 aim** [éim]
自 ねらう　他 に向ける, をねらう　名 目的
aim at ～　～にねらいをつける

**1052 achieve** [ətʃíːv]
他 を達成する　⇒派 achievement 名 達成
achieve one's aim　目的を遂げる

**1053 reduction** [ridʌ́kʃən]
名 減少；割引　⇒派 reduce 他 を減少させる
price reduction　値引き

**1054 overtime** [óuvərtàim]
形 時間外の　副 時間外で　名 時間外労働, 超過勤務
work overtime　超過勤務をする

私の名前はマーガレット・フィッチと言います。まだお知り合いでない方のために申し上げますが，人事部の部長です。私たちは定期的に方針を見直しますが，今四半期の私たちの目標は，残業費の一律20パーセント削減を達成することに向けられています。このために，本日は全部長にお集まりいただきました。皆さんには，当該の業務が定時勤務時間内には終わらないことが確かであるとするやむにやまれぬ理由がない限り，残業費を承認なさらないようにお願いします。

---

### 1055 authorize
[ɔ́:θəràiz]

他 に権限を与える；を認可する

authorize ~ to do 〜に…する権限を与える
authorized by the government 政府の認可を受けた

### 1056 expenditure
[ikspénditʃər, eks-]

名 支出額, 経費；支出

at a minimum expenditure of time and effort
最小限の時間と努力で

### 1057 compelling
[kəmpéliŋ]

形 やむにやまれぬ；説得力のある
⇒派 compel 他 を強いる

a compelling argument 説得力のある議論

### 1058 complete
[kəmplí:t]

他 を完成させる，仕上げる 形 完全な
⇔反 incomplete 形 不完全な
⇒派 completely 副 完全に

be complete with ~ 〜を完備している

---

**Q** The word "completed" in line 8 is closest in meaning to

(A) perfected
(B) finished
(C) assembled
(D) won

解答は p. 336

## 5 Speech 3 新事業への投資募集

Here's a **noteworthy** development in casual restaurant dining. Health First is a chain of eateries available to purchase on a **franchise basis**. The Los Angeles, Chicago and New York test markets are the best indicators that you can invest in this project with confidence. We forecast that it will **eventually** become a number one player in the fast food arena. The concept is healthy food served quickly. The organization has been **endorsed** by doctors around the country. The advertisement **tag** line is "First not Fast!" If you're **seeking** a sound investment that represents the wave of the future, look no further. There is a **prospectus** you can look at and a potential investor **kit** is **forthcoming**.

(116 words)

---

**1059 noteworthy** [nóutwə̀ːrði]
形 注目に値する, 顕著な
≒類 notable 形 注目すべき
noteworthy achievement　注目に値する業績

**1060 franchise** [fræntʃaiz]
名 フランチャイズ, 営業権；選挙権
他 にフランチャイズを与える
a franchise store　フランチャイズ店

**1061 basis** [béisis]
名 基礎, 共通基盤
on ~ basis　~に基づいて

**1062 eventually** [ivéntʃuəli]
副 (問題はあったが)結局, ついには
≒類 at last ついに

**1063 endorse** [endɔ́ːrs]
他 を承認する；を推奨する；〈小切手〉に裏書きする
⇒派 endorsement 名 承認
endorse a proposal　提案を是認する

**1064 tag** [tǽg]
名 名札, 荷札, (車の)ナンバープレート
他 に札をつける
a good tag line　すばらしいキャッチフレーズ

これはカジュアルレストランでの食事における注目すべき進展です。ヘルス・ファーストはフランチャイズ方式で購入できるレストランチェーンです。ロサンゼルスとシカゴ，ニューヨークのテスト市場が，この事業は自信を持って投資できるものだということを最もよく示しています。私たちは，これが最終的には，ファーストフード業界でトップの地位を得ることになると予測します。コンセプトは，体によい食事がすばやく提供されるということです。この組織は全国の医師たちから推奨されています。広告のキャッチフレーズは「ファーストフードではなく，ファーストクラスの食事！」です。もし将来の流れを象徴する確かな投資先を探しているのなら，もうこれ以上はその必要はありません。目を通していただくための趣意書をご用意しています。また，投資希望者用の説明書類一式が近々発行されます。

---

### 1065 seek
[síːk]

他 を探す，求める

seek employment　職を探す

### 1066 prospectus
[prəspéktəs]

名 案内書；計画説明書

a company prospectus　会社の事業内容説明書

### 1067 kit
[kít]

名 道具一式

a first-aid kit　救急用品一式

### 1068 forthcoming
[fɔ̀ːrθkʌ́miŋ]

形 やがて来る，来たる

a forthcoming book　近刊書

---

**Q** The word "seeking" in line 9 is closest in meaning to
(A) talking about
(B) recommending
(C) achieving
(D) looking for

解答は p. 336

## 6 Message 留守番電話メッセージ

Thank you for calling Woodward Appliances. The regular business hours at our Main Street location are from 7:00 A.M. to 10:00 P.M. **daily**. You can find answers to **frequently** asked questions about the products we carry at www.woodwardappliances.com. Please listen carefully and choose from one of the **following options**. For 24-hour **technical** support, press "1." For **corporate** sales, press "2." For returns, press "3." To hear an employee list and leave **voicemail** for **individual** employees, press "4." For all other **inquiries**, press "5."  (83 words)

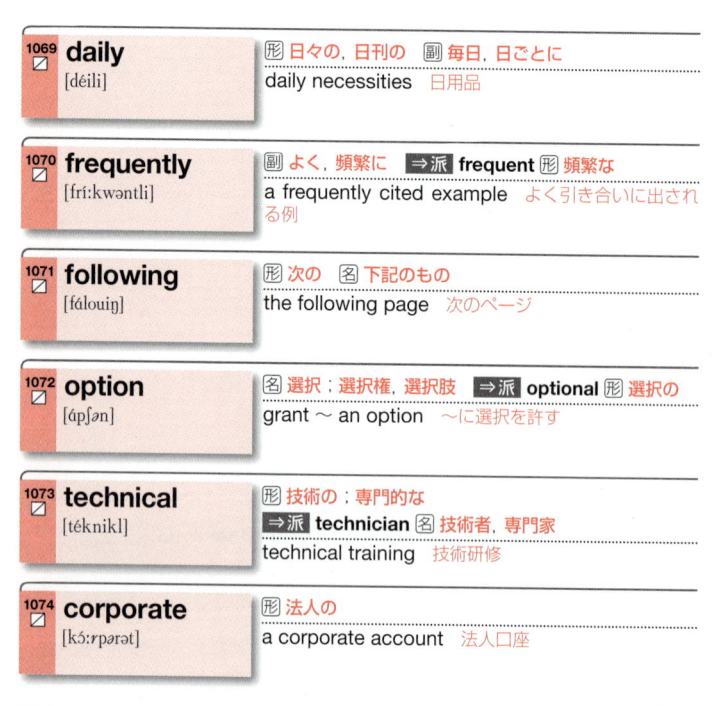

---

**1069 daily** [déili]
形 日々の, 日刊の　副 毎日, 日ごとに
daily necessities　日用品

**1070 frequently** [frí:kwəntli]
副 よく, 頻繁に　⇒派 **frequent** 形 頻繁な
a frequently cited example　よく引き合いに出される例

**1071 following** [fálouiŋ]
形 次の　名 下記のもの
the following page　次のページ

**1072 option** [ápʃən]
名 選択；選択権, 選択肢　⇒派 **optional** 形 選択の
grant ~ an option　~に選択を許す

**1073 technical** [téknikl]
形 技術の；専門的な
⇒派 **technician** 名 技術者, 専門家
technical training　技術研修

**1074 corporate** [kɔ́:rpərət]
形 法人の
a corporate account　法人口座

ウッドワード電器店にお電話いただきありがとうございます。当メインストリート店の通常の営業時間は毎日午前7時から午後10時までです。当店で扱っている商品についてのよくある質問に対する回答は，www.woodwardappliances.com にてご確認いただけます。注意深くお聞きになって，次の選択肢の中から1つお選びください。24時間の技術サポートは「1番」，法人向けの販売については「2番」，返品については「3番」，従業員のリストをお聞きになって従業員個人に伝言を残される場合は「4番」，その他のお問い合わせはすべて「5番」を押してください。

---

**1075 voicemail** [vɔ́ismèil]
名 ボイスメール，留守番電話
voicemail messages 音声メッセージ

**1076 individual** [ìndəvídʒuəl]
形 個々の，個人的な 名 個人
in the individual case 個々の場合において

**1077 inquiry** [ínkwəri, inkwáiəri]
名 質問，照会；調査 ⇒派 inquire 他自 (を) 尋ねる
an inquiry into ～ ～に関する質問〔調査〕

---

**Q** The word "following" in line 5 is closest in meaning to
(A) behind
(B) believing
(C) upcoming
(D) resulting

解答は p. 336

## 7  Advertisement 1  コンピュータ業者の宣伝

Lyle Edwards here for Edwards Computer Repair Services. We'll visit your home or office and remove computer **viruses**, troubleshoot and **resolve software** issues, build local **access** networks, or install new **hardware**. Ready to upgrade? We can build you a new **state-of-the-art** system or offer you a simpler, inexpensive computer that we have **refurbished** ourselves. All of our systems come with our special, easy-to-read Edwards owner's manuals as well as the most **reliable** anti-virus and maintenance software on the market to help you **protect** your **investment**. Give us a call today at 555-7667.

(92 words)

---

**1078 virus** [váiərəs]
名 ウイルス
a computer virus　コンピュータウイルス

**1079 resolve** [rizálv]
他 を決議〔決定〕する；を解決する　自 決意する
⇒派 **resolution** 名 決議；決意
resolve to do　…することを決心する

**1080 software** [sɔ́(:)ftwèər]
名 ソフトウェア
software engineering　ソフトウェア工学

**1081 access** [ǽkses]
名 入る権利；アクセス, 接近；通路　他 にアクセスする
access to the house　その家へ行く道

**1082 hardware** [hɑ́:rdwèər]
名 ハードウェア；金物類
a hardware vendor　ハードウェアの製造元

**1083 state-of-the-art** [stéitəvðiɑ́:rt]
形 最新式の　≒類 **latest** 形 最新の
state-of-the-art technology　最先端技術

こちらはエドワーズ・コンピュータ修理サービスのライル・エドワーズです。私たちはご家庭やオフィスまで出向いてコンピュータ**ウイルス**を駆除したり，故障点検をして**ソフトウェア**の問題**を解決**したり，LAN の設定や新しい**ハードウェア**のインストールを行ったりします。アップグレードをお考えですか。私たちは**最先端**システムの構築，自社で**新装した**よりシンプルで安価なコンピュータの提供などを行っています。当社のシステムにはすべて，読みやすいエドワーズの発注者向け特別説明書がついています。また，皆様の**投資を保護する**お手伝いをするために，現在販売されている中で最も**信頼できる**ウイルス防止ソフトとメンテナンスソフトもすべてにおつけしております。555-7667 に，今日お電話ください。

---

### 1084 refurbish
[riːfə́ːrbiʃ]

他 を更新する；を改装する
refurbish a building　建物を修復する

### 1085 reliable
[riláiəbl]

形 信頼できる；期待通りの
⇒派 reliability 名 信頼性, 確実性
reliable information　確かな情報

### 1086 protect
[prətékt]

他 を保護する　⇒派 protection 名 保護
protect ~ from harm　~に危害が及ばないようにする

### 1087 investment
[invéstmənt]

名 投資 (の対象)；投下資本；投入
⇒派 invest 他 を投資する
make a large investment　多額の投資をする

---

**Q** The word "resolve" in line 3 is closest in meaning to
(A) correct
(B) achieve
(C) gain
(D) divide

解答は p. 336

## 8  Advertisement 2　格安ツアーの宣伝

Have you always dreamed of an **excursion** to the Caribbean? Here's your opportunity. Travel Pro has a super deluxe all-inclusive package vacation to Jamaica at the **exclusive** Sandcastle Resort for the unbelievably low price of $480 per person. Go ahead and **comparison**-shop, you won't find this level of **comfort** this inexpensive from any other vendor. This includes **roundtrip** air **fare**, all **lodging** and meal expenses for four nights at the resort with a motor coach tour of the island. Be kind to yourself, be kind to your wallet! As they say in Jamaica, "Don't worry, be happy." Make your reservation by calling our very hot Jamaica Tours Hotline at 555-7711. Our **agents** are standing by.　(115 words)

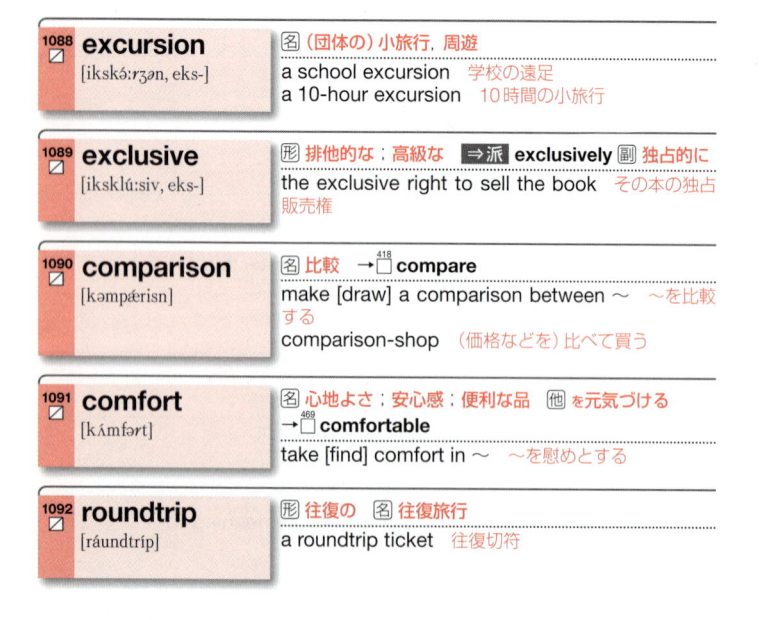

---

**1088 excursion**
[ikskə́:rʒən, eks-]
图 (団体の)小旅行, 周遊
a school excursion　学校の遠足
a 10-hour excursion　10時間の小旅行

**1089 exclusive**
[iksklú:siv, eks-]
形 排他的な；高級な　⇒派 **exclusively** 副 独占的に
the exclusive right to sell the book　その本の独占販売権

**1090 comparison**
[kəmpǽrisn]
图 比較　→ compare
make [draw] a comparison between ～　～を比較する
comparison-shop　(価格などを)比べて買う

**1091 comfort**
[kʌ́mfərt]
图 心地よさ；安心感；便利な品　他 を元気づける
→ **comfortable**
take [find] comfort in ～　～を慰めとする

**1092 roundtrip**
[ráundtríp]
形 往復の　图 往復旅行
a roundtrip ticket　往復切符

カリブ海への旅行をいつも夢に見ていたあなた。さあ、チャンスがやってきました。トラベル・プロでは高級サンドキャッスル・リゾートでの、すべて込みの超デラックスなジャマイカへのパッケージツアーを、お一人様480ドルという信じられないような安さでご用意しております。どうぞほかの旅行社と比べてみてください。この快適さでこれだけお安いものは、他社では見つかりません。ここには、往復航空運賃、現地での4泊分のすべての宿泊費と食費、および島内のバスツアーが含まれます。あなた自身に優しく、あなたの財布にも優しく！ジャマイカのことわざにある通り、「あれこれ悩まず楽しくやりましょう」。話題沸騰の当社のジャマイカツアー・ホットライン、555-7711までお電話の上ご予約ください。係員がお待ちしております。

---

**1093 fare** [féər]
名 運賃、料金　自〈人が〉やっていく、暮らす
≒類 fee 名 報酬；料金
at a reduced fare　割引料金で

**1094 lodging** [ládʒiŋ]
名 宿泊；宿
lodging facilities　宿泊施設

**1095 agent** [éidʒənt]
名 代理人、代行業者、代理店；係員；作用物質
≒類 agency 名 代理店；機関
an agent commission　代理店手数料

---

**Q** The word "agents" in line 11 is closest in meaning to
(A) instruments
(B) police
(C) substances
(D) representatives

解答は p. 336

## 9  Instructions　エクササイズ器具の付属 CD

Use this **audio** CD along with the **booklet** to help you with your exercise program. This program explains how to use DAG, the Dream Abs Gym. Sit on the seat, extend your arms and the DAG **apparatus** will help you contract your **abdomen** and bring your **knees** to your **chest**. If you're like most of our **subscribers**, you have been **desperately** trying to tone up your abs, without much success. Let DAG do most of the work for you, just pull and **bend**. The other tracks on the CD give you music to work out by. Questions? Just call our **toll**-free support number at 800-55-2225.

(105 words)

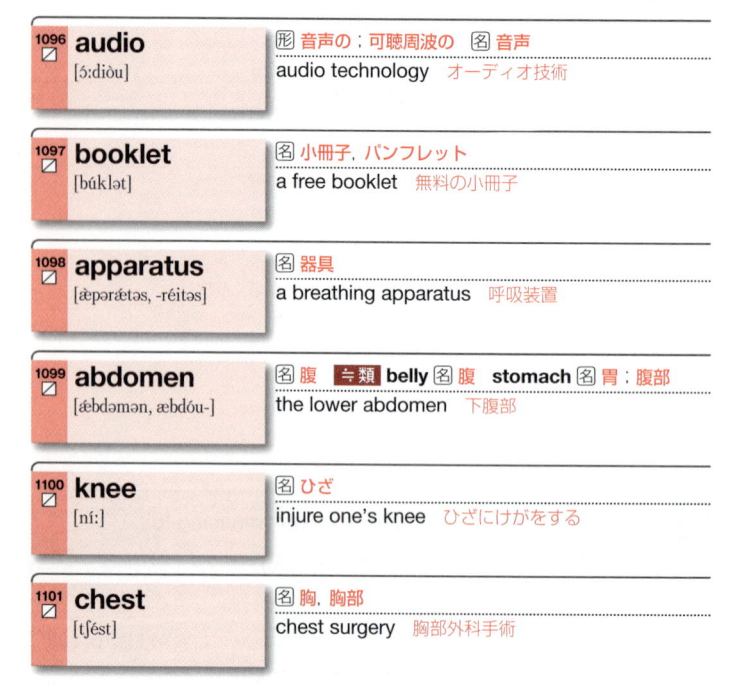

---

**1096 audio** [ɔ́:diòu]
形 音声の；可聴周波の　名 音声
audio technology　オーディオ技術

**1097 booklet** [búklət]
名 小冊子, パンフレット
a free booklet　無料の小冊子

**1098 apparatus** [æpərǽtəs, -réitəs]
名 器具
a breathing apparatus　呼吸装置

**1099 abdomen** [ǽbdəmən, æbdóu-]
名 腹　≒類 belly 名 腹　stomach 名 胃；腹部
the lower abdomen　下腹部

**1100 knee** [ní:]
名 ひざ
injure one's knee　ひざにけがをする

**1101 chest** [tʃést]
名 胸, 胸部
chest surgery　胸部外科手術

エクササイズプログラムの補助として、パンフレットとともにこの音声CD をお使いください。このプログラムは、DAG、ドリーム・アブス・ジムの使い方を説明しています。いすに座り両腕を伸ばせば、DAG 器具の助けで腹部を収縮させ、ひざを胸につけることができます。もしあなたが、ほとんどのお申し込み者の皆様と同じなら、必死で腹筋を強化しようとしてあまりうまくいかなかったことでしょう。エクササイズはDAG に全面的にお任せください。あなたはただ引っ張ったり身体を曲げたりすればよいのです。CD のほかのトラックには、トレーニング用のBGM が入っています。ご質問がございましたら、通話料無料のサポートダイヤル 800-55-2225 までお気軽にお電話ください。

---

### 1102 subscriber
[səbskráibər]

名 定期購読者；加入者, 申し込み者；署名者

a subscriber to a newspaper　新聞の予約購読者

### 1103 desperately
[déspərətli]

副 必死に, やけになって；絶望的に

try desperately to do　必死に…しようとする

### 1104 bend
[bénd]

自 身体を曲げる
他 〈物〉を曲げる；〈規則など〉を曲げる

bend one's back　背を曲げる

### 1105 toll
[tóul]

名 (道路・橋などの) 通行料, 料金；長距離通話料

a toll booth　料金所
a toll-free call　フリーダイヤル通話

---

**Q** The word "chest" in line 5 is closest in meaning to
(A) box
(B) dresser
(C) upper body
(D) account

解答は p.336

## 10 Weather Report 気象情報

Tropical Storm Hazel has caused tens of thousands of dollars in damage to homes along the coast. Residents living along the shoreline of North Beach were forced to evacuate their homes because of high winds last night, but no injuries have been reported. Winds that exceeded 200 miles per hour were reported along with strong waves crashing up on the shore. The National Weather Bureau issued a severe weather advisory at 1:00 A.M. Throughout the night, rescue workers help move elderly residents to the nearest shelter. (86 words)

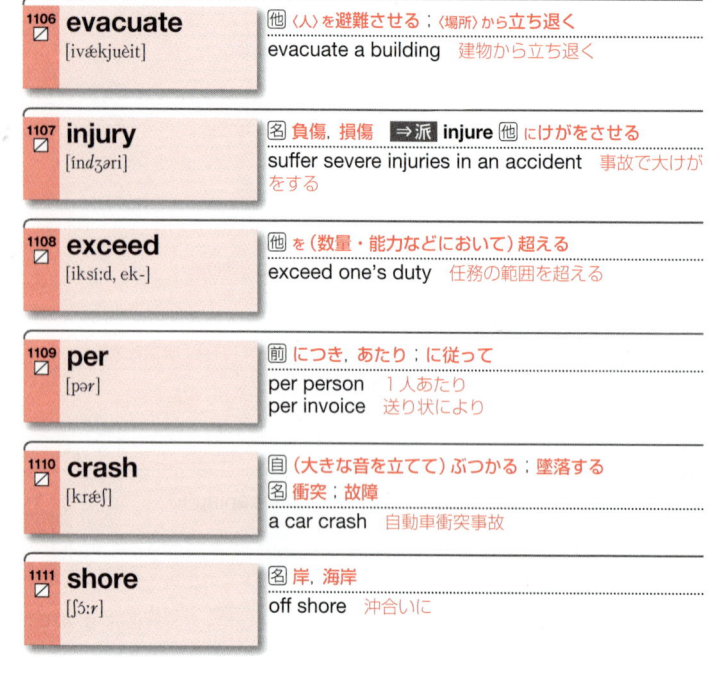

---

**1106 evacuate** [ivǽkjuèit]
他 〈人〉を避難させる;〈場所〉から立ち退く
evacuate a building　建物から立ち退く

**1107 injury** [índʒəri]
名 負傷, 損傷　⇒派 injure 他 にけがをさせる
suffer severe injuries in an accident　事故で大けがをする

**1108 exceed** [iksí:d, ek-]
他 を(数量・能力などにおいて)超える
exceed one's duty　任務の範囲を超える

**1109 per** [pər]
前 につき, あたり；に従って
per person　1人あたり
per invoice　送り状により

**1110 crash** [kræʃ]
自 (大きな音を立てて)ぶつかる；墜落する
名 衝突；故障
a car crash　自動車衝突事故

**1111 shore** [ʃɔ́:r]
名 岸, 海岸
off shore　沖合いに

熱帯低気圧ヘーゼルは海岸沿いの住宅に何万ドルもの被害を出しています。ノースビーチの海岸沿いの住人たちは昨夜強風のために強制的に住宅から避難させられましたが，負傷は報告されていません。強い波が海岸に轟音を立てて打ちつけており，風は1時間につき200マイルを超す速さであることが報告されました。気象庁は午前1時に荒天注意報を発しました。救助隊員たちは夜を徹して，高齢の住民を最寄りの避難所に移動させる救護活動を行っています。

---

**1112 advisory**
[ədváizəri]

图 報告；(気象などの)注意報
形 助言を与える，顧問の
an advisory board　諮問機関

**1113 rescue**
[réskju:]

图 救出；救助　他 を救助する
a rescue corps　救助隊

**1114 elderly**
[éldərli]

形 年配の，高齢の
the elderly population　老齢〔高齢者〕人口

---

**Q** The word "shore" in line 6 is closest in meaning to
(A) support
(B) hometown
(C) coast
(D) shelter

解答は p.336

## 11 News Report 1　盗難事件

Thieves broke into McKenna Variety Store last night and **stole** about 5,000 dollars **worth** of **merchandise**. This is the third **burglary** in the downtown area in two weeks. All three of the break-ins had similar patterns. In what is described as a "high tech" **crime**, the alarm systems at each of the shops seem to have been **electronically** canceled. After turning off the alarms, the burglars took small **quantities** of the most expensive items in the stores. In all three cases, stores were using older alarm systems. Police say that local **merchants** are advised to upgrade their burglar alarm systems and install **security** cameras. If the stores had had security cameras, the thieves may have already been **apprehended**. (118 words)

---

**1115 steal** [stíːl]
他 を盗む
have one's purse stolen　財布を盗まれる

**1116 worth** [wə́ːrθ]
形 価値がある　名 価値
appraise the worth of ～　～の価値を評価する

**1117 merchandise** [mə́ːrtʃəndàiz]
名 商品　他 の販売を促進する
make merchandise of ～　～を売り物にする

**1118 burglary** [bə́ːrɡləri]
名 押し込み, 窃盗；不法侵入事件
⇒派 burglar 名 強盗
burglary insurance　盗難保険

**1119 crime** [kráim]
名 犯罪
prevention of crime　犯罪防止

**1120 electronically** [ilèktránikli]
副 電子装置で
⇒派 electronic 形 電子の, ネットワークを利用した
electronic transfer　電信振替

昨夜マッケナ・バラエティー・ショップに泥棒が入り，約5,000ドル相当の商品が盗まれました。これはここ2週間に町の中心部で起こった3件目の窃盗事件です。3件の侵入事件すべてに類似したパターンがあります。「ハイテク」犯罪と呼ばれるように，各店舗の警報システムが電子器具を用いて解除されていたものと見られます。警報装置を止めたあと，窃盗犯は店にある最も高価な品物を少数盗みました。3件とも共通して，店舗は古い警報システムを使用していました。警察によると，現地で店を営んでいる人々は，盗難警報システムをバージョンアップし，防犯カメラを設置することをお勧めするとのことです。もしこれらの店に防犯カメラがあったら，すでに泥棒を逮捕できていた可能性があります。

---

**1121 quantity** [kwɑ́ntəti]
名 分量, 数量；量
in quantity 大量に

**1122 merchant** [mə́ːrtʃənt]
名 商店主, 商人 形 商業の
retail merchant 小売業者

**1123 security** [sikjúərəti]
名 安全；防犯 ⇒派 secure 他 を獲得する；を安全にする 形 安全な
a security firm 警備会社

**1124 apprehend** [æprihénd]
他 を逮捕する, 捕える ⇒派 apprehension 名 懸念
apprehend a suspect 容疑者を逮捕する

---

**Q** The word "merchants" in line 9 is closest in meaning to
(A) products
(B) commerce
(C) military
(D) shopkeepers

解答は p. 336

## 12 News Report 2　爆発事件

In other news, an **explosion** occurred at a **warehouse** near the **docks** early this morning. What appears to be a homemade bomb caused a fire to break out and two wings of a warehouse **owned** by Martin Communications were destroyed. The company was in between shipments of **inventory** and the location was **virtually empty**, so police are having a difficult time **determining** the cause. **Authorities** are questioning **witnesses** and taking statements. Anyone who was near the docks between 4:00 and 6:00 A.M. is asked to call the Crime Control Assist number at 555-6100.　　　　　　　　　　　　　　　　　　　　(93 words)

---

**1125 explosion** [iksplóuʒən, eks-]
名 爆発　⇒派 explode 自 爆発する
a gas explosion　ガス爆発

**1126 warehouse** [wéərhàus]
名 倉庫
a warehouse store　ウェアハウスストア（倉庫を店舗にするなどして経費を抑えた安売り店）

**1127 dock** [dák]
名 波止場, 埠頭；ドック；積荷場
in dock　（船が）ドックに入って

**1128 own** [óun]
他 を所有する　形 自分自身の
the cost of owning a car　車を持つのにかかる費用

**1129 inventory** [ínvəntɔ̀:ri]
名 商品目録, 棚卸表；在庫　他 の目録を作る
take (an) inventory of ～　～の一覧表〔目録〕を作る

**1130 virtually** [vɔ́:rtʃuəli]
副 ほとんど, 実質上, 事実上
⇒派 virtual 形 実質上の
be virtually unknown　ほとんど無名である

次のニュースです。今朝早く、波止場近くの倉庫で爆発がありました。炎を燃え上がらせたのは手製の爆弾と見られるもので、マーティン・コミュニケーションズ所有の倉庫2棟が破壊されました。会社は在庫品の出荷の最中で、現場はほぼ無人であったため、警察は原因の特定に苦慮しています。当局は目撃者に事情を聴取して調書をとっているところです。午前4時から6時の間に波止場近くにいた人は、555-6100の犯罪取り締まり支援番号にご一報ください。

---

**1131 empty** [émpti]
形 何も入っていない；無人の
an empty box　空箱

**1132 determine** [ditə́ːrmin]
他 …しようと決める；に決意させる；と結論付ける
be determined to do　…することを堅く決意している

**1133 authority** [əθɔ́ːrəti, əθɑ́ːr-]
名 権威(者)；当局；権限
the proper authorities = the authorities concerned　関係当局〔官庁〕

**1134 witness** [wítnəs]
名 目撃者　他 を目撃する
witness an accident　事故を目撃する

---

**Q** The word "virtually" in line 6 is closest in meaning to
(A) electronically
(B) nearly
(C) imaginarily
(D) nobly

解答は p.336

## 13 Talk 1 ラジオ番組の料理紹介

You're listening to *What's Happening Around Town*. This is Cary Claymore. All this week, the announcers here at WDDQ are sharing our personal favorite recipes with listeners. In conjunction with this, thanks to the **charitable** nature of our **sponsor**, Klein's Market, you can find all the **ingredients** we **mention** on sale! My favorite side dish is called Country Carrot Salad. **Peel** and **shred** three to four carrots. Mix in two tablespoons of mayonnaise, a teaspoon of orange peel, two teaspoons of **chopped** parsley, and a third of a cup each of raisins and walnuts. If you'd like, you can **replace** the walnuts with pecans. **Chill** and **serve**. (107 words)

---

**1135 charitable** [tʃǽritəbl]
形 慈悲深い；慈善の　⇒派 charity 名 慈善事業
a charitable act　慈善行為

**1136 sponsor** [spánsər]
名 スポンサー；保証人；支持者
他 のスポンサーとなる
the sponsor of a proposal　提案の主唱者

**1137 ingredient** [ingríːdiənt]
名 材料, 構成要素
an active ingredient　有効成分

**1138 mention** [ménʃən]
他 に言及する　名 言うこと, 言及すること
as I mentioned before　前に申し上げた通り

**1139 peel** [píːl]
他 の皮をむく
peel ~ off ...　…から~をはがす

**1140 shred** [ʃréd]
他 を細かく切る；をシュレッダーにかける　名 切れ端
shred documents　書類をシュレッダーにかける

お送りしているのは,「街での出来事」です。ケアリー・クレイモアです。今週いっぱいは,ここ WDDQ のアナウンサーたちが自分のお気に入りのレシピをリスナーに紹介しています。これに関連して,私たちの**スポンサー**,クラインズ・マーケットの**寛大な**心根のおかげで,私たちが番組で**挙げる材料**がすべて割引価格となっています! 私のお気に入りの副菜は田舎風にんじんサラダといいます。にんじん3,4本**の皮をむき**,**千切りにします**。マヨネーズ大さじ2杯,オレンジピール小さじ1杯,**刻み**パセリ小さじ2杯,干しぶどうとクルミそれぞれ3分の1カップを混ぜ合わせます。お好みによって,ピーカンナッツをクルミ**に代用**していただいても結構です。**冷やしてお出しください。**

---

## 1141 chop
[tʃáp]

他 を切り刻む 名 一撃;厚切りの肉片

chop ~ into small pieces　~をみじん切りにする

## 1142 replace
[ripléis]

他 に取って代わる;を交代させる;を取り替える
⇒派 **replacement** 名 代替;交代

replace the broken window　割れた窓を取り替える

## 1143 chill
[tʃíl]

他 を冷やす 自 冷える;寒気がする 名 寒さ
⇒派 **chilly** 形 冷えびえする

have a chill　寒くてぞくぞくする

## 1144 serve
[sə́ːrv]

他 〈飲食物〉を出す;〈人〉の役に立つ;に(商品・サービスなどを)提供する 自 役立つ

serve breakfast　朝食を出す

---

**Q** The word "mention" in line 5 is closest in meaning to
(A) name
(B) detail
(C) perform
(D) honor

解答は p.336

## 14 Talk 2 実演販売の説明

To **facilitate** your Hurricane 3000 **demonstration**, ask the customer to bring out their current **vacuum** cleaner. Explain that the **typical** vacuum cleaner only works for the first 15 minutes and then the dirt is **clogged** in the bag. Smile and be **confident**. Open their **canister** and show them how dirt gets clogged. Compare theirs to ours by cleaning once with theirs and then showing how the Hurricane still finds dirt. **Emphasize** that our system uses water to **trap** dirt. The water is the filter. Talk about the lifetime **warranty** and say they can receive a discount if they give us their old machine as a down payment for the Hurricane.

(110 words)

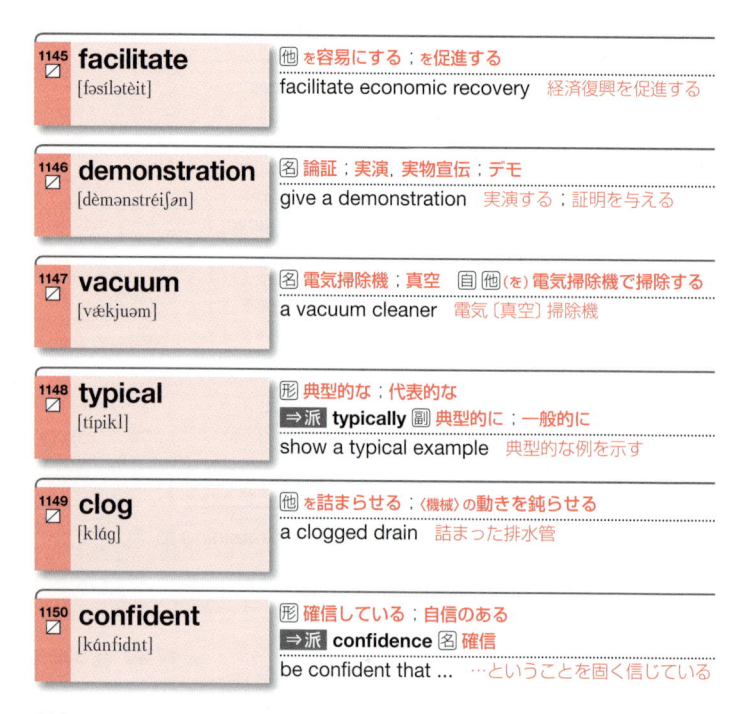

---

### 1145 facilitate
[fəsílətèit]

他 を容易にする；を促進する

facilitate economic recovery　経済復興を促進する

### 1146 demonstration
[dèmənstréiʃən]

名 論証；実演, 実物宣伝；デモ

give a demonstration　実演する；証明を与える

### 1147 vacuum
[vækjuəm]

名 電気掃除機；真空　自他 (を)電気掃除機で掃除する

a vacuum cleaner　電気〔真空〕掃除機

### 1148 typical
[típikl]

形 典型的な；代表的な
⇒派 **typically** 副 典型的に；一般的に

show a typical example　典型的な例を示す

### 1149 clog
[klάg]

他 を詰まらせる；〈機械〉の動きを鈍らせる

a clogged drain　詰まった排水管

### 1150 confident
[kάnfidnt]

形 確信している；自信のある
⇒派 **confidence** 名 確信

be confident that ...　…ということを固く信じている

ハリケーン3000の実演販売を簡単にするために，顧客に現在使っている掃除機を持ってくるよう頼んでください。代表的な掃除機は最初の15分間しかうまく働かず，その後はごみで袋が詰まってしまうということを説明してください。ほほえんで，自信を示すように。掃除機を開け，ごみが詰まっている様子を見せてください。一度顧客の掃除機で掃除をし，それからハリケーンがまだごみを見つけることを示して，顧客の掃除機と当社の掃除機を比べてください。当社のシステムは，ごみを中に閉じ込めるのに水を使うということを強調してください。水がフィルターです。永久保証について話をし，ハリケーンの頭金として古い掃除機を当社に提供してくれれば値引きが受けられると説明してください。

---

**1151 canister** [kǽnəstər]
名 小箱，缶；箱型電気掃除機
a film canister フィルム容器

**1152 emphasize** [émfəsàiz]
他 を強調する ⇒派 emphasis 名 強調
emphasize the importance of ～ ～の重要性を強調する

**1153 trap** [trǽp]
他 をわなで捕える；を閉じ込める 名 わな
be caught in a trap わなにかかる

**1154 warranty** [wɔ́:rənti]
名 保証；根拠；認可
⇒派 warrant 名 認可 他 を正式に認可する
be under warranty 保証期間内にある

---

**Q** The word "typical" in line 3 is closest in meaning to
(A) ideal
(B) ordinary
(C) essential
(D) descriptive

解答は p. 336

# Chapter 4-2 TOEIC 形式の長文で覚える

学校英語 ▶▶▶ TOEIC® TEST  Part 7 形式

## 1  E-mail 1  オンライン登録の確認

From: Customerconnection@support.kendallprint.com
To: Jdavisconsultants@maplewood.sbb.com
Subject: Registration
Date: Mon, 6 Feb 12:54:24-700

Dear Corporate Customer,
We thank you for registering your product online and providing us with your corporate **profile** information. Your profile is the easiest way to **ensure** fast, convenient access to Kendall information and assistance. This information often helps us **ascertain** the most efficient way to serve you, as well. Being a registered user also **entitles** you to take advantage of various databases and **storage** on the Kendall Web site.

You may view or edit your profile information anytime on our Web site. We **adhere** to a strict privacy policy, so your information is never shared with our affiliate companies unless you've provided your **consent** to do so. We've provided a link to access and **retrieve** your profile here.

(130 words)

---

**1155 profile** [próufail]
名 横顔, 側面；人物紹介；概要
in profile  側面から

**1156 ensure** [enʃúər, -ʃɔ́ːr]
他 を請け合う；を確実にする
ensure that ...  確実に…であるようにする

**1157 ascertain** [æ̀sərtéin]
他 を確かめる；を突き止める
ascertain that ...  …であることを確かめる

**1158 entitle** [entáitl]
他 に資格〔権利〕を与える
be entitled to do  …する権利が与えられている

**1159 storage** [stɔ́ːridʒ]
名 保管；保管スペース；メモリ, 記憶装置
put ~ in storage  ~を倉庫に保管する

差出人：Customerconnection@support.kendallprint.com
宛先：Jdavisconsultants@maplewood.sbb.com
件名：登録
日付：2/6（月）12:54:24 -700

法人会員様
貴社製品のオンライン登録および，会社**概要**情報のご提供をありがとうございます。貴社の概要は，ケンドールの情報および支援へのすばやく便利なアクセス**を確実にする**ための最も簡単な方法です。この情報は，当社が貴社のお役に立つための最も効果的な方法**を確かめる**のにもしばしば役に立ちます。また，会員登録をいただきましたので，ケンドールのウェブサイト上のさまざまなデータベースや**記憶装置**などのご利用**資格を差し上げます。**

貴社の概要情報は，いつでも当社のウェブサイト上でご覧になり，編集していただけます。当社は厳しいプライバシー方針を**忠実に守っておりますので**，貴社の**同意**なしに，情報が当社の系列会社に漏れることは決してありません。こちらに貴社の概要にアクセスし，**検索する**ためのリンクを記載いたしました。

---

**1160 adhere**
[ədhíər, æd-]

自 くっつく；固守する
adhere to the wall　壁にくっつく

**1161 consent**
[kənsént]

名 同意　自 承諾する，同意する
consent to do　…することを承諾する

**1162 retrieve**
[ritríːv]

他 を取り戻す，回収する；を検索する
retrieve data from a computer　コンピュータからデータを引き出す

---

**Q** The word "consent" in line 16 is closest in meaning to
(A) permission
(B) gratitude
(C) ability
(D) current

解答は p. 336

## 2  E-mail 2　日程変更の連絡

From: Tom@phytonutrientsformulas.com
To: Emily@phytonutrientsformulas.com
RE: Schedule
Date: Mon, 10 Oct

Emily,

My **suspicions** were correct. The Lynwood Laboratory is in an absolute state of **upheaval**. Two of the key **chemists** continued to argue about the process instead of working to meet the end-of-the-year **deadline** for the new **formula**. Then, both of them decided to **resign**. Since I'm the only one here who understands the chemistry and the **agenda** of our corporate **headquarters**, I need to stay on for at least the next week, sort things out and hire some new scientists. I'd like you to reschedule all of my appointments for the next week and **apologize** to everyone for the unexpected **delay** in my return from Philadelphia. Thanks in advance.
Tom

(121 words)

---

**1163 suspicion** [səspíʃən]
名 疑い、いぶかり
above [beyond] suspicion　（確固として）疑いの余地がない

**1164 upheaval** [ʌphíːvl]
名 激変、動乱
an emotional upheaval　感情の激変

**1165 chemist** [kémist]
名 化学者
⇒派 chemistry 名 化学　chemical 形 化学の
organic chemistry　有機化学

**1166 deadline** [dédlàin]
名 期限、締切
meet a deadline　締切に間に合わせる

**1167 formula** [fɔ́ːrmjələ]
名 決まり文句；公式；解決策；（薬などの）調剤法
the formula for weight loss　ダイエットの秘訣

**1168 resign** [rizáin]
自 他 (を)辞職する
resign on account of age　老齢のため辞職する

差出人：Tom@phytonutrientsformulas.com
宛先：Emily@phytonutrientsformulas.com
件名：スケジュール
日付：10月10日（月）

エミリー
私の疑念は当たっていました。リンウッド研究所は完全に激変状態です。中心的な役割を持つ化学者の2人は，年末の新しい調剤法の締切を守るために働くことをせず，その過程についての口論を続けていました。そして，2人ともが辞める決断をしました。ここで化学のことと我が社の本部の議事についてわかっているのは私1人だけなので，少なくとも来週はここに残って事態を整理し，新しい科学者を何人か雇い入れなくてはなりません。来週の私の約束をすべて調整し直して，私がフィラデルフィアから戻るのが予定外に遅れることをみんなに謝っておいてくれますか。よろしくお願いします。
トム

---

**1169 agenda**
[ədʒéndə]

名 議題，議事；予定表

high on the agenda　最初に議論すべき

**1170 headquarters**
[hédkwɔ̀rtərz]

名 本社；本部

transfer to headquarters in London　ロンドンの本社に転勤する

**1171 apologize**
[əpálədʒàiz]

自 謝罪する　⇒派 apology 名 謝罪

apologize for ～　～のことで謝る
apologize to ～　～に謝る

**1172 delay**
[diléi]

名 延期；遅れ　他 を遅らせる

traffic delays　交通の遅れ

---

**Q** The word "upheaval" in line 7 is closest in meaning to
(A) damage
(B) movement
(C) confusion
(D) lifting

解答は p.336

## 3  Letter 1  希望就職先への連絡

Ralph Peters
Omega Group
65090 Palm Blvd.
Boynton Beach, FL

Dear Mr. Peters,
I attempted to phone you several times. I believe my Uncle Walter contacted you a few weeks ago on my **behalf**. It seems we are all **alumni** of the University of Technology Sydney. I graduated in the spring of 2004, but then I took a year off to spend time traveling around the European **continent** to experience a variety of cultures and **broaden** my horizons. My uncle indicated that there may be the possibility of employment within your organization. I have enclosed a **résumé** and I would be very grateful if you would take a look at it. Please do not **hesitate** to contact me if I can answer any questions or provide **additional** information.
**Sincerely**,
Bradley Shaw

(131 words)

---

**1173 behalf** [bihǽf]
名 利益；大義
on behalf of ～　～のために；～の代理で、～を代表して

**1174 alumni** [əlʌ́mnai]
名 同窓生（alumnus の複数形）
an alumni association　同窓会

**1175 continent** [kάntənənt]
名 大陸　⇒派 continental 形 大陸(性)の
the entire continent　大陸全体

**1176 broaden** [brɔ́:dn]
他 を広げる　⇒派 broad 形 広い
broaden one's mind　見聞を広げる

**1177 résumé** [rézəmèi]
名 履歴書；概要
résumé of ～　～の概要

ラルフ・ピーターズ
オメガグループ
フロリダ州ボイントンビーチ
パーム大通り 65090 番地

ピーターズ様
何度かお電話いたしました。叔父のウォルターが私の代わりに何週間か前にご連絡したと思います。私たちは皆シドニー技術大学の同窓生のようです。私は 2004 年春に卒業しましたが，その後 1 年間休みを取って，さまざまな文化を体験し，見聞を広めるためにヨーロッパ大陸を旅行して過ごしました。叔父は，貴社での就職の可能性があるかもしれないと示唆してくれました。履歴書を同封しましたので，目を通していただけると大変光栄に存じます。疑問にお答えできることや，追加情報をご提供できることがありましたら，遠慮なくご連絡ください。

敬具

ブラッドリー・ショー

---

**1178 hesitate** [hézitèit]
自 ためらう ⇒派 hesitation 名 ためらい
I hesitate to ask you but ... お願いしにくいのですが…

**1179 additional** [ədíʃənl]
形 追加の ⇒派 add 他 を追加する
an additional fee 追加料金

**1180 sincerely** [sinsíərli, sən-]
副 心から，誠意を持って
⇒派 sincere 形 正直な；誠実な
Sincerely yours [Yours sincerely]. 敬具

---

**Q** The word "broaden" in line 11 is closest in meaning to
(A) follow
(B) increase
(C) clarify
(D) expand

解答は p.336

## 4  Letter 2　出版社への投書

Dear Editor,

In reaction to the recent media **coverage** on the brawl that broke out after the football game last week at Central High School, many people have spoken out to criticize our youth. I live in a retirement home and a lovely group from that very high school **volunteers** to spend time with elderly people like myself. I am grateful to Sarah, Peter and Lindsey who share their Thursday afternoons with me. These **youngsters** are wonderful role models, yet your articles seem to **lump** them together with the kids involved in the scandal. Not all students are the same. Sarah is now **ashamed** to say where she goes to school, as there has been so much public **scorn**. This should be a wake-up call for us. Why don't we **seize** this opportunity to think of students who take part and volunteer and do well in academics as heroes instead of always giving such **overwhelming** acclaim to sports players?

Sincerely,
Gladys Underwood

(162 words)

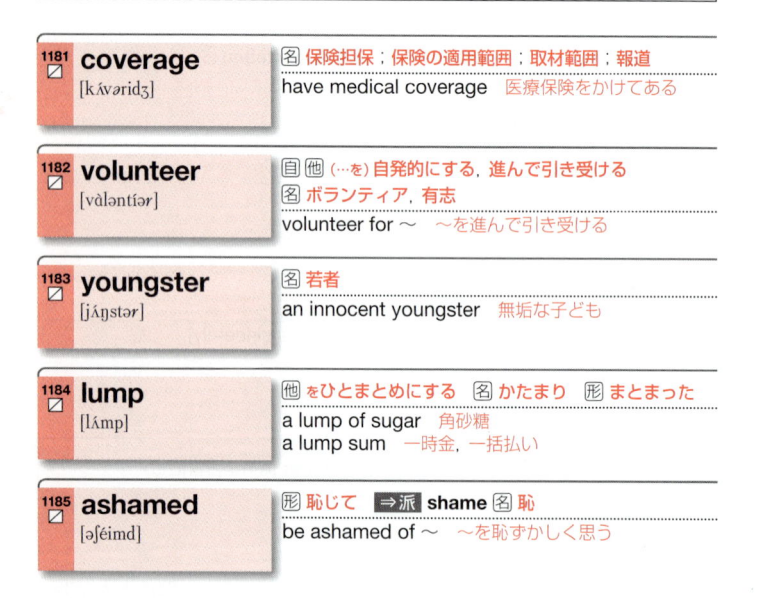

---

**1181 coverage** [kʌ́vəridʒ]
名 保険担保；保険の適用範囲；取材範囲；報道
have medical coverage　医療保険をかけてある

**1182 volunteer** [vɑ̀ləntíər]
自他 (…を)自発的にする, 進んで引き受ける
名 ボランティア, 有志
volunteer for ～　～を進んで引き受ける

**1183 youngster** [jʌ́ŋstər]
名 若者
an innocent youngster　無垢な子ども

**1184 lump** [lʌ́mp]
他 をひとまとめにする　名 かたまり　形 まとまった
a lump of sugar　角砂糖
a lump sum　一時金, 一括払い

**1185 ashamed** [əʃéimd]
形 恥じて　⇒派 shame 名 恥
be ashamed of ～　～を恥ずかしく思う

編集者様
先週セントラル・ハイスクールでのフットボールの試合後に起きた乱闘に関する最近のマスコミ報道に反発して，若者について批判を口にする人が多くなりました。私は老人ホームに住んでおり，まさにその問題の高校に所属しているすばらしいグループが，私のような高齢者と一緒に過ごすことを買って出てくれています。私は，木曜日の午後を私と過ごしてくれるサラ，ピーターとリンゼイに感謝しています。この若者たちは模範的なすばらしい人たちなのに，あの記事では例のスキャンダルにかかわった子どもたちと彼らをひとまとめに扱っているように思います。すべての生徒たちが同じではありません。世間からの軽蔑があまりに激しいので，サラは今ではどこの学校へ行っているか言うことを恥ずかしく思っています。これは私たちに対する警鐘でしょう。この機会をとらえて，スポーツ選手たちばかりに圧倒的な賞賛を送る代わりに，ボランティア活動に参加して学業も優秀な生徒たちをヒーローと考えてはいかがでしょうか。

敬具

グラディス・アンダーウッド

---

**1186 scorn** [skɔ́ːrn]
名 軽蔑；軽蔑の的　⇒派 **scornful** 形 軽蔑した
with scorn　軽蔑して

**1187 seize** [síːz]
他 をつかむ；〈意味など〉を理解する
seize an idea　考えをはっきりと理解する

**1188 overwhelming** [òuvərhwélmiŋ]
形 圧倒的な，抗しがたい
an overwhelming disaster　不可抗力の災害

---

**Q** The word "seize" in line 12 is closest in meaning to
(A) take
(B) arrest
(C) acquire
(D) create

解答は p. 336

## 5  Memo 1  社屋の増築工事のお知らせ

This is to **inform** you that **construction** is to begin on the new wing of this building on Wednesday. We recognize the potential **disruption** from noise, but we trust that you will manage to carry out your daily duties without **undue hardship**. We have devised a **contingency** plan for client meetings, however. We were fortunate to find a **vacancy** in a small **suite** of offices on the 9th floor of the Winchester Building across the street that will serve as our temporary **conference** rooms. You can reserve meeting space on a first-come-first-served basis, by calling Rhonda Neal in the **personnel** department at extension 5509.　　　　(104 words)

---

**1189 inform** [infɔ́ːrm]
他 に知らせる，通知する
inform ～ of ...　～に…を知らせる

**1190 construction** [kənstrʌ́kʃən]
名 建設；建設工事
under [in the course of] construction　建設中で

**1191 disruption** [disrʌ́pʃən]
名 混乱；分裂
⇒派 **disrupt** 他 を混乱させる；を分裂させる
a major disruption　大きな混乱

**1192 undue** [ʌndjúː]
形 過度の；不当な
undue profit　不当な利得

**1193 hardship** [hάːrdʃip]
名 苦労，困難
bear hardship　困苦に耐える

**1194 contingency** [kəntíndʒənsi]
名 偶然のこと；予期される緊急事態
⇒派 **contingent** 形 偶然の
prepare for the contingency　万一の場合に備える

水曜日にこのビルの新しい棟の建設工事が始まることをお知らせいたします。騒音による混乱の可能性はあると思いますが，皆さんはそれほどひどい苦労なしに日々の業務をこなせるものと信じています。しかしながら，顧客との会合についての緊急時対策も考案しました。幸い，向かいのウィンチェスタービルの9階に，当座の会議室として使えるような，小ぢんまりとした続き部屋の事務所の空きがあることがわかりました。内線5509，人事部のロンダ・ニールに電話をいただければ，先着順で会議スペースを予約することができます。

---

### 1195 vacancy
[véikənsi]

名 空室；(職・地位などの)空席，欠員
⇒派 **vacant** 形 空いている
have a vacancy for ～　～に欠員がある

### 1196 suite
[swíːt]

名 (ホテルなどの)ひと続きの部屋，スイート；ひと揃いの家具
a hotel suite　ホテルのスイートルーム

### 1197 conference
[kánfərəns]

名 会議
hold a conference　会議を開催する
attend a conference　会議に出席する

### 1198 personnel
[pɜ̀ːrsənél]

名 職員；人事部
excessive personnel costs　多すぎる人件費

---

**Q** The word "vacancy" in line 6 is closest in meaning to
(A) disturbance
(B) opening
(C) insignificance
(D) equipment

解答は p. 336

## 6  Memo 2  共同募金のお知らせ

**TO ALL EMPLOYEES**

As you know every year the chairman of our company endorses a charity for our **annual** corporate **fundraiser**. The members of the fundraiser committee collaborate to offer an event that is both enjoyable and **inspiring**. Our support this year is for the American **Lung** Association. We will have a formal dinner dance at the Whitmore Hotel downtown that will include a silent auction. The entertainment this year will be a one-woman show by comedienne Rita Kowalski. Tickets to the show are $75.00 per person. $50 of the total cost is tax-**deductible**. In addition, we have **enclosed** an envelope in this notice for those who wish to **donate** additional funds. These donations are also tax-deductible. For anyone wishing to make an **anonymous** donation, please feel free to leave the taxpayer information blank.

(134 words)

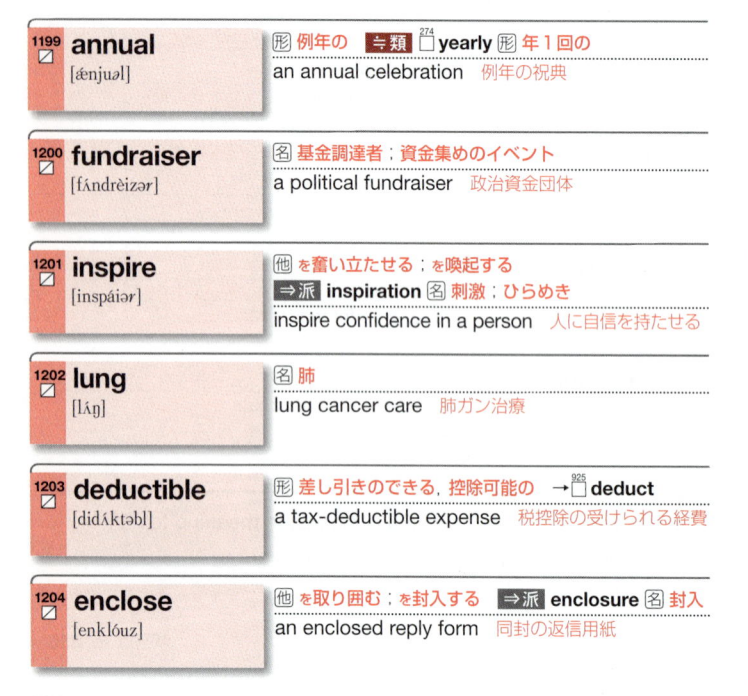

---

**1199 annual** [ǽnjuəl]
形 例年の　≒類 yearly 形 年1回の
an annual celebration　例年の祝典

**1200 fundraiser** [fʌ́ndrèizər]
名 基金調達者；資金集めのイベント
a political fundraiser　政治資金団体

**1201 inspire** [inspáiər]
他 を奮い立たせる；を喚起する
⇒派 inspiration 名 刺激；ひらめき
inspire confidence in a person　人に自信を持たせる

**1202 lung** [lʌ́ŋ]
名 肺
lung cancer care　肺ガン治療

**1203 deductible** [didʌ́ktəbl]
形 差し引きのできる，控除可能の　→ deduct
a tax-deductible expense　税控除の受けられる経費

**1204 enclose** [enklóuz]
他 を取り囲む；を封入する　⇒派 enclosure 名 封入
an enclosed reply form　同封の返信用紙

従業員各位

ご存じの通り，毎年当社の代表は**年1回**の共同**募金イベント**のためのチャリティを支援しています。募金委員会のメンバーは協力して，楽しくかつ**意識を高めるような**イベントを実施します。今年我々が支援するのは，アメリカ**肺**協会です。町の中心部にあるホイットモアホテルで正式なディナーダンスパーティがあり，そこで入札式オークションも行われます。今年の余興はコメディエンヌのリタ・コワルスキーによるワンマンショーです。ショーのチケットは1人75ドルです。全費用のうち50ドルは税金の**控除対象**になります。さらに，この案内状には，追加資金の**寄付**を希望される方のために封筒**を同封**しています。その寄付も控除対象となります。**匿名による**寄付をご希望の方は，遠慮なく納税者情報を空白にしておいてください。

---

### 1205 donate
[dóuneit, -́-]

他 を寄付する；を提供する 自 寄付する
⇒派 donation 名 寄付
donate 〜 to ... 〜を…に寄付する

### 1206 anonymous
[ənánəməs]

形 匿名の
an anonymous telephone cal 匿名の電話

---

**Q** The word "anonymous" in line 13 is closest in meaning to
(A) illegal
(B) unusual
(C) infamous
(D) unnamed

解答は p.336

## 7  Memo 3  コンピュータ購入のお知らせ

From: Harold R. Marley, Personnel
Notice to All Employees

Computer **Upgrades**
We have recently purchased 50 Jonas Notebook PCs. Any employee whose laptop is more than 15 months old may be **eligible** for a new **unit**. Jonas is up-and-coming in the computer field and all of their units have high **quality displays** with an **unconditional guarantee**. If even one bright dot is found, you can exchange it for a new model! These computers have built-in Bluetooth wireless **capabilities** that make it easy to be online anywhere or to **transfer** data from your cell phones and PDAs. They also have a DVD-RW drive and a built-in media reader. To apply for a new computer, log in on the employee Web site and open page users/newpc.htm. Make sure to include your cell phone number so that the tech advisor to the personnel department can contact you directly **regarding** this replacement.  (148 words)

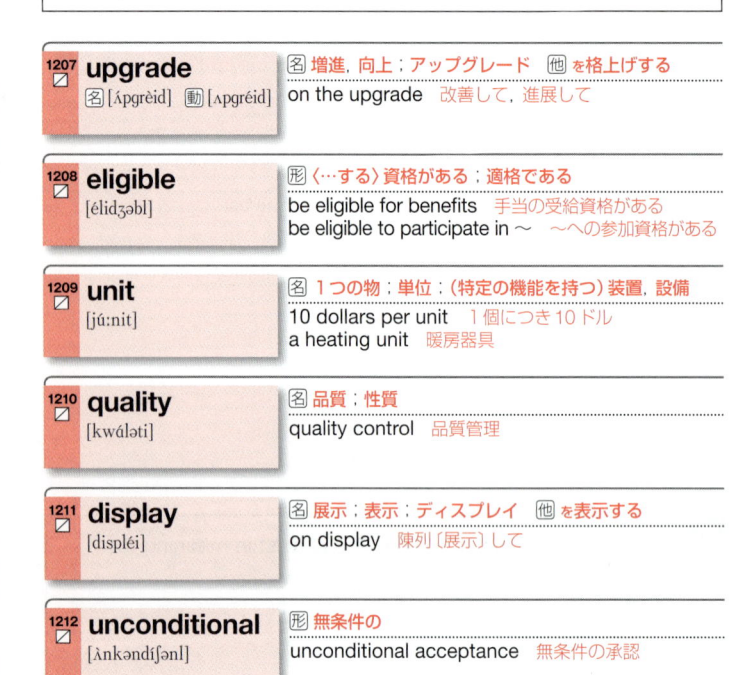

---

**1207 upgrade**
名 [ʌ́pgrèid]  動 [ʌpgréid]

名 増進, 向上；アップグレード　他 を格上げする
on the upgrade　改善して, 進展して

---

**1208 eligible**
[élidʒəbl]

形 〈…する〉資格がある；適格である
be eligible for benefits　手当の受給資格がある
be eligible to participate in ～　～への参加資格がある

---

**1209 unit**
[júːnit]

名 1つの物；単位；(特定の機能を持つ)装置, 設備
10 dollars per unit　1個につき10ドル
a heating unit　暖房器具

---

**1210 quality**
[kwɑ́ləti]

名 品質；性質
quality control　品質管理

---

**1211 display**
[displéi]

名 展示；表示；ディスプレイ　他 を表示する
on display　陳列〔展示〕して

---

**1212 unconditional**
[ʌ̀nkəndíʃənl]

形 無条件の
unconditional acceptance　無条件の承認

差出人:人事部　ハロルド・R・マーリー
全社員への連絡

コンピュータの**アップグレード**
先日ジョナスのノートパソコンを 50 台購入しました。15 か月以上前のノートパソコンを使っている方には，新しい**機器**にする**資格があります**。ジョナスはコンピュータ分野において有望で，すべての製品に，**条件なしの保証**付きの**高品質**の**ディスプレイ**が付いています。1 つでも明るい色の点が見つかれば，新しいモデルに交換できます！このコンピュータにはブルートゥースのワイヤレス**性能**が組み込まれており，どこでも容易にオンライン接続したり，携帯電話や PDA からデータ**を転送**したりできます。DVD-RW ドライブと内蔵型のメディアリーダーも付いています。新しいコンピュータを申し込むには，従業員用ウェブサイトにログインし，users/newpc.htm のページを開いてください。この交換**に関して**，人事部の技術アドバイザーが直接連絡できるように，携帯電話の番号を必ず記入してください。

### 1213 guarantee
[gæ̀rəntíː]
名 保証；保証書　他 を保証する，確約する
a guarantee fund　保証積立金

### 1214 capability
[kèipəbíləti]
名 能力；才能；性能　⇒派 capable 形 有能な；〈…する〉能力がある　≒類 ability 名 能力
the capability to deal with 〜　〜を処理する能力

### 1215 transfer
動 [trænsfə́ːr, ´−−]
名 [trǽnsfər]
他 を移す；を異動させる；を乗り換えさせる
自 乗り換える；異動する　名 移動
transfer to another department　別の部に異動になる

### 1216 regarding
[rigáːrdiŋ]
前 については，に関しては
regarding your recent inquiry　先日のお問い合わせに関して

---

**Q** The word "unit" in line 6 is closest in meaning to
(A) part
(B) group
(C) team
(D) machine

解答は p. 336

## 8 Memo 4 休暇調査実施のお知らせ

To: All **Executives**
From: Personnel

It has come to our attention that the average executive in our organization has two weeks or more vacation time available at the **current** moment. We understand the **popularity** of taking fewer, longer vacations and why this is an option that is **commonly favored**, but we are concerned about the **distinct** possibility that a large number of you will decide to take time off **simultaneously**. We do not wish to do away with the system of saving up vacation time to take extended time off, so we have **devised** a **survey** that asks each of you when you will be likely to take your next leave. As this is an informal gathering of data, we have done our best to **simplify** the process. Simply indicate the month in which you wish to take time off and whether your vacation is likely to be in the first or second half of the month. Thank you for your cooperation.

(162 words)

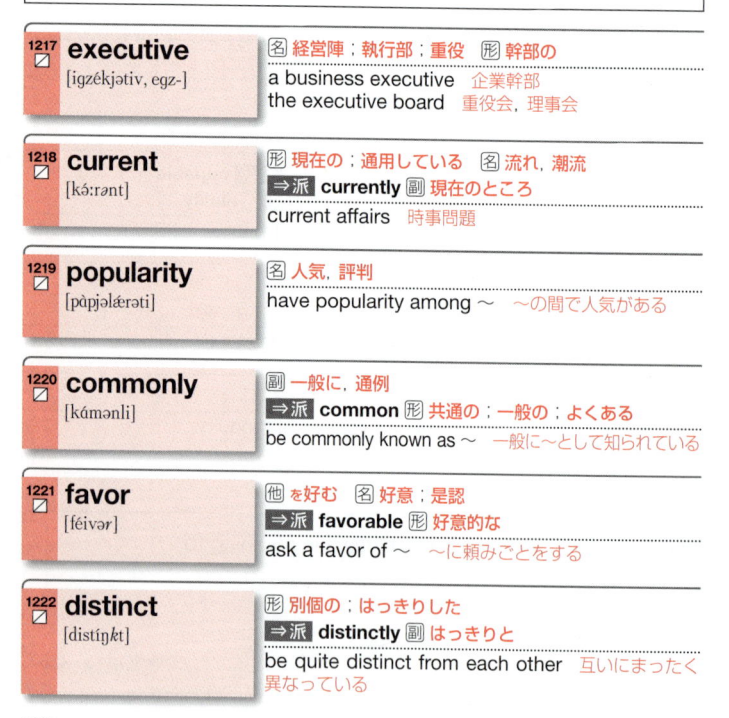

---

**1217 executive** [iɡzékjətiv, eɡz-]
名 経営陣；執行部；重役　形 幹部の
a business executive　企業幹部
the executive board　重役会, 理事会

**1218 current** [kə́ːrənt]
形 現在の；通用している　名 流れ, 潮流
⇒派 currently 副 現在のところ
current affairs　時事問題

**1219 popularity** [pɑ̀pjəlǽrəti]
名 人気, 評判
have popularity among 〜　〜の間で人気がある

**1220 commonly** [kɑ́mənli]
副 一般に, 通例
⇒派 common 形 共通の；一般の；よくある
be commonly known as 〜　一般に〜として知られている

**1221 favor** [féivər]
他 を好む　名 好意；是認
⇒派 favorable 形 好意的な
ask a favor of 〜　〜に頼みごとをする

**1222 distinct** [distíŋkt]
形 別個の；はっきりした
⇒派 distinctly 副 はっきりと
be quite distinct from each other　互いにまったく異なっている

宛先：全**重役**
差出人：人事課

我が社の平均的な重役は，**現**時点で2週間またはそれ以上の休暇を取れるということが私たちの注目するところとなりました。より長い休暇をより少ない回数で取るのが**人気だということ**と，なぜそれが**一般的に**好まれる選択肢なのかということは承知しています。けれども，私たちは，皆様方のうちの多くが**同時に**休むことを決定なさる可能性が**はっきりしている**ことを懸念しております。皆様がより長い休暇を取るため，休暇日数をためておくというシステムを撤廃したくはありませんので，皆様が次の休暇をだいたいいつごろ取ることになりそうかをお一人お一人に伺うという**調査を考案**いたしました。これは公式のデータ収集ではありませんので，なるべく手続き**を簡単に**いたしました。休暇を希望なさる月と，休暇がその月の初旬になりそうか下旬になりそうかということのみ，簡単にお知らせください。ご協力ありがとうございます。

---

**1223 simultaneously**
[sàiməltéiniəsli, sì-]
副 同時に　⇒派 **simultaneous** 形 同時に起こる
simultaneously with 〜　〜と同時に

**1224 devise**
[diváiz]
他 を考案する，考え出す
devise a long-term strategy　長期戦略を考案する

**1225 survey**
名 [sə́rvei, sərvéi]
動 [—́—, —́—]
名 調査；調査報告書；概観
他 を調査する；の全体を眺める
carry out a survey of 〜　〜の調査を実行する

**1226 simplify**
[símpləfài]
他 を単純にする；を容易にする
⇒派 **simple** 形 単純な
simplify procedures for 〜　〜の手続きを簡単にする

---

**Q** The word "favored" in line 7 is closest in meaning to
(A) honored
(B) trusted
(C) preferred
(D) served

解答は p.336

## 9 Advertisement 1　旅行会社のサービス案内

Edgerton Specialty Travel Agency can **customize** any trip to your needs, to make your next excursion unforgettable. Why plan your trip alone? At Edgerton, we have an **extensive** travel resource room with a **multitude** of **brochures** and guidebooks. We even have research **cubicles** where you can make notes from our materials or go online. Unlike making reservations and arrangements from home, our friendly and **courteous** agents are right on **site** here to consult with you and serve as your personal travel advisers. **Established** in 1965, we **celebrate** our 40th **anniversary** this year. Come in for a consultation and enter our anniversary sweepstakes where you could win a trip for two to Australia. We're located in the First Street Mall in the heart of town. Call us at 555-1119.　　　　　　　　　　　(128 words)

---

**1227 customize** [kʌ́stəmàiz]
他 をカスタマイズする, 好みに合わせて変更する
customized software　特別仕様のソフトウェア

**1228 extensive** [iksténsiv, eks-]
形 広い；広範囲にわたる；大規模な
extensive market research　広範囲にわたる市場調査

**1229 multitude** [mʌ́ltət(j)ùːd]
名 多数；[the multitude] 大衆
appeal to the multitude　大衆に訴えかける

**1230 brochure** [brouʃúər]
名 パンフレット, 小冊子
a travel brochure　旅行案内のパンフレット

**1231 cubicle** [kjúːbikl]
名 間仕切りで小さく区切った場所；小部屋
office cubicles　オフィスの小部屋

**1232 courteous** [kə́ːrtiəs]
形 礼儀正しい；親切な　→ 37 courtesy
be courteous in wording　言葉遣いが丁寧である

エッジャートン・スペシャルティ旅行社は，ご要望に応じてどんな旅行も**カスタマイズし**，お客様の今度の旅行を忘れられないものにすることができます。一人で旅行の計画を立てる必要などありません。エッジャートンには，**パンフレット**やガイドブックを**多数**備えた**広い**旅行資料スペースがあります。さらに，資料からメモを取ったり，インターネットに接続したりできる検索用**ブース**もご用意しております。ご自宅で予約や手配をするのと違って，ここでは当店の親しみやすくて**親切な**担当者がその**場**におり，お客様の相談に乗り，個人の旅行アドバイザーとしてお手伝いいたします。当店は1965年に**設立され**，今年40**周年を祝います**。旅行相談にお越しになり，40周年記念懸賞にご応募ください。2名様にオーストラリア旅行が当たります。当店は町の中心部にあるファーストストリート商店街にあります。お問い合わせは555-1119まで。

---

**1233 site** [sáit]
名 敷地；場所；(インターネット上の)サイト
on site　現場で；現地で

**1234 establish** [istǽbliʃ, es-]
他 を設立する　⇒派 **establishment** 名 設立
establish one's fame　名声を確立する

**1235 celebrate** [séləbrèit]
他〈特定の日・出来事〉を祝う
celebrate her promotion　彼女の昇進を祝う

**1236 anniversary** [ænəvə́ːrsəri]
名 (例年の)記念日
celebrate one's wedding anniversary　結婚記念日を祝う

---

**Q** The word "extensive" in line 3 is closest in meaning to
(A) costly
(B) comprehensive
(C) luxurious
(D) frequent

解答は p. 336

## 10 Advertisement 2　料理講習会の案内

The Crawford Hotel is proud to announce its new **Culinary** Studies Weekends. Every other month, Chef David, senior chef of the hotel's **premier** restaurant, The Peacock Grille, is offering a two-day seminar. Learn to prepare **authentic** restaurant fare at home. To make the program appeal to as wide an audience as possible, Chef David asks that you indicate your skill level on the application form. A highly **skilled** chef will be placed in the advanced group. The chef will assign tasks according to each participant's ability. David Wentworth is the **former** head chef of The Sojourner's Bistro. Headhunted by the chairman of the Crawford Hotel, who fell in love with his Caesar salad, Chef David began working at The Peacock Grille in 1999. Receiving much **acclaim** for his concern for **nutrition**, Chef David's **recipes** are also **hearty**, healthy, and low-fat.　　　　　　　　　　　　　　　　　　　　　(140 words)

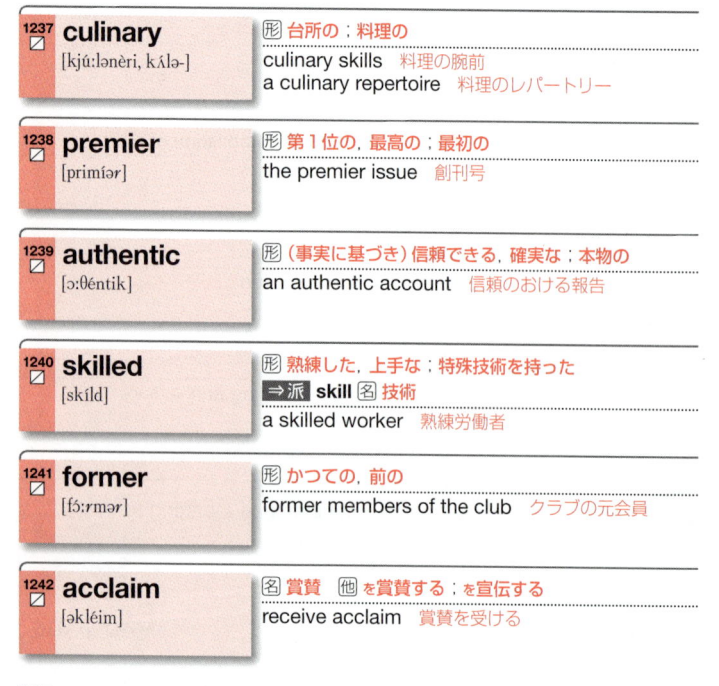

---

**1237 culinary** [kjú:lənèri, kʌ́lə-]
形 台所の；料理の
culinary skills　料理の腕前
a culinary repertoire　料理のレパートリー

**1238 premier** [primíər]
形 第1位の, 最高の；最初の
the premier issue　創刊号

**1239 authentic** [ɔːθéntik]
形 (事実に基づき) 信頼できる, 確実な；本物の
an authentic account　信頼のおける報告

**1240 skilled** [skíld]
形 熟練した, 上手な；特殊技術を持った
⇒派 **skill** 名 技術
a skilled worker　熟練労働者

**1241 former** [fɔ́:rmər]
形 かつての, 前の
former members of the club　クラブの元会員

**1242 acclaim** [əkléim]
名 賞賛　他 を賞賛する；を宣伝する
receive acclaim　賞賛を受ける

クロフォード・ホテルから新しく始まるウィークエンド料理講習会をご案内できることを光栄に思います。1か月おきに，当ホテルの最高級レストラン，ピーコック・グリルのベテランシェフ，デイビッドシェフが2日間のセミナーを行います。本格的なレストランの料理をご家庭で作れるようになります。このプログラムができるだけ多くの参加者の方々にご満足いただけるようにと，デイビッドシェフは申込書にご自身の技術レベルを記入してほしいと言っています。上級グループには高い技術を持ったシェフが担当します。シェフは，それぞれの参加者の能力に応じて，作業を割り当てます。デイビッド・ウェントワースはソジュルナーズ・ビストロの前主任シェフです。彼のシーザーサラダにほれ込んだクロフォード・ホテルの支配人に引き抜かれて，デイビッドシェフは1999年にピーコック・グリルで働き始めました。デイビッドシェフのレシピは，栄養への配慮について多くの賞賛を得ており，栄養たっぷりのうえ，ヘルシーで低脂肪です。

---

### 1243 **nutrition**
[n(j)u:tríʃən]

名 栄養摂取；栄養；栄養学

an expert in nutrition　栄養学の専門家
a source of nutrition　栄養源

### 1244 **recipe**
[résəpi]

名 調理法, レシピ

a recipe for 〜　〜の調理法
a recipe using milk　牛乳を使った調理法

### 1245 **hearty**
[hárti]

形 心からの；(栄養)たっぷりの

hearty congratulations　心からのお祝い

---

**Q** The word "former" in line 9 is closest in meaning to
(A) oldest
(B) previous
(C) first
(D) overdue

解答は p. 336

## 11 Information 薬の使用説明

The purpose of this medication is to keep blood glucose levels within the target range. In the **majority** of cases, your physician will have had you **undergo** a fasting blood test **beforehand** to determine baseline levels. This blood draw provides your doctor with **invaluable** information. By examining the blood sample in a laboratory, it is possible to **assess** your condition from both your blood glucose score and your score on a test called Hemoglobin A1C (HA1C), which offers an **accurate** indication of your condition over the past three months. Your physician uses this data to **evaluate** your condition and will instruct you to be retested periodically. If your HA1C score goes above 7.0, your doctor may suggest changes in your **diet** and if it falls below 7.0, it may be necessary to **adjust** the **dose** of the medication. (138 words)

---

### 1246 majority
[mədʒɔ́(:)rəti]
名 大多数, 大部分
⇒派 major 形 多数の；大きい 自 専攻する
an overall majority 絶対多数

### 1247 undergo
[ʌ̀ndərɡóu]
他 を経験する；〈検査・手術など〉を受ける
undergo surgery 手術を受ける

### 1248 beforehand
[bifɔ́:rhænd]
副 あらかじめ ≒類 in advance あらかじめ
⇔反 afterward 副 あとで
let ~ know beforehand ~にあらかじめ知らせる

### 1249 invaluable
[invǽljuəbl, -væljubl]
形 計り知れないほど貴重な
an invaluable art collection 貴重な美術コレクション

### 1250 assess
[əsés]
他 を評価〔査定〕する；〈税金など〉を課す
assess a fine on ~ ~に罰金を科す

### 1251 accurate
[ǽkjərət]
形 正確な ⇒派 accuracy 名 正確さ
to be accurate 正確に言えば

この薬の目的は、血糖値を目標範囲内に抑えることです。**大多数**の場合、担当医は、最低値を決めるために、あなたに**前もって**絶食を伴う血液検査**を受け**させることになります。この採血は担当医にとって**貴重**な情報源となります。血液サンプルを研究所で調べることにより、血糖値とヘモグロビン A1C（HA1C）と呼ばれる検査の値の両方を利用して、あなたの状態**を査定する**ことができます。HA1C は過去 3 か月間のあなたの状態**を正確に**示してくれます。あなたの担当医は、このデータを使ってあなたの状態**を評価し**、定期的に再検査を受けるように指示します。あなたの HA1C 値が 7.0 を超えるようなら、担当医はあなたに**食事**の変更を指示し、7.0 を下回るようなら、薬の**服用量を調整する**ことが必要となるでしょう。

---

### 1252 evaluate
[ivæljuèit]

他〈価値・能力など〉を判断〔評価〕する
⇒派 **evaluation** 名 評価
evaluate property　財産を評価する

### 1253 diet
[dáiət]

名 規定食；食事；ダイエット
on a diet　ダイエット中で

### 1254 adjust
[ədʒʌ́st]

他 を合わせる、適合させる、調整する
⇒派 **adjustment** 名 調整
adjust oneself to ～　～に順応する

### 1255 dose
[dóus]

名（薬の 1 回の）服用量
a lethal [fatal] dose　致死量

---

**Q** The word "assess" in line 6 is closest in meaning to
(A) charge
(B) value
(C) adjust
(D) judge

解答は p. 336

## 12 Review 新作映画の論評

*Unexpected Visitor*, Melwood Studio's latest thriller, is an unexpected surprise among the summer films. Starring Tiffany Winters and Justin Marx, the film **revolves** around a mistaken address. Instead of going to a meeting at 75 W. 63rd St., the protagonist ends up at 75 E. 63rd St. where he becomes involved in one **amazing** situation after the other. In this film, producer-director Avery Shaw proves that a good **psychological** thriller can still **capture** the imagination of today's movie-goer. There are no special effects, and the soundtrack is melodic, yet **devoid** of classic rock hits, as has become popular among recent films. Winters and Marx are **relative newcomers** to Hollywood, but both actors have clear "star" quality. There are a few rocky areas in the storyline where **continuity** could be better, but **overall**, this film deserves a big thumbs-up. (138 words)

---

**1256 unexpected** [ʌ̀nɪkspéktɪd]
形 予期しない ⇒派 **expect** 他 を予期する
make an unexpected visit 突然訪問する

**1257 revolve** [rɪvɑ́lv]
自 回転する；展開する 他 を回転させる
revolve around ～ ～の周りを回転する；～を中心に展開する

**1258 amazing** [əméɪzɪŋ]
形 驚くべき
an amazing amount of ～ 驚くほどの量の～

**1259 psychological** [sàɪkəlɑ́dʒɪkl]
形 心理学の；心理の ⇒派 **psychology** 名 心理学 **psychologist** 名 心理学者
a psychological burden 心理的負担

**1260 capture** [kǽptʃər]
他 をとらえる；〈人の心・注意など〉を引き付ける
capture one's attention ～の注意を引き付ける

**1261 devoid** [dɪvɔ́ɪd]
形 欠いている，まったくない
devoid of objectivity 客観性に欠ける

メルウッドスタジオの最新のスリラー,『予期せぬ訪問者』は, 夏の映画の中の予期せぬ驚きである。ティファニー・ウィンターズとジャスティン・マークスが主演するこの映画は, 住所の間違いを巡って展開する。主人公は, 63番街ウェスト75番地での会合に行く代わりに, 63番街イースト75番地に行ってしまい, そこで次々と驚くべき状況に巻き込まれる。この映画で製作者兼監督のエイブリー・ショーは, 良質のサイコスリラーが今なお現代の映画ファンの心をとらえることができるということを証明している。特殊効果はなく, サウンドトラックは, 美しいものの, 最近の映画で人気が出てきたようなクラッシックロックのヒット曲はそこにはまったくない。ウィンターズとマークスはハリウッドでは比較的新人であるといえるが, 両俳優とも明らかに「スター」の素質を持っている。話の展開にいくつかぎこちなく, もう少し連続性が求められる箇所があるものの, 全体的にいえば, 大いに賞賛に値する。

## 1262 relative
[rélətiv]

形 相対的な, 比較上；関係する 名 親類
⇒派 **relatively** 副 比較的
relative to 〜 〜に関して；〜と比較して

## 1263 newcomer
[n(j)úːkʌmər]

名 新人；初心者
introduce a newcomer 新人を紹介する

## 1264 continuity
[kàntən(j)úːəti]

名 連続(性)
break the continuity of one's speech 〜の話の腰を折る

## 1265 overall
副 [òuvəróːl]
形 [óuvəròːl]

副 全体としては 形 全体の
overall cost 総経費

---

**Q** The word "devoid" in line 9 is closest in meaning to
(A) useless
(B) without
(C) composed
(D) available

解答は p. 336

## 13 Article 1　アルゼンチン経済

Argentina plans to begin **negotiations** next month with the International **Monetary** Fund for a new loan agreement. Argentina already **owes** about $11.7 billion to the IMF making it the third largest **debtor** after Brazil and Turkey. **Apparently**, Argentina needs a new loan to help **boost** central bank reserves and extend the nation's economic recovery. The Argentine economy has expanded more than 8% in each of the past two years, after contracting 11% in 2002. Since Argentina is able to meet the payments, such an agreement with the IMF is more important to the country for **prestige** than for financing. Loan agreements from the IMF give Argentina a sort of "**seal** of **approval**" that looks good to **potential** foreign investors.　　　　　（119 words）

---

**1266 negotiation** [nigòuʃiéiʃən]
名 交渉, 折衝　⇒派 negotiate 自他 (を)交渉する
enter into negotiations with ～　～と交渉を開始する

**1267 monetary** [mánətèri]
形 通貨の；財政の　⇒派 money 名 金；通貨
in monetary difficulties　財政困難で

**1268 owe** [óu]
他〈人〉に〈金額〉の借りがある；〈人〉に〈親切など〉を受けている
owe money on mortgages　抵当に入れた借金がある

**1269 debtor** [détər]
名 債務者, 負債者　⇒派 debt 名 借金, 負債
pay back a debt　借金を返す

**1270 apparently** [əpǽrəntli, əpéər-]
副 どうも…らしい；見たところ…らしい
⇒派 apparent 形 明白な；見たところ
apparently small difference　一見小さな違い

**1271 boost** [bú:st]
他 を押し上げる；〈生産・売上など〉を増やす　名 上昇
boost sales　売上を伸ばす
a boost in prices　価格の引き上げ

アルゼンチンは来月，新しい貸し付け合意について国際**通貨**基金と**交渉**を始めることを計画している。アルゼンチンはすでに IMF から約 117 億ドル**の貸し付けを受け**ており，ブラジル，トルコに次いで世界 3 位の**債務国**になっている。**聞くところによると**，アルゼンチンは中央銀行の予備金**を増やし**，国内経済の復興をさらに進めるために新しい貸し付けを必要としているとのことである。アルゼンチン経済は，2002 年に 11 パーセント縮小して以来，過去 2 年とも前年より 8 パーセント以上拡大している。アルゼンチンには返済能力があるため，IMF とのこのような合意は，同国にとって，資金調達のためというよりもむしろ，**威信**のために重要である。IMF からの貸付合意は，海外の**潜在的**投資家にとって魅力のある，ある種の「**承認の印**」をアルゼンチンに与えるだろう。

---

### 1272 prestige
[prestíːʒ, -tíːdʒ]

名 名声，威信

add prestige to 〜　〜に威信を添える

### 1273 seal
[síːl]

名 印章；封印；密封　他 に封をする；を密封する

the official seal of approval　公的な認可の印
seal registration　印鑑登録

### 1274 approval
[əprúːvl]

名 承認；賛成

⇒派 approve 他 自 (を)認める，賛成する

prior approval　事前の承認

### 1275 potential
[pəténʃəl, pou-]

形 可能性のある，潜在的な　名 可能性，見込み；素質

a potential customer　顧客になる可能性のある人，潜在顧客

---

**Q** The word "seal" in line 11 is closest in meaning to
(A) decoration
(B) sign
(C) glue
(D) rubber

解答は p. 336

## 14 Article 2 会社統合の現況

In the 1980s, profit-seekers with deep pockets were able to charge in and **gain** control of companies through what was known as a "**hostile takeover**." The situation quieted down considerably in the 90s. Globalization became the goal and the violent images of corporate raiders seemed to disappear gradually, making the more **global** world of **mergers** and **acquisitions** appear friendlier. In reality, American corporations today have been so **thoroughly downsized** and restructured, there is little surplus available for a 1980s-type raider to squeeze out and turn a short-term profit. Companies used to be funded by junk bonds, a high-risk **commodity**, which is a rarity today. Nowadays, companies expend most of their energy trying to stay big and strong enough to weather the current of globalization and **deregulation**.

(126 words)

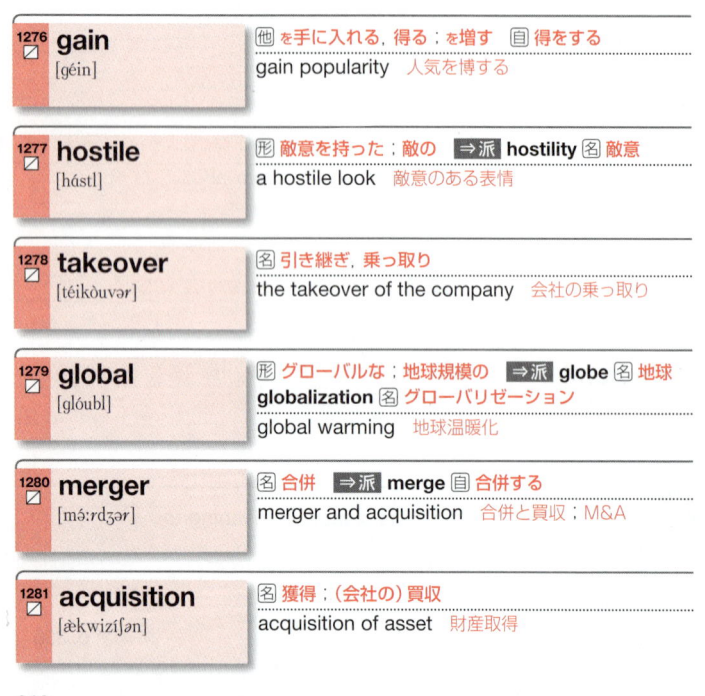

---

**1276 gain** [géin]
他 を手に入れる, 得る；を増す 自 得をする
gain popularity　人気を博する

**1277 hostile** [hάstl]
形 敵意を持った；敵の　⇒派 hostility 名 敵意
a hostile look　敵意のある表情

**1278 takeover** [téikòuvər]
名 引き継ぎ, 乗っ取り
the takeover of the company　会社の乗っ取り

**1279 global** [glóubl]
形 グローバルな；地球規模の　⇒派 globe 名 地球
globalization 名 グローバリゼーション
global warming　地球温暖化

**1280 merger** [mə́:rdʒər]
名 合併　⇒派 merge 自 合併する
merger and acquisition　合併と買収；M&A

**1281 acquisition** [æ̀kwizíʃən]
名 獲得；(会社の) 買収
acquisition of asset　財産取得

1980年代には，十分な資力を持った利益追求者たちは，攻め込んでいって「敵対的買収」として知られる方法で会社に対する支配力を手に入れることができた。90年代には状況はかなり落ち着いた。グローバリゼーションが目標となり，会社の乗っ取り者という強暴なイメージは徐々になくなり，合併と買収という，よりグローバルな世界が友好的に見えるようになった。実際，現在アメリカの会社は徹底的に規模が縮小され，再構築されて，1980年代タイプの乗っ取り者が会社を廃業に追い込み，短期的収益を出すために使える余剰資金はほとんどなくなっている。かつて会社はジャンクボンドやリスクの高い商品を資金として持っていたが，現在ではそれはまれである。今日，会社はグローバリゼーションと規制緩和の流れを切り抜けるのに十分なだけ大きく，強くあるために大いに心血を注いでいる。

---

**1282 thoroughly** [θə́:rouli, θə́:rə-]
副 徹底的に，まったく；入念に
⇒派 thorough 形 徹底的な
a thoroughly competent lawyer　非常に有能な弁護士

**1283 downsize** [dáunsàiz]
他〈人員など〉を削減する；を小型化する
downsize the workforce by 10%　10パーセント人員を削減する

**1284 commodity** [kəmάdəti]
名 日用品；物品，(サービスと対比して)商品
prices of commodity　物価

**1285 deregulation** [di:règjəléiʃən]
名 規制緩和，自由化　⇔反 878 regulation 名 規制
deregulation of prices　価格統制の廃止

---

**Q** The word "gain" in line 2 is closest in meaning to
(A) seize
(B) earn
(C) raise
(D) grow

解答は p.336

## 15 Article 3 ハワイの農業

A good **portion** of our local residents in Kona, Hawaii are farmers or hobby farmers. As produce grows **rapidly** in the climate, people often have more mangos or bananas than they consume themselves. A recent noteworthy trend is for those with plenty of fruit and vegetables to become **grocery** store **vendors**. Several stores in the **vicinity** now **accept** spot sales of popular produce. Some growers find this very **lucrative**. The only requirement seems to be getting a Hawaii General Excise Tax number, which is relatively **inexpensive**. People with more exotic products, such as dragon fruit actually go to the stores and demonstrate to customers how to cut and eat the product. With commonly available items like mangos and avocados, marketing is about appearance or timing. For example, visitors want bananas without spots. In June mangos are **abundant**, but anyone who can deliver them in July meets with great demand. (149 words)

---

**1286 portion** [pɔ́ːrʃən]
名 一部分；一人前の料理；分担
the major portion of the yield 収穫高の大部分

**1287 rapidly** [rǽpidli]
副 速やかに，迅速に ⇒派 rapid 形 速やかな
rapidly changing technology 急速に変化する科学技術

**1288 grocery** [gróusəri]
名 食料雑貨店；[groceries] 食料雑貨類
a grocery store = a grocery 食料雑貨店

**1289 vendor** [véndər, -dɔːr]
名 製造供給元；供給メーカー；売る人，露天商人
a retail vendor 小売り商人
a computer vendor コンピュータメーカー

**1290 vicinity** [visínəti]
名 付近，周辺；近接
in close vicinity to the office 会社のすぐ近くに

**1291 accept** [əksépt, æk-, ik-]
他 を受け取る，受け入れる
⇒派 acceptance 名 受け入れ
accept a proposal 申し出を受け入れる

ハワイ州コナの地元住民の**大部分**が農園や家庭菜園を所有しています。農産物はこの気候の中で**急速に**育つので，人々はしばしば自分たちが消費しきれないほどのマンゴーやバナナを収穫します。最近の特記すべき傾向は，たっぷりと果物や野菜を持っている人が，**食料品**店の**販売人**となることです。今では，**付近**の店のいくつかが，人気のある農産物をその場で販売すること**を受け入れています**。生産者の中には，これはとても**もうかる**と考えている人もいます。必要な条件は，ハワイ一般物品税番号を取得することのみであるようです。これには比較的**費用がかかりません**。ドラゴン・フルーツのように，より珍しい産物を持っている人は，実際に店に出かけて行って，客にその産物の切り方や食べ方を実演しています。マンゴーやアボカドのような一般に手に入るような品物については，販売は外観やタイミングにかかっています。例えば，買い物客は傷のないバナナを欲しがります。6月にはマンゴーは**あり余るほど出回り**ますが，7月にそれを届けられる人はだれでも，大きな需要を受けることになります。

---

### 1292 lucrative
[lúːkrətiv]

形 利益が得られる

a lucrative business　もうかる商売

### 1293 inexpensive
[inikspénsiv]

形 費用がかからない，安い

relatively inexpensive　比較的費用が安い

### 1294 abundant
[əbʌ́ndənt]

形 豊富な

be abundant in ～　～が豊富にある

---

**Q** The word "accept" in line 6 is closest in meaning to
(A) exclude
(B) import
(C) tolerate
(D) allow

解答は p.336

## 16 Article 4　気象情報

Miami, Florida (Global News Service) — Hurricane Ronald reached Category 4 strength Wednesday night as it churned just off the coast of Cuba. Florida **officials** ordered a **mandatory** evacuation of the lower Florida Keys. Many of those forced to evacuate have traveled north to Miami. The **governor** declared a state of emergency in order to mobilize resources to handle the impending storm which has already had **sustained** winds of 135 mph. After the Keys, the forecast indicates that the storm could affect the U.S. Gulf Coast anywhere from Southwest Florida to Southeast Louisiana. The pattern of the storm appears **roughly** the same as Hurricane Betsy, which occurred four years ago. The recommendation of the National Weather **Bureau** is to prepare **plenty** of drinking water and emergency **rations**. Many people are choosing to invest in battery-operated TVs and radios and individual power **generators** that run on gas.　　(145 words)

---

**1295 official** [əfíʃl]
- 名 公務員　形 職務上の；公職にある
- official documents　公文書

**1296 mandatory** [mǽndətɔ̀ːri]
- 形 命令の；義務的な；必須の
- a mandatory clause　必須条項
- mandatory retirement　定年退職

**1297 governor** [gʌ́vənər]
- 名 州知事, 理事
- appoint 〜 to the office of governor　〜を知事に任命する

**1298 sustain** [səstéin]
- 他 を持続させる；に耐える；を支持する
- ⇒派 **sustainable** 形 持続可能な
- sustain interest　興味を持続させる

**1299 roughly** [rʌ́fli]
- 副 おおよそ；手荒に　⇒派 **rough** 形 おおよその
- roughly speaking　大ざっぱに言えば

**1300 bureau** [bjúərou]
- 名 (政府の)省；局；事務所
- bureau chief　支局長

フロリダ州マイアミ（グローバル・ニュースサービス）——ハリケーン・ロナルドは水曜日の夜キューバの沿岸を激しい勢いで通過した際に，カテゴリー4の強さに発達した。フロリダ州の職員はフロリダキーズ南部に強制避難を命じた。強制的に避難させられた人たちの多くは，マイアミへ北上した。知事は，すでに風速毎時135マイルを維持しつつ接近している嵐に対処する人材を動員するために，非常事態を宣言した。予報によれば，キーズの次に，嵐はフロリダ南西部からルイジアナ州南東部にいたるまで，アメリカのメキシコ湾岸のいたるところに影響を与える可能性があるとのことである。嵐の型は4年前に発生したハリケーン・ベッツィとほぼ同じであるとの見方である。気象局は十分な量の飲み水と非常食を用意しておくように勧めている。バッテリー式のテレビやラジオ，ガソリンで動く個人用発電機に投資するという選択をしている人も多い。

---

**1301 plenty**
[plénti]

名 たくさん，十分な量

plenty of ～　たくさんの～

**1302 ration**
[ræʃən]

名 支給，配給；食料

on ration　配給を受けて

**1303 generator**
[dʒénərèitər]

名 発電機

an electric generator　発電機

---

**Q** The word "roughly" in line 10 is closest in meaning to
(A) approximately
(B) difficultly
(C) forcefully
(D) carelessly

解答は p.336

## 17 Article 5 空港検査の厳格化

In this age of **uncertainty**, many citizens are willing to **sacrifice** their **civil** rights and subject themselves to all sorts of **scrutiny** at the hands of airport officials. **Widespread** global **terrorism** has made the treatment at the airport something like **criminal** processing. There is no point in dressing respectably to board a plane, at least not when it comes to footwear, as you may be asked to remove your shoes before stepping through the security scanner. You also want to keep an eye on your hand luggage. If you accidentally leave it in the restroom or the sandwich shop, security personnel may **confiscate** it and you may never see your favorite hairbrush or razor again. Safety, of course, is a **priority**, but some of us can still remember when air travel customers were actually treated with a smile and respect. (140 words)

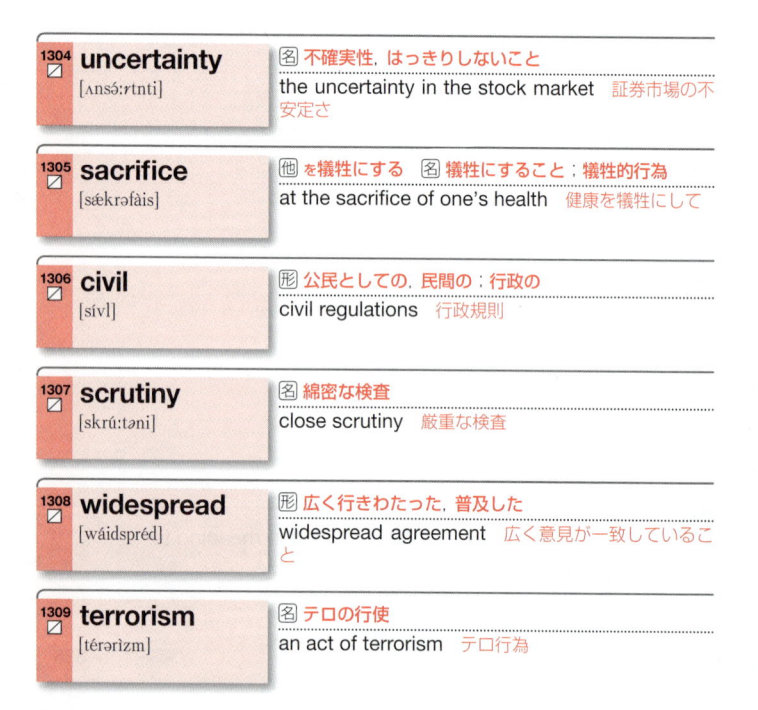

---

**1304 uncertainty** [ʌnsə́ːrtnti]
名 不確実性，はっきりしないこと
the uncertainty in the stock market　証券市場の不安定さ

**1305 sacrifice** [sǽkrəfàis]
他 を犠牲にする　名 犠牲にすること；犠牲的行為
at the sacrifice of one's health　健康を犠牲にして

**1306 civil** [sívl]
形 公民としての，民間の；行政の
civil regulations　行政規則

**1307 scrutiny** [skrúːtəni]
名 綿密な検査
close scrutiny　厳重な検査

**1308 widespread** [wáidspréd]
形 広く行きわたった，普及した
widespread agreement　広く意見が一致していること

**1309 terrorism** [térərìzm]
名 テロの行使
an act of terrorism　テロ行為

この**不安定**な時代にあって，多くの国民は喜んで**市民としての**権利を**犠牲にし**，空港職員の手によるあらゆる種類の**綿密な検査**に身を任せている。地球規模で**広がっているテロリズム**のために，空港での待遇は**犯罪者**の処理手続のようなものになってきている。飛行機に乗るときに，上品に着飾っても意味がない。少なくとも，靴についてはそうだ。セキュリティー探査装置を通る前に靴を脱ぐようにと求められるかもしれないからだ。手荷物についても，目を離さないようにしたいところだ。もしたまたまトイレかサンドイッチ店に置き忘れたりすれば，警備担当者がそれ**を没収し**，あなたは二度とお気に入りのヘアブラシやカミソリにお目にかかれないかもしれない。安全はもちろん**優先事項**だが，私たちの中には，今でも，飛行機の旅客たちが実際に笑顔と敬意を持って接してもらえたころを思い出すことができる人がいるのだ。

---

**1310 criminal**
[kríminl]

形 犯罪の 名 犯罪者 →crime

a criminal case　刑事事件

**1311 confiscate**
[kánfiskèit]

他 を没収する ⇒派 confiscation 名 没収

be confiscated by ～　～に没収される

**1312 priority**
[praiɔ́(:)rəti]

名 優先事項；優先（権）

of high priority　最優先の

---

**Q** The word "civil" in line 2 is closest in meaning to
(A) polite
(B) friendly
(C) citizen's
(D) government's

解答は p. 336

## 18 Article 6 容疑者の脱走事件

Al Morrison and Richard Sommerville escaped from Centerville Prison this afternoon. Morrison is considered **armed** and dangerous. In **jail** on suspicion of murdering his girlfriend, Carmen Flores, Morrison has been **awaiting trial**. Sommerville is a repeat offender doing time for drug trafficking. The two used a high-tech stun **device** to overpower the guards in the cell block. They switched clothing with the prison employees and walked out of the gate. Throughout his **imprisonment**, Morrison has maintained that he is **innocent** of the murder charges. When asked to comment, Morrison's **attorney**, Jeffrey Osborne said that his client was feeling impatient with the **judicial** process and this frustration drove him to such extreme measures. Osborne says that if his client contacts him, he will urge him to **surrender**. (126 words)

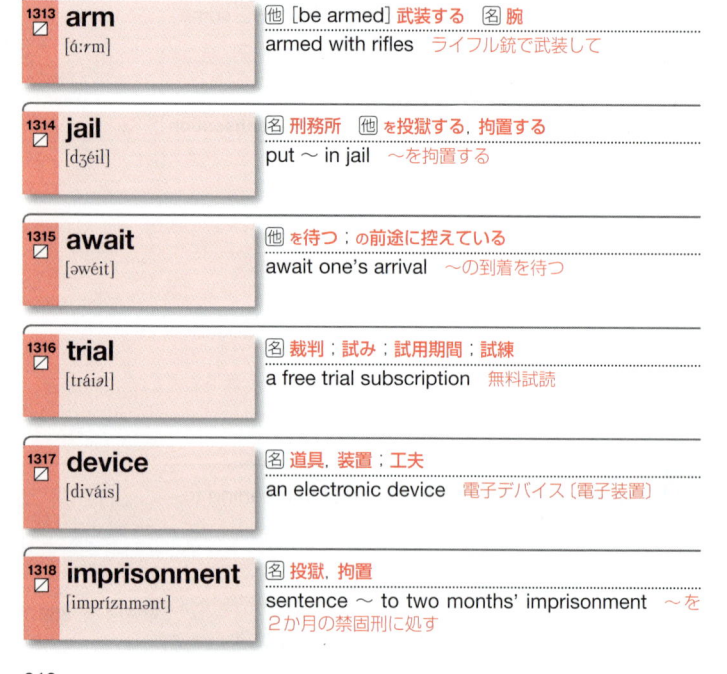

---

**1313 arm** [á:rm]
他 [be armed] 武装する 名 腕
armed with rifles　ライフル銃で武装して

**1314 jail** [dʒéil]
名 刑務所　他 を投獄する,拘置する
put ~ in jail　~を拘置する

**1315 await** [əwéit]
他 を待つ；の前途に控えている
await one's arrival　~の到着を待つ

**1316 trial** [tráiəl]
名 裁判；試み；試用期間；試練
a free trial subscription　無料試読

**1317 device** [diváis]
名 道具, 装置；工夫
an electronic device　電子デバイス〔電子装置〕

**1318 imprisonment** [impríznmənt]
名 投獄, 拘置
sentence ~ to two months' imprisonment　~を2か月の禁固刑に処す

今日の午後，センタービル刑務所からアル・モリソンとリチャード・ソマービルが脱走した。モリソンは武器を所持しており，危害を及ぼす可能性があると思われる。モリソンは恋人のカーメン・フローレスを殺害した疑いで拘置中であり，裁判を待っていた。ソマービルは麻薬売買で服役している常習犯である。2人は，高性能のスタン装置を使って独房棟の看守を打ち負かした。彼らは刑務所の職員と衣服を取り替え，門から歩いて逃亡した。モリソンは拘置中一貫して殺人罪については無実であると主張していた。モリソンの弁護士のジェフリー・オズボーンはコメントを求められ，依頼人は裁判の進行状況にいらいらしており，そのフラストレーションからこのような極端な手段に出たと話している。オズボーンは，もし依頼人が連絡してきたら，抵抗をやめるように説得すると話している。

---

**1319 innocent** [ínəsənt]
形 無罪の；悪気のない
⇒派 **innocence** 名 無罪であること
an innocent question　他意のない質問

**1320 attorney** [ətə́ːrni]
名 弁護士，法律家
power of attorney　代理権

**1321 judicial** [dʒuːdíʃəl]
形 司法の，裁判の
a judicial decision　判決

**1322 surrender** [səréndər]
自 降伏する；委ねる　他 を引き渡す；を放棄する；〈保険〉を解約する　名 引き渡し；降伏
cash surrender value　解約返戻金

---

**Q** The word "innocent" in line 9 is closest in meaning to
(A) guiltless
(B) naïve
(C) childish
(D) moral

解答は p. 336

## 19 Notice 1 救済活動への協力者募集

The Turtle Valley Disaster Volunteer Center is looking for local **residents** to help with **earthquake** relief work. So far, we have had a number of volunteers from the outlying **districts** answer the call, but we are in the process of creating long term programs and it is important that we **involve** Turtle Valley residents in that **effort**. We must be the ones to **revitalize** our own community!
Needed:
Local residents who can help the relief effort for 3-5 **consecutive** days.
Volunteer Center Location:
9569 Ocean Dr. (Behind the Turtle Valley Police Station)
Phone: 555-8104
There are half a **dozen** parking spaces in front of the center and there is a soccer field on the north side of the police station that can be used for **spillover** parking. (127 words)

---

**1323 resident** [rézidənt]
名 居住者 形 居住する ⇒派 residence 名 住宅
resident tax 住民税

**1324 earthquake** [ə́:rθkwèik]
名 地震
the frequency of earthquakes 地震の回数

**1325 district** [dístrikt]
名 地区；地域
a residential district 住宅地

**1326 involve** [inválv]
他 をかかわらせる
be involved in ～ ～に参加する

**1327 effort** [éfərt]
名 努力；活動
make efforts 努力する

**1328 revitalize** [riváitəlaiz]
他 に新しい活力を与える，を活性化する →1030 vital
revitalize business activities 経済活動を活性化させる

タートルバレー災害ボランティアセンターでは，地震救援活動を支援してくださる地元の住民の方々を募集しています。これまで，遠隔地の多くのボランティアの方々に電話の応対をしていただいていますが，私たちは長期的なプログラムを作り上げようとしており，タートルバレーの住民の皆さんにその活動に参加していただくことが重要です。自分たちのコミュニティーは自分たちで再生しなければなりません。

募集：
援助活動を連続して3～5日手伝ってくださる地元の方
ボランティアセンターの場所：
オーシャンドライブ9569番地（タートルバレー警察署裏）
電話：555-8104
センターの前に6台分（＝12台の半分）の駐車スペースがあり，警察の北側にあるサッカー場も，停めきれなかった分の駐車スペースとして使用できます。

### 1329 consecutive
[kənsékjətiv]

形 連続した，続いて起こる

for 24 consecutive hours　24時間連続で
consecutive numbers　通し番号

### 1330 dozen
[dʌ́zn]

名 形 ダース(の)，12個(の)

pack eggs in dozens　卵を1ダースずつ詰める

### 1331 spillover
[spílòuvər]

名 あふれること；あふれ出たもの；過剰；余波

have a spillover effect on ～　～への波及効果がある

---

**Q** The word "effort" in line 5 is closest in meaning to
(A) force
(B) action
(C) artwork
(D) effect

解答は p.336

## 20 Notice 2　ホテルのサービスの案内

Welcome to the Monument Hotel. We hope that you have a pleasant stay. If there is anything we can do to make you more comfortable, please do not hesitate to call on us. If you did not receive your **complimentary coupon** book when you **checked in**, press the **Concierge** button on your phone and request it. The **vouchers** are **honored** by many of the merchants and restaurants in this area, including the Castaway Restaurant and Mindy's, the gift shop in the lobby. Your entertainment system includes a variety of **cutting-edge** technology including on-demand movies, interactive restaurant **reservations**, video games, broadband Internet service and, of course, **broadcast** TV. You can also use your system to check out the night before your departure. Many of these services are free, while others carry a **nominal** charge that will be added to your hotel bill. (141 words)

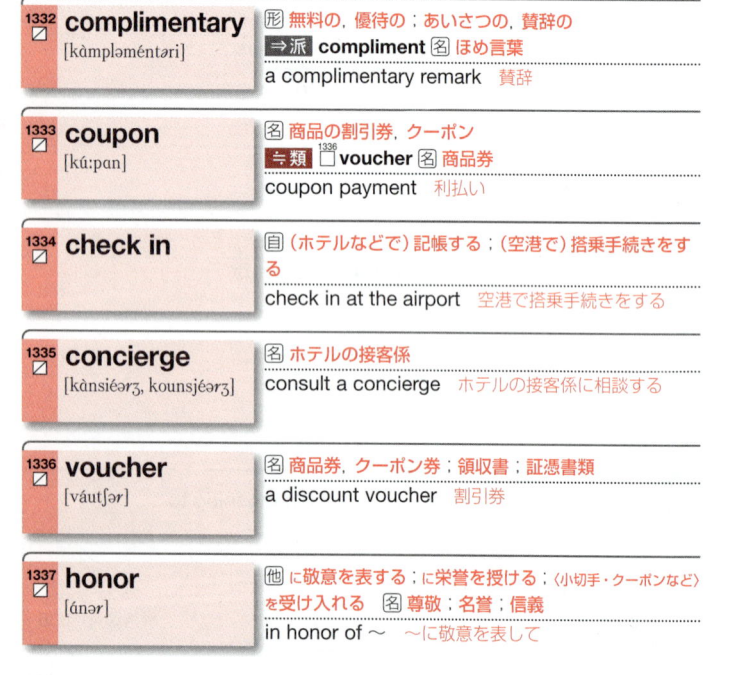

---

**1332 complimentary** [kàmpləméntəri]
形 無料の, 優待の；あいさつの, 賛辞の
⇒派 compliment 名 ほめ言葉
a complimentary remark　賛辞

**1333 coupon** [kúːpɑn]
名 商品の割引券, クーポン
≒類 voucher 名 商品券
coupon payment　利払い

**1334 check in**
自 (ホテルなどで)記帳する；(空港で)搭乗手続きをする
check in at the airport　空港で搭乗手続きをする

**1335 concierge** [kὰnsiéərʒ, kounsjéərʒ]
名 ホテルの接客係
consult a concierge　ホテルの接客係に相談する

**1336 voucher** [váutʃər]
名 商品券, クーポン券；領収書；証憑書類
a discount voucher　割引券

**1337 honor** [ánər]
他 に敬意を表する；に栄誉を授ける；〈小切手・クーポンなど〉を受け入れる 名 尊敬；名誉；信義
in honor of ～　～に敬意を表して

モニュメントホテルにようこそ。気持ちよくご滞在いただけるように願っております。もし皆様にもっと心地よく滞在していただくためにできることがございましたら、どうぞ遠慮なくお申しつけください。**チェックイン**のときに**優待クーポン**の冊子を受け取っていらっしゃらない場合は、電話機の「**接客係**」のボタンを押してご請求ください。**割引クーポン**はキャストアウェイレストランや、ロビーにあるギフトショップのミンディーズを含む、このあたりの店やレストランの多くで**お使いいただけます**。娯楽装置には、さまざまな**最先端の**技術が含まれます。オンデマンドの映画、対話型のレストラン**予約**、テレビゲーム、ブロードバンド・インターネットサービスと、もちろんテレビ**放送**もございます。また、ご出発の前夜にこの装置を使ってチェックアウトすることもできます。これらのサービスの多くは無料ですが、**少し費用がかかるものもあります**。その費用はホテルの請求書に加算されます。

---

**1338 cutting-edge** [kʌ́tiŋ édʒ]
形 最先端の
be on the cutting edge　最新の技術を駆使している

**1339 reservation** [rèzərvéiʃən]
名 予約　⇒派 reserve 他 を予約する
reconfirm one's reservation　予約を再確認する

**1340 broadcast** [brɔ́:dkæst]
他 〈番組〉を放送する　自 放送する
broadcast-broadcast-broadcast　名 放送
a radio broadcast　ラジオ放送

**1341 nominal** [nάmənl]
形 名目だけの；わずかな
a nominal leader　名ばかりの指導者

---

**Q** The word "nominal" in line 13 is closest in meaning to
(A) small
(B) famous
(C) grammatical
(D) valuable

解答は p. 336

## 21 Notice 3　薬のオンライン処方の案内

Holbrook **Pharmacy** Online **Prescription Refill** Center
If you have **purchased** a refillable prescription at any of our 12 stores throughout the **metropolitan** area, you can use our handy, **interactive**, online order form to order a refill. This system allows you to fill up to four prescriptions at a time and pick them up at the Holbrook Pharmacy location that is most convenient for you. All that is required is that you have the phone number of the pick-up location on hand. All information is stored in our centralized system, so you do not need to pick up your prescription at your regular branch every time. If you don't know the telephone number of the pharmacy that you wish to use this time, go to: www.holbrookpharmacy.com/storelocator.html and locate the **appropriate** number. Always **inspect** your prescription thoroughly and read all directions. If you notice a **discrepancy**, or if you have any questions, please consult the **pharmacist** on duty.

(156 words)

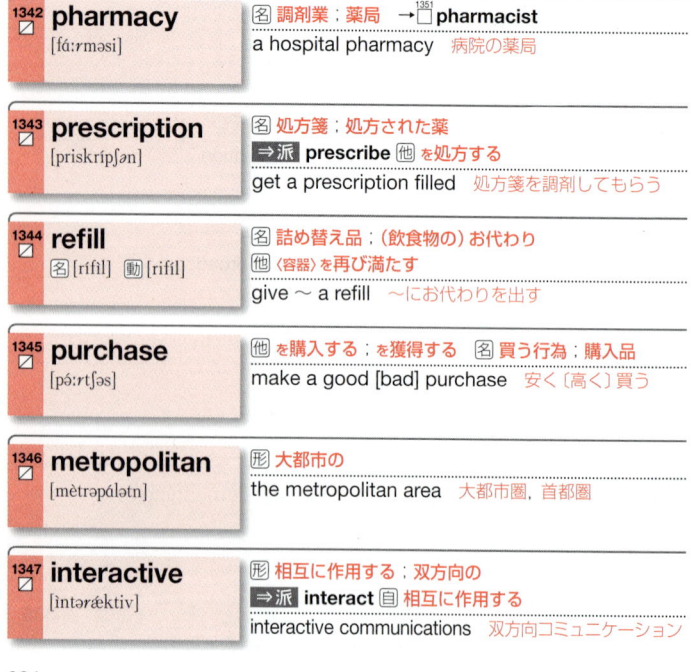

---

**1342 pharmacy** [fá:rməsi]
名 調剤業；薬局　→ 1351 pharmacist
a hospital pharmacy　病院の薬局

**1343 prescription** [priskrípʃən]
名 処方箋；処方された薬
⇒派 prescribe 他 を処方する
get a prescription filled　処方箋を調剤してもらう

**1344 refill** 名[rí:fil] 動[ri:fíl]
名 詰め替え品；(飲食物の)お代わり
他 〈容器〉を再び満たす
give ～ a refill　～にお代わりを出す

**1345 purchase** [pə́:rtʃəs]
他 を購入する；を獲得する　名 買う行為；購入品
make a good [bad] purchase　安く〔高く〕買う

**1346 metropolitan** [mètrəpálətn]
形 大都市の
the metropolitan area　大都市圏, 首都圏

**1347 interactive** [ìntəræktiv]
形 相互に作用する；双方向の
⇒派 interact 自 相互に作用する
interactive communications　双方向コミュニケーション

ホルブルック薬局オンライン処方再調剤センター

私どもの都市部の 12 店舗のいずれかで再調剤可能な処方薬を購入された場合，当店の便利な，双方向のオンライン注文書を利用して再調剤の注文が可能です。このシステムを利用して，一度に４つまでの処方を受け，最もご都合のよい場所にあるホルブルック薬局で受け取ることができます。受け取り店の電話番号を手元に置いておけばよいのです。すべての情報は私どもの中央のシステムに集積されていますので，毎回決まった支店で処方薬を受け取る必要はありません。もし今回ご利用希望の薬局の電話番号をご存じでなければ，www.holbrookpharmacy.com/storelocator.html をご確認いただき，該当する番号をお探しください。処方箋は常に丁寧にお調べになり，指示はすべてお読みください。何か不一致に気づかれたり，ご質問がありましたら，当番の薬剤師にご相談ください。

---

### 1348 appropriate
[əpróupriət]

形 適切な

be appropriate for ～ ～に適している，妥当である

### 1349 inspect
[inspékt]

他 を検分〔調査〕する ⇒派 inspection 名 調査

inspect the scene of the fire 火災の現場を調査する

### 1350 discrepancy
[diskrépənsi]

名 相違，食い違い ≒類 difference 名 相違

resolve the discrepancy 食い違いを修正する

### 1351 pharmacist
[fá:rməsist]

名 薬剤師

a licenced pharmacist 免許を持つ薬剤師

---

**Q** The word "inspect" in line 13 is closest in meaning to
(A) visit
(B) interview
(C) examine
(D) respect

解答は p. 336

## 22 Notice 4 株を購入する際の注意

Buying Stock — First of all, anyone who is attempting to sell you investments over the phone should be considered your **enemy**. These phone salespeople have high-pressure sales **tactics**, and present effective, believable arguments. Don't let this **presentation convince** you. They are not doing you any favors, no matter how wonderful they make an investment sound. They are operating in their own best interest to **dump** over-the-counter stock on you. The money you pay in will go into their own pockets, or the pockets of their company. Up-and-coming, honest companies don't need to **resort** to these types of tactics; this is the well-known approach of **disreputable**, shady companies. If you choose to **ignore** this advice you **deserve** your fate! As the **shareholder** of questionable stock, you may also have difficulty trying to find a buyer for your shares once you decide the time has come to sell.

(146 words)

---

**1352 enemy** [énəmi]
名 敵
a common enemy 共通の敵

**1353 tactics** [tæktiks]
名 作戦；戦術　≒類 strategy 名 戦略
marketing tactics マーケティング戦術

**1354 presentation** [prì:zəntéiʃən, -zen-, prèzən-]
名 発表, プレゼンテーション；提示, 提出；贈呈, 授与
presentation of documents 書類の提示
make a presentation プレゼンテーションをする

**1355 convince** [kənvíns]
他 〈人に〉…ということを納得させる
⇒派 convincing 形 説得力のある
convince ~ of ... ~に…を納得させる

**1356 dump** [dʌ́mp]
他 を投げ捨てる；を投げ売りする　名 ごみ捨て場
dump garbage at an official site 定められた場所にごみを捨てる

**1357 resort** [rizɔ́:rt]
自 訴える, 頼る　名 行楽地, リゾート；頼ること
the resort industry リゾート産業

株の購入——まず最初に，電話であなたに投資物件を売ろうとする人はだれであろうと，敵だと考えるべきです。これらの電話の営業者は強い圧力をかけるような営業手法を持っており，効果的でもっともらしい論拠を提示してきます。この売り込みに納得させられてはいけません。彼らが投資をどんなにすばらしく思えるようにしようと，彼らはあなたに何ら尽くしてはくれません。彼らは自分たちに最も都合がよいように，あなたに店頭取引の株を投げ売りしようと働きかけているのです。あなたが支払うお金は彼ら自身か，彼らの会社の懐に入ります。有望で誠実な会社はこの種の手法に訴える必要がありません。つまり，これはいかがわしく，うさんくさい会社でよく知られるアプローチなのです。もしあなたがこの忠告を無視することに決めれば，あなたは破滅にいたるに値します！ 売り時だと判断したときに，問題のある株の株主として，自分の株の買い手を探そうとして苦労することにもなるでしょう。

---

### 1358 disreputable
[dísrépjətəbl]

形 たちの悪い；評判の悪い

a disreputable agency　評判の悪い代理店

### 1359 ignore
[ignɔ́ːr]

他 を無視する

ignore insulting remarks　侮辱的な意見を無視する

### 1360 deserve
[dizə́ːrv]

他 に値する

deserve praise [punishment]　賞賛〔刑罰〕に値する

### 1361 shareholder
[ʃéərhòuldər]

名 株主

a major shareholder　大株主

---

**Q** The word "resort" in line 10 is closest in meaning to

(A) travel
(B) employ
(C) relocate
(D) convene

解答は p. 336

## 23 Notice 5 奨学金の給付の案内

When you **enroll** for any type of financial aid at Maxwell College, the Office of **Scholarship Review** (OSR) confirms your enrollment, student **status** and other eligibility **criteria**. You must be carrying 12 course credit hours to be considered a full-time student eligible for aid. The OSR then authorizes payment of all grants, loans and scholarships directly to your student account. Your award may increase, decrease, or be canceled, depending on these eligibility reviews. If your aid is canceled for any reason, you will be responsible for paying all **tuition** and fees on your own account. Funds are applied toward your **outstanding** balance first. If your credited aid exceeds your student charges, the Business Office will mail you a check for the balance within 14 days of the credit being approved. All balance checks are mailed to the student's current address as recorded in our system. We ask that you **notify** the Business Office **immediately** of any change of address.

(159 words)

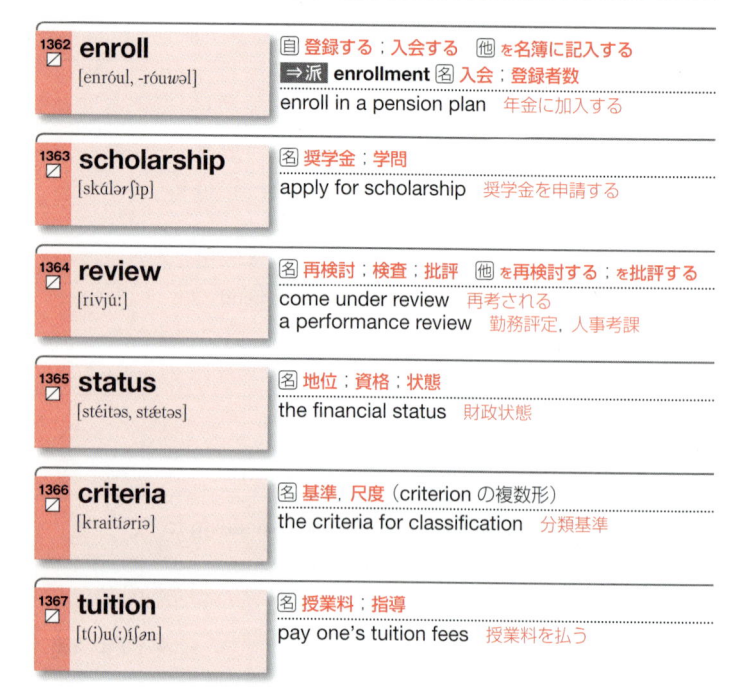

---

**1362 enroll** [enróul, -róuwəl]
自 登録する；入会する 他 を名簿に記入する
⇒派 **enrollment** 名 入会；登録者数
enroll in a pension plan 年金に加入する

**1363 scholarship** [skálərʃip]
名 奨学金；学問
apply for scholarship 奨学金を申請する

**1364 review** [rivjúː]
名 再検討；検査；批評 他 を再検討する；を批評する
come under review 再考される
a performance review 勤務評定, 人事考課

**1365 status** [stéitəs, stǽtəs]
名 地位；資格；状態
the financial status 財政状態

**1366 criteria** [kraitíəriə]
名 基準, 尺度（criterion の複数形）
the criteria for classification 分類基準

**1367 tuition** [t(j)u(ː)íʃən]
名 授業料；指導
pay one's tuition fees 授業料を払う

マックスウェルカレッジでは，どのようなタイプのものであれ経済援助に登録すると，奨学金審査事務所（OSR）があなたの登録と学生としての状況，その他の適格基準を確認します。援助の資格を持つ正規の学生と見なされるためには，12 単位時間を履修していなければなりません。その後 OSR はすべての給付金，貸与金，奨学金を学生口座に直接支払うことを認可します。奨学金は，資格再審査によって，増額，減額，取り消しとなることがあります。もし何らかの理由で援助が取り消された場合は，自力ですべての授業料や費用を支払う責任があります。資金はまずあなたの未払いの差引残高に充てられます。もし貸し付けられた援助金が学費を超えた場合は，振込みの実施から 14 日以内に，事務所から差引額の小切手が郵送されます。差引額の小切手はすべて，我々のシステムに登録されている学生の現住所に送られます。いかなる住所変更も，ただちに事務所に届け出ていただくようお願いします。

---

### 1368 outstanding
[àutstǽndiŋ]

形 未払いの；傑出した

an outstanding loan　貸付残高

### 1369 notify
[nóutəfài]

他 〈人〉に知らせる，を通知する

notify ~ in writing　~に書面で通知する

### 1370 immediately
[imí:diətli]

副 ただちに，すぐ　⇒派 immediate 形 即時の

come home immediately　すぐに帰宅する

---

**Q** The word "outstanding" in line 10 is closest in meaning to
(A) noticeable
(B) superior
(C) unpaid
(D) projecting

解答は p. 336

## 24 Notice 6 年次会議の議長あいさつ

Dear Participant,

Welcome to the annual Modern Engineering Society conference. It is **customary** for the chairman of the organization to speak at the annual conference, but as this year's chairperson, I have selected to do away with this formality. Instead, I believe that participants should use the time previously **devoted** to senseless speeches to **linger** after the sessions and interact with colleagues or **browse** the New **Inventions**, Publications and Media booths in the display hall where we have given publishers and **manufacturers** the opportunity to **disseminate** information about their latest products. Each afternoon from 5:00 to 5:45, we have invited dynamic speakers from every **sector** to deliver the last speech of the day.

Wishing you a fruitful conference,
Sonia Heller, Ph.D.  2005-2006 Chair
Modern Engineering Society

(126 words)

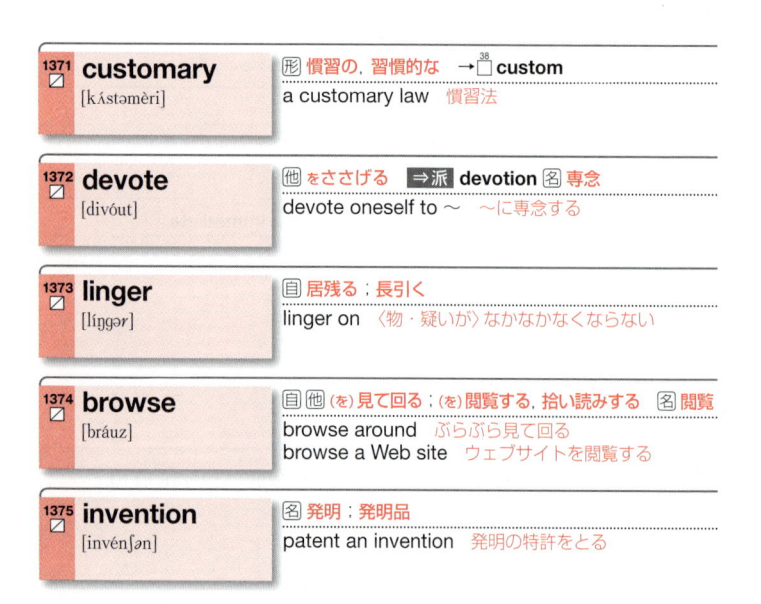

---

**1371 customary** [kʌ́stəmèri]
形 慣習の, 習慣的な →custom
a customary law  慣習法

**1372 devote** [divóut]
他 をささげる ⇒派 devotion 名 専念
devote oneself to 〜  〜に専念する

**1373 linger** [líŋgər]
自 居残る；長引く
linger on 〈物・疑いが〉なかなかなくならない

**1374 browse** [bráuz]
自他 (を)見て回る；(を)閲覧する, 拾い読みする 名 閲覧
browse around  ぶらぶら見て回る
browse a Web site  ウェブサイトを閲覧する

**1375 invention** [invénʃən]
名 発明；発明品
patent an invention  発明の特許をとる

参加者の皆様
モダンエンジニアリング協会の年次会議にようこそおいでくださいました。組織の議長が年次会議でごあいさつをするのが慣例ではありますが，私は今年の議長として，この儀礼を廃止することにいたしました。そうする代わりに，参加者の皆さんは，これまで意味のないスピーチに充てられていた時間を使って，会議後に残って同僚たちと交歓したり，展示ホールで新発明や出版，メディアなどの展示ブースを見て回ったりして過ごすべきだと思うのです。展示ホールでは，出版社やメーカーの方々が自社の最新製品についての情報を広める機会をご提供しております。毎日午後 5 時から 5 時 45 分には，その日の最後の講演をしていただくために，あらゆる分野から精力的な講演者の方々をお呼びしております。実りある会議となることをお祈りしております。
ソーニャ・ヘラー博士　2005-2006 年　議長
モダンエンジニアリング協会

---

### 1376 manufacturer
[mæ̀njəfǽktʃərər]

名 製造業者
⇒派 manufacture 名 製造　他自 (を) 製造する
an electronics manufacturer　電子機器メーカー

### 1377 disseminate
[disémənèit]

他 を広める
disseminate information　情報を広める

### 1378 sector
[séktər]

名 (社会や国家の経済における) 部門；分野
the private [public] sector　民間〔公共〕部門

---

**Q** The word "customary" in line 3 is closest in meaning to
(A) legal
(B) sacred
(C) taxable
(D) traditional

解答は p. 336

## 25 Notice 7 子どもの保護者募集

The Child Protection **Agency** seeks new **foster** parents. We're looking for people to be **advocates** for children who, due to unsuitable family conditions are currently **wards** of the agency. **Orientation** groups will be meeting from the beginning of October. Call 555-2000. Please be aware that children **removed** from abusive homes may take years to recover from the abuse. While we hope that someone will eventually adopt these children, we recognize that the average home may not be able to accommodate children with such **severe** problems. Some act up, while others just shut down completely, so they require constant **supervision**. Recent research by psychologists shows that the development of the part of the brain that regulates **compassion** may become **impaired** if not used when the child is very, very young.

(129 words)

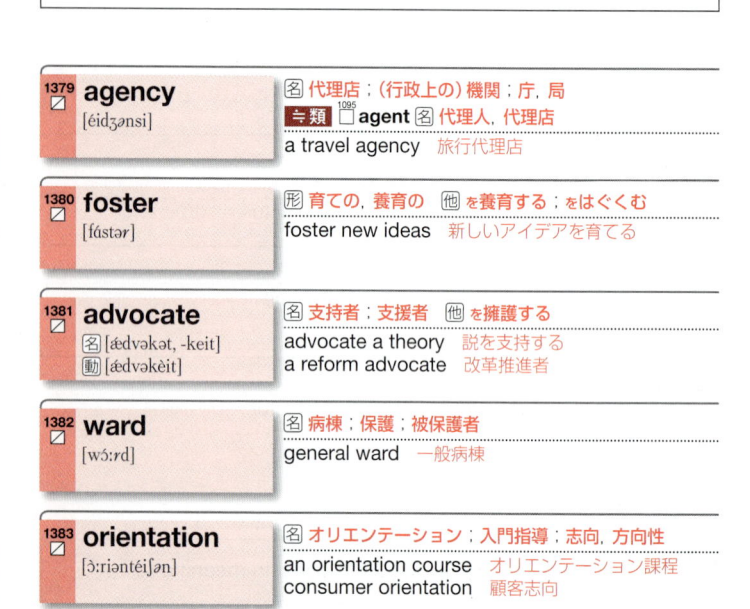

---

**1379 agency** [éidʒənsi]
名 代理店；(行政上の)機関；庁, 局
≒類 agent 名 代理人, 代理店
a travel agency　旅行代理店

**1380 foster** [fɔ́(ː)stər]
形 育ての, 養育の　他 を養育する；をはぐくむ
foster new ideas　新しいアイデアを育てる

**1381 advocate**
名 [ǽdvəkət, -keit]
動 [ǽdvəkèit]
名 支持者；支援者　他 を擁護する
advocate a theory　説を支持する
a reform advocate　改革推進者

**1382 ward** [wɔ́ːrd]
名 病棟；保護；被保護者
general ward　一般病棟

**1383 orientation** [ɔ̀ːriəntéiʃən]
名 オリエンテーション；入門指導；志向, 方向性
an orientation course　オリエンテーション課程
consumer orientation　顧客志向

**1384 remove** [rimúːv]
他 を取り去る, 移動する；を取り除く；を解雇する
⇒派 removal 名 除去
remove a stain　しみを消す

児童保護機関では，新しい里親を探しています。私たちが探しているのは，不遇な家庭環境のために現在機関の被保護者となっている子どもの支援者になってくださる方です。オリエンテーショングループは10月初旬から会合を開きます。555-2000にお電話ください。虐待をする家庭から離された子どもたちは，虐待から回復するのに何年もかかることがあるということを申し上げておきます。私たちは，だれかが最終的にこういった子どもたちを養子にしてくれることを望んではいますが，平均的な家庭にこのような厳しい問題を抱えた子どもを受け入れることは不可能かもしれないということはわかっています。過激な行動をとる子どももいれば，完全に殻に閉じこもってしまう子どももいるため，常に監督が必要です。心理学者の最近の研究では，子どもが非常に小さいときに脳の中の同情をつかさどる部分を使わなければ，その部分が損なわれてしまう可能性があるということが明らかになりました。

## 1385 severe
[sivíər]

形 深刻な；厳しい；険しい

a severe shortage　深刻な不足

## 1386 supervision
[sùːpərvíʒən]

名 監督，指揮　⇒派 supervise 他 を監督する
supervisor 名 監督者

under the supervision of ～　～の監督下に

## 1387 compassion
[kəmpǽʃən]

名 同情，あわれみ

compassion for others　他人への思いやり

## 1388 impair
[impéər]

他 〈価値など〉を損なう

impair one's credit　～の信用を損ねる

---

**Q** The word "severe" in line 9 is closest in meaning to
(A) strict
(B) disciplined
(C) extreme
(D) plain

解答は p. 336

333

## 26 Policy 契約決定の際の法的規約

This contract is subject to English Law. ICC rules are to be observed under existing CIGS guidelines and UCC Law will supersede ICC in the event of a **conflict**. The Seller and Buyer will attempt to **settle** all **disputes** amicably. Either party may serve notice on the other requiring any dispute be settled within 30 (thirty) days after such notice and, if the dispute is not settled refer it to **arbitration** in accordance with this contract, unless breach of payment occurs by the buyer or there is failure to post a Letter of Credit. The arbitration will be heard by one or more **arbitrators appointed** by **mutual** agreement of the parties and in accordance with the Arbitration Act of 1996. The seat of arbitration shall be England. The **award** shall be enforceable in any country, and a formal request to judiciary officials shall be **deemed** accepted without contest or protest. (150 words)

---

### 1389 conflict
[kánflikt] / [kənflíkt]
名 争い, 衝突　自 衝突する
a conflict between 〜　〜の間の対立

### 1390 settle
[sétl]
他 を解決する；を払う；を決定する　自 和解する；定住する；落ち着く　⇒派 **settlement** 名 合意, 和解
settle a bill　勘定を払う

### 1391 dispute
[dispjúːt, ́ー]／[－́ー]
名 論争, 言い争い　他自 (を)論争する
in dispute　論争中の
a labor dispute　労働争議

### 1392 arbitration
[àːrbətréiʃən]
名 調停, 仲裁
go to arbitration　仲裁に委ねる

### 1393 arbitrator
[áːrbətrèitər]
名 仲裁人, 調停者
arbitrator's fees　仲裁人手数料

### 1394 appoint
[əpɔ́int]
他 を任命する；〈時間・場所など〉を指定する
⇒派 **appointment** 名 (面会の)約束, 予約；任命
appoint new members　新メンバーを指名する

この契約はイギリスの法律に従うものとする。また，ICC 法は現存の CIGS ガイドラインのもとに守られるべきものであり，UCC 法と ICC 法が対立した場合には UCC 法が ICC 法に取って代わる。売却者と購入者は，友好的にあらゆる争議を解決するよう試みるものとする。いずれの側も，いかなる争議についても，相手側に通知を出し，その通知から 30 日以内に解決するよう求めねばならない。もし解決されない場合には，購入者による支払いの不履行が発生した場合や信用状を送付しなかった場合以外，この契約に鑑みて調停に持ち込むこととする。調停は，両者双方の合意により指名された，1 人またはそれ以上の調停者により審議され，1996 年の調停法に従うものとする。調停地はイギリスとする。裁定はいずれの国においても強制力を持ち，法務官に対する公式の要請は論争や抗議なしに受諾されるものと考えられる。

### 1395 mutual
[mjúːtʃuəl]
形 相互の, お互いの；共通の, 共有する
mutual fund 投資信託会社

### 1396 award
[əwɔ́ːrd]
名 賞；裁定；奨学金　他〈賞など〉を与える
present an award 賞を贈呈する

### 1397 deem
[díːm]
他 と見なす, 判断する
be deemed to be 〜　〜と思われている

---

**Q** The word "settle" in line 4 is closest in meaning to
(A) establish
(B) sink
(C) reside
(D) resolve

解答は p. 336

# 解答一覧

## Chapter 4-1

1. (A)
2. (C)
3. (A)
4. (B)
5. (D)
6. (C)
7. (A)
8. (D)
9. (C)
10. (C)
11. (D)
12. (B)
13. (A)
14. (B)

## Chapter 4-2

1. (A)
2. (C)
3. (D)
4. (A)
5. (B)
6. (D)
7. (D)
8. (C)
9. (B)
10. (B)
11. (D)
12. (B)
13. (B)
14. (A)
15. (D)
16. (A)
17. (C)
18. (A)
19. (B)
20. (A)
21. (C)
22. (B)
23. (C)
24. (D)
25. (C)
26. (D)

# MEMO

# Index

### 単 語

単語太字（**abc**）：見出し語（例文付き）
単語細字（abc）：見出し語以外

### ページ数

数字はページ数を表しています。
数字太字（**123**）：見出し語，または ⇒派 （派生語）として出てきたページ
数字細字（123）： ≒類 （類義語）， ⇔反 （反意語）， →（参照）， ♂ （関連語）など，参考語として出てきたページ

## A

- **abdomen** ···· **272**
- **abide** ········ **204**
- **ability** ···· **69**, 297
- able ·········· 69
- **absence** ····· 157
- **absent** ······ **157**
- absolute ····· 157
- **absolutely** ··· **157**
- **abstract** ···· **167**
- **abundant** ···· **313**
- **abuse** ········ **10**
- **accelerate** ··· **230**
- **accept** ······ **312**
- acceptance ··· 312
- **access** ······ **268**
- **accessory** ··· **230**
- **accident** ···· **42**
- accidental ··· 42
- accidentally ··· 42
- **acclaim** ····· **302**
- **accommodate**
  ··········· **42**, **145**
- **accommodation**
  ··········· 42, 145
- **accompany** ··· **103**
- **accomplish** ··· **145**
- accomplishment
  ············· 145
- **account** ···· **10**, **42**
- **accountant** 10, 42
- **accounting** 10, **42**
- **accumulate** ··· **181**
- accumulation · 181
- **accuracy** ···· **304**
- **accurate** 159, **304**
- accusable ··· 204
- accusation ··· 204
- **accuse** ······ **204**
- accustom ··· 230
- **accustomed** · **230**
- **achieve** ····· **262**
- achievement · 262
- **acquaintance**
  ············· **262**
- **acquire** ····· **145**
- **acquisition** ··· **310**
- **acting** ······· **10**
- actual ······· 119
- **actually** ····· **119**
- **ad** ··········· **43**
- **adapt** ······· **181**
- **add** ········· **289**
- **additional** ··· **289**
- **address** ····· **103**
- **adequate** ···· **195**
- **adhere** ····· **285**
- **adjacent** ···· **230**
- **adjust** ······· **305**
- adjustment ··· 305
- **administration**
  ············· **129**
- **admission**
  ··········· **43**, 145
- **admit** ···· **43**, 145
- **adopt** ········ **10**
- **advance** ····· **11**
- advancement ··· 11
- **advantage** ··· **69**
- **advertise** ···· **69**
- **advertisement**
  ··········· 43, **69**
- **advisory** ···· **275**
- **advocate** ···· **332**
- **affect** ······· **103**
- **affection** ···· **167**
- **affluent** ····· **230**
- **afford** ······· **43**
- **affordable** ··· **43**
- **afterward** ··· **304**
- **agency** ··· 271, **332**
- **agenda** ····· **287**
- **agent** ···· **271**, 332
- **agree** ········ **11**
- **agreement** ··· **11**
- **aid** ········· **129**
- **aim** ········· **262**

338

- [ ] **aisle** · 259
- [ ] **allege** · 231
- [ ] allegedly · 231
- [ ] **alleviate** · 231
- [ ] **allocate** · 231
- [ ] allot · 231
- [ ] allow · 43
- [ ] **allowance** · 43
- [ ] **alter** · 43, 44, **181**
- [ ] alteration · 181
- [ ] **alternate** · 43
- [ ] **alternative** · 44
- [ ] **altitude** · 204
- [ ] **alumni** · 288
- [ ] **amazing** · 306
- [ ] **amend** · 44
- [ ] **amenity** · 231
- [ ] **amount** · 69
- [ ] **ancient** · 195
- [ ] **anniversary** · 301
- [ ] **announce** · 103
- [ ] announcer · 103
- [ ] **annoy** · 181
- [ ] **annual** · 65, **294**
- [ ] **anonymous** · 295
- [ ] **anticipate** · 181
- [ ] anticipation · 181
- [ ] **apologize** · 287
- [ ] apology · 287
- [ ] **apparatus** · 272
- [ ] apparel · 238
- [ ] **apparent** · 308
- [ ] **apparently** · 308
- [ ] **appeal** · 145
- [ ] **appear** · 129
- [ ] **appearance** · 129
- [ ] **appliance** · 69
- [ ] **applicable** · 44
- [ ] **applicant** · 44, **103**
- [ ] **application** · 11, **103**
- [ ] **apply** · 11, 44, **103**
- [ ] **appoint** · 334
- [ ] appointment · 334
- [ ] **appreciate** · 11
- [ ] appreciation · 11
- [ ] **apprehend** · 277
- [ ] apprehension · 277
- [ ] **approach** · 103
- [ ] **appropriate** · 325
- [ ] **approval** · 309
- [ ] **approve** · 309
- [ ] **approximate** · 256
- [ ] **approximately** · 256
- [ ] **arbitration** · 334
- [ ] **arbitrator** · 334
- [ ] **argue** · 103
- [ ] **arise** · 145
- [ ] **arm** · 318
- [ ] **arrange** · 103
- [ ] arrangement · 103
- [ ] **arrest** · 231
- [ ] **article** · 11
- [ ] **ascend** · 232
- [ ] **ascertain** · 284
- [ ] **ashamed** · 290
- [ ] **aspect** · 129
- [ ] **assemble** · 12
- [ ] **assembly** · 12
- [ ] **assert** · 204
- [ ] **assess** · 304
- [ ] **asset** · 204
- [ ] **assign** · 145
- [ ] **assignment** · 12, **145**
- [ ] **assist** · 105
- [ ] assistance · 105
- [ ] assistant · 105
- [ ] **associate** · 12
- [ ] **association** · 12
- [ ] **assume** · 145
- [ ] **assurance** · 181
- [ ] **assure** · 181
- [ ] at last · 264
- [ ] **athlete** · 129
- [ ] athletic · 129
- [ ] **atmosphere** · 129
- [ ] **attach** · 12, **147**
- [ ] **attachment** · 12, **147**
- [ ] **attain** · 181
- [ ] **attempt** · 147
- [ ] **attend** · 44, **105**
- [ ] **attendant** · 44, **105**
- [ ] **attention** · 189, **256**
- [ ] **attitude** · 129
- [ ] **attorney** · 319
- [ ] attract · 69
- [ ] **attraction** · 69
- [ ] **attractive** · 69
- [ ] **audience** · 69
- [ ] **audio** · 272
- [ ] **audit** · 205
- [ ] **auditor** · 205
- [ ] **authentic** · 302
- [ ] **author** · 71
- [ ] **authority** · 279
- [ ] **authorize** · 263
- [ ] availability · 13
- [ ] **available** · 13
- [ ] **average** · 119
- [ ] **avoid** · 105
- [ ] **await** · 318
- [ ] **award** · 335
- [ ] aware · 45
- [ ] **awareness** · 45

## B

- [ ] **background** · 129
- [ ] **baggage** · 217

- [ ] **balance** ······· 13
- [ ] **ban** ············ 167
- [ ] **bankrupt** ····· 205
- [ ] bankruptcy ···· 205
- [ ] **banquet** ······ 205
- [ ] **barrel** ········· 232
- [ ] **basement** ···· 205
- [ ] **basis** ··········· 264
- [ ] **bear** ············ 13
- [ ] **beat** ············ 147
- [ ] **beforehand** ··· 304
- [ ] **behalf** ·········· 288
- [ ] belly ············· 272
- [ ] **bend** ············ 273
- [ ] **benefit** ········ 13
- [ ] besides ········· 199
- [ ] **beverage** ····· 205
- [ ] **bid** ·············· 206
- [ ] **bidder** ········· 206
- [ ] **bill** ·············· 13
- [ ] **blame** ·········· 147
- [ ] **block** ··········· 258
- [ ] **board** ··········· 14
- [ ] **bond** ············ 131
- [ ] **booklet** ········ 272
- [ ] **boost** ··········· 308
- [ ] **booth** ·········· 206
- [ ] bore ············· 157
- [ ] **boring** ·········· 157
- [ ] **bother** ········· 147
- [ ] **bound** ·········· 157
- [ ] **boundary** ····· 131
- [ ] **brand** ··········· 258
- [ ] **breakdown** ··· 232
- [ ] **breakthrough** ··· 232
- [ ] **bribery** ········ 232
- [ ] **brief** ············ 157
- [ ] briefly ·········· 157
- [ ] broad··········· 288
- [ ] **broadcast** ···· 323
- [ ] **broaden** ······ 288
- [ ] **brochure** ····· 300
- [ ] **browse** ········ 330
- [ ] **budget** ········· 71
- [ ] **bulk** ············ 233
- [ ] **burden** ········ 131
- [ ] **bureau** ········ 314
- [ ] burglar ········· 276
- [ ] **burglary** ······ 276

## C

- [ ] **cabinet** ········ 71
- [ ] **calculate** ······ 147
- [ ] calculation ···· 147
- [ ] **campaign** ····· 71
- [ ] **cancel** ·········· 105
- [ ] cancellation ··· 105
- [ ] **candidate** ····· 71
- [ ] **canister** ······· 283
- [ ] **capability** ····· 297
- [ ] capable ········ 297
- [ ] **capacity** ······· 131
- [ ] **capital** ·········· 14
- [ ] **capture** ········ 306
- [ ] **career** ·········· 71
- [ ] **cargo** ··········· 206
- [ ] **carrier** ·········· 206
- [ ] **cash** ············ 71
- [ ] **cast** ············· 181
- [ ] **catalog** ········· 71
- [ ] **catering** ······· 206
- [ ] **cause** ··········· 73
- [ ] **caution** ···· 56, 131
- [ ] cautious ······· 131
- [ ] cautiously····· 131
- [ ] **celebrate** ······ 301
- [ ] **certificate** ···· 207
- [ ] **certify** ·········· 207
- [ ] **chair** ········ 14, 73
- [ ] **chairman** ······ 73
- [ ] **challenge** ····· 73
- [ ] **chance** ········· 14
- [ ] change··········· 181
- [ ] **channel** ········ 14
- [ ] **characteristic** 167
- [ ] **charge**
 ····· 15, 47, 55, 63
- [ ] **charitable** ···· 280
- [ ] charity ········· 280
- [ ] **chart** ··········· 73
- [ ] **check** ······ 15, 45
- [ ] **check in** ······ 322
- [ ] **checkout** ····· 45
- [ ] **checkup** ······ 45
- [ ] **chemical** ······ 286
- [ ] **chemist** ······· 286
- [ ] chemistry ······ 286
- [ ] **chest** ·········· 272
- [ ] **chill** ············ 281
- [ ] **chilly** ·········· 281
- [ ] **choice** ········· 73
- [ ] **choose** ········ 73
- [ ] **chop** ··········· 281
- [ ] **circumstance**
 ················· 131
- [ ] **cite** ············· 207
- [ ] **civil** ············ 316
- [ ] **claim** ··········· 15
- [ ] **clarify** ·········· 233
- [ ] **class** ······ 73, 105
- [ ] **classify** ··· 73, 105
- [ ] clear············ 45
- [ ] **clearance** ····· 45
- [ ] **clerical** ········ 233
- [ ] **clerk** ············ 73
- [ ] **client** ··········· 73
- [ ] **climate** ········ 15
- [ ] **clog** ············ 282
- [ ] close ············ 45
- [ ] **closure** ········ 45
- [ ] **clue** ············ 167
- [ ] **code** ············ 75
- [ ] **collaborate** ··· 260

340

- ☐ collaboration ··· 260
- ☐ collapse ······ 167
- ☐ colleague ······ 75
- ☐ column ······· 167
- ☐ combine ······ 147
- ☐ comfort ·· 119, 270
- ☐ comfortable
  ········· 119, 270
- ☐ comfortably ··· 119
- ☐ commensurate
  ················ 233
- ☐ comment ······ 75
- ☐ commerce ····· 119
- ☐ commercial ··· 119
- ☐ commission ··· 15
- ☐ commit ········ 16
- ☐ commitment ···· 16
- ☐ committee ····· 75
- ☐ commodity ··· 311
- ☐ common ······ 298
- ☐ commonly ···· 298
- ☐ commute······ 207
- ☐ commuter ····· 207
- ☐ company ······ 75
- ☐ compare 105, 270
- ☐ comparison
  ········· 105, 270
- ☐ compassion ··· 333
- ☐ compatible ··· 207
- ☐ compel········ 263
- ☐ compelling ··· 263
- ☐ compensate ···· 16
- ☐ compensation
  ················· 16
- ☐ compete ········ 46
- ☐ competent ··· 208
- ☐ competitor ····· 46
- ☐ complain········ 75
- ☐ complaint ····· 75
- ☐ complement ·· 208
- ☐ complete ·· 51, 263

- ☐ completely····· 263
- ☐ complex ······· 16
- ☐ compliance ···· 233
- ☐ complicated ··· 157
- ☐ compliment ···· 322
- ☐ complimentary
  ·················· 322
- ☐ comply ······· 233
- ☐ component ··· 208
- ☐ compose ······ 147
- ☐ comprehensive
  ·················· 208
- ☐ compromise ··· 167
- ☐ concern ········ 75
- ☐ concerning ···· 195
- ☐ concierge ····· 322
- ☐ conclude······ 131
- ☐ conclusion ···· 131
- ☐ condition ······ 16
- ☐ conduct ······ 105
- ☐ conference ··· 293
- ☐ confidence ···· 282
- ☐ confident ···· 282
- ☐ confidential ··· 208
- ☐ confirm ··· 59, 105
- ☐ confiscate ···· 317
- ☐ confiscation ···· 317
- ☐ conflict ········ 334
- ☐ conform ······ 234
- ☐ confront ······ 183
- ☐ confrontation ··· 183
- ☐ confuse ······ 107
- ☐ confusion ····· 107
- ☐ congratulate··· 234
- ☐ congratulation
  ·················· 234
- ☐ connect ··· 47, 107
- ☐ conscious ····· 195
- ☐ consecutive ··· 321
- ☐ consent ······· 285
- ☐ consequent····· 157

- ☐ **consequently**
  ················ 157
- ☐ **conservation** ·· 169
- ☐ conserve······· 169
- ☐ **consider**······ 107
- ☐ **considerable**
  ················ 157
- ☐ consideration·· 107
- ☐ **consist** ········ 183
- ☐ **consistent** ···· 209
- ☐ **consolidate** ··· 234
- ☐ **constitute** ···· 183
- ☐ constitution ···· 183
- ☐ **construction** ·· 292
- ☐ **consult** ········ 16
- ☐ consultation ···· 16
- ☐ consume······· 75
- ☐ **consumer** ····· 75
- ☐ consumption ··· 75
- ☐ **contact** ········ 77
- ☐ **contain** ········ 107
- ☐ **contemporary**
  ················ 195
- ☐ **content** ······· 131
- ☐ **continent** ····· 288
- ☐ continental····· 288
- ☐ **contingency** ·· 292
- ☐ **contingent** ··· 292
- ☐ continue ········ 47
- ☐ **continuity** ···· 307
- ☐ **contract** ······· 77
- ☐ **contrary** ······ 195
- ☐ **contribute**
  ············ 17, 183
- ☐ **contribution** ··· 17
- ☐ **control** ····· 46, 77
- ☐ **controller** ····· 46
- ☐ controversial ··· 169
- ☐ **controversy**··· 169
- ☐ **convenience**
  ············ 51, 77

341

- [ ] convenient ····· **77**
- [ ] **convention** ····· **77**
- [ ] **convey** ······ **183**
- [ ] **convince** ····· **326**
- [ ] **convincing** ····· **326**
- [ ] **cooperation** ···· **209**
- [ ] **cooperative** ···· **209**
- [ ] **coordinate** ····· **209**
- [ ] cordial ········ **209**
- [ ] **cordially** ······ **209**
- [ ] **corporate** ····· **266**
- [ ] **corporation** ····· **77**
- [ ] **correct**
    ······ **17**, 51, **159**
- [ ] **cost** ···· 46, **77**, **83**
- [ ] **costly** ······ **46**, **77**
- [ ] **count** ········ **149**
- [ ] **counter** ······· **107**
- [ ] **counterpart** ···· **133**
- [ ] **countless** ····· **149**
- [ ] **coupon** ······· **322**
- [ ] **courier** ······· **209**
- [ ] **courteous**
    ············ **17**, **300**
- [ ] **courtesy** ··· **17**, 300
- [ ] **coverage** ····· **290**
- [ ] co-worker ····· 75
- [ ] **crack** ········· **169**
- [ ] **crash** ········· **274**
- [ ] **create** ········ **107**
- [ ] credit ·········· 46
- [ ] **creditor** ······· 46
- [ ] **crew** ·········· **77**
- [ ] **crime** ···· **276**, 317
- [ ] **criminal** ······· **317**
- [ ] **criteria** ········ **328**
- [ ] critic ··········· **195**
- [ ] **critical** ········ **195**
- [ ] **crowded** ······· 55
- [ ] **cubicle** ·· **206**, **300**
- [ ] **cuisine** ········ **210**
- [ ] **culinary** ········ **302**
- [ ] **currency** ······· **133**
- [ ] **current** ········ **298**
- [ ] currently ······· **298**
- [ ] **custom** ···· **17**, **330**
- [ ] **customary** ····· **330**
- [ ] **customer** ······· **79**
- [ ] **customize** ····· **300**
- [ ] **cutting-edge**
    ················ **323**

# D

- [ ] **daily** ·········· **266**
- [ ] **damage** ········ **79**
- [ ] date ············ 64
- [ ] **deadline** ······· **286**
- [ ] **deal** ··········· **17**
- [ ] dealer ·········· **17**
- [ ] **debate** ········· **133**
- [ ] debt ············ **308**
- [ ] **debtor** ········· **308**
- [ ] **decade** ········· **133**
- [ ] decide ······ 46, **79**
- [ ] **decision** ········ **79**
- [ ] **decisive** ········ 46
- [ ] declaration ····· **149**
- [ ] **declare** ········ **149**
- [ ] **decline** ········· **18**
- [ ] decrease ··· 85, 185
- [ ] **deduct** ··· **234**, **294**
- [ ] **deductible** ····· **294**
- [ ] **deem** ·········· **335**
- [ ] **defect** ········· **210**
- [ ] **deficit** ·········· **210**
- [ ] **define** ········· **149**
- [ ] definite ········· **210**
- [ ] **definitely** ······· **210**
- [ ] **degree** ········· **79**
- [ ] **delay** ·········· **287**
- [ ] **deliberate** ······ **210**
- [ ] deliberately ····· **210**
- [ ] **delicate** ······· **195**
- [ ] **delighted** ······ **197**
- [ ] deliver ·········· **79**
- [ ] **delivery** ········· **79**
- [ ] **demand** ········· **79**
- [ ] **demonstrate** ···· **18**
- [ ] **demonstration**
    ············ **18**, **282**
- [ ] denial ·········· **183**
- [ ] **dental** ········· **159**
- [ ] **deny** ·········· **183**
- [ ] depart ·········· **18**
- [ ] **department** ····· **18**
- [ ] **departure** ······ **18**
- [ ] **depend** ········ **107**
- [ ] **dependent**
    ············ **18**, **107**
- [ ] **deposit** ········· **19**
- [ ] **depress** ······· **183**
- [ ] **depression**
    ············ **19**, **183**
- [ ] **deregulation** · **311**
- [ ] descend ······· 232
- [ ] **describe** ·· **19**, **107**
- [ ] **description**
    ············ **19**, 107
- [ ] **deserve** ······· **327**
- [ ] **designate** ····· **257**
- [ ] **desire** ·········· **133**
- [ ] **desperately** ····· **273**
- [ ] **despite** ········ **119**
- [ ] **destination** ····· **79**
- [ ] **detail** ··········· **19**
- [ ] **detergent** ····· **258**
- [ ] **deteriorate** ··· **234**
- [ ] **determine** ····· **279**
- [ ] **device** ········· **318**
- [ ] **devise** ········· **299**
- [ ] **devoid** ········ **306**
- [ ] **devote** ········ **330**
- [ ] devotion ······· **330**

- [ ] **diagnosis** ···· 235
- [ ] **diet** ········ 305
- [ ] **difference** ···· 325
- [ ] different ···· 52, 127
- [ ] **dig** ············ 183
- [ ] **diligent** ······· 235
- [ ] **diminish** ······· 185
- [ ] **director** ········ 79
- [ ] **directory** ······ 211
- [ ] **disaster** ······· 133
- [ ] disastrous ······· 133
- [ ] **discard** ········ 235
- [ ] **discharge** ······ 47
- [ ] **discipline** ······ 169
- [ ] **disclose** ······· 235
- [ ] **disconnect** ······ 47
- [ ] **discontinue** ···· 47
- [ ] **discount** ········ 81
- [ ] **discrepancy** ·· 325
- [ ] **discuss** ········ 109
- [ ] discussion ······· 109
- [ ] **disease** ········ 169
- [ ] **dismiss** ···· 47, 185
- [ ] **dismissal** ·· 47, 185
- [ ] **disorder** ········ 47
- [ ] **display** ········ 296
- [ ] **disposal** ······· 185
- [ ] **dispose** ······· 185
- [ ] **dispute** ········ 334
- [ ] **disregard** ·· 48, 191
- [ ] **disreputable** ·· 327
- [ ] **disrupt** ········ 292
- [ ] **disruption** ····· 292
- [ ] **dissatisfy** ······· 48
- [ ] **disseminate** ·· 331
- [ ] **distinct** ········ 298
- [ ] distinctly ········ 298
- [ ] **distribute** ······· 19
- [ ] distribution ······· 19
- [ ] distributor ······· 19
- [ ] **district** ········· 320

- [ ] **disturb** ········ 257
- [ ] disturbance ···· 257
- [ ] **diverse** ···· 48, 197
- [ ] **diversify** ········ 48
- [ ] **divide** ······ 20, 20
- [ ] **dividend** ······· 211
- [ ] **division** ····· 20, 20
- [ ] **dock** ·········· 278
- [ ] **document** ······ 81
- [ ] **domestic** ······· 20
- [ ] **dominant** ······ 211
- [ ] **donate** ········· 295
- [ ] donation ········· 295
- [ ] **dose** ··········· 305
- [ ] **down payment**
  ················ 235
- [ ] **downsize** ······ 311
- [ ] **downtown** ····· 119
- [ ] **dozen** ·········· 321
- [ ] **draft** ············ 211
- [ ] **drain** ············ 211
- [ ] **drawer** ········· 212
- [ ] **due** ·········· 20, 56
- [ ] **dump** ·········· 326
- [ ] **duplicate** ······ 236
- [ ] **durable** ········ 236
- [ ] **duration** ········ 212
- [ ] **duty** ············· 20

# E

- [ ] **eager** ·········· 159
- [ ] **earn** ············ 109
- [ ] **earthquake** ···· 320
- [ ] **ecology** ········ 169
- [ ] **economize** ······ 48
- [ ] economy ········· 48
- [ ] **effect** ··········· 81
- [ ] **effective** ········ 81
- [ ] **efficiency** ······ 119
- [ ] **efficient** ········ 119
- [ ] **effort** ··········· 320

- [ ] **elderly** ········· 275
- [ ] electronic ······· 276
- [ ] **electronically**
  ················ 276
- [ ] **elegant** ········ 197
- [ ] **element** ········ 169
- [ ] **eligible** ········ 296
- [ ] **eliminate** ······ 109
- [ ] **embrace** ······· 236
- [ ] **emerge** ········ 185
- [ ] **emergence** ···· 258
- [ ] **emergency** ···· 258
- [ ] **eminent** ········ 236
- [ ] **emission** ······ 171
- [ ] **emit** ············ 171
- [ ] **emphasis** ······ 283
- [ ] **emphasize** ···· 283
- [ ] **employee** ······· 81
- [ ] **employer** ······ 133
- [ ] **employment** ···· 63
- [ ] **empty** ·········· 279
- [ ] **enclose** ········ 294
- [ ] **enclosure** ······ 294
- [ ] **encounter** ····· 185
- [ ] **encourage** ····· 109
- [ ] **endorse** ········ 264
- [ ] **endorsement** ·· 264
- [ ] **enemy** ·········· 326
- [ ] **enforce** ········· 48
- [ ] **enforcement** ···· 48
- [ ] **engage** ···· 49, 109
- [ ] **engagement** ···· 49
- [ ] **engineer** ········ 81
- [ ] **engineering** ···· 81
- [ ] **enhance** ······· 212
- [ ] **enlarge** ········· 49
- [ ] **enormous** ······ 197
- [ ] **enormously** ···· 197
- [ ] **enroll** ·········· 328
- [ ] **enrollment** ····· 328
- [ ] **ensure** ········· 284

343

| | | |
|---|---|---|
| ☐ enter ············ **81** | ☐ exclude ········ 109 | **F** |
| ☐ enterprise ······· 49 | ☐ **exclusive** ····· **270** | ☐ **fabric** ··········· **237** |
| ☐ **entertain** ········ **81** | ☐ exclusively ···· 270 | ☐ **facilitate** ······· **282** |
| ☐ **entertainment** | ☐ **excursion** ····· **270** | ☐ **facility** ········ **213** |
| ············ **81** | ☐ **excuse** ········· **83** | ☐ **failure** ········· **135** |
| ☐ **enthusiasm** ··· **171** | ☐ **executive** ····· **298** | ☐ **fame** ············ **171** |
| ☐ **entire** ·········· **119** | ☐ **exemption** ···· **236** | ☐ **fare** ············ **271** |
| ☐ **entitle** ········· **284** | ☐ **exhaust** ········ **149** | ☐ **fascinate** ······ **237** |
| ☐ **entrance** ··· **81**, 81 | ☐ exhausted ····· **149** | ☐ **fasten** ········· **213** |
| ☐ **entrepreneur** · 49 | ☐ **exotic** ········· **212** | ☐ **fatigue** ········· **237** |
| ☐ **entry** ············ **81** | ☐ **expand** ········· **21** | ☐ **favor** ············ **298** |
| ☐ **environment** ··· **259** | ☐ **expansion** ······ **21** | ☐ **favorable** ······ **298** |
| ☐ environmental | ☐ expect ·········· **306** | ☐ **fax** ············· **83** |
| ············ **259** | ☐ **expedition** ····· **212** | ☐ **feasible** ······· **237** |
| ☐ **environmentally** | ☐ **expenditure** ··· **263** | ☐ **feature** ·········· **22** |
| ············ **259** | ☐ **expense** ········ **83** | ☐ **fee** ······ **213**, 271 |
| ☐ **equal** ··········· **185** | ☐ **experience** ····· **83** | ☐ **feed** ············ **149** |
| ☐ equip ··········· **256** | ☐ **experiment** ··· **133** | ☐ **fierce** ··········· **238** |
| ☐ **equipment** ···· **256** | ☐ **expert** ······ 49, **83** | ☐ **figure** ············ **22** |
| ☐ **essential** ······ **159** | ☐ **expertise** ··· 49, 83 | ☐ **file** ·············· **22** |
| ☐ **establish** ······ **301** | ☐ **expire** ········· **213** | ☐ **finalize** ········· **238** |
| ☐ establishment | ☐ **explain** ········ **109** | ☐ **finance** ········ **121** |
| ············ **301** | ☐ **explanation** ··· **109** | ☐ **financial** ······ **121** |
| ☐ **estate** ········· **83** | ☐ **explode** ········ **278** | ☐ **finding** ········· **171** |
| ☐ **estimate** ······· **83** | ☐ **exploration** ··· **149** | ☐ **fine** ············· **22** |
| ☐ **evacuate** ······ **274** | ☐ **explore** ········ **149** | ☐ **fire** ·············· **22** |
| ☐ **evaluate** ······ **305** | ☐ **explosion** ····· **278** | ☐ **firm** ············· **23** |
| ☐ evaluation ····· **305** | ☐ **export** ·········· **109** | ☐ **fiscal** ··········· **213** |
| ☐ **evaporate** ······ 49 | ☐ **expose** ········ **185** | ☐ **fit** ··········· 50, **111** |
| ☐ **eventually** ····· **264** | ☐ exposure ······· **185** | ☐ **fitness** ··· 50, **111** |
| ☐ **evolution** ······ **185** | ☐ **exquisite** ······ **237** | ☐ **fix** ············· **111** |
| ☐ **evolve** ········· **185** | ☐ **extend** ····· 21, **109** | ☐ **flat** ············· **23** |
| ☐ **exact** ··········· **159** | ☐ **extension** ·· **21**, 109 | ☐ **flavor** ·········· **135** |
| ☐ exactly ·········· **159** | ☐ **extensive** ····· **300** | ☐ **flaw** ········· 50, **171** |
| ☐ **examine** ········ **21** | ☐ **extent** ·········· **135** | ☐ **flawless** ··· **50**, 171 |
| ☐ **exceed** ········ **274** | ☐ external ········ 199 | ☐ **flexibility** ······ **135** |
| ☐ except ·········· **171** | ☐ **extinct** ·········· **171** | ☐ flexible ········· **135** |
| ☐ **exception** ····· **171** | ☐ **extinction** ····· **171** | ☐ **float** ············ **187** |
| ☐ **excess** ········· **121** | ☐ **extra** ············ **21** | ☐ **flood** ············ **83** |
| ☐ excessive ······ **121** | ☐ extreme ········ **121** | ☐ flourish ········· 251 |
| ☐ **exchange** ······ **21** | ☐ extremely ····· **121** | ☐ **fluctuate** ······ **260** |

344

- ☐ fluctuation ····· **260**
- ☐ **fluid** ········ **23**
- ☐ **fold** ········· **214**
- ☐ **folder** ······· **214**
- ☐ **following** ···· **266**
- ☐ **forbid** ···· **167**, **238**
- ☐ **force** ··········· 48
- ☐ **formal** ········· 197
- ☐ **former** ······· **302**
- ☐ **formula** ······ **286**
- ☐ **forthcoming** ·· **265**
- ☐ **forward** ······ **23**
- ☐ **foster** ········ **332**
- ☐ **found** ········ **111**
- ☐ **foundation** ···· **23**
- ☐ **fragile** ········ **214**
- ☐ **frame** ········ **24**
- ☐ **franchise** ····· **264**
- ☐ **fraud** ········· **214**
- ☐ **freight** ······· **214**
- ☐ **frequent** ····· **266**
- ☐ **frequently** ··· **266**
- ☐ **front** ·········· **24**
- ☐ **frustrate** ····· **187**
- ☐ **fuel** ··········· **85**
- ☐ **fulfill** ········ **187**
- ☐ fulfillment ····· **187**
- ☐ **function** ····· **171**
- ☐ **fundraiser** ···· **294**
- ☐ **further** ······ **121**
- ☐ furthermore ··· 199

## G

- ☐ **gain** ·········· **310**
- ☐ **garment** ····· **238**
- ☐ **gather** ······· **149**
- ☐ **gauge** ······· **238**
- ☐ gaze ··········· 260
- ☐ **general** ······ **121**
- ☐ generally ······ **121**
- ☐ **generate** ····· **187**

- ☐ **generator** ······· **187**, **315**
- ☐ **generous** ····· **214**
- ☐ **genuine** ······ **197**
- ☐ **glance** ······· 173
- ☐ **global** ········ **310**
- ☐ globalization ··· **310**
- ☐ globe ·········· **310**
- ☐ **government** ··· **85**
- ☐ **governor** ····· **314**
- ☐ **grab** ········· **239**
- ☐ **grade** ········ 173
- ☐ **graduate** ··· **24**, **63**
- ☐ **grant** ········· **24**
- ☐ **grateful** ······ **260**
- ☐ **grocery** ······ **312**
- ☐ **guarantee** ···· **297**

## H

- ☐ **hail** ·········· **239**
- ☐ **hallway** ······ **256**
- ☐ **halt** ·········· **239**
- ☐ hand ··········· 50
- ☐ **handwriting** ··· 50
- ☐ **hang up** ····· **239**
- ☐ **hardly** ······· **159**
- ☐ **hardship** ····· **292**
- ☐ **hardware** ···· **268**
- ☐ **harsh** ········ **239**
- ☐ **harvest** ······ 135
- ☐ **hazard** ······· **240**
- ☐ **headquarters** · **287**
- ☐ **hearty** ······· **303**
- ☐ **help** ········· **121**
- ☐ **helpful** ······ **121**
- ☐ **hesitate** ····· **289**
- ☐ hesitation ····· **289**
- ☐ **high** ········· **121**
- ☐ **highly** ······· **121**
- ☐ **hire** ·········· **111**
- ☐ **honor** ······· **322**

- ☐ **host** ············ **24**
- ☐ **hostile** ······· **310**
- ☐ hostility ······· **310**
- ☐ **household** ···· **259**
- ☐ however ······· 161
- ☐ **human** ········ **85**
- ☐ **humanity** ····· **85**
- ☐ **humid** ······· **215**
- ☐ **humidity** ····· **215**

## I

- ☐ **ideal** ········· **197**
- ☐ **identification** ·· **50**
- ☐ **identify** ···· 50, **149**
- ☐ **ignore** ········ **327**
- ☐ ill ··············· **85**
- ☐ **illegal** ····· 123, **159**
- ☐ **illness** ········· **85**
- ☐ **immediate** ···· **329**
- ☐ **immediately** ·· **329**
- ☐ **impact** ········ **85**
- ☐ **impair** ········ **333**
- ☐ **impatient** ·· **50**, 257
- ☐ **imperfection** ··· **51**
- ☐ **implement** ···· **240**
- ☐ **implication** ········· **51**, 151
- ☐ **imply** ····· 51, **151**
- ☐ **import** ········ 109
- ☐ **impose** ······· **187**
- ☐ **impress** ······ **187**
- ☐ impression ···· **187**
- ☐ **imprisonment** ············· **318**
- ☐ **in advance** ··· 304
- ☐ **in spite of ~** ·· 119
- ☐ **incentive** ····· **215**
- ☐ **incidental** ····· **25**
- ☐ **income** ········ **85**
- ☐ **incomplete** ············· **51**, 263

345

- [ ] **inconvenience** ········· **51**
- [ ] **incorporate** ····· **240**
- [ ] **incorrect** ······· **51**
- [ ] **increase** ····· 52, **85**
- [ ] **incredible** ····· **197**
- [ ] incredibly ····· **197**
- [ ] **increment** ····· **52**
- [ ] incur ········· **215**
- [ ] indecisive ······ 46
- [ ] independence ········· **121**
- [ ] **independent** ····· **121**
- [ ] **indicate** ····· 52, **111**
- [ ] **indicator** ····· **52**, 111
- [ ] **indifferent** ····· **52**
- [ ] **indispensable** ········· **240**
- [ ] **individual** ····· **267**
- [ ] **induce** ········· **215**
- [ ] industrial ········· **25**
- [ ] **industry** ········· **25**
- [ ] **inexpensive** ····· **313**
- [ ] **infer** ············· **240**
- [ ] **influence** ········· **85**
- [ ] **inform** ····· 52, **292**
- [ ] **informal** ········· **197**
- [ ] information ······ 52
- [ ] **informative** ····· **52**
- [ ] **ingredient** ····· **280**
- [ ] **initial** ············· **25**
- [ ] initially ········· **25**
- [ ] **initiative** ····· **173**
- [ ] **injection** ····· **241**
- [ ] injure ········· **274**
- [ ] **injury** ········· **274**
- [ ] innocence ····· **319**
- [ ] **innocent** ····· **319**
- [ ] **innovation** ····· **173**
- [ ] inquire ········· **267**
- [ ] **inquiry** ········· **267**
- [ ] **insert** ········· **215**
- [ ] **insist** ········· **187**
- [ ] **inspect** ········· **325**
- [ ] inspection ········· **325**
- [ ] inspiration ········· **294**
- [ ] **inspire** ········· **294**
- [ ] **install** ········· **25**
- [ ] installation ········· **25**
- [ ] **institute** ········· **135**
- [ ] **instruct** ········· **187**
- [ ] instruction ········· **187**
- [ ] **instrument** ········· **135**
- [ ] **insufficient** ········· 52, **201**
- [ ] **insurance** ····· 53, **87**
- [ ] **insure** ········· **53**
- [ ] **intense** ····· 53, **199**
- [ ] **intensive** ····· 53, **199**
- [ ] interact ········· **324**
- [ ] **interactive** ········· **324**
- [ ] **interfere** ········· **256**
- [ ] **interior** ········· **135**
- [ ] **intern** ········· **216**
- [ ] **internal** ········· **199**
- [ ] **interrupt** ········· **189**
- [ ] interruption ········· **189**
- [ ] **intersection** ········· **216**
- [ ] **intervene** ········· **216**
- [ ] **intervention** ········· **216**
- [ ] **interview** ········· **25**
- [ ] **interviewee** ········· **25**
- [ ] **interviewer** ········· **25**
- [ ] **invalid** ········· **229**
- [ ] **invaluable** ········· **304**
- [ ] **invention** ········· **330**
- [ ] **inventory** ········· **278**
- [ ] **invest** ········· **269**
- [ ] **investigate** ········· **137**
- [ ] **investigation** ········· **137**
- [ ] **investment** ········· **269**
- [ ] **invitation** ········· **87**
- [ ] **invite** ········· **87**
- [ ] **invoice** ········· **216**
- [ ] **involve** ········· **320**
- [ ] **issue** ········· **26**
- [ ] **item** ········· **87**
- [ ] **itinerary** ········· **216**

## J

- [ ] **jail** ········· **318**
- [ ] **jam** ········· **26**
- [ ] **jeopardize** ········· **241**
- [ ] **join** ········· **53**
- [ ] **joint** ········· **53**
- [ ] **judge** ········· **137**
- [ ] **judicial** ········· **319**
- [ ] **justify** ········· **189**

## K

- [ ] **kit** ········· **265**
- [ ] **knee** ········· **272**

## L

- [ ] **label** ········· **137**
- [ ] **labor** ········· **26**
- [ ] **laboratory** ········· **87**
- [ ] **lack** ········· **87**
- [ ] **lag** ········· **151**
- [ ] **land** ········· **53**
- [ ] **landmark** ········· **53**
- [ ] **landscape** ········· **137**
- [ ] **large** ········· **49**
- [ ] **latest** ········· **268**
- [ ] **launch** ········· **26**
- [ ] **laundry** ········· **258**
- [ ] **law** ········· **53**
- [ ] **lawmaker** ········· **53**
- [ ] **layout** ········· **173**
- [ ] **leak** ········· **217**
- [ ] **lean** ········· **123**
- [ ] **lease** ········· **217**
- [ ] **legal** ········· **123**, 159

- [ ] legislation ···· 241
- [ ] length ········ 54
- [ ] lengthen ······ 54
- [ ] level ·········· 26
- [ ] liability ······ 241
- [ ] liaison ······· 241
- [ ] likely ········ 123
- [ ] limit ·········· 87
- [ ] line ··········· 62
- [ ] linger ········ 330
- [ ] load ······ 27, 65
- [ ] loan ··········· 87
- [ ] lobby ·········· 87
- [ ] local ········· 123
- [ ] locate ··· 27, 59, 89
- [ ] location ···· 27, 89
- [ ] lodging ······· 271
- [ ] log ············ 27
- [ ] logical ········ 199
- [ ] lose ··········· 89
- [ ] loss ··········· 89
- [ ] low ··········· 189
- [ ] lower ········· 189
- [ ] lucrative ······ 313
- [ ] luggage ······· 217
- [ ] lump ········· 290
- [ ] luncheon ····· 217
- [ ] lung ·········· 294

## M

- [ ] machine ······ 137
- [ ] machinery ···· 137
- [ ] maintain ······· 27
- [ ] maintenance ···· 27
- [ ] major ········· 304
- [ ] majority ······ 304
- [ ] maker ········· 53
- [ ] mandatory ···· 314
- [ ] manual ········ 89
- [ ] manufacture ··· 331
- [ ] manufacturer · 331

- [ ] manuscript ··· 217
- [ ] margin ········ 27
- [ ] mark ·········· 53
- [ ] marketing ····· 89
- [ ] marry ·········· 28
- [ ] material ······· 89
- [ ] maximum ····· 123
- [ ] measure ······ 111
- [ ] mechanic
  ············ 137, 159
- [ ] mechanical ···· 159
- [ ] medical ······· 123
- [ ] medication ···· 218
- [ ] medicine ······ 137
- [ ] mend ·········· 44
- [ ] mention ······· 280
- [ ] merchandise
  ················· 276
- [ ] merchant ····· 277
- [ ] merge ········ 310
- [ ] merger ········ 310
- [ ] merit ········· 173
- [ ] method ········ 89
- [ ] metropolitan ·· 324
- [ ] minimum ····· 123
- [ ] misuse ········ 54
- [ ] moderate ····· 218
- [ ] modest ······· 242
- [ ] modify ········ 189
- [ ] monetary ····· 308
- [ ] money ········ 308
- [ ] monitor ········ 28
- [ ] monopolize ··· 242
- [ ] monopoly ···· 242
- [ ] morale ········ 242
- [ ] moreover ····· 199
- [ ] motivate ······ 218
- [ ] motive ········ 218
- [ ] mount ········· 28
- [ ] multinational ··· 54
- [ ] multiple ······· 199

- [ ] multitude ····· 300
- [ ] municipal ····· 218
- [ ] mutual ········ 335

## N

- [ ] name ·········· 54
- [ ] namely ········ 54
- [ ] narrow ········ 28
- [ ] nation ········· 54
- [ ] national ······· 54
- [ ] nationwide ···· 54
- [ ] native ········ 137
- [ ] neglect ······· 189
- [ ] negotiate ····· 308
- [ ] negotiation ··· 308
- [ ] nervous ······ 199
- [ ] net ··········· 159
- [ ] nevertheless ·· 161
- [ ] new ··········· 59
- [ ] newcomer ···· 307
- [ ] night ·········· 56
- [ ] nominal ······ 323
- [ ] nonetheless ·· 161
- [ ] notable ···· 55, 264
- [ ] note ······· 55, 111
- [ ] noteworthy ··· 264
- [ ] notice ·········· 28
- [ ] notify ········· 329
- [ ] novel ········· 123
- [ ] numerous ···· 161
- [ ] nutrition ······ 303

## O

- [ ] object ········· 151
- [ ] objection ······ 218
- [ ] objective ····· 173
- [ ] obligation
  ············· 55, 173
- [ ] obligatory ····· 55
- [ ] oblige ···· 55, 173
- [ ] observation ···· 29

- observe ····· 29
- obsolete ····· 242
- obtain ········ 111
- occupation ········ 57, 139
- occupy ·· 139, 151
- occur ········ 113
- odd ·········· 29
- offend ····· 55, 219
- offender ··· 55, 219
- offense ······· 219
- offer ·········· 89
- official ········ 314
- online ········· 161
- operate ········ 89
- operation ······ 89
- opinion ········ 91
- opponent ····· 175
- opportunity ··· 256
- optimism ····· 261
- optimistic ···· 261
- option ········ 266
- optional ······ 266
- order ······· 29, 47
- organization ··· 91
- organize ······ 113
- orientation ··· 332
- otherwise ···· 123
- outage ······· 242
- outcome ····· 175
- outdated ········ 242, 243
- outline ······· 139
- outlook ······ 243
- outrageous ··· 243
- outstanding ·· 329
- overall ········ 307
- overcharge ···· 55
- overcome ···· 113
- overcrowded ·· 55
- overdue ······· 56

- overhead ····· 243
- overlook ····· 219
- overnight ····· 56
- oversee ······ 219
- overtime ····· 262
- overwhelming ········ 291
- owe ··········· 308
- own ·········· 278

## P

- package ······ 91
- packet ······· 219
- panel ········· 29
- panelist ······ 29
- parallel ···· 64, 161
- participant ········ 91, 113
- participate ········ 91, 113
- party ·········· 29
- passenger ····· 91
- patent ······· 219
- path ········· 139
- patience ····· 139
- patient ········ 50, 139, 257
- patron ······· 243
- patronage ···· 243
- paycheck ····· 220
- payroll ······· 220
- pedestrian ··· 220
- peel ·········· 280
- pending ······ 220
- pension ······ 244
- per ··········· 274
- perceive ····· 189
- perception ··· 189
- perfection ···· 51
- perform ······· 30
- performance ·· 30

- period ········· 56
- periodically ···· 56
- perishable ···· 244
- permission ···· 30
- permit ········· 30
- personnel ···· 293
- perspective ·· 175
- pessimistic ··· 261
- petition ······ 220
- pharmacist ········ 324, 325
- pharmacy ···· 324
- phase ········ 175
- philosophy ···· 30
- physical ····· 125
- physically ··· 125
- physician ····· 91
- pier ·········· 221
- pile ······· 175, 226
- plan ··········· 91
- plant ·········· 30
- plate ·········· 91
- pledge ······· 221
- plenty ······· 315
- poll ·········· 221
- popularity ··· 298
- portable ····· 161
- portfolio ····· 221
- portion ······ 312
- portrait ······· 56
- portray ······· 56
- position ······· 30
- possess ····· 189
- postage ····· 221
- postpone ···· 113
- potential ···· 309
- pour ········· 189
- practical ···· 161
- practice ····· 161
- praise ········ 191
- precaution ···· 56

- [ ] precede · · · · · · · · 244
- [ ] **preceding** · · · · · 244
- [ ] **precise** · · 159, 161
- [ ] precisely · · · · · · 161
- [ ] **predict** · · · · · · · 113
- [ ] prediction · · · · · · 113
- [ ] **prefer** · · · · · · · · 244
- [ ] **preferred** · · · · · 244
- [ ] **preliminary** · · · 244
- [ ] **premier** · · · · · · 302
- [ ] **premium** · · · · · 245
- [ ] **preoccupation**
  · · · · · · · · · · · · · · · 57
- [ ] **preparation** · · · 175
- [ ] **prepare** · · · · · · 175
- [ ] **prescribe** · · · · · 324
- [ ] **prescription** · · · 324
- [ ] **presentation** · · · 326
- [ ] **preserve** · · · · · · 31
- [ ] **president** · · · · · · 31
- [ ] **press** · · · · · · · · · 31
- [ ] **prestige** · · · · · · 309
- [ ] presumable · · · · 245
- [ ] **presumably** · · · 245
- [ ] **presume** · · · · · 245
- [ ] **prevail** · · · · · · · 191
- [ ] **prevent** · · · · · · 151
- [ ] **previous** · · · · · · 125
- [ ] previously · · · · · 125
- [ ] primarily · · · · · · 161
- [ ] **primary** · · · · · · 161
- [ ] **principle** · · · · · 175
- [ ] **prior** · · · · · · · · · 222
- [ ] **priority** · · · · · · 317
- [ ] **private** · · · · · · · 125
- [ ] **privilege** · · · · · 139
- [ ] **probable** · · · · · 245
- [ ] **probably** · · · · · 245
- [ ] **procedure** · · · · · 93
- [ ] **proceed** · · · · · · · 31
- [ ] **process** · · · · · · · 93

- [ ] produce · · · 93, 163
- [ ] **product** · · · · · · · 93
- [ ] **production**
  · · · · · · · · · · · · 93, 93
- [ ] **productive** · · · · 163
- [ ] **profession** · · · · 139
- [ ] professional · · · 139
- [ ] **profile** · · · · · · · 284
- [ ] **profit** · · · · · · 57, 93
- [ ] **profitable** · · · · · 57
- [ ] **profound** · · · · · 199
- [ ] **prohibit** · · · · · · 222
- [ ] **project** · · · · · · · · 93
- [ ] **prolong** · · · · · · 191
- [ ] **prominent** · · · · 199
- [ ] promise · · · · · · · · 57
- [ ] **promising** · · · · · 57
- [ ] promote · · · · · · · 31
- [ ] promotion · · · · · · 31
- [ ] **prompt** · · · · · · · 222
- [ ] proof · · · · · · 57, 151
- [ ] **proper** · · · · · · · 163
- [ ] properly · · · · · · · 163
- [ ] **property** · · · · · · 32
- [ ] **proportion** · · · · 175
- [ ] **proposal** · · · · · · 93
- [ ] propose · · · · · · · 93
- [ ] **prospect** · · · · · 177
- [ ] prospective · · · · 177
- [ ] **prospectus** · · · · 265
- [ ] **prosperity** · · · · 261
- [ ] **protect** · · · · · · · 269
- [ ] protection · · · · · 269
- [ ] **prove** · · · · · 57, 151
- [ ] **provide**
  · · · · · · · 57, 58, 113
- [ ] **provider** · · · · 57, 113
- [ ] **province** · · · · · 177
- [ ] **provision** · · · · · 58
- [ ] **proximity** · · · · · 245
- [ ] **psychological**
  · · · · · · · · · · · · · · · 306
- [ ] psychologist · · · 306
- [ ] psychology · · · · 306
- [ ] **publication** · · · · 93
- [ ] **punctual** · · · · · 201
- [ ] punctuality · · · · 201
- [ ] **purchase** · · · · · 324
- [ ] **purpose** · · · · · · · 95
- [ ] **pursue** · · · · · · · 139
- [ ] **pursuit** · · · · · · · 139

## Q

- [ ] **qualification** · · 222
- [ ] **qualified** · · · · · 245
- [ ] **quality** · · · · · · · 296
- [ ] **quantity** · · · · · · 277
- [ ] **quarter** · · · · · 32, 58
- [ ] **quarterly** · · · · · · 58
- [ ] **quest** · · · · · · · · 246
- [ ] question · · · · · · · 58
- [ ] **questionnaire** · · 58
- [ ] **quit** · · · · · · · · · 113
- [ ] **quota** · · · · · · · · 246
- [ ] quotation · · · · · 177
- [ ] **quote** · · · · · · · · 177

## R

- [ ] **raise** · · · · · · · · · 32
- [ ] random · · · · · · · 246
- [ ] **randomly** · · · · · 246
- [ ] rapid · · · · · · · · · 312
- [ ] **rapidly** · · · · · · · 312
- [ ] **rate** · · · · · · · · · · 32
- [ ] **ration** · · · · · · · · 315
- [ ] **raw** · · · · · · · · · · 163
- [ ] react · · · · · · · · · 139
- [ ] **reaction** · · · · · · 139
- [ ] **readily** · · · · · · · 58
- [ ] ready · · · · · · · · · 58
- [ ] **reasonable** · · · 201
- [ ] **rebate** · · · · · · · 246

- ☐ **recall** ············ 32
- ☐ **receipt** ········ 58, **95**
- ☐ receive ······· 58, **95**
- ☐ **reception** ········ 223
- ☐ receptionist ····· 223
- ☐ **recession** ········ 223
- ☐ **recipe** ············ 303
- ☐ **recipient** ········· 58
- ☐ recognition ······· 33
- ☐ **recognize** ········· 33
- ☐ **recommend** ··· 115
- ☐ recommendation
  ·················· 115
- ☐ **reconfirm** · 59, **105**
- ☐ **recover** ·········· 151
- ☐ recovery ········· 151
- ☐ **recruit** ············ 246
- ☐ **reduce** ············ 262
- ☐ **reduction** ········ 262
- ☐ **refer** ········ 33, **141**
- ☐ **reference** ·· 33, **141**
- ☐ **refill** ·············· 324
- ☐ **reflect** ····· 151, **177**
- ☐ **reflection**
  ············ 151, **177**
- ☐ **reform** ··········· 223
- ☐ **refrain** ············ 260
- ☐ refresh ············ 247
- ☐ **refreshment** ···· 247
- ☐ **refund** ············ 223
- ☐ **refurbish** ········ 269
- ☐ **refuse** ············· 33
- ☐ **regard** ······ 48, **191**
- ☐ **regarding** ········ 297
- ☐ **region** ············ 125
- ☐ **regional** ·········· 125
- ☐ **register** ·········· 115
- ☐ **registration** ····· 115
- ☐ **regret** ······ 115, **247**
- ☐ **regrettably** ······ 247
- ☐ **regular** ··········· 125

- ☐ **regulate** ········· 224
- ☐ **regulation**
  ··············· 224, 311
- ☐ **reimburse** ······· 224
- ☐ **reinforce** ········ 191
- ☐ reinforcement
  ····················· 191
- ☐ **reject** ·············· 33
- ☐ **relative** ··········· 307
- ☐ relatively ·········· 307
- ☐ **release** ············ 33
- ☐ **relevant** ·········· 224
- ☐ reliability ·········· 269
- ☐ **reliable** ··········· 269
- ☐ **relief** ··············· 34
- ☐ **relocate** ··········· 59
- ☐ relocation ········· 59
- ☐ **reluctant** ········· 201
- ☐ **remain** ····· 59, **115**
- ☐ **remainder**
  ·············· 59, **115**
- ☐ **remark** ··· 177, **201**
- ☐ **remarkable** ····· 201
- ☐ **remedy** ·········· 224
- ☐ **remind** ·········· 115
- ☐ **remote** ············ 34
- ☐ removal ·········· 332
- ☐ **remove** ·········· 332
- ☐ **renew** ············· 59
- ☐ renewal ············ 59
- ☐ **renovate** ········· 225
- ☐ renovation ······· 225
- ☐ **renown** ·········· 247
- ☐ **renowned** ······· 247
- ☐ **rent** ·········· 34, **59**
- ☐ **rental** ·············· 59
- ☐ **repair** ······ 34, **111**
- ☐ **replace** ··········· 281
- ☐ replacement ···· 281
- ☐ **reply** ··············· 95
- ☐ **report** ············· 95

- ☐ **represent** ·· 34, **60**
- ☐ **representative**
  ················ 34, **60**
- ☐ **reputation** ······ 141
- ☐ **require** ····· 60, **115**
- ☐ **requirement**
  ············· **60**, 115
- ☐ **reschedule** ······ 60
- ☐ **rescue** ············ 275
- ☐ **research** ·········· 95
- ☐ **resemble** ········ 191
- ☐ **reservation** ····· 323
- ☐ **reserve** ··········· 323
- ☐ **residence** ········ 320
- ☐ **resident** ·········· 320
- ☐ **resign** ············· 286
- ☐ **resolution** ······· 268
- ☐ **resolve** ··········· 268
- ☐ **resort** ············· 326
- ☐ **resource** ·········· 95
- ☐ **respective** ······· 247
- ☐ respectively ····· 247
- ☐ **respond** ········· 115
- ☐ **response** ········ 115
- ☐ **responsibility** ·· 127
- ☐ **responsible** ···· 127
- ☐ **restore** ··········· 191
- ☐ **restrain** ·········· 247
- ☐ **restrict** ··········· 191
- ☐ restriction ········ 191
- ☐ **résumé** ·········· 288
- ☐ **retail** ·············· 225
- ☐ **retain** ············· 153
- ☐ **retire** ··············· 95
- ☐ **retirement** ······· 95
- ☐ **retrieve** ·········· 285
- ☐ **return** ············· 35
- ☐ **reunion** ············ 60
- ☐ **reveal** ············· 153
- ☐ **revenue** ·········· 225
- ☐ **reverse** ··········· 193

- review ········ 328
- **revise** ······ 44, 262
- revision ········ 262
- **revitalize** ······ 320
- **revolve** ········ 306
- **reward** ········ 35
- **rigid** ············ 201
- **risk** ············ 141
- rough············ 314
- **roughly** ········ 314
- **roundtrip** ···· 270
- **routine** ········ 141
- **row** ············ 141
- royal············ 35
- **royalty** ········ 35
- **ruin** ············ 193
- **rural** ····· 163, 165
- **rush** ············ 115

# S

- **sacrifice** ······ 316
- **salary** ·········· 95
- sale··············· 64
- satisfaction ···· 117
- **satisfy** ····· 48, 117
- satisfying ······ 117
- **save** ············ 35
- **scatter** ········ 225
- schedule········ 60
- **scholarship** ··· 328
- **scorn** ·········· 291
- scornful ········ 291
- **scrutiny** ······ 316
- **seal** ············ 309
- **search** ········ 153
- **sector** ········ 331
- secure·········· 277
- **security** ······ 277
- **seek** ············ 265
- **seize** ·········· 291
- **select** ········ 163

- selective ······ 163
- **seminar** ········ 97
- **senior** ······ 35, 60
- **seniority** ········ 60
- **sensible** ········ 36
- **separate** ······ 163
- separately ······ 163
- separation ······ 163
- **serial** ············ 61
- series ············ 61
- **serve** ·········· 281
- **session** ········ 97
- **settle** ········ 334
- settlement ···· 334
- **severe** ········ 333
- shame·········· 290
- **share** ·········· 36
- **shareholder** ·· 327
- **ship** ········ 36, 61
- **shipment** ·· 36, 61
- **shore** ·········· 274
- **shortage** ······ 141
- **shred** ·········· 280
- shut ············· 61
- **shutdown** ······ 61
- sign ·············· 61
- **signature** ······ 61
- significance···· 163
- **significant** ······ 163
- **similar** ········ 127
- similarity ······ 127
- **simple**·········· 299
- **simplify** ········ 299
- simultaneous ·· 299
- **simultaneously**
  ················ 299
- sincere ·········· 289
- **sincerely** ······ 289
- **sink** ············ 36
- **site** ············ 301
- **skeptical** ······ 248

- skill ············ 302
- **skilled** ········ 302
- **skyscraper** ···· 248
- slight ············ 165
- **slightly** ········ 165
- **snack** ·········· 141
- **soar** ············ 248
- **software** ······ 268
- **solid** ············ 36
- **solution** ······ 141
- **solve** ····· 117, 141
- **sophisticated**
  ················ 165
- **source** ·········· 97
- space ············ 61
- **spacious** ······ 61
- **special** ····· 37, 62
- **specialize** ······ 37
- **specialty** ······ 62
- **specific** ··· 37, 226
- specifically······ 37
- **specification**
  ················ 226
- **specify** ········ 226
- **spectacular** ···· 248
- **spectator** ···· 248
- **spillover** ······ 321
- **sponsor** ······ 280
- **spread** ········ 153
- **square** ········ 37
- stability ······ 165
- **stable** ········ 165
- **stack** ·········· 226
- **stage** ·········· 143
- **stain** ············ 249
- **stance** ········ 249
- **standard** ······ 97
- **staple** ·········· 249
- stapler ·········· 249
- **stare** ············ 260
- **state** ········ 37, 37

351

- statement ..... 37
- state-of-the-art ..... 268
- stationary ..... 249
- stationery ..... 226
- statistic ..... 177
- statistics ..... 177
- status ..... 328
- steadily ..... 127
- steady ..... 127
- steal ..... 276
- stimulate ..... 153
- stock ..... 38
- stomach ..... 272
- storage ..... 284
- store ..... 38
- strategy ..... 97, 326
- stream ..... 62, 179
- streamline ..... 62
- stress ..... 97
- structure ..... 143
- struggle ..... 193
- stunning ..... 249
- subject ..... 97
- submission ..... 38
- submit ..... 38
- subordinate ..... 250
- subscribe ..... 227
- subscriber ..... 227, 273
- subscription ..... 227
- substance ..... 62
- substantial ..... 62
- substantiate ..... 250
- substitute ..... 143
- subtract ..... 250
- suburb ..... 179
- succeed ..... 62
- succeeding ..... 62
- success ..... 127
- successful ..... 127
- suffer ..... 193
- sufficient ..... 52, 201
- suggest ..... 117
- suggestion ..... 117
- suit ..... 117, 165
- suitable ..... 165
- suite ..... 293
- summarize ..... 227
- summary ..... 227
- superior ..... 38
- supervise ..... 333
- supervision ..... 333
- supervisor ..... 333
- supplement ..... 227
- supplier ..... 38, 62
- supply ..... 38, 62, 79
- support ..... 63, 117
- supportive ..... 63, 117
- suppose ..... 117
- surcharge ..... 63
- surface ..... 39
- surpass ..... 227
- surplus ..... 39
- surrender ..... 319
- surround ..... 193
- survey ..... 299
- suspect ..... 39
- suspend ..... 250
- suspicion ..... 286
- sustain ..... 314
- sustainable ..... 314
- sweep ..... 155
- symptom ..... 179
- systematic ..... 250
- systematically ..... 250

## T

- tactics ..... 326
- tag ..... 264
- take part in ..... 113
- takeover ..... 310
- talented ..... 201
- target ..... 39
- task ..... 97
- technical ..... 266
- technician ..... 266
- technique ..... 99
- technological ..... 99
- technology ..... 99
- temperature ..... 99
- temporary ..... 39
- tenant ..... 228
- tend ..... 179
- tendency ..... 179
- tension ..... 179
- tentative ..... 251
- term ..... 40
- terminate ..... 228
- terrorism ..... 316
- testimony ..... 251
- that is to say ..... 54
- thorough ..... 311
- thoroughly ..... 311
- thrive ..... 251
- ticket ..... 99
- toast ..... 40
- toll ..... 273
- tool ..... 143
- total ..... 127
- totally ..... 127
- tough ..... 40
- toxic ..... 228
- track ..... 99
- traffic ..... 99
- trail ..... 251
- trailer ..... 251
- transact ..... 228
- transaction ..... 228
- transcript ..... 251

- [ ] transfer · 297
- [ ] transit · 229
- [ ] transition · 252
- [ ] transmission · 229
- [ ] transmit · 229
- [ ] transport · 101
- [ ] transportation · 101
- [ ] trap · 283
- [ ] tray · 101
- [ ] treasure · 63
- [ ] treasury · 63
- [ ] treatment · 143
- [ ] tremendous · 201
- [ ] trial · 318
- [ ] tuition · 328
- [ ] turnover · 252
- [ ] typical · 282
- [ ] typically · 282

## U

- [ ] unanimous · 252
- [ ] uncertainty · 316
- [ ] unconditional · 296
- [ ] undergo · 304
- [ ] undergraduate · 63
- [ ] undertake · 193
- [ ] undue · 292
- [ ] unemployment · 63
- [ ] unexpected · 306
- [ ] unfortunately · 247
- [ ] union · 60
- [ ] unique · 165
- [ ] unit · 296
- [ ] unparalleled · 64
- [ ] unprecedented · 252

- [ ] update · 64
- [ ] upgrade · 296
- [ ] upheaval · 286
- [ ] urban · 163, **165**
- [ ] urge · 64, **193**
- [ ] urgent · 64
- [ ] use · 54

## V

- [ ] vacancy · 293
- [ ] vacant · 293
- [ ] vacuum · 282
- [ ] valid · 229
- [ ] validate · 229
- [ ] valuable · 40
- [ ] value · 40
- [ ] vapor · 49
- [ ] variety · 101
- [ ] vary · 155
- [ ] vehicle · 258
- [ ] vendor · 312
- [ ] venture · 143
- [ ] venue · 252
- [ ] verification · 253
- [ ] verify · 253
- [ ] vicinity · 312
- [ ] violate · 64
- [ ] violation · 64
- [ ] virtual · 278
- [ ] virtually · 278
- [ ] virus · 268
- [ ] visibility · 40
- [ ] visible · 40
- [ ] vital · 257, **320**
- [ ] vitally · 257
- [ ] vivid · 260
- [ ] voicemail · 267
- [ ] volatile · 253
- [ ] volunteer · 290
- [ ] vote · 155
- [ ] voucher · 322, **322**

- [ ] vulnerable · 253

## W

- [ ] wage · 101
- [ ] waive · 253
- [ ] ward · 332
- [ ] warehouse · 278
- [ ] warn · 101
- [ ] warning · 101
- [ ] warrant · 283
- [ ] warranty · 283
- [ ] waste · 41
- [ ] weigh · 155
- [ ] weight · 155
- [ ] welfare · 179
- [ ] whole · 64
- [ ] wholesale · 64
- [ ] wide · 54, **65**
- [ ] widespread · 316
- [ ] wildlife · 143
- [ ] withdraw · 41
- [ ] withdrawal · 41
- [ ] withhold · 253
- [ ] witness · 279
- [ ] work · 65
- [ ] workload · 65
- [ ] workshop · 229
- [ ] world · 65
- [ ] worldwide · 65
- [ ] worth · 276
- [ ] writing · 50

## Y

- [ ] year · 65
- [ ] yearly · 65, **294**
- [ ] yield · 41
- [ ] youngster · 290

# MEMO

# MEMO

# MEMO

# MEMO

【執筆・校閲協力】
（英文・問題執筆）Shari Berman, Alice Bratton, Kevin Glenz
　　　　　　　　Michael Howard Maesaka, Terrence Young
【音声吹き込み】Howard Colefield（アメリカ）, Lindsay Nelson（アメリカ）
　　　　　　　　Andree Dufleit（カナダ）, Steven Ashton（イギリス）
　　　　　　　　James House（イギリス）, Sarah Greaves（オーストラリア）
　　　　　　　　Jason Takada-Latchford（オーストラリア）

# TOEIC® テスト 大学生のための頻出英単語

初版第1刷発行 … 2013年11月10日
編者 …………………… Ｚ会編集部
発行人 ………………… 藤井孝昭
発行 …………………… 株式会社 Ｚ会ＣＡ
発売 …………………… 株式会社 Ｚ会
　　　　　　　　　　〒411-0943　静岡県駿東郡長泉町下土狩105-17
　　　　　　　　　　TEL 055-976-9095
　　　　　　　　　　http://www.zkai.co.jp/books/
装丁 …………………… Concent, inc.
執筆・編集協力 …… 株式会社 シー・レップス
録音・編集 ………… 一般財団法人 英語教育協議会（ELEC）
印刷・製本 ………… 日経印刷株式会社

© Ｚ会ＣＡ 2013　★無断で複写・複製することを禁じます
定価はカバーに表示してあります
乱丁・落丁はお取り替えいたします
ISBN978-4-86290-137-8 C0082